WALKING

KEY

- - - - **Garden Walk** About 15 Minutes

● ● ● ● **River & Garden Walk** About 30 Minutes

✱✱✱✱ **Porters Lodge** About 30 Minutes

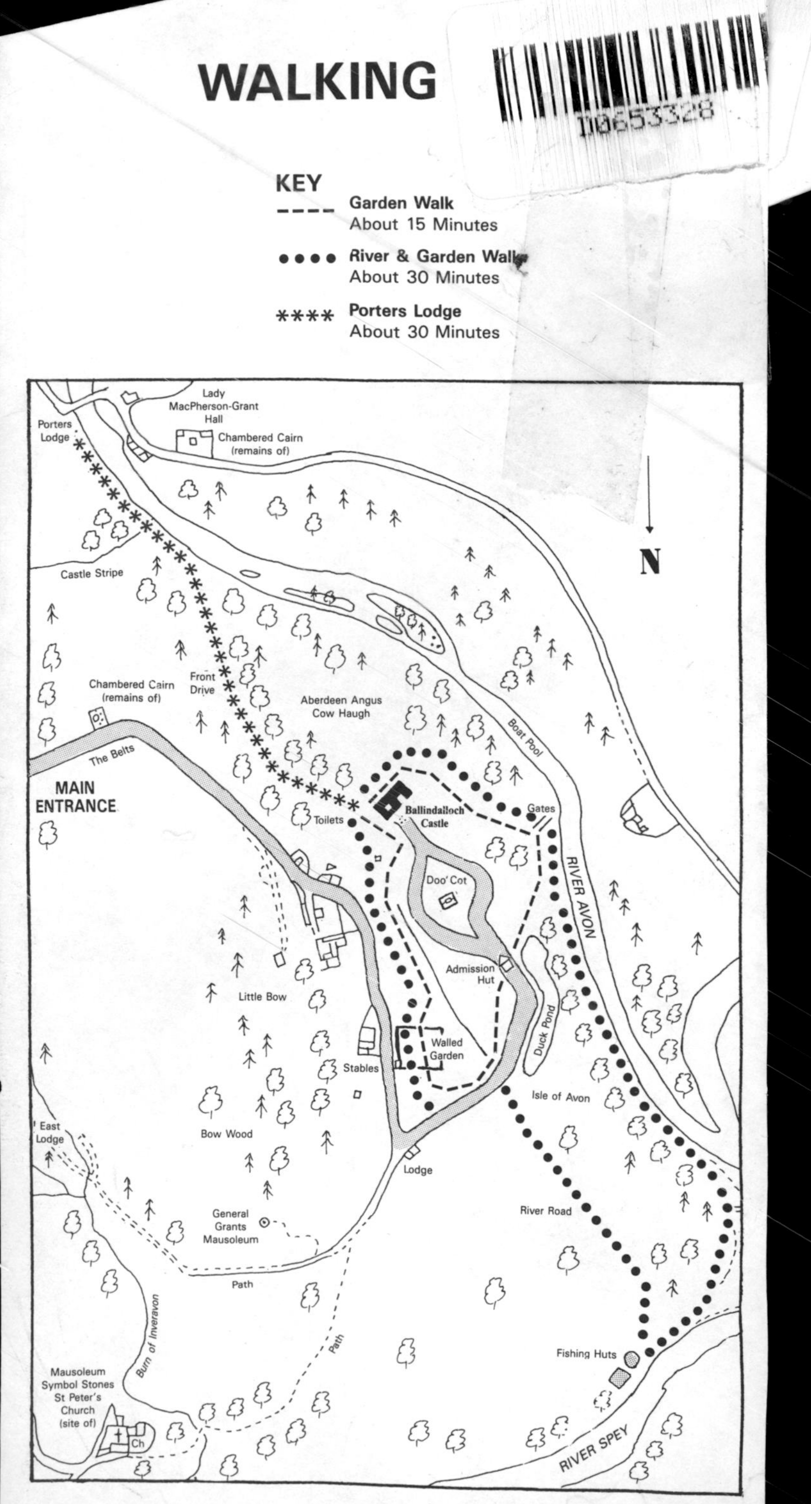

Printed by Moravian Press Ltd., South Street, Elgin.

lcome to lloch Castle

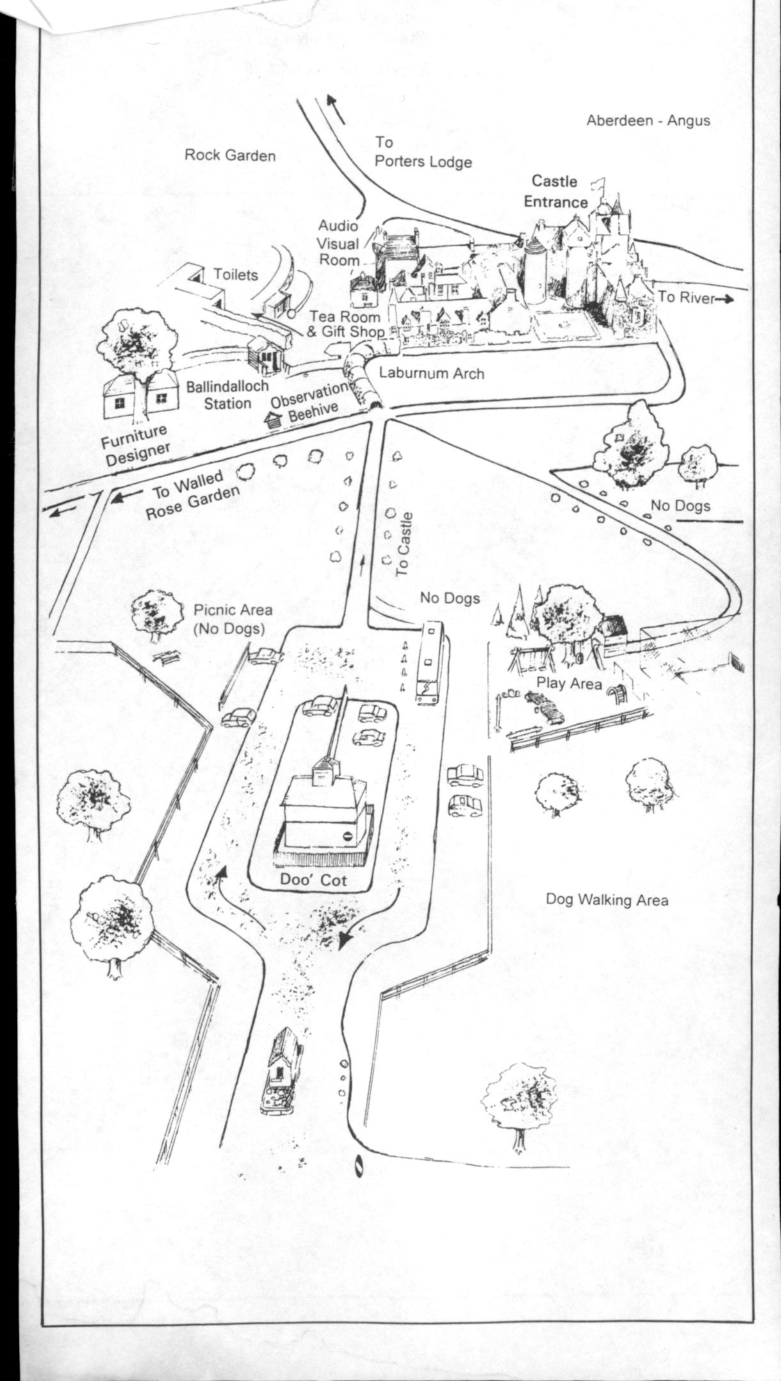

Scalp Dance

Also by the author:

Black Flag

Bloody Dawn

Scalp Dance

Indian Warfare on the High Plains 1865–1879

Thomas Goodrich

Composition by Doric Lay Publishers

Printed in the United States of America

ISBN 0-8117-1523-X

To Donald Danker

Professor Emeritus, Washburn University

Indian warfare is, of all warfare, the most dangerous, the most trying, and the most thankless. Not recognized by the high authority of the United States Senate as war, it still possesses for you the disadvantages of civilized warfare, with all the horrible accompaniments that barbarians can invent and savages execute. In it you are required to serve without the incentive to promotion or recognition; in truth, without favor or hope of reward.

—Captain Charles King

Contents

List of Illustrations *viii*
Introduction by Albert Castel *ix*

Prologue—November 29, 1864 1

1 Thicker Than Fiddlers in Hell 7
2 A Perfect Silence 21
3 The Last Bullet 35
4 The Man, The Monster, The War 47
5 One Equals One 61
6 More Tears Than Dollars 77
7 Island in the Sand 93
8 A Fate Worse Than Death 115
9 Old Men Laugh 131
10 If I Were an Indian . . . 159
11 A Lease on Hell 181
12 The Girl I Left Behind Me 197
13 Red is the Rosebud 215
14 Garry Owen . . . in Glory 233
15 Death Song 265
16 Bloody Road Back 295

Epilogue 307

Notes *311*
Bibliography *329*
Index *336*

List of Illustrations

John Chivington, *page 2*
The Battle of Platte Bridge, *11*
Map—The northern Plains, *17*
Red Cloud, *23*
Margaret Carrington, *26*
Henry Palmer, *44*
Map—The southern Plains, *51*
Elizabeth and George Custer, *54*
Attack on the Overland Route, *63*
Frederick Wyllyams after the fight at Fort Wallace, *67*
The Kidder Massacre, *72*
James Butler "Wild Bill" Hickok, *81*
William F. "Buffalo Bill" Cody, *88*
George Forsyth, *95*
The Battle of the Arickaree, *104*
Sigmund Shlesinger, *113*
Catherine German, *123*
Albert and Jennie Barnitz, *134*
Satanta, *150*
A Pawnee tepee, *160*
A Comanche warrior, *169*
The Scalp Dance, *175*
Map—Southern battleground, *184*
Addie and Julia German, *192*
Frank and Alice Baldwin, *204*
Washakie, *208*
George Crook, *228*
The Battle of the Rosebud, *230*
Edward Godfrey, *237*
Marcus Reno, *243*
Charles Windolph, *252*
Stanislas Roy, *255*
John Finerty, *269*
Map—Northern battleground, *271*
Sitting Bull, *289*

Introduction

In the summer of 1846 young Francis Parkman of Boston and Harvard traveled across the High Plains with the object of "observing the Indian character" in preparation for writing a multi-volumed account of the rise and fall of the French empire in North America, a work destined to become the greatest narrative history ever produced by an American author. On a June afternoon Parkman and his companions came upon a Sioux encampment along Horse Creek, a tributary of the Platte River in what is now Colorado. He described the scene in *The Oregon Trail*, published in 1849:

> On the farther bank stood a large and strong man, nearly naked, holding a white horse by a long cord, and eyeing us as we approached. This was the chief . . . called "Old Smoke." Just behind him, his youngest and favorite squaw sat astride a fine mule, covered with caparisons of white skins, garnished with blue and white beads, and fringed with little ornaments of metal that tinkled with every movement of the animal. The girl had a light clear complexion, enlivened by a spot of vermilion on each cheek; she smiled, not to say grinned, upon us, showing two gleaming rows of white teeth. In her hand she carried the tall lance of her unchivalrous lord, fluttering with feathers; his round white shield hung at her back. Her dress was a tunic of deerskin, made beautifully white by means of a species of clay found on the prairie, ornamented with beads, arranged in figures more gay than tasteful, and with long fringes at all of the seams. Not far from the chief stood a group of stately figures, their white buffalo robes thrown over their shoulders, gazing coldly upon us; and in the rear, for several

> acres, the ground was covered with a temporary encampment. Warriors, women, and children swarmed like bees; hundreds of dogs, of all sizes and colors, ran restlessly about; and close at hand, the wide shallow stream was alive with boys, girls, and young squaws, splashing, screaming, and laughing in the water.

Parkman and his party, however, were not the only whites present.

> At the same time a long train of emigrants with their heavy wagons was crossing the creek, and dragging on in slow procession by the encampment of the people whom they and their descendants, in the space of a century, are to sweep from the face of the earth.

What had been a description suddenly turned into a prediction—a prophecy of doom for the Indians laughing and splashing in the creek. Moreover, this prediction came true in essence and did not require a century to do so. By the time Parkman died in 1893 the Sioux and all of the other Great Plains tribes between the Missouri River and Rocky Mountains, although not swept from the face of the earth, had been reduced to a pathetic remnant confined to squalid reservations. Where they had hunted buffalo, white farmers grew wheat and white ranchers herded cattle. On their former campsites stood fast-growing towns with names such as Cheyenne and Sioux Falls—sole, ironic reminders of what had been but no longer was.

Writing in his final report as commanding general of the U.S. Army before retiring in 1883, General William T. Sherman explained how and why it happened:

> The Army has been a large factor in producing this result, but it is not the only one. Immigration and the occupation by industrious farmers and miners of lands vacated by the aborigines have been largely instrumental to that end, but the railroad which used to follow in the rear now goes forward with the picketline in the great battle of civilization with barbarism, and has become the greater cause.

The only error in Sherman's explanation is a curious one for a general to commit: Not only was the army a "large factor" in dispossessing the Indians, it was a necessary one. Without it, the lands occupied by the "industrious farmers and miners" would not have been vacated and it would have taken far more time and cost much more blood to build the railroads that transported them and other settlers onto those lands in ever-increasing, ultimately overwhelming numbers. The Plains Indians were proud, courageous, and above all, fierce warriors. When, instead of just a few hunters and trappers, hundreds of farmers, ranchers, miners, and railroad and town builders began moving into their lands, they struck back. They did so in the same way as against enemy tribes—murdering, mutilating, raping, torturing, and occasionally sparing women and boys to be turned into squaws and warriors. Panic-stricken and crying for vengeance, the surviving whites demanded protection and retaliation, a clamor taken up by Western newspapers and politicians. That meant sending in the army—to be precise, the regulars. Wasn't that what they were paid for?

And so the soldiers went off to "pacify" the "hostiles." It was not easy. Unless they had greatly superior numbers the Indians avoided pitched battles, preferring to hit and run, ambush detachments, and cut off stragglers. They were good at guerrilla war, given their intimate knowledge of the country, their swift and hardy ponies, and a skill at riding that made them, in the words of one officer, the "best light cavalry in the world." The only way to subdue them was to carry out surprise attacks on their villages, which unfortunately but inevitably resulted in the slaying of women and children as well as warriors. This tactic, along with the virtual extermination of the buffalo that sustained the Indians, ultimately led to their subjugation. It was "total war" before the term was coined.

It also was brutal, vicious, and nasty. Indians neither gave nor expected quarter when they fought; the concept was unknown to them. They almost always scalped dead soldiers, and often mutilated their bodies in a variety of "unspeakable" ways. If they did take prisoners, it merely was for the purpose of torturing them to death by means that caused the victims to wish they never had been born. Such practices could have but one effect on the soldiers. Atrocities begot atrocities, massacres produced massacres, and savagery incited savagery. The older image of the frontier regular typified by John Wayne contains no more truth than modern cinematic portrayals of Plains Indians as peace-loving sages living in mystic harmony with nature.

The story of the army's climactic struggle with the Plains Indians has been told often, starting while it occurred and continuing ever since. *Scalp Dance* does not pretend to offer any startling new facts or interpretations. So vast is the historical (and pseudohistorical) literature on the subject that this would be a virtual impossibility. What it does is present the story in the words of those who lived it and sometimes died in it—soldiers and settlers, their wives, and occasionally reporters who accompanied the army into battle. By doing so it puts the reader into the action psychologically via the accounts of the men and women who were there physically. As a result the reader experiences something of what they experienced. This is not always pleasant; in fact, it can be horrifying. But it is informative and interesting, which is what history should be, and most of the time it is as gripping as anything you have ever read. If you don't believe me, read what follows. I am confident you will agree.

—Albert Castel

Prologue—November 29, 1864

He sat in his saddle, staring intently to the north. Beneath a broad hat brim, his small, dark eyes worked feverishly. His hard, handsome face, aglow in the first rays of dawn, moved not a muscle. Ahead, where the road dipped gently to the valley, he could see clearly the thin belt of timber that marked the course of the creek. Beyond the trees, gleaming white in the sun, there they stood, more than 100 of them. He had heard they would be here. And, as the forty-mile night ride had proven, he had placed great faith in the story. On a long campaign like this, however, many things might go wrong and one could never be sure until the very last moment. But there they were, just as he had been told, just as he had hoped, just as he had prayed.

Sitting straight and stiff on his mount, scanning the scene below, the big, burly colonel was a striking figure. Even if one had been unacquainted and cast a curious eye on him for the first time they might have easily guessed him for the man of the cloth that he was—an air of the Old Testament clung unmistakeably about his bearded, humorless face. Stern and intense, John Chivington was, at a glance, a no-nonsense sort of man who brooked no opposition. Good and bad, right and wrong, were black and white issues to the colonel's mind, and there was no room in his makeup for any gray middle ground. This morning, down there along the banks of Sand Creek, John Chivington was going to right a great wrong.

Behind the colonel, the waiting column of horsemen cast long, stark shadows over the brown and barren prairie. Anxiously sitting their tired and steaming mounts, the men and officers watched their commander closely,

John Chivington. DENVER PUBLIC LIBRARY, WESTERN HISTORY DEPARTMENT.

waiting for his signal. Everyone knew that the time had come—the hour of the avenger was at hand. After nearly three years of fear and frustration the opportunity to smite their foe had finally arrived.

Since 1861 the people of Colorado had lived a nightmare. Separated from civilization and "the States" by hundreds of miles of wilderness, the struggling territory was left largely to fend for itself when civil war erupted in the East. First came the Confederate threat from Texas in 1862, a strong expedition that pushed north, intent on seizing the mountains and their golden treasury. Only through the dogged determination of the miners, teamsters, and ranchers of the region, led by men such as John Chivington, was the gray tide stemmed in New Mexico and finally forced back. Later, Rebel guerrillas, again from Texas, made small but ominous forays into the territory. Farther east, Missouri bushwhackers repeatedly threatened to sever the overland lifelines to Colorado. Then, in 1864, the greatest and most terrifying threat of all suddenly arose.

Beginning in the spring and continuing throughout the summer, several Indian tribes unleashed a string of attacks that all but paralyzed the Plains and sent the small and scattered population of Colorado fleeing in terror back to the foot of the mountains. Efforts by local militias and Federal cavalry to pursue and punish the fleet raiders were to no avail. For those who had only heard tales of Indian atrocities, there were now plenty of examples.

Revealed a Denver man who, with two friends, stumbled upon the aftermath of one Indian raid:

> About 100 yards from the desolated ranch [we] discovered the body of the murdered woman and her two dead children, one of which was a little girl of four years and the other an infant. The woman had been stabbed in several places and scalped, and the body bore evidences of having been violated. The two children had their throats cut, their heads being nearly severed from their bodies.[1]

Later that autumn, a band of Southern Cheyenne and Arapahoe under Black Kettle, aware of looming winter and weary of war, ceased their raiding and sued for peace. Although territorial authorities refused to treat with the Indians until the remaining hostiles surrendered, Black Kettle's band was given a voucher of safety from a young Federal officer and allowed to camp in peace.

The people of Colorado were outraged. That Indians, whose hands yet dripped with blood, should be granted immunity during the winter only to resume their raids in the summer, seemed a mockery of justice. Punishment, not peace, should be the raiders' reward, most whites felt, and none was more violent on the matter or more determined to punish than the Reverend John Chivington. Thus, above Sand Creek this bright winter morning in 1864, as the big colonel and his rough and raw Coloradans removed their great coats and drew their deadly weapons, the thought uppermost on the minds of all was a swift and terrible judgment for the crimes of the past.

"Remember the murdered women and children!" cried Chivington as he and his nine hundred screaming horsemen charged toward the village. Sure of their safety, the sleeping Indians were caught completely by surprise. According to one witness:

> When I looked toward the chief's lodge, I saw that Black Kettle had a large American flag up on a long lodgepole as a signal to the troops that the camp was friendly. Part of the people were rushing about the camp in great fear. All the time Black Kettle kept calling out not to be frightened; that the camp was under protection and there was no danger. Then suddenly the troops opened fire on this mass of men, women, and children, and all began to scatter and run . . . . At last Black Kettle, seeing that it was useless to stay longer, started to run.[2]

Though most of the 600 Indians, including Black Kettle, miraculously escaped, many were not so fortunate. Besieged for three years with their backs to the wall, harassed and humiliated by a wily, elusive foe that simply defied pursuit, when the Coloradans finally gained control of the camp all their hate and fury exploded in a fiery flash. Running through the village the troops mowed down men, women, and children in heaps. Vengeful and murderous as many were, some soon discovered they had no stomach for what then ensued.

"[T]hey were scalped, their brains knocked out," said one horrified soldier. "[T]he men used their knives, ripped open women, clubbed little children, knocked them in the head with their guns, beat their brains out, [and] mutilated their bodies in every sense of the word."[3] Recalled another trooper:

> There was one little child, probably three years old, just big enough to walk through the sand. The Indians had gone ahead, and this little child was behind following after them. The little fellow was perfectly naked . . . . I saw one man get off his horse, at a distance of about seventy-five yards, and draw up his rifle and fire—he missed the child. Another man came up and said, "Let me try the son of a bitch; I can hit him." He got down off his horse, kneeled down and fired at the little child, but he missed him. A third man came up and made a similar remark, and fired, and the little fellow dropped.[4]

When the carnage had ended, one officer noted:

> In going over the battle-ground . . . I did not see a body of a man, woman, or child but what was scalped, and in many instances, their bodies were mutilated in a most horrible manner—men, women, and children's privates cut out . . . . I heard one man say that he had cut a woman's private parts out, and had them for exhibition on a stick . . . . I also heard of numerous instances in which men had cut the private parts of females, and stretched them over their saddle-bows, and some of them over their hats.[5]

While many were stunned and sickened by the slaughter, most felt justified after it was done.

> I saw some of the men opening bundles or bales. I saw them take therefrom a number of white persons' scalps—men's, women's, and children's . . . . I saw one scalp of a white woman in particular . . . . It had been taken entirely off the head; the head had been skinned, taking all the hair; the scalp had been tanned to preserve it; the hair was auburn and hung in ringlets; it was very long hair. There were two holes in the scalp in front, for the purpose of tying it on their heads when they appeared in the scalp dance.[6]

When John Chivington and his victorious column returned to Denver a short time later, the city erupted in a "glorification."

"[They] have won for themselves," rang a local editor, "the eternal gratitude of dwellers on these plains."[7]

Even as one great war was winding down, the seeds for another were being deeply sown by both sides. Unlike the one just ending, however, this next war would last much longer. And unlike the war now ending, this new fight would be waged with a hatred and fury that would soon make the world shudder.

1

Thicker Than Fiddlers in Hell

By the spring of 1865, the bloody American Civil War was all but over. For four years the eyes of the North had seldom strayed from the land of sun, slaves, and secession. Whereas the great and absorbing preoccupation of the United States before the Rebellion had been growth and prosperity and empire, from 1861 to 1865 the sole concern of the young republic was nothing less than its own survival. But then, in April, with the sudden surrender of the main Rebel armies, the Union found itself free to turn its conquering energies west once again.

Beyond the great rivers and mountains a vast new realm of incredible wealth was rising on the Pacific coast. If America was to fulfill its dream of Manifest Destiny, this western half must be firmly and forever bound to the East. Already, a number of well-worn trails spanned the continent, including the historic road to California and Oregon, its graceful windings now wedded to the first telegraph line. Between the Missouri River and the Rocky Mountains were the Great Plains, a generally treeless expanse, home to cactus and sage, buffalo and wolf, and also to some of the fiercest people on Earth. Here, the Sioux, Cheyenne, Arapahoe, Kiowa, and Comanche held dominion. Though leaders of some bands seemed reconciled to the inevitability of the white man and his passage through the region, others bitterly resented the invasion and were determined to oppose it at all costs. The government of the United States was just as determined to guarantee the safety of the overland routes and the railroads soon to follow, some of which were already inching west at war's end.

While most Civil War veterans returned to homes and families, thousands of Northerners were retained for post-war service. Some were posted in the occupied South. Others were ordered west. In the meantime, hundreds of soldiers were already on the Plains fighting Indians. For many Americans, it came as a shock to discover that while their attention had been riveted on the conflict at their doorstep, half a continent away troops were engaged in a smaller, though vastly more savage contest.

"Do tell me what is the popular opinion of this indian war, in the States," wrote Corporal Hervey Johnson to his sister in the summer of 1865. "[N]o news papers we get ever speak of us, they all gloating over the close of the war in the south and dont seem to remember the soldiers out here fighting a race, whom it would be flattering to call men."[1]

Like Johnson and others guarding the crucial telegraph line through Wyoming, those who had served part or all of their Civil War years in the West felt they were engaged in a hopeless, thankless, inglorious fight, and were all but forgotten by the government and those they loved. Many, like Private George Saunders, were bitter over their treatment and now only longed to escape. "We don't give a red [cent] if the Red Devils take every post in the country," Saunders scratched in his diary, "if only they take care to keep out of our way."[2] Johnson felt the same.

> I dont care who does the fighting, I dont want any more of it "in mine." The boys out here have all come to the conclusion that fighting indians is not what it is cracked up to be, especially when it is fighting on the open prarie against five to one, we always have to fight at such a disadvantage, we always have to shoot at them running, they wont stand and let a fellow shoot at them like a white man.[3]

As Johnson suggested, throughout the summer thousands of Sioux and Northern Cheyenne carried out hit-and-run raids along the North Platte River in an attempt to cut the telegraph and halt traffic on the road to California. Unlike the great battles of the late war, where earth-shaking violence was often followed by weeks, even months, of relative quiet, Indian fighting was an unpredictable, unending, and utterly unnerving war where the front line was very often as close as the next ravine.

"[T]he indians came to see us again," Corporal Johnson continued. "I was on 'lookout' that day on top of the buildings."

> When I saw them coming I fired and then jumped off the house to run and help drive in the mules which were about a hundred yards

> off. The other boys ran out towards the indians and fired at them, they turned and ran off to a bluff about half a mile and stopped. They stood there expecting we would follow them . . . when they would lead us into ambush, at least that's what we thought. They soon got tired of standing there and concluded to come back to the road, they tried hard to draw us out making all the fun of us they could, but we "couldent see it," finding they were not going to succeed by the means they were trying they went to tearing down the telegraph. We didnt like to see it of course but we had to stand and look at them. we could have driven them off by going out on foot but they would have gone off and cut the line somewhere else.[4]

One section of the overland route that received special attention from the Sioux was in central Wyoming, where the road crossed the North Platte River over a long wooden span. To guard this vital link were a mere 110 soldiers, deficient not only in mounts, but weapons. One of those at Platte Bridge Station was Lieutenant William Drew.

> Just after dinner on the 25th of July . . . someone called out, "Indians!" and all hands, seizing their arms, ran out to see where they were . . . . On the north side of the river about fifteen or twenty Indians on horseback were moving leisurely along. In a few minutes about a dozen men were mounted, and crossing the bridge they commenced skirmishing with the enemy. As fast as our men moved on, the Indians fell back, until our men had gone about three miles from the bridge. All this time the Indians were increasing in numbers, until there were about forty in plain sight . . . . At this time an order was received from the station for the men to come back . . . . As our men fell back toward the bridge, Indians kept coming out of the ravine, until there were about fifty in sight, showing that their maneuvering had been for the purpose of leading our men as far away from all support as possible, and to then wipe them out by superior numbers. Our men reached the station without any loss . . . . In one of the charges the boys shot a Cheyenne chief through the bowels. He threw his arm over the neck of his pony . . . and went into a thicket of brush, where the chief fell off. Two of the boys rode into the thicket and found the chief lying apparently dead. One man jumped off his horse and stabbed the Indian about the heart. He did not give the least sign of life. Then the trooper commenced to scalp him. As soon as the knife touched his head, the Indian began to beg, when another man shot him through the brain. The Indian's belief is that if a warrior loses his scalp, he can-

not go to the happy hunting ground. Indians will lose their lives without the least sign of fear, but want to save their scalps . . . .

About ten days before this, the Indians had captured one of our men, and had tortured and mangled his body in a shocking manner. Our boys swore that if they ever got hold of an Indian they would cut him all to pieces, and they did.[5]

With nightfall, the fighting along the North Platte ceased. Many at the bridge, however, were now anxious over the fate of a wagon supply train due the following day. Once again, Lieutenant Drew:

The next morning . . . as soon as we could distinguish objects, we scanned the surrounding country to see if we could find any of our previous day's opponents. We did not make out any on our side of the river, but on the north side there were some moving about, with others scattered on the hills. Altogether there seemed to be about ninety in sight—just about the number we had been fighting the day before . . . . We breakfasted, and then Major [Martin] Anderson ordered Lieutenant Caspar Collins . . . to take command of a detail of twenty-five men and reinforce the train to prevent their being surprised by the savages.

The detail moved out in fine spirits, crossed the bridge and then rode leisurely along the bottom-land up on to the bluff . . . . On reaching the top of the bluffs, two Indians were seen by the detail at the top of the telegraph poles a little over a quarter of a mile away, cutting the wires. As soon as they saw our men, they slid down the poles, mounted their ponies and started for the back country as fast as the animals could carry them. Their mounts appeared to be very lame, and they did not appear to make much headway. It looked like a soft snap to "take them in," and Lieutenant Collins ordered the boys to go for them before the Indians could reach their friends. This charge, of course, took them off the road and away from the sight of the river. The instant the last man disappeared from view, from behind the screen of willows west of the bridge, about four hundred Cheyennes, on horseback, appeared, and with loud yells charged over the bottom-land and up on to the bluff in the direction in which our men had gone. The instant they reached the top of the bluff, from behind every sandhill and out of every hollow, Indians appeared.[6]

"N., E., S., W., and every point of the compass, the savages came," recalled one of those trapped with Collins. "It appeared as though they sprang up out

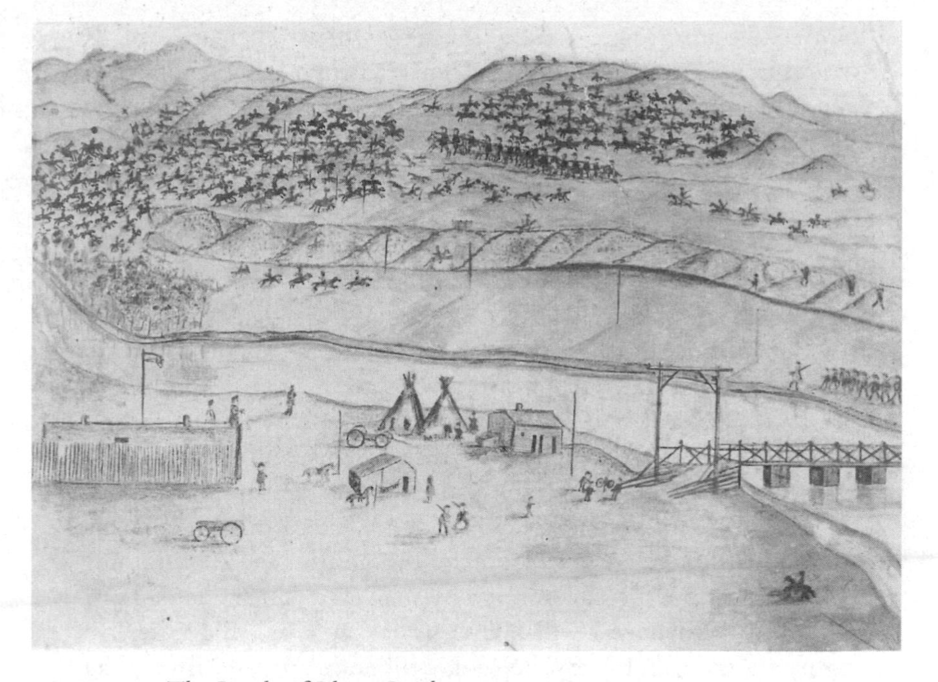

The Battle of Platte Bridge. KANSAS STATE HISTORICAL SOCIETY.

of the ground. They completely surrounded us . . . . We turned and charged into the thickest of them, drawing our pistols and doing the best we could."[7] Another man involved in the dash for the bridge was Ferdinand Erhardt.

> We were in close quarters; every man for himself. In the mixup the Indians quit firing, as they were hitting one another. About a dozen or more confronted me, and the nearest brave struck at me with his tomahawk. I dodged the blow and with my carbine close to his body I let him have the charge and he fell from his horse. There was no time to reload. I dropped my carbine on the sling to my side and drew my revolver, pointing it at one, then at another, which had the effect to make them dodge right and left. I rode a good horse . . . and a lively race followed, with a horde of savages on either side. It seemed to me that I was bringing up the rear and . . . I was about to give up hope, when another trooper came along. They made a rush for him which left a gap through which my horse shot . . . towards the bridge to safety. In the meantime our men at the stockade had not been idle . . . . [T]hey came across the bridge to our rescue and opened fire among the redskins which

> cleared the immediate vicinity without which relief none of us would have escaped . . . . Corp'l [Henry] Grimm came in with several arrows sticking in his back. Many of the redskins bit the dust but they held their ground [and] mutilated and danced around the dead bodies of our comrades.[8]

"One of our men had fallen on the edge of the bluff," noted Lieutenant Drew, "fully a thousand yards from the bridge."

> An Indian rode up to his body and commenced shooting arrows into it. After firing four or five arrows the Indian dismounted, took his tomahawk and commenced to hack him with it. The boys at the bridge were very much excited about this, and some of them wanted to rush up and save the body from further mutilation, but . . . they were forbidden to undertake it. One of the boys put his gun to his shoulder and fired at the Indian, but the shot did not seem to disturb his equanimity in the least. Then Hank Lord remarked: "I believe I will take a whack at him." Elevating his sight to a thousand yards, he took deliberate aim and fired. The Indian had his hatchet raised at the time, and was just about to strike it into the head of the dead soldier; but the bullet was too quick for him. It struck him in some vital part, for the hatchet dropped from his hand and he fell over on the ground. Pretty soon he managed to stagger to his feet, and succeeded in getting on his pony and started away, but he was badly hurt and swayed from side to side on his pony. He was just about to fall off, when two of the Indians noticing his condition, rode up, one on each side, and supported him off the field.
>
> For about an hour there were no new developments, except that the Indians, by one means or another, tried to decoy some of us away from the bridge . . . . As soon as the Indians saw they could not draw us out in that manner, they commenced to call us all the vile names they could think of, using language they had picked up among the whites previous to the breaking out of the war, or had learned from the renegrade [*sic*] whites among them. Just at this time, one of the boys sang out: "There comes the train!" And sure enough, there it was in sight, coming over the hills about four miles from the station. The Indians had perceived it about the same time, and in a minute every one of them was on his pony and urging his animal at its fastest pace in that direction . . . .
>
> Sergeant [Amos] Custard, in command of the train, had sent five of his escort about a quarter of a mile ahead of the others as an

> advance guard. Quite a body of Indians came suddenly up a ravine between this advance guard and the train. The corporal in charge of the advance at first attempted to get back to the train, but seeing the large force he had to contend with . . . he ordered his men to turn to the right and gallop as fast as possible to the river . . . . Just as they reached the river, one of the soldiers fell, shot through the heart. The rest plunged into the stream. When about four rods from the opposite shore, another man was shot and fell from his horse into the river. The others reached the shore in safety and headed toward the station.[9]

With perhaps one thousand Sioux and Cheyenne in the area, the men atop the buildings of the tiny garrison watched in helpless horror as the supply train was surrounded.

"The Indians forced the wagons into a shallow ravine," remembered Lieutenant George Walker. "With field glasses we saw . . . the smoke from the men's carbines as the Indians charged on them."[10]

The unequal contest continued for nearly four hours. Finally, the sound of the last gunshot echoed across the hills and the troops at Platte Bridge saw only black smoke billowing from the wagon train.

As a grief-stricken William Drew later wrote:

> Never in all our service as soldiers had we experienced anything like this before. To know that about twenty of our comrades . . . were . . . within two and one-half miles of us, surrounded by an overwhelming number of savage enemies . . . and we not able to do anything for their relief, was heart-rending. Some of us went to Major Anderson and requested that forty or fifty of us be allowed a rescue, but the major . . . realized that an attempt at relief . . . would doubtless mean the destruction of the entire party, in which event it would have been an easy matter for the Indians to have taken the station and massacred all who were left.[11]

The following day, after the Indians had withdrawn, reinforcements reached Platte Bridge and together the troops set out for the scene of the attack. "On arriving there a horrible sight met our gaze," Drew recounted. "Twenty-one of our dead soldiers were lying on the ground, stripped naked and mangled in every conceivable way. I noticed one poor fellow with a wagon tire across his bowels, and from appearances, it had been heated red-hot and then laid upon him while still alive."[12]

In all, twenty-seven corpses were recovered from the two battlefields, including that of Caspar Collins. "Lieut. Collins was horribly mutilated," reported a correspondent for the *Chicago Journal*, "his hands and feet cut off, throat cut, heart taken out, scalped, and one hundred arrows in him."[13]

Even as the Indians relentlessly assailed the road, several strong army columns were marching for the heart of hostile country to punish the Sioux, Northern Cheyenne, and Arapahoe as well as open new roads north. Mincing no words, the expedition commander, Brigadier General Patrick Connor, informed his men: "You will not receive overtures of peace or submission from Indians but will attack and kill every male Indian over twelve years old."[14]

For many soldiers, the Powder River Campaign was their first glimpse of the Far West. For most, it was not pleasant. As he struggled with a train of wagons through Nebraska, teamster Albert Holman groaned:

> [E]very mile took us deeper into the sand hills and the sun of a July day pouring its hot rays upon the burning sand, glistened so that we were nearly blinded. By afternoon it was impossible to go but a few rods at a time, it being necessary to stop often and let the cattle breath and rest, for the poor creatures were suffering so from want of water that their tongues protruded from their mouths, and several of them died. The men, too, were nearly prostrated from the heat, and in fact, some of them were so nearly overcome that they had to be placed in the wagons. The expedition's official thermometer reached 103 at noon, 106 at 2:00 p.m.[15]

"We marched 25 miles and over desolate and rough ground," Lieutenant Charles Springer recorded in his diary. "Nothing but wild sage and prickly pears grow there. The heat was intense, and the dust rolled in one white thick cloud thro' the column. Not a drop of water along our route."[16]

Looking like "a lot of chimney sweeps" when the dusty day's march was done, many men, Springer included, found the "musketos" so thick that sleep was "out of the question." Before long there was more to occupy the troops than heat, sand, and insects.

In the middle of August, as one of the far-flung columns entered hostile country, a large band of Cheyenne appeared. Mindful of the two deadly howitzers the whites possessed—the "guns that shoot twice"—the raiders were content to stampede horses, surprise a straggler or two, and hinder the army's advance in every way possible. Though never decisive, the tactic was effective, as Albert Holman admitted.

> A feeling of forlorn hopelessness seemed to spread over our entire party, not from fear that the Indians could take us, but because of our inability to proceed, or to cope with and drive them away . . . .

> On the two highest hills, one north and one south, were gathered large numbers of Indians and from each group came the most hideous noises. They blew blasts from cavalry bugles . . . danced, yelled, and taunted us in a most aggravating manner . . . . Some few of them could speak enough English to call us all the vile names imaginable, very profane language to embellish their sentences.[17]

The Indians finally withdrew after several days of such harassment. Like the bitter taste of sage, however, the memory of these first encounters lingered with many a young soldier. Meanwhile, on the evening of August 28, the main column led by General Connor learned that a large band of Arapahoe was camped not far away on the Tongue River. A night march was quickly ordered. The following morning Connor's advance spotted a large pony herd grazing quietly on a mesa. In the words of Private Charles Adams:

> General Conner [*sic*] made us a speech saying we were near the Indian village. He had no idea what force was there, but had confidence in the men and expected each man to do his duty. Should we get in close quarters the men should group in fours and stay together, and use their guns (carbines) as long as possible and under no circumstances use their revolvers unless there was no other chance. We were to make every shot count and be sure to leave one shot for ourselves rather than fall into the hand of the Indians . . . . We were to avoid killing women and children as much as possible. It was about eight o'clock when we saw an Indian on a high point, riding in a circle, their signal of danger. The bugle sounded forward, and away we went.[18]

Captain Henry Palmer continues:

> Gen. Conner [*sic*] then took the lead . . . and dashed out across the mesa . . . . [E]very man followed as closely as possible. At first sight of the general, the ponies covering the table land in front of us set up a tremendous whinneying and galloped down toward the Indian village, more than a thousand dogs commenced barking, and more than seven hundred Indians made the hills ring with their fearful yelling. It appeared that the Indians were in the act of breaking camp. The ponies, more than three thousand, had been gathered in, and most of the warriors had secured their horses; probably half of the squaws and children were mounted, and some had taken up the line of march up the stream for a new camp . . . . The general watched the movements of his men until he saw the last men

> emerge from the ravine, when he wheeled on the left into line. The whole line then fired a volley from their carbines into the village without halting their horses, and the bugle sounded the charge . . . . [N]ot a man but what realized that to charge into the village without a moment's hesitation was our only salvation. We already saw that we were greatly outnumbered, and that only desperate fighting would save our scalps.[19]

"As we neared the village," noted Private Adams, "the command divided, some turning to the right, others to the left. The Indians had some of their tepees down and packs on their ponies and some of the ponies were so heavily packed that when they tried to run the packs pulled them over and they could not get up."[20] Returning to Henry Palmer:

> My horse carried me forward almost against my will, and . . . I was in the village in the midst of a hand to hand fight with warriors and their squaws, for many of the female portion of this band did as brave fighting as their savage lords. Unfortunately for the women and children, our men had no time to direct their aim; bullets from both sides and murderous arrows filled the air; squaws and children, as well as warriors, fell among the dead and wounded . . . . One of our men . . . a fine looking soldier with as handsome a face as I ever saw on a man, grabbed me by the shoulder and turned me about so that I might assist him in withdrawing an arrow from his mouth. The point of the arrow had passed through his open mouth and lodged in the root of his tongue. Having no surgeon with us . . . it was . . . decided that to get the arrow out from his mouth, the tongue must be, and was, cut out.[21]

At length, with most of the Indians managing to escape, the troopers took control of the camp. Well aware that his force would be overwhelmed should the warriors return, Connor wisely ordered a withdrawal. Concluded Captain Palmer:

> Two hundred and fifty lodges had been burned with the entire winter supply of the Arapahoe band. The son of the principal chief (Black Bear) was killed, sixty-three warriors were slain, and about eleven hundred head of ponies captured . . . . We brought back to camp . . . eight squaws and thirteen Indian children, who were turned loose a day or two afterwards . . . . Two of our soldiers . . . were found among the dead and three or four died of their wounds.[22]

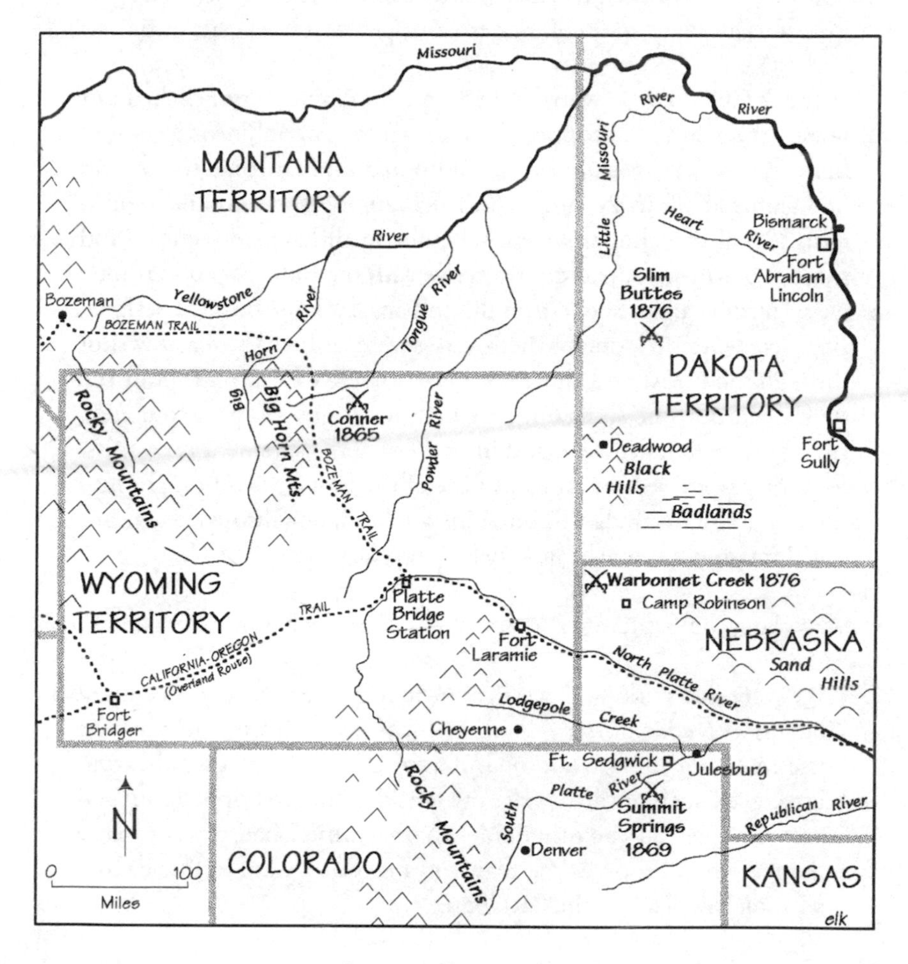

The northern Plains.

Although Connor hoped to press on against the more formidable Sioux and Cheyenne, he first had to link up with his other two columns. Unfortunately, while both units were now united, they were also lost. If Connor had difficulty locating his men, the Indians did not. During the first days of September, the errant command was assailed almost constantly as it struggled its way south. The diary of Lt. Charles Springer describes the initial attack.

> [A]bout 50 Sioux . . . warriors had dashed in among our picked out horses, the guard . . . dropped their guns and run, only 2 or 3 showed fight. Before any assistance from camp had time to come the thieves had gathered about 20 horses and fled among the hills and mountains. Small detachments were sent out in different directions and some of our men . . . had quite a tussle with the Indians. 5 of our men were killed by arrow shots from the Indians, and one of them scalped, two were wounded, one of them very severe, as he had an arrow shot through the breast and the attempt was made to scalp him, but the fiends had no time to fulfill their hellish designs. Some of our men run upon them killed two, and in the heat and excitement (also thirst for revenge) scalped the Indians. One of the Indians was brought into camp. He had one bullet through his forehead, one through the heart, one through the throat, a little below the collar bone.[23]

Four days later, on September 5, Springer's diary took a more personal turn.

> [W]e were just done with a frugal breakfast when the cry was raised "Indians" "to your horses." I shouted [to] my men [to] run for their horses, when a small troop of Indians dashed down toward camp, but received such a warm welcome that they never stopped, but ran across the river on the other side. By that time I had my company mounted, and as soon as the regiment moved forward in line of battle, I took my place in the battalion.[24]

With ten men Springer was ordered to hold the northwest edge of camp.

> I deplyed [*sic*] them as skirmishers and moved forward through the woods until I gained the river bank; there I found some Indians on the other side and we commenced shooting at them and drove them off . . . . Lieut. [Philip] Smiley . . . with 6 men went on the . . . east side of the river, and stopped there about 300 yards from the bank. I intended to join them and moved up the river, when I discoverd a strong party of Indians galloping across the river . . . and going for

> the little squad . . . I shouted "charge" to my men and we went at full gallop to their assistance. We run the chaps off, [but] another . . . large squad galloped towards us [and] I hollered to Lieut. Smiley that I was going to charge [and] he should follow; again my little squad of ten men went with a yell at them, but the Indians never budged, we let a well directed volley fly at them; after the discharge a yell arose which appeared to have broke loose in the infernal regions, and a shower of arrows accompanied the yelling. I shouted "fire" and again a volley hailed among them . . . . I gave the order to fall back at the squad of Lieut. Smiley[.] we stopped wheeled around and again let loose at them, which turned them in a hurry. We followed up our advantage while the squad of Smiley's remained on the hill. Then I observed that the Indians were growing stronger, and tried to cut us off from the hill. I again shouted to fall back, but their number increased every moment. They appeared to grow out of the ground. We were compelled to fall back, but my God, now commenced a scene hard to describe; I noticed a little fellow by the name of Charley Elliott of my company pursued by two tall warriors; I went to his assistance, just as Charley shot the one who struck at him with a tommy hawk. I killed the one with my revolver which shot him in the back; he just rolled from his pony and Charley escaped with a little wound in the small of the back. The arrow had struck the sling belt which saved his life . . . . [T]he one I killed was not over 7 feet from me, hanging on the side of the pony. All his dodging did not help him anything . . . . I still kept shooting with my pistol amongst the pursuing crowd. Lots of the Indians dropped from their saddles to rise no more . . . . Sergt. James Kelly told me afterwards that [another] Indian was close behind me, taking cool and deliberate aim and firing at me. He waited, or expected every minute to see me fall, but luckily I was not touched . . . . Now came two little mountain howitzers . . . and commenced to throw shells amongst them. Of all the running and scampering away I ever saw that beat all. They struck a bee line for the next hill, and never stopped until they reached a point of safety.[25]

Although several comrades were dead or wounded and he himself had come within a hair of death, Springer treated the affair as little more than an adventure. "We had a good deal of fun with the Indians," he confided to his diary, "or, as the men called them the Idaho Militia; how they dodged when they saw the smoke of the artillery . . . and what excellent horsemanship they displayed."[26]

Though the Indians continued their attacks and swarmed about the soldiers "thicker than fiddlers in hell," Springer's party did eventually reach Connor and safety. With the approach of winter, however, the commander prudently moved his column south and the campaign came to a close. Except for the lone victory on the Tongue, the grand expedition had proven "a fizzle." Dozens of men had been killed and wounded and hundreds of horses lost or stolen; all the while, the main aim of the campaign, the mighty Sioux and Northern Cheyenne, had hardly been touched. The U.S. government was coming to the grim realization that only a permanent presence in the heart of Indian country could bring the defiant warriors to terms.

2

A Perfect Silence

With the arrival of fresh troops freed by Appomattox, the overland trail to California was, for the most part, secure. By the spring of 1866 the entire road from the Missouri River to the Pacific was open and traffic moved in relative safety. Other routes, however, including the Santa Fe and Smoky Hill roads in Kansas and the Bozeman Trail from Fort Laramie to the mines of Montana, were still largely under Indian control.

In an effort to resolve the issue of the latter route, a U.S. peace commission, headed by Nathaniel Taylor, met at Fort Laramie with the tribes over whose land the road ran. Among all Indians assembled, Sioux chief Red Cloud stood out from the rest. Wrote one young officer:

> Red Cloud . . . was one of the most picturesque red men I ever saw, a model of physical excellence standing over six feet in height, straight as an arrow, with the impress of command stamped on every line of his powerful face and revealed in his every movement, so full of dignity that he appeared like a Chesterfield of the Plains. Untutored in the ways of civilization, he was a splendid creation of the earth and air and sunshine.[1]

When the conference opened on June 5, a correspondent of the Denver *Rocky Mountain News* was on hand.

[T]he Peace Commission convened in front of headquarters under a very large covering festooned with cedar . . . . Nineteen chiefs in a circle fronted them . . . . After smoking the pipe of peace, the Post Chaplain . . . made a very appropriate prayer, which was replied to by Red Cloud, who prayed to the Great Spirit for peace, and then presented Taylor with a very fine redstone pipe with an embroidered tobacco pouch. Then, with a general hand-shaking, Red Cloud . . . said: "We have come to hear our Great Father."

Taylor replied by reading: "We have come here as special messengers from your Great Father . . . . [He] desires to be at peace with you, also to make a treaty. You know that war brings trouble, and in war sometimes bad white men and bad Indians do bad things. What we want your people to remember is that this treaty is the last one, not made for a day, but for all time. We are willing to listen with patience, in council, to what you have to say. We will tell you all we have to say, keeping nothing back. You know that the Great Father . . . has treated you well. He has given you provisions.

"In the mountains there are many people; they all get their provisions by [wagon] trains. They want a road by which they can travel. White men will go about as they always have done. It is true they drive off game; therefore, we are willing to pay liberally for the damage done. The Great Father does not wish to keep many soldiers in this country. He will be satisfied if the mails and telegraph are not molested. We do not ask you to give up the country or sell it. We only ask for roads to travel back and forth, and no roads will be made except by orders from the Great Father, so as not to disturb the game; and whatever damage is done by the roads would be paid by the Great Father."

At the conclusion of the address, Red Cloud shook hands with the commissioners and said that "he had nothing to say, as he wished to get all the Indians together and have a talk." The council then adjourned.[2]

In truth, Red Cloud and many other chiefs wanted no part of the proposed treaty. The land through which the Bozeman passed was some of the best hunting ground on the northern Plains. Though the talks continued the following day, little was gained. "[I]t is transparent that the Indians will with great reluctance consent to roads being made through the country," the Denver reporter concluded. "It does not look reasonable that they will give up this western country to the white man and suffer a gradual extermination, for it is sure that wherever the white man goes, the game will disappear."[3]

Red Cloud. Nebraska Historical Society.

When Colonel Henry Carrington arrived in the middle of the council, and Red Cloud heard that the officer and his seven hundred men were already under orders to march up the Bozeman and build forts, the talks came to a sudden and dramatic end. Pointing his finger at the colonel, the enraged chief glared.

> You are the white eagle who has come to steal the road. The Great Father sends us presents and wants us to sell him the road, but the white chief comes with soldiers to steal it, before the Indian says yes or no. I will talk with you no more. I and my people will go now, and we will fight you. As long as I live I will fight for the last hunting grounds of my people.[4]

Despite the declaration of war, Carrington's column boldly departed Fort Laramie and soon established a permanent camp at the foot of the Bighorn Mountains, adjacent to the Bozeman Trail. Within weeks, the log palisades of Fort Phil Kearny had arisen. A short time later, half of Carrington's command marched north ninety miles and constructed Fort C. F. Smith. Together with Fort Reno to the south, a chain of military posts now straddled the road to Montana at the very seat of Sioux country. True to his word, Red Cloud began the war in earnest. Margaret Carrington, wife of the colonel, noted but a few of the incidents along the Bozeman that summer of 1866.

> **July 22d.** At Buffalo Springs . . . a citizen train was attacked, having one man killed and another wounded.
> **July 23d.** A citizen train was attacked at Dry Fork . . . and two men were killed.
> **July 29th.** A citizen train was attacked at Brown Springs . . . and eight men were killed, two were wounded, and one of these died of his wounds.
> **August 14th.** Joseph Postlewaite and Stockley Williams were killed within four miles of Fort Reno.
> **September 13th.** At midnight a summons came from the hay contractors . . . for help, as one man had been killed, hay had been heaped upon five mowing-machines and set on fire, and two hundred and nine cattle had been stolen by the Indians . . . . The same day at 9 o'clock, Indians stampeded a public herd, wounding two of the herders . . . . Private Donovan came in . . . with an arrow in his hip.
> **September 14th.** Private Gilchrist was killed.
> **September 16th.** Peter Johnson, riding a few rods in advance of his party . . . was suddenly cut off by Indians. Search was made . . . but his remains were not recovered.
> **September 27th.** Private Patrick Smith was scalped . . . but crawled a half mile to the block-house, and survived twenty-four hours.
> Two of the working party in the woods were also cut off from their comrades . . . and were scalped before their eyes.[5]

Although free to come and go, contractors, laborers, and other civilians attached to the army were cautioned not to stray far from the fort. Ridgeway Glover, an artist for *Frank Leslie's Illustrated Weekly*, was one of those in the habit of ignoring such advice. "This morning," Colonel Carrington reported on September 17, "[he] was found two miles from the fort naked, scalped, and his back cleft with a tomahawk."[6] Two days later, an officer's wife, Frances Grummond, recorded the Sioux's increasing boldness:

> Quite a large body of Indians suddenly appeared at the summit of the hill in full war paint, brandishing their spears, giving loud yells and lifting their blankets high in the air as they moved down in an

attempted charge upon the miner's camp. Between one and two hundred Indians were scattered along the crest of that hill.[7]

Red Cloud's campaign continued despite the advent of winter. Writing to his brother on December 15, 1866, Surgeon C. M. Hines describes one incident:

> A few days ago a wagon train had gone up to the mountain five or six miles from this post for the purpose of cutting pine timber for buildings. On their return they were attacked by about 300 Indians. We have a mounted guard on post on top of a very high point near the fort, who telegraphed to us by means of a flag of the condition of the wood train. The mounted cavalry and infantry were immediately ordered out to relieve them. They started in two parties, Colonel Carrington and fourteen men going in one direction, and about thirty in another. The larger party . . . came upon the Indians suddenly, and charged them. The fight continued for a distance of eight miles or more . . . . [I]n the fight the cavalry broke and were brought back (some of them) by Captain [Frederick] Brown and Lieutenant [Alfred] Wands levelling their guns at them, and telling them that they would shoot them . . . . This was just what the Indians wanted. [The officers] with ten or eleven men, remained and fought the whole of them, and whipped them . . . . [T]hey and three or four men started in the pursuit of about thirty Indians, who were apparently retreating; an Indian's horse had almost given out, and Lieutenant [Horatio] Bingham wounded the horse by a pistol shot . . . . The Indian then took to his heels, they following him, cutting at him with their swords . . . . At this time they saw two large bodies of Indians flanking them, when they concluded to run through them; drawing their swords, they laid about them right and left. Lieutenant Bingham did not follow . . . . All got through; but Sergeant [G. R.] Bowers no doubt turned around and fired upon his pursuers; they overtook and put an arrow in him and split his skull open above the eyes . . . . Our people found him a short time afterwards; he was living and in great agony, but died in a short time.[8]

After a search, Lieutenant Bingham also was finally found "in the brush . . . shot with over fifty arrows, lying over an old stump."[9]

With much of his meager force narrowly averting disaster, it was clear to Carrington that decoys were trying to lure troops from the stockade. As a result, he consistently ordered his men to break off hot pursuits, especially those that might lead over Lodge Trail Ridge, a long slope several miles northwest of the post.

"From the 6th to the 19th of December Indians appeared almost daily about the wood party or within sight of the fort," Carrington wrote. "December 19 the picket on Pilot Hill reported the train as corralled and threatened by a large force. I sent Brevet Major James Powell with a detachment to relieve the train. He did his work—pressed the Indians towards Lodge Trail Ridge, but having peremptory orders not to cross it, he returned with the train, reporting the Indians in large force, and that if he had crossed the ridge he never would have come back with his command."[10]

December 21 dawned bright and beautiful and much warmer than normal. In the words of Margaret Carrington:

> Though snow covered the mountains, and there was every indication of the return of severe weather, the morning was quite pleasant. Men only wore blouses at their work, and the train, although much later than usual, went to the Pinery with a strong guard, so that the teamsters, choppers, and escort, all armed, numbered not far from ninety men.
>
> The children ran in about 11 o'clock, shouting "Indians!" and the pickets on Pilot Hill could be distinctly seen giving the signal of "many Indians," on the line of the wood road; and news was also furnished that the train was in corral only a short distance from the garrison.

Margaret Carrington. MADGE SULLIVAN COLLECTION.

> The officers and all the ladies were soon watching for other usual demonstrations, while a detail was being organized to relieve the train.[11]

Private Timothy O'Brien was one of those with the wood crew.

> I was in Wagon No. 2. We were about one mile out from the fort on our way to the mountains to get our load of logs, when we were attacked by the Indians, about fifty or sixty of them . . . . [A]fter repulsing the Indians, we held a consultation and decided to go on to the mountains for our load of logs . . . . Bringing our wood train to the mountains, we hurriedly pulled logs down the mountain sides through the deep snow and after loading our wagons, we started for the fort.[12]

In the meantime, Captain William Fetterman had marched hastily from the post with more than fifty foot soldiers. A newcomer to Fort Kearny, Fetterman was openly contemptuous of his wild adversary. The fact that he and a group of comrades had one day been fired upon by concealed warriors at close range without receiving a scratch left him laughing at the Indians' marksmanship; the ease with which he and a few men had routed a large band the week before caused the captain to sneer at his foe's fighting ability. "A company of regulars," he was heard to say, "could whip a thousand, and a regiment could whip the whole array of hostile tribes."[13] Additionally, after Carrington refused his late request to lead a hundred soldiers against a Sioux encampment that contained perhaps ten times that number, Fetterman's opinion of his commander's courage also plummeted.

In spite of Carrington's standing order—"Support the wood train . . . . Do not engage or pursue Indians at its expense"—William Fetterman could be counted upon to act as his conscience and circumstances dictated.[14]

Soon after the captain left, a nervous Carrington directed a group of horsemen to saddle up. According to Lieutenant Wands:

> The cavalry company, numbering about twenty-seven men, were all mounted and awaiting orders . . . . Colonel Carrington directed me to inform Lieutenant George Grummond that his orders were to join . . . Fetterman's command, report to and receive all his orders from [him] . . . and under no circumstances were they to cross the Bluff in pursuit of Indians. I gave those instructions to Lieutenant Grummond, and while the Corporal of the Guard was unlocking the gate, I returned to Lieutenant Grummond and repeated them,

and asked him if he thoroughly understood them. He replied he did, and would obey them to the letter.

Lieutenant Grummond left the Post with his detachment of cavalry and had proceeded about two hundred yards when he was called back by Colonel Carrington, who was on the sentinel's platform at the time, and who called out in a loud voice, repeating the same instructions given to Lieutenant Grummond by me, and asking him if he understood them. He replied I do.[15]

"The health of Mrs. Grummond was such," revealed Margaret Carrington, "that Lieutenant Wands and other friends urged him, for his family's sake, to be prudent, and avoid all rash movements and any pursuit that would draw them over Lodge Trail Ridge."[16] After a short ride the cavalry joined Fetterman's foot soldiers. Colonel Carrington:

Just as the command left, 5 Indians reappeared at the [creek] crossing. The glass revealed others in the thicket, having the apparent object of determining the watchfulness of the garrison or cutting off any small party that should move out. A case-shot dismounted 1 and developed nearly 30 more, who broke for the hills and ravines to the north.[17]

Eager for the chase, Fetterman did not turn west toward the beleaguered wood train as ordered but promptly charged after the fleeing Indians. Shortly, the entire command disappeared over the forbidden ridge. "At 12 o'clock firing was heard . . . beyond Lodge Trail Ridge," Carrington recalled. "A few shots were followed by constant shots, not to be counted. Captain [Tenodor] Ten Eyck was immediately dispatched with infantry and the remaining cavalry and two wagons to join . . . Fetterman at all hazards."[18] The colonel's wife continued:

Every shot could be heard, and there was little doubt that a desperate fight was going on . . . . Wagons and ambulances were hurried up; the whole garrison was on the alert; extra ammunition for both parties was started, and even the prisoners were put on duty to give the guard and all available men their perfect freedom for whatever might transpire. Couriers were sent to the woods to bring back the train and its guard, to secure its support, as well as from fear that the diversion of Captain Fetterman from his orders might still involve its destruction . . . . [T]he whole force of armed men left at the post, including guard and everything, was but one hundred and nineteen men.

> Until the wagons galloped out of the gate, we could see a solitary Indian on the highest part of Lodge Trail Ridge; but he soon disappeared. All this time firing was increasing in intensity, and in little more than thirty minutes—after one or two quick volleys . . . and a few scattering shots—a perfect silence ensued. There were then many anxious hearts, and waiting was perfectly terrible! The movements of Captain Ten Eyck were watched with intensest interest . . . . Soon [an] orderly was seen to break away from the command and make for the fort . . . on the run. He brought the message that the valleys were full of Indians, and that several hundred were on the road below, yelling and challenging them to come down; but nothing could be seen of Fetterman.[19]

The wood train arrived without loss, but throughout the increasingly cold day, those inside the fort watched and waited in dreadful anticipation. It was after dark when, with a sense of relief, Ten Eyck's company safely rode through the gates. Inside his wagons, however, lay the white, marble-like corpses of forty-nine men. The captain sadly announced that Fetterman's entire command had been wiped out.

The night of December 21 was one of sleepless terror at Fort Phil Kearny. Recorded an officer:

> We had ten women and several children with us. The colonel gave orders that as soon as the Indians made the expected attack, the women and children should enter the magazine, and the men should hold the fort as long as possible. When they could hold it no longer, they were to get behind the wagons that surrounded the magazine, and when the colonel saw that all was lost, he would himself blow up the magazine and take the lives of all, rather than allow the Indians to capture any of the inmates alive.[20]

Although such an attack did not materialize, Carrington was determined to act. "The following morning," the colonel explained, "believing that failure to rescue [the remaining bodies] would dishearten the command and encourage the Indians . . . I took 80 men and went to the scene of action." What he found on that wind-swept ridge was staggering. Naked, frozen hard as stone, all the bodies had been hacked to pieces.

> Eyes torn out and laid on the rocks; noses cut off; ears cut off; chins hewn off; teeth chopped out; joints of fingers; brains taken out and placed on rocks with other members of the body; entrails taken out

> and exposed; hands cut off; feet cut off; arms taken out from sockets; private parts severed and indecently placed on the person; eyes, ears, mouth, and arms penetrated with spear-heads, sticks, and arrows; ribs slashed to separation with knives; skulls severed in every form, from chin to crown; muscles of calves, thighs, stomach, breast, back, arms, and cheek taken out. Punctures upon every sensitive part of the body, even to the soles of the feet and palms of the hand. All this only approximates to the whole truth.
>
> I found citizen James S. Wheatly and Isaac Fisher . . . who with "Henry rifles" felt invincible, but fell, one having 105 arrows in his naked body . . . . Fetterman and [Frederick] Brown had each a revolver shot in the left temple . . . . The latter went out without my consent or knowledge, fearless to fight Indians with any adverse odds, and determined to kill one at least before joining his company [back east] . . . . As Brown always declared he would reserve a shot for himself as a last resort, so I am convinced that these two brave men fell each by the other's hand rather than undergo the slow torture inflicted upon others . . . . The road on the little ridge where the final stand took place was strewn with arrowheads, scalp poles, and broken shafts of spears. The arrows that were spent harmlessly from all directions show that the command was suddenly overwhelmed, surrounded, and cut off while in retreat . . . . A few bodies were found at the north end of the divide [but] . . . nearly all were heaped near four rocks . . . inclosing a space about 6 feet square, having been the last refuge for defense.[21]

As others passed over the field they noticed that, of all the dead, only one had not been chopped to bits—the bugler, Adolph Metzler. "The bravery of our bugler is much spoken of," remarked a comrade, "he having killed several Indians by beating them over the head with his bugle . . . . [He] fought so courageously that his remains were left untouched but covered with a buffalo robe."[22]

The corpses were loaded in wagons and hauled back to the fort "like you see hogs brought to market," noted one witness.[23]

While the understrength garrison at Phil Kearny nervously manned the walls and the women and children huddled in horror, Carrington sped a courier to Fort Laramie with a desperate plea for help.

> Promptness will save the line, but our killed shows that any remissness will result in mutilation and butchery beyond precedent . . . . Depend upon it that the post will be held so long as a round or a man is left. Promptness is the vital thing. Give me officers and

> men . . . . [T]he Indians are desperate; I spare none, and they spare none.[24]

Reinforcements did arrive, but Red Cloud's assault on the Bozeman Trail rose to such heights that the forts along the road were cut off not only from the outside world but from one another as well. As desperate as the situation was at Phil Kearny, it could have been worse. "We were not as badly off as the men at Fort C. F. Smith," recalled Private William Murphy. "They were abandoned from the middle of November, 1866 until March, 1867 . . . . I am of the opinion that [our] officers thought that the men [there] were all killed at the time of the massacre and no one was left."[25]

"The rations were getting low, and matters were looking very gloomy," acknowledged one of those inside Fort Smith, drummer James Lockwood.

> There was no way of obtaining news from the outside world, and the officers caused a bulletin board to be erected in a public place in the barrack square and upon this they would daily post clippings from newspapers, which they happened to have in their baggage; this served to break the dull, gloomy monotony which seemed to pervade everything, and in some measure to distract their attention from their desperate situation. The snow was very deep and the weather remained bitter cold; the rations gave out entirely, and they were compelled to take the grain which was brought for the animals and boil it to make food with which to sustain the lives of the garrison.[26]

While two volunteers from Fort Phil Kearny did reach Smith that winter, they were intercepted by Indians on the return trip and lost their horses, guns, and supplies. One who knew them remembered:

> Their sufferings were indescribable. They evaded the Indians but, without food, their lot was indeed a hard one. They managed to kill one rabbit, and this they ate raw. Their shoes gave out and they were obliged to take their coats and wrap them about their feet. Their indomitable pluck saved them, however, for about eleven o'clock one night they reached the fort, but they were in a frightful condition.[27]

With the arrival of summer 1867, the Sioux, Cheyenne, and Arapahoe assailed the Bozeman Trail with increased ferocity. Forts C. F. Smith to the north and Reno to the south came in for their share of blood and death but, again, it was Phil Kearny that was the center of attention. On August 2, a large war party surprised a wood crew five miles from the fort. Throughout the morning, fewer than forty men fought from behind a corral of wagon beds against the repeated assaults of more than a thousand Indians. After beating back one attack, Captain James Powell looked down to see yet another horror approaching.

> It chilled my blood. Hundreds and hundreds of Indians [were] swarming up a ravine about ninety yards to the west of the corral . . . . Immediately we opened a terrific fire upon them. Our fire was accurate, cooly delivered and given with most telling effect, but nevertheless it looked for a minute as though our last moment on earth had come.[28]

After hours of fighting under a blazing sun, and with more than ten of their number dead or wounded, the fate of the powder-blackened crew seemed to be sealed. Unbeknownst to the men, a small force with a cannon was bravely making its way toward the battle. In the words of Major Benjamin Smith:

> On nearing the corral of the Wood Party . . . I discovered that a high hill near the road and overlooking the corral . . . was occupied by a large party of Indians, in my estimation five or six hundred were in sight . . . . The grass was burning in every direction . . . . I fired a shot from the Howitzer . . . . The shell . . . fell short . . . but seemed to disconcert them as a number of mounted Indians who were riding rapidly toward my command turned and fled.[29]

Terrified by the "thunder wagon," the Indians broke off their attack. As one of the besieged soldiers later wrote:

> The boom of the big gun was heard, and again, and again, and towards the east we could see the glorious caps on the heads of our comrades in the long skirmish line. We jumped to our feet; we yelled; we threw our caps in the air and hugged each other and some of us cried. The strain was over![30]

In more ways than one, the "strain" was over. Admitting defeat, Ulysses Grant, general-in-chief, concluded in the spring of 1868 that the cost of holding the isolated forts was simply too great. Built to protect the Bozeman Trail, the three posts had barely protected themselves. Though many diehards were outraged—Major Andrew Burt begged to lead a mere 200 men against as many as four thousand warriors camped on the Little

Bighorn—Grant's word was final. The forts were abandoned and Red Cloud's victorious Sioux swept in. After two full years of defiance, the hated symbols were burned to the ground. As the debacle along the Bozeman proved, great campaigns would be necessary before the U.S. Army could hope to vanquish the powerful tribes of the northern Plains.

3

The Last Bullet

"He must not think of enlisting in the regular army. He will regret such a move as long as he is in the ranks. I speak of what I know when I advise against such a move."[1] Thus wrote an army officer to his mother, warning a young relative against making a terrible mistake. After years of scrutiny and growing dismay, the soldier expressed a tacit fact about life in the military—a man could go no lower.

Following the Civil War, an emotionally drained public was in no mood to support another war, especially a dirty, undeclared war far from its doorstep. The patriotic fervor that had filled the ranks of the Grand Army of the Republic early in the conflict was totally lost after the guns fell silent in 1865 and life in the military was seen as an utterly unappealing occupation. Consequently, most who enlisted after Appomattox joined for reasons other than patriotism.

Many German and Italian immigrants with language barriers, as well as Irish day laborers, viewed the army as a ticket to improve their life. The chronically unemployed and those fleeing debt or marital mismatches also thought they saw a haven in the military. Additionally, there were the "Bummers, shirkers [and] Dead Heads," said cynics, the "very off-scouring of all creation" who somehow gravitated to the ranks. Indeed, not a few common criminals and fugitives from justice enlisted simply to obtain free passage west. Once there, many struck off for mining camps at the first opportunity. There were, of course, many decent and upright individuals who entered the post-war army. If recruits were not aware of their lowly status upon enlisting, however, the fact was made abundantly clear soon after.

For most new arrivals the transition to military life could hardly have been more extreme. Whether they came from the steaming, stinking slums of the cities or the sweet, green pastures of the country, many frontier soldiers began their new life amid a miserable collection of mud and stick huts called "forts" dropped down in a strange, daunting world of wind, sand, and sage. "The post was . . . about as dreary as any spot on earth," one writer noted of Fort Wallace in western Kansas. "There were no trees; only the arid plain surrounded it, and the sirocco winds drove the sands of that desolate desert into the dug-outs that served for the habitation of officers and men."[2]

At Fort Sedgwick, Colorado, William T. Sherman witnessed soldiers living in "hovels in which a negro would hardly go." The major general protested, "Surely, had the Southern planters put their negroes in such hovels a sample would, ere this, be carried to Boston and exhibited as illustrative of the cruelty and inhumanity of the man-masters."[3] And the incredible isolation of many prairie posts was almost absolute. Wrote Captain Albert Barnitz from Fort Hays, Kansas:

> The latest paper that has reached this post, so far as I am aware, is a copy of the Washington *Chronicle* of March 22, over a month old!—and it has been read by every body in the regiment I suppose, as, when I last saw it, it had the appearance of an old spelling book where little thumbs have worn through its pages![4]

"The arrival of the coach at the fort was the occasion of a general turnout of the officers of the garrison," an amused New York reporter noted at Fort Wallace in 1868.

> The first inquiry was after the mail and while that was being assorted, in the sutler's store, a group assembled around asking after every item of news from Sheridan, as if that enterprising "city" were in the heart of business, trade, and fashion . . . . The nearest settlement was Pond City, quite an extravagant appellation for a relay station with a community of about a half a dozen semi-barbarous inhabitants. Exclusive of this frontier emporium and Sheridan, about fifteen miles distant, there was not a settlement within a hundred miles of the fort.
>
> As may be imagined, the arrival of a stranger . . . was a rare and important event in the daily routine of the garrison.[5]

Because of the distances involved, supplying the frontier forts was cumbersome and costly. Argued General Sherman:

> If the army could be concentrated and quartered in the region of supplies, the expenses could be kept down to a comparatively small sum; or if we had, as in former years, a single line of frontier a little in advance of the settlements, the same or similar would be the result; but now, from the nature of the case, our troops are scattered by companies to posts in the most inhospitable parts of the continent, to which every article of food, forage, clothing, ammunition, &c., must be hauled in wagons hundreds of miles at great cost. For the same reason this department is heavily taxed by the cost of fuel and materials for making huts, sometimes at a distance of one or two hundred miles from a place where a growing twig as large as a walking stick can be found.[6]

Rancid bacon and wormy bread soon became a staple of the men's diet, resulting in much sickness and disease. Given the dreary conditions—and with the drudgery of drill, the monotony of garrison duty, and the paltry pay a soldier received—it is not surprising that after gaining his first glimpse of military life, many a new recruit did not wait around for a second.

"The desertions were unceasing," one officer's wife admitted. "The nearer the troops approached the mountains, the more the men took themselves off to the mines . . . . At one company post on the South Platte . . . the captain woke one morning to find that his first-sergeant and forty out of sixty men that composed the garrison, had decamped, with horses and equipments, for the mines."[7]

Among those who decided to make the most of a bad situation, there were more surprises. Newcomers soon discovered that the weather on the Plains was one of incredible extremes. Without the buffer of mountain or forest, prairie winds delivered some of the coldest winters and hottest summers on earth. In addition to the perils overhead—blizzards in winter, tornadoes in summer, ferocious hailstorms at any time—there were the hazards below: scorpions, tarantulas, rattlesnakes, and, near any body of Western water, multitudes of mosquitos. Scribbled Hervey Johnson from the banks of the North Platte:

> Just now is the height of the musketo season, I dont think I ever saw any thing to exceed it. The boys all go about with handkerchiefs tied round their faces and a brush in one hand. [O]f an evening we build

> smokes all about the parade [ground] and in the quarters to drive out the "varmints" I can scarcely write for them.[8]

Occasionally, there were more serious hazards, as a soldier at Fort Larned, Kansas, graphically made note:

> [A] mad wolf, a very large grey wolf, entered the post and bit one of the sentinels—ran into the hospital and bit a man lying in bed—passed another tent, and pulled a man out of his bed, biting him severely—bit one man's finger nearly off—bit at some woman, and I believe one or two other persons in bed . . . . [He] passed through the hall of [a] house, and pounced upon a large dog which he found there, and whipped him badly in half a minute, and then passed on to where there was a sentinel guarding the haystacks, and tried to bite the sentinel, but did not succeed—the sentinel shooting and killing him on the spot! He proved to be of a very unusual size, and there appears to be no doubt that he had the hydrophobia. The Indians say that they have never known any one bitten by a mad wolf to recover.[9]

One of the few bright spots in any recruit's month was payday. It was also one of the worst days of the month for officers. "I wish it did not come so often," fretted one officer's wife. "The men are almost unmanageable as soon as they have a dollar."[10]

Situated near almost every frontier fort was a squalid huddle of tents, shacks, and dugouts that specialized in fleecing the soldier. In the numerous "gambling hells," greenhorns soon were separated from their money. Bordellos were also popular on payday, though the better resorts were beyond the means of most lowly "soger bois." As a result, many privates frequented "hog ranches"—filthy, dark dens where disease was rampant and a "case of the clap" was often the consequence.

Of all the problems encountered by officers on payday, however, liquor was by far the greatest source of woe. Under nearly every roof from the Missouri River to the Rockies was ensconced a barrel or two of "the meanest whisky on earth."

"Plains whisky is usually very rapid in its effects," noted one expert. "A barrel of tolerably good whiskey sent from the States was, by the addition of drugs, made into several barrels after it reached the Plains."[11] At Hays City, Dobytown, Julesburg, Sheridan, and other lawless towns near forts, drunken troops ran amok, rioting, fighting, murdering one another, even assaulting their own officers.

"The Officer of the Day came in and ordered the men to camp," wrote a soldier following payday in Dodge City, Kansas. "One of the men, full of liquor and beer, grabbed the Officer . . . took his belt off and threw him under the billiard table."[12]

Many officers tried mightily to keep the men and whiskey apart by threatening saloon keepers, dumping barrels into the streets, and flogging enterprising peddlers who slipped into camp. As one frontier editor made clear, however, it was an impossible task:

> [T]he other day a squad of soldiers from Fort Laramie went to a ranche five miles distant, demanded whisky, and, being refused, fired a volley into the building. The affair ended in the burning of the ranche and robbing of the safe, the owner losing $60,000. Now, the crime of the ranche-man lay in not selling whisky to the soldiers, but as in Fort Sedgewick [*sic*], the other day, a man received one hundred lashes with a plaid thong because he did sell whisky to soldiers . . . . The case seems to stand now like this: If you don't sell whisky to soldiers you are shot, your house is burned, and your money is stolen; if you do sell it, you get a hundred lashes well laid on.[13]

Punishment for unruly troops might range from the "month and a month"—thirty days in the guardhouse and thirty days without pay—to being branded and drummed out of the service. Generally, the penalty fell somewhere in between. A sutler's clerk in Montana happened upon one group of payday prisoners.

> [T]hey have some tied up by their thumbs, some by the arms, ala spread eagle; one fellow, whom they couldn't manage any other way, bucked and gagged and laid out in the snow four hours; a most severe and almost cruel punishment; but he deserved it richly.[14]

"At the guard tent . . . four stakes were driven into the ground; and the drunken soldier was stretched out full length and tied to them," recounted Private William Murphy from Wyoming. "Sun beating down on him, flies eating him up (in eyes, nose, mouth, ears). It was reported that he died."[15]

"For about a week after pay day," wrote another trooper from Fort Hays, "it would be nothing for a company to have half a dozen enlisted men in the guard house. I remember on one encampment after pay day there were about seventy-five men walking around in a circle, keeping step, and each man had a log of cord wood on his shoulders, and the procession was headed by a sergeant major with a log on his shoulder."[16]

Another soldier added, "They make them carry them sometimes till they cannot stand any longer, but it doesn't do much good . . . they will get drunk again the next day."[17]

Though they tried to regulate the drinking habits of their men, the commanders themselves set poor examples. "I should be sorry," admitted an army surgeon to his sister, "to see you married to an officer [for it would lead] not only to privations but to a life with confirmed drunkards and blackguards."[18] Many officers drank to excess. After listing in his journal the numerous "physical and intellectual" reasons why he should swear off liquor, Captain Albert Barnitz did. "Besides," he mused, "the example of an officer who does not drink at all is much needed in the regiment, and I might almost say in the Army at large!"[19]

In a letter to his wife, Barnitz described his circle of friends.

> Capt. Gillette and Major Beebe are confirmed inebriates, and the same may be said of Col. Keogh—they are seldom sober. The same is true of Col. West. He was drunk all the time that we were on the late expedition, and had to be hauled in an ambulance. He has been drunk for a week past, and . . . I might name a good many others who are addicted to intemperance!—Sam Robbins and "Salty" Smith are not always duly sober, and Captain Hamilton winks with unusual rapidity at times!—I cannot say that I ever know him to be more seriously affected by liquor. Brevet Major Asbury . . . who is here, is drunk nearly all the time! The fact is Jennie, there appears to be a premium offered for drunkenness in the army![20]

While drinking was far and away the favorite pastime of officers and men, guarding the frontier and fighting hostile tribes was their profession. For the new arrival to the Plains, first exposure to Indians was usually the "Hangs-around-the-forts," those who set up tepees near the gates and lived a semi-permanent existence. To soldiers steeped in the novels of James Fenimore Cooper and the image of the "noble red man," the reality was a severe setback. Sleeping, loafing, begging, pilfering, and above all, drinking, formed the daily routine of many male hang-arounds. "Lo, the poor Indian," began the sympathetic though distant Englishman, Alexander Pope, in a philosophical poem enumerating the trials, misfortunes, and virtues of the native. After several weeks in the West, most soldiers simply dropped the "poor Indian" and facetiously dubbed him "Lo." And for those, like Lieutenant James Steele, who harbored romantic notions of sharing breathtaking sunsets with beautiful Indian princesses, their dreams were blasted to shreds.

> There is really no more beauty to be found among Indian "maidens" than there is among gorillas . . . . More false than ever Cooper's wonderful tales, are the poems which descant upon the charms of dusky love and the romance of wilderness affection . . . . The man who invented those charming but phenomenally false Indian ideals, and first crowned the universal squaw—squat, angular, pig-eyed, ragged, wretched, and insect haunted—with the roses of love, ought to see the woman once, and as a punishment, to be subjected for a session to her indescribable blandishment.[21]

And for those not shackled by Steele's standards, there were other surprises as well. "[T]he class of Indians that settle round a post have a large number of worthless, lewd women along, who are more or less diseased," revealed an officer from Montana. "Two-thirds of the inmates of the post hospital have been placed there by the effects of diseases, contracted with these Indian women."[22]

If soldiers had too many encounters with "friendlies," once in the field, most did everything in their power to avoid meeting "hostiles." Private Alson Ostrander:

> As we got farther into the Indian country, I found that the enthusiasm for the wilds of the West I had gained from Beadle's dime novels gradually left me. The zeal to be at the front to help my comrades subdue the savage Indians . . . also was greatly reduced. My courage had largely oozed out while I listened to the blood-curdling tales the old-timers recited. But I was not alone in this feeling. When we got into the country where Indian attacks were likely to happen any moment, I found that every other person in the outfit, including our seasoned scouts, was exercising all the wit and caution possible to avoid contact with the noble red man. Instead of looking for trouble and a chance to punish the ravaging Indians, the whole command was trying to get through without a fight.[23]

When encounters unavoidably arose, it was almost always on the Indians' terms. Though pitched battles and dramatic charges did occur, especially when the odds favored them, hit-and-run tactics were the warriors' forte. And, after years of practice, the Indian had become a master of them. Expecting the open and "manly" combat displayed in the Civil War, many novices at first laughed at what they construed as "Lo's" cowardly behavior.

"I only wish you could witness the Indian mode of fighting; it really is amusing sometimes!" Albert Barnitz wrote to his wife, Jennie. "The Indians maneuver so much like wolves! They always ride at full speed, whooping, and . . . are no sooner driven from one sand hill, than they pop up on another, always passing around its base, and ascending it from the far side."[24]

If Barnitz initially found Indian tactics amusing, he and many others soon discovered that they were engaged in deadly serious work.

> [They are] always watching for a chance to make a dash, and cut off some straggler, or drive through some thin part of a line! One morning, just as we were breaking camp, a party dashed down suddenly and cut off two men of "F" Troop, and 4 horses and were off like a flash, carrying off the men—whom they had wounded—on their ponies—a vigorous and immediate pursuit forced them to drop one of the men, who although badly wounded will probably recover, but the other could not be rescued, and if he lived long enough they doubtless had a war dance around and tortured him to death.[25]

"[I]n less time than it takes to write this, six Indians dashed up out of that hidden gully, filled Blair with arrows, took his scalp, and then tomahawked him right before our eyes."[26] So wrote Alson Ostrander, sketching a scene he and hundreds of horrified soldiers would witness during their years on the Plains. As Ostrander, Barnitz, and others learned firsthand, those who treated Indian tactics lightly did so at their peril. Moreover, any who at first glance discounted the warriors' weapons gained new respect after suddenly facing them. Although hostiles increasingly carried firearms, the bow and arrow remained their weapon of choice. As one astute observer of Indian warfare, Margaret Carrington, noted:

> Popular opinion has regarded the Indian bow and arrow as something primitive . . . and quite useless in a contest with the white man. This idea would be excellent if the Indian warriors would calmly march up in line of battle and risk their masses . . . against others armed with the rifle . . . . At fifty yards, a well-shapen, iron-pointed arrow is dangerous and very sure. A handful drawn from the quiver and discharged successively will make a more rapid fire than that of a revolver, and at very short range will farther penetrate a piece of plank or timber than the ball of an ordinary Colt's navy pistol.[27]

Added Captain Eugene Ware:

> While a revolver could shoot six times quickly . . . it could not be reloaded on horseback on a run with somebody pursuing. But the

> Indian could shoot six arrows that were as good as six shots from a revolver at close range and then he could shoot twenty-four more in rapid succession. And so, when a soldier had shot out all his cartridges he was a prey to the Indian with a bow and arrow who followed him.[28]

There was another item about which newcomers were soon made aware: Of all the horrors the Plains had to offer, falling into hostile hands was the most terrible. "Save the last bullet for yourself" was stock advice uttered in deadly earnest. "The great real fact is," declared Colonel Henry Carrington, "that these Indians take alive when possible, and slowly torture."[29]

"You could always tell which casualties had been wounded [first]," one sergeant reminisced, "because the little Indians and the squaws, after removing the clothes, would shoot them full with arrows and chop them in the faces with hatchets. They never mutilated a dead man, just those who had been wounded."[30]

"A favorite method of torture was to 'stake out' the victim," revealed Colonel Richard Dodge.

> He was stripped of his clothing, laid on his back on the ground and his arms and legs, stretched to the utmost, were fastened by thongs to pins driven into the ground. In this state he was not only helpless, but almost motionless. All this time the Indians pleasantly talked to him. It was all kind of a joke. Then a small fire was built near one of his feet. When that was so cooked as to have little sensation, another fire was built near the other foot; then the legs and arms and body until the whole person was crisped. Finally a small fire was built on the naked breast and kept up until life was extinct.[31]

While such torture could take hours, hideous mutilation might occur in the blink of an eye. Soon after two soldiers left their column to cut hay near Julesburg, Colorado, drummer James Lockwood and his companions watched in disbelief as the men were jumped by Indians. "[I]n less time than it takes to read this," Lockwood later wrote, "they were stripped of their clothing, mutilated in a manner which would emasculate them, if alive, and their scalps torn from their heads."[32]

Ghastly mutilation and torture of comrades was terrible enough. When the young soldier had seen the results of an Indian raid on unsuspecting settlers, however, he often became a different sort of man. Captain Henry Palmer:

Henry Palmer. Kansas State Historical Society.

> We found the bodies of three little children who had been taken by the heels by the Indians and swung around against the log cabin, beating their heads to a jelly. Found the hired girl some fifteen rods from the ranch staked out on the prairie, tied by her hands and feet, naked, body full of arrows and horribly mangled.[33]

Not surprisingly—and in spite of attempts by officers to stop it—many men were quick to respond in kind. "We were bewhiskered savages living under canvas," admitted one soldier. After a fight with troops near Fort C. F. Smith in 1867, Sioux warriors were forced to retire, leaving one of their slain behind. The whites soon decamped but, according to one witness, "before leaving the ground they scalped the dead Indian in the latest and most artistic western style, then beheaded him, placing his head upon a high pole, leaving his carcass to his friends or the wolves."[34]

Because Indians commonly dug up bodies and scalped them, when army columns moved out they marched over graves to obliterate all trace. Again, the violation of burial sites was a ghoulish game some soldiers were not slow to learn. After discovering an Indian burial ground in Montana, Lieutenant Edward Godfrey recounted with disgust:

A number of their dead, placed upon scaffolds or tied to the branches of trees, were disturbed and robbed of their trinkets. Several persons rode about exhibiting their trinkets with as much gusto as if they were trophies of their valor, and showed no more concern for their desecration than if they had won them at a raffle.[35]

"Ten days later," Godfrey added with a note of ironic satisfaction, "I saw the bodies of these same persons dead, naked and mutilated."[36]

Considering the unspeakable fate awaiting them should they fall into hostile hands, it is not surprising that, when facing Indians, many soldiers "skedaddled." Occasionally, officers too showed the "white feather." Recalled Captain R. G. Carter:

Once a detail was sent out scouting under Lt. _____. They were attacked by Indians outnumbering the men two to one. This officer ran—unqualifiedly ran, begging his men to follow and "not fire a shot for fear of angering the Indians." [Sergeant] Charlton rode beside him and said: "Lt., if we stop and make a stand they will run." "No! no! we can do nothing but try to out-run them," _____ said. Charlton then took command and also chances of being tried for disobedience of orders, made a stand with the men, who were more experienced in such warfare than this young untried officer, and drove the Indians off. This officer came to him afterwards and asked him not to say anything about this at the post, and Charlton told me that he never did.[37]

For every coward, though, there was a hero. Courage in a gallant, popular conflict was often rewarded with fame, fortune, and rapid promotion. In a vicious, forgotten war waged in the wilderness, however, the reward for valor was often nothing more than a painful death, a dusty grave, and a simple memory that burned in a man's soul forever. Lieutenant Charles Springer:

We buried Morris in the morning . . . . No head board, nor marble catafalk marks the spot of a good soldier who died in the noble and generous act of helping a comrade to get out of the hands of the foe; no soldier salute sounded war like over the grave, no muffled drum solemnized the burial, no tears of relations were shed upon the grave. Was buried upon an open ground, the body scented with turpentine, then the whole wagon train drove over his grave to prevent the Indians from finding his grave and scalping him. I read a chapter from the Bible and acted the preacher—James Morris is no more—Requiscat in pace.[38]

4

The Man, The Monster, The War

Pawnee Rock, Santa Fe Trail, June 11:

> About two miles further on, we found another body filled with arrows, the hands taken off at the wrists, the feet taken off at the ankles, the heart taken out, and the head scalped. The third body was found . . . filled with arrows, hands and feet taken off, the head skinned and heart taken out and laid on the body. About a hundred yards off a wolf was scampering off with a hand.[1]

Downner's Station, Smoky Hill Road, November 19:

> The body of one lay in front of the ranch, stripped of all clothing, and from his chest protruded more than twenty arrows . . . . Not far away lay another, also nude, his body pierced with many arrows, his tongue cut out, and he was otherwise namelessly mutilated. In the rear of the ranch a still more sickening sight met our view. Here the fiends had made a fire . . . and across the yet smouldering embers lay the body of a man half consumed from the knees to the shoulders. The arms were drawn to the chest, the hands clenched, and every feature of the face indicated that the man had died in agony. Without doubt he had been burned alive.[2]

Thus ran the reports from Kansas, 1865. After the slaughter on Sand Creek the year before, the outraged tribes of the southern Plains swept the prairie with a wave of robbery, rape, and murder. Commerce and communication on the overland routes thinned to a trickle and westward immigration halted altogether. Although Coloradans and Westerners in general heartily endorsed the results of Sand Creek, many in the East were horrified. Indeed, a tremor of shock and revulsion shook many Americans and thousands cried for a more humane solution to the Indian question. Additionally, with victory in the Civil War and the end of slavery, the powerful forces of Abolitionism suddenly turned their impulses toward helping the Indian.

Bowing to the pressure and its own sincere desire to end the war, the U.S. government assembled a peace commission to deal with the tribes of the southern Plains. In October 1865, the two parties, with frontiersmen Kit Carson and William Bent serving as interpreters, met on the Little Arkansas River in southern Kansas. After several days of talks the council came to an agreement and signed a treaty. In exchange for gifts, annuities, and large reservations in the Indian Territory, the tribes agreed to vacate the land between the Arkansas and Smoky Hill rivers, the country through which the overland routes ran and over which the railroads would soon follow. With both sides in accord, the council adjourned.

"The consultations were harmonious & friendly," one white participant jotted in his journal. "They will probably keep the terms if we do."[3] Hardly had the ink dried, however, when reality set in. What red and white leaders said was one thing; what their young men did was another. Reckless young men, seeking plunder and adventure, had no intention of living within a reservation; at the same time, white outlaws from Kansas and Texas viewed Indian pony herds as easy marks. Throughout 1866 numerous violations of the treaty were recorded by both sides. Although generally random, incidents involving young warriors became increasingly menacing until, by the winter of 1866–67, many on the frontier feared a general uprising. After talking in January 1867 with a Kiowa peace chief, Major Henry Douglas reported darkly from Fort Dodge, Kansas.

> He says . . . all the tribes north and south of the Arkansas will be in the outbreak; his own tribe among them. He also states that Satante [*sic*] . . . a principal chief of the Kiowas, is always talking of war; that they have already had a council at the Kiowa camp, in which the Cheyennes, Sioux, Arapahoes, Kiowas, Comanches, and [Plains] Apaches were represented, and it was agreed that as soon as the grass was old enough they would commence war.[4]

In addition to the threats and taunts from the Southern Arapahoe, two months later Douglas received a list of demands from Satanta.

> [H]e gave me ten days to move from this post . . . . That all white men must move east of Council Grove by the spring . . . . [T]hat he wanted the mules and cavalry horses fattened, as he would have use for them, for he intended to appropriate them; that all Indians had agreed to stop the railroads and roads at Council Grove; that no roads or railroads would be allowed west of that point . . . . No wagons will be allowed on the road except those that bring presents.[5]

As a result of such threats, as well as the increasing number of Indians prowling about the Santa Fe and Smoky Hill trails, Major General Winfield Scott Hancock was ordered to march from Fort Leavenworth, Kansas, and compel the hostile tribes to remain at peace. Acting promptly, Hancock assembled an infantry, cavalry, and artillery force of about 1,500. Joining the general was the newly formed 7th Cavalry. While the normally absent colonel, A. J. Smith, was its nominal commander, the "boy general" of the Civil War, Lieutenant Colonel George Armstrong Custer, was the regiment's leader in fact.

"We go prepared for war," Hancock announced to his men. "No insolence will be tolerated from any band of Indians who we may encounter. We wish to show them that the government is ready and able to punish them if they are hostile."[6] After calling for a council at Fort Larned with the various tribal chieftains, Hancock was chagrined when only Tall Bull, White Horse, and a dozen Cheyenne warriors appeared. Nevertheless, on April 12, the general addressed the small assemblage.

> The Great Father has heard that some Indians . . . are trying to get up war, to try to hunt the white man. That is the reason I came down here. I intend, not only to visit you here, but . . . visit you in your camp. The innocent, and those who are truly our friends, we shall treat as brothers. If we find, hereafter, that any of you have lied to us, we will strike them . . . . I have heard that a great many Indians want to fight. Very well; we are here, and we come prepared for war . . . . We are building railroads, and building roads through the country. You must not let your young men stop them; you must keep your men off the roads . . . . You know very well, if you go to war with the white man you would lose. The Great Father has plenty more warriors. It is true, you might kill some soldiers and

> surprise some small detachments, but you would lose men, and you know that you have not a great many to lose. You cannot replace warriors lost; we can . . . . Let the guilty, then, beware, I say to you, to show you the importance of keeping treaties made with us, and of letting the white man travel unmolested.[7]

After the chiefs had spoken, the council adjourned. As Albert Barnitz revealed, however, the parley had settled nothing.

> The Big war Chiefs did not talk altogether pleasantly to night I thought—they used some "circumlocution!" . . . . It was obvious that they were not at all satisfied with the prospect of being forced into making a treaty, (and I noticed that . . . "Tall Bull," while making a speech . . . or rather while the interpreter was translating . . . stood tapping the ground with his foot, in a very defiant manner) . . . . We march at 7 o'clock tomorrow morning to the Cheyenne camps—without invitation!—to visit them at home, and talk war or peace to them, as they may elect.[8]

Despite the plea of Cheyenne agent Edward Wynkoop, who insisted that after Sand Creek the Indians would stampede at the approach of an army column, Hancock set out the following day for the village, situated somewhere up the Pawnee Fork. Next morning, April 14, the general's advance was suddenly barred by several hundred Sioux and Cheyenne warriors.

"[O]ne of the finest and most imposing military displays . . . which has ever been my lot to behold," praised George Custer, describing his first confrontation with the braves.

> It was nothing more nor less than an Indian line of battle drawn directly across our line of march; as if to say: thus far and no farther. Most of the Indians were mounted; all were bedecked in their brightest colors, their heads crowned with the brilliant war bonnet, their lances bearing the crimson pennant, bows strung, and quivers full of barbed arrows. In addition to these weapons . . . each one was supplied with either a breech-loading rifle or revolver, sometimes with both . . . . General Hancock . . . coming suddenly in view of the wild fantastic battle array . . . hastily sent orders to the infantry, artillery, and cavalry to form line of battle . . . . The cavalry . . . came into line on a gallop, and, without waiting to align the ranks carefully, the command was given to draw saber. As the bright blades

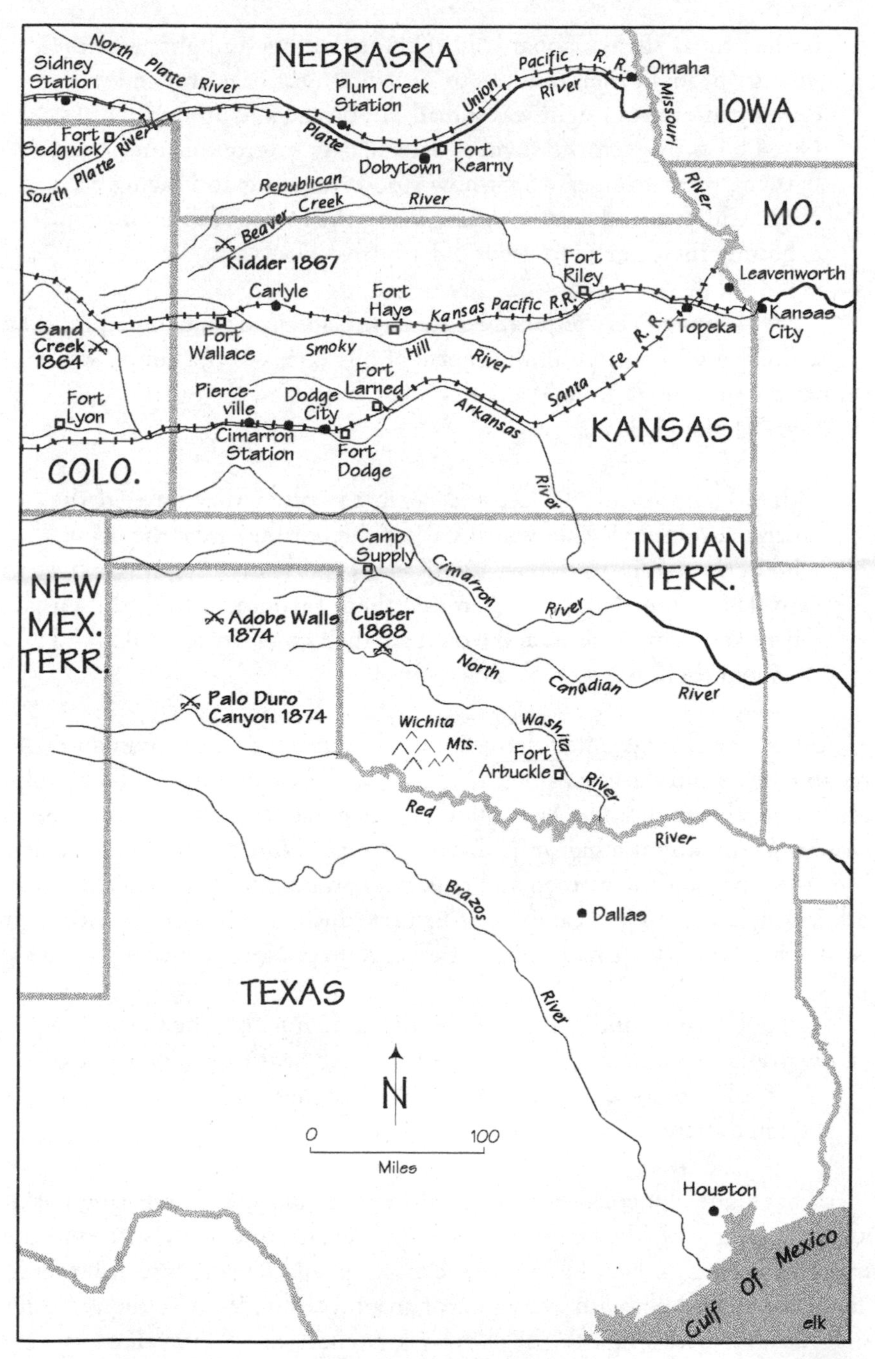

The southern Plains.

> flashed from their scabbards into the morning sunlight, and the infantry brought their muskets to a carry, a most beautiful and wonderfully interesting sight was spread out before and around us . . . . Not a bush or even the slightest irregularity of ground intervened between the two lines which now stood frowning and facing each other. Chiefs could be seen riding along the line as if directing and exhorting their braves to deeds of heroism.[9]

"They kept at a very respectful distance," Captain Barnitz noted, "until a big white flag was hoisted in the centre of our line, when a couple of them ventured near enough to hold a parley."[10]

General Hancock:

> [T]hey came on until I ordered them to halt. I then invited the chiefs to an interview, in which I asked them if they were the people who were anxious to fight—saying that I was ready if such was the case. They replied, "No." I then told them I would go toward their village and camp near it, and would see their chiefs in council . . . . I then told them to go on to their camp.[11]

After the Indians had left, Hancock reformed the command and resumed his bold advance along the Pawnee. "We came up to their camp, after a march of ten and a half miles," the general continued. "I encamped close to them, about a half mile distant. Roman Nose . . . and other chiefs informed me that the women and children had become frightened and run off, leaving everything in camp."[12] When asked why the people had fled, as it was obvious the whites had come in peace, Roman Nose replied:

> Are not women and children more timid than men? The Cheyenne warriors are not afraid, but have you ever heard of Sand Creek? Your soldiers look just like those who butchered the women and children there.[13]

That night Hancock learned that the entire village was preparing to slip away. Moving quickly, he ordered the 7th Cavalry to quietly surround the camp. Crawling on hands and knees, expecting wild screams and a shower of arrows to greet them with every foot of ground covered, the soldiers, Custer included, crept through the black toward the lodges. "While all of us were full of the spirit of adventure," Custer remembered, "there was scarcely one of us who would not have felt more comfortable if we could have got back to our horses without loss of pride."[14] When the troops finally reached the edge of the village, it became apparent that, in Custer's words, "the bird had flown." Accompanied by an army surgeon, the relieved officer explored the deserted tepees.

> I had entered several without discovering anything important . . . . There were dogs of all ages, sexes and sizes. In one of the lodges we found young puppies, in another we found in a camp-kettle a mess of stewed dogs . . . . Finally, in company with the doctor I arrived at one the interior of which was quite dark, the fire having almost died out. Procuring a lighted fagot, I prepared to explore it as I had done the others; but no sooner had I entered the lodge than my fagot failed me, leaving me in total darkness. Handing it out to the doctor to be relighted, I began feeling my way about the interior of the lodge. I had almost made the circuit when my hand came in contact with a human foot.[15]

After some anxious moments, the doctor finally arrived with the torch.

> [T]here, directly between us, wrapped in a buffalo robe, lay . . . a little Indian girl, probably ten years old; not a full-blood, but a half-breed. She was terribly frightened at finding herself in our hands, with none of her people near. Why was she left behind in this manner? . . . [O]ur half-breed interpreter, was called in . . . . [A]fter recovering sufficiently to talk she said "the Indian men did her bad."[16]

The terrified child was examined by the physician, who determined that she had indeed been "violated and most shamefully abused."[17]

"Woe be unto these Indians, if ever I overtake them," Custer vowed.[18]

At dawn Hancock ordered the 7th Cavalry to pursue the Sioux and Cheyenne and by force, if necessary, compel them to return and resume talks. Although he wisely delayed burning the lodges until more was heard from Custer, the general grudgingly admitted that "this looks like the commencement of war."

Had he a hundred officers to choose from, Hancock could have found no better man to chase Indians than Custer. "Custer is precisely the man for the job," wrote newspaper reporter and future African explorer Henry Morton Stanley. "A certain impetuosity and undoubted courage are his principal characteristics."[19] Stanley might have added that Custer was energetic, ambitious, and full of fight. More than anything else, what others did for pay and patriotism, the young colonel did from sheer lust for adventure. Already a hero at twenty-seven, following the Civil War the brevet major

Elizabeth and George Custer. KANSAS STATE HISTORICAL SOCIETY.

general might have figured his own salary with any of a dozen concerns eager to fix their name to his national star. Instead, Custer took a reduction in rank, a cut in pay, and set out on a high-risk, low-reward life in the "peacetime" cavalry. Neither he nor his devoted wife, Elizabeth, ever regretted the decision.

From their first step among the cactus and sage, "Autie" and "Libbie" fell at once and forever in love with the Plains. The absolute freedom they felt when riding together over the open spaces enabled their own free spirits to soar. An avid hunter, Custer marvelled that the seemingly sterile prairie actually teemed with what appeared to be an inexhaustible supply of game. By nature an outdoorsman, the colonel savored each day anew the clean air and healthy climate. Custer's fascination with the inhabitants of the Plains was boundless. While other Westerners regarded the Indian as little more than vermin fit for extermination, Custer was intrigued by the customs, traditions, and lore of the tribes. Indeed, fellow officers complained that the lieutenant colonel spent more free time among his Indian scouts than with white men.

When she could not be with him, as was the case during the Hancock campaign, Custer, brimming with boyish enthusiasm, shared with Libbie his daily adventures by prodigious letter writing.

April 20, 1867

The first member of the buffalo family that I saw was a calf about four weeks old. I was riding alone with one of the Delaware Indians we employ as scouts, and the dogs with me. The calf jumped up out of the tall grass and started to run off. The dogs all followed and soon overtook it, each one taking hold, while the calf set up a terrible bellowing; and they held it till I rode up, dismounted, and killed it. I took off one quarter with my hunting-knife, and left the remainder on the ground. Just then one of my guides, a half-breed Cheyenne, came up, and before the blood had ceased flowing, while the carcass was still warm, he cut out the heart and kidneys and ate them at once . . . just as you would eat an apple.[20]

April 30, 1867

I have the funniest pet now. It is a young beaver. He is quite tame; runs about the tent, follows me, and when I lie down in the bed to read, he cuddles up under my gown or on my arm and goes to sleep. He cries exactly like a baby two days old. A person outside the tent would think there was a nursery in here, if he could hear it about 2 o'clock in the morning. I feed it from my hand at the table. Its tail is perfectly flat. I am going to tell Eliza that it used to be round but a wagon ran over it.[21]

Though the Indians had a running start, Custer and the 7th Cavalry steadily closed in on the fleeing Sioux and Cheyenne. Wrote the colonel the following day:

> We continued to gain on them, and were so close that, although the heat of the sun was quite high, the earth disturbed by the feet of their ponies and by dragging their lodge poles was still damp and fresh. I had strong hopes of overtaking them before dark . . . . Seeing that we were gaining upon them, the Indians now began breaking into small bands and separating. I followed the main trail . . . . [M]ost of the bands in leaving seemed to bear to the right, as if being directed toward the Smoky Hill. The trail gradually grew less and more faint, until about 5 p.m., we could only trace them singly and with difficulty.[22]

Custer, who had been so successful against Rebel cavalry that would turn and fight when pressed hard enough, soon learned that if he hoped to bag Indians, surprise, not pursuit, was the key. The next morning Custer and his hapless column reached the Smoky Hill River. There, the troopers saw for themselves that the hostiles had already crossed the overland trail. At one stage stop, two tenders "had been in a state of siege for several days," Albert Barnitz scratched in his diary, "shut up in a little 'Fort' of about the size and appearance of a potato hill!"[23] Custer continued:

> We found, in passing over the route on our eastward march that only about every fourth station was occupied. The occupants of the other three having congregated there for mutual defense against the Indians, the latter having burned the deserted stations . . . . [I]t was not until we reached Lookout Station, a point about fifteen miles west of Fort Hays, that we came upon the first real evidences of an Indian outbreak. Riding some distance in advance of the command, I reached the station only to find it and the adjacent buildings in ashes, the ruins still smoking. Nearby I discovered the bodies of three station-keepers, so mangled and burned as to be scarcely recognizable as human beings. The Indians had evidently tortured them before putting an end to their sufferings . . . . Some men had been up the day before . . . and partly buried the corpses. But the wolves had been there, uncovered the bodies, and eaten the flesh from the legs. The hair was burned from their heads . . . . The flesh was roasted and crisped from their faces and bodies, and altogether it was one of the most horrible sights imaginable.[24]

Learning of the Smoky Hill attacks, Hancock reluctantly ordered the camp on the Pawnee destroyed and whatever hope there had been for avoiding a general Indian war swiftly went up in smoke. Although a soldier bound by duty, Custer was one of those who felt the coming conflict totally unnecessary. "I regarded the outrages that have been committed lately as not the work of a tribe, but of small and irresponsible parties of young men, who are eager for war," he confided to Libbie. "My opinion is, that we are not yet justified in declaring war."[25] Cheyenne agent Wynkoop agreed.

> The nation knows and I know who General Hancock is—know him for the good, brave, faithful soldier who has won the proud position he now holds through gallant and meritorious services; but the Indians were not aware of General Hancock's antecedents, and had no means of discriminating between him and Colonel Chivington, or distinguishing the man from the monster.[26]

With the razing of the village and the onset of a new prairie war, the great national debate flared even greater. Not since the massacre at Sand Creek had the Eastern outcry for a just and humane Indian policy been so forceful. Although the impulse might vary and the venue shift, the Eastern argument was usually the same. One entreaty to Congress was signed by Henry Ward Beecher and other crusaders, including the powerful pacifists, the Quakers:

> It has long been the conviction of the humane amongst us, that our aboriginal inhabitants have been the victims of great wrongs, cruelties and outrage; but it is only recently that the particular nature, the atrocious character, and the frightful results of these crimes have been brought distinctly before us . . . . No nation can safely disregard the just claims of even the humblest class of its citizens . . . . No nation is more sensitive to the claims and obligations of justice than our own; and we are sure that when the true history of the Indian's wrongs is laid before our countrymen, their united voice will demand that the honor and the interests of the nation shall no longer be sacrificed to the insatiable lust and avarice of unscrupulous men.[27]

An erstwhile abolitionist, Wendell Phillips, added:

> Our treatment of the Indian is one of the foulest blots in our history . . . . We shall never be able to be just to other races, or reap the full benefit of their neighborhood till we "unlearn contempt." . . . The popular indifference to this whole question, combined with the selfish greed and bloodthirstiness of the frontier, is obstacle enough to the adoption of this policy . . . . God bless such barbarians and make us like them.[28]

Not surprisingly, such "shad-bellied" sentiments were held in contempt by most Westerners. "Those who never saw [an Indian] think he is a high toned chivalrous character—loving his friends, hating his enemies, never doing a dishonorable action and in every way worthy of the highest respect," a Colorado editor hissed. "Those of us unfortunate western people, who have met the gentleman, don't believe anything about it. We know him to be a dirty, drunken, ignorant, lousey, treacherous, thieving scoundrel. Born a thief, he thinks it is high tallent to lie, and to kill his enemy when asleep, is his glory."[29] Echoed an outraged Kansas journalist:

> Go . . . and point a houseless, impoverished man to the smoking embers of his dwelling, the work of savage hands, where but yesterday he had stock, grain and plenty, after years of hardships and say to him, "the triumph of humanitarian principles!" Kneel beside the dying victim on the plains, scalped and disemboweled, and to his ear whisper—"peace!" Clasp a maniac sister in your arms, upon whose body sixty savage monsters have glutted their passions, restore her purity and call reason to its throne again with words of "peace!"
>
> Could the arrow and tomahawk but reach a few of the "peace" men in our national councils, their blood would color this Indian question with a hue that even Congressmen could understand.[30]

Far removed from the frontier and chained to romantic ideals, few Easterners appreciated the intense hatred Westerners reserved for Indians. Occasionally the poles touched, as when a peace advocate, Senator James R. Doolittle of Wisconsin, rhetorically asked a Denver audience "What should we do with the red man?"

"[T]here suddenly arose," recalled the stunned senator, "such a shout as is never heard unless upon some battle field;—a shout almost loud enough to raise the roof of the Opera House.—'Exterminate them! Exterminate them!' "[31]

When word later arrived that Doolittle's coach had been attacked by Indians on its return east and that the shaken senator, after viewing the remains of several murdered whites, admitted that perhaps his attitudes were wrong, one Denver editor expressed hope. "[B]ut," growled the angry newsman a short time later, "as soon as he reached safety, the dog returned to his vomit again."[32]

"It is doubtful if there be a people on earth concerning whom there is so wide a difference of opinion as the North American Indians," commented Colonel Richard Dodge, expressing what was perhaps the most accurate view of the issue.

> Eastern people, educated by reading Cooper's and other similar novels, to a romantic admiration for the "red man," misled by the travellers' tales of enthusiastic missionaries, or the more interested statements of agents and professional humanitarians; and indulging in a philanthropy safe because distant, and sincere because ignorant, are ready to believe all impossible good, and nothing bad, of the "noble savage." The western frontier people who come in contact with him, who suffer from his depredations, and whose life is made a nightmare by his vicinity, have no words to express their detestation of his duplicity, cruelty and barbarism. No amount of reason, no statement of facts, will ever change the opinion of either eastern or western people on this subject.[33]

In the meantime, as the arguments between east and west continued, the Indians and soldiers of the southern Plains engaged in their own brand of debate.

5

One Equals One

Following the Indian outbreak in April 1867 and the ensuing attacks along the Smoky Hill, a wave of horror swept the southern Plains. Settlers who had arrived but the year before repacked their families and furniture and fled east in terror while frightened station hands along the overland route kept watch from barricaded dugouts. "If Indians come within shooting distance, shoot them," ran a directive from the American Express Company to its employees. "Show them no mercy, for they will show you none."[1]

Although May passed in relative quiet while the hostiles fattened their ponies on spring grass, nervous rumormongers saw with every dust cloud of antelope an approaching war party. Such breathless reports and the patrols they elicited did nothing to help the undermanned military on their increasingly taxed mounts. In an effort to halt the false alarms, an angry George Custer issued a warning:

> The frequency with which fake and startling reports of the presence and movements of bodies of hostile Indians are made . . . demands that in [the] future all persons whether civilians or soldiers who are guilty of bringing in false information, or who through fear, imagination or maliciousness originate reports . . . shall be considered stampeders and at once subjected to summary punishment . . . . It is the duty of officers as well as men, who see objects resembling Indians, to ascertain positively before reporting.[2]

Despite the threat, false alarms persisted in northern Kansas. Farther south, however, there was no need to issue such orders because the reports of raids were almost always true. Even while he was reassuring General Hancock of his friendship, the Kiowa chief Satanta was leading forays up and down the Arkansas Valley that all but closed the Santa Fe Trail. Although strong detachments were posted, every stage stop but two between forts Dodge and Lyon was struck. After losing his horse herd—as Satanta had promised in March—the despair in Major Henry Douglas's plea for help is hardly concealed.

> The country in this vicinity is alive with Indians . . . . There is no doubt but that all the Indians of this country are at war with us. Their peace promises were only mere pretexts to gain time . . . . With the Cheyennes and Sioux to the north of us and the Kiowas and Arapahoes all around us, we have more work in hand than our little garrison can perform.[3]

Simultaneous with the Santa Fe attacks, the Sioux and Cheyenne swooped down on the Smoky Hill. While stage lines struggled to stay running, coaches were compelled to travel in pairs—one for travellers, one for soldiers. Even so, there was no guarantee of safety. "On June 15th, five and a half miles east of Big Timber, while crossing a ravine," the *Colorado Tribune* reported on two coaches travelling together, "they were suddenly attacked by about 100 Indians."

> They immediately got out of the coach to give them battle. Part of the soldiers in the extra coach, including the sergeant, behaved in a cowardly manner, and refused to get out. After fighting a few minutes, the coach in which the cowards were, started, the driver says, because he could not hold the mules. Then the rest commenced piling in, and soon the other coach commenced moving. All, except Mr. Brownell and one soldier, succeeded in getting into it. They were cut off, and both cut and scalped by the Indians. Then commenced a race . . . . One soldier after being wounded at once got out to whip up. On attempting to get in again he made a mis-step and fell, and was immediately tomahawked and scalped . . . . Mr. Blake got out to whip up and caught a ball in his arm . . . . The Indians kept up a running fire for four miles, and finally withdrew.[4]

Crossing the Plains by stage was not the only perilous proposition. As construction of the Union Pacific in the north and the Kansas Pacific to the south continued apace, each tie laid took the tracks deeper into hostile terri-

Attack on the Overland Route. KANSAS STATE HISTORICAL SOCIETY.

tory. Late one summer day in 1867, near Plum Creek Station, Nebraska, a band of Cheyenne tore down the telegraph wire along the Union Pacific. Instead of moving on as usual, the Indians paused. "In these big wagons that go on the metal road," one pointed, "there must be things that are valuable—perhaps clothing. If we could throw these wagons off the iron they run on and break them open, we could find out what [is] in them and could take whatever might be useful to us."[5]

Heaving ties on the track, the warriors withdrew a short distance to await results. William Thompson:

> About 9 o'clock [that] night, myself and five others left Plum Creek Station, and started up the track on a hand car to hunt up where the break in the telegraph was. When we came to where the break proved to be, we saw a lot of ties piled up on the track, but at the same moment Indians jumped up from the grass all around, and fired on us. We fired two or three shots in return, and then, as the Indians pressed on us, we ran away. An Indian on a pony singled me out, and galloped up to me. After coming within ten feet of me he fired, the bullet entering my right arm; seeing me still run, he

> "clubbed his rifle" and knocked me down. He then took out his knife, and stabbed me in the neck, and then making a twirl round his fingers with my hair, he commenced sawing and hacking away at my scalp. Though the pain was awful, and I felt dizzy and sick, I knew enough to keep quiet. After what seemed to be half an hour he gave me the last finishing cut to my scalp on my left temple, and as it still hung a little he gave it a jerk . . . . I could have screamed my life out. I can't describe it to you. I just felt as if the whole head was taken right off. The Indian then mounted and galloped away, but as he went he dropped my scalp within a few feet of me . . . . While lying down I could hear the Indians moving around whispering to each other . . . . After . . . about an hour and a half, I heard the low rumbling of the [freight] train as it came tearing along.[6]

By the time the engineer spotted the obstruction, it was too late. With a hiss of steam and a screech of steel, the locomotive jumped the track and went thundering into the ditch. Swarming over the wreck the Indians immediately shot the engineer; when the stunned fireman appeared swinging a lantern he too was killed. Inside the cars the excited warriors found shoes, sugar, sacks of flour, bolts of silk, and best of all, whiskey. After a lengthy revel around the burning debris the raiders staggered to their ponies and were off into the night. As soon as it was safe, Thompson also staggered away into the night, clutching his own bloody scalp.

When the seven victims of the Plum Creek massacre were brought to Omaha a short time later, a large crowd, including Henry Morton Stanley, was waiting at the station. One of the charred corpses, noted the newsman, had been reduced to a "trunk about two feet in length, resembling a half-burnt log of the same size." Stepping feebly from the train was the only survivor of the affair, William Thompson. "In a pail of water by his side," the incredulous Stanley later wrote, "was his scalp about nine inches in length and four in width, somewhat resembling a drowned rat as it floated, curled up, on the water."[7]

As a result of this attack and others—one bold warrior actually lassoed a speeding locomotive and was dragged over the prairie—passenger trains became rolling arsenals. Consequently, most Indians quickly learned to give the "chee-chee wagons" a wide berth. The roads were another matter, however, and hostiles continued to tear down miles of telegraph wire, topple water tanks, and kill section workers by the score.

As with stage stations, Indians on the warpath found the valuable property at lonely railroad depots irresistible. The decision of two off-duty conductors to spend a few hours fishing at a creek near Sidney Station, Nebraska, coincided almost exactly with an aborted attack on the depot by a small band of Sioux. According to the Cheyenne, Wyoming, *Argus*:

> [T]he Indians crossed the track and were riding at full speed for the bluffs, when they apparently caught sight of the conductors, for they all changed their course abruptly and swept down on them. One of the conductors, named William Edmundson, had a small pocket pistol with him and managed to keep the Indians at a little distance from him while he retreated towards the station. He was shot in four or five places with arrows, one of them passing entirely through his body. When about half way to the station, he dropped exhausted from loss of blood. His unfortunate companion, Thomas Cahoon, had no weapon, and the savages rode up to him and sent eight arrows into his body. One arrow went right through his body about one and a half inches above the heart . . . . The Indians then scalped him, tearing off the skin and flesh from around the forehead back to the neck.
>
> After leaving the conductors the Indians went up to [Lodge] Pole Creek, striking the track three miles west of the station, where they found two section men at work. One of them fortunately had a shot gun, which he kept pointed at the Indians until he reached the station. The other was not armed and was riddled with arrows and afterwards scalped.[8]

While frontier forts were expected to protect the railroads and trails in their vicinity, many garrisons, like Fort Wallace in far western Kansas, were so remote and weak that their own safety was often in doubt. On June 21, a large band of Indians brazenly tried to drive off the post's livestock and then assailed several stage stations in the area for good measure. Three days later, accompanied by a detachment of the 7th Cavalry, Albert Barnitz reached the beleaguered garrison. Hardly had he time to unpack his pen and paper before the sturdy captain found himself the lead actor in, as he phrased it to his wife, "quite a desperate little fight."

> [O]n the morning of Wednesday, June 26, just as I was about starting to breakfast, I saw a commotion at the Post, men running to and fro, and emerging from their quarters and tents with arms . . . . I learned that the Indians were approaching in considerable force, and that a large party were already running off the mules and stage horses from the Ponds-creek Stage Station. In less than a minute my

> horses were coming in, and I at once ordered them to be saddled, and the command formed for action, and mounting my horse . . . I rode out to the North West, to the high ground to reconnoitre . . . . I had not ridden more than half a mile, and completed some hasty observations (discovering small parties of Indians on the ridges . . . and a cloud of dust arising from the direction of the Stage Station), when I saw my company approaching, at a gallop, and also a small party of cavalry coming out from the Post to join me.[9]

After aligning his forty-nine men, Barnitz sounded the charge and raced toward an estimated two hundred warriors. "The Indians fell back to the brow of a hill two miles from the fort," reported a writer for *Harper's Weekly*, "then turned and awaited the attack. The cavalry charged at a gallop, and were met by a counter charge. The Indians, with lances poised and arrows on the string, rode at them with great speed, and a hand-to-hand fight followed."[10] Barnitz continues:

> Corporal [Prentice G.] Harris says that he saw an Indian, who appeared to be a chief, swing a pole which he carried, with a bunch of feathers tied to a string, on the end, rapidly around his head five or six times, and then point it at me, when instantly half a dozen Indians started for me, each firing a number of shots, but I was not touched. One Indian dashed towards me . . . and fired several shots at me over his pony's head, and then when opposite me turned, and rode parallel with me . . . lying lengthwise on his pony, and firing from under his pony's neck . . . . The shots came very close! But I was just then too much concerned for the fate of my command to pay much heed to his firing. I only pointed my revolver at him, a few times, as if I was about to fire, and thus disconcerted him a little . . . . [Pvt. John G.] Hummell was wounded severely—a bullet wound through the thigh, and a lance thrust in the side . . . . Sergeant [Frederick] Wyllyams . . . was killed. The Indians stripped, scalped, and horribly mutilated his body . . . . He had fought bravely, but had incautiously become separated from the command, and was surrounded by overwhelming numbers. The Indians stripped, or partially stripped all the dead . . . almost instantly. When [Charles] Clarke, the chief Bugler . . . fell from his horse . . . a powerful Indian was seen to reach down, as he rode at full speed, seize the body with one hand, and jerk it across his pony, strip off the clothes in an instant, dash out the brains with a tomahawk, and hasten on for another victim![11]

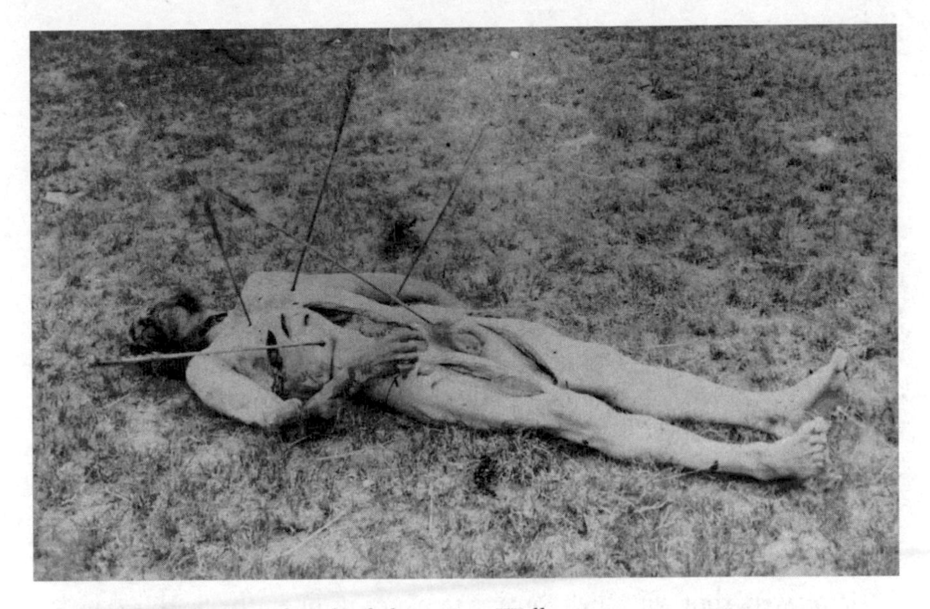

Frederick Wyllyams after the fight at Fort Wallace. Kansas State Historical Society.

"[T]he savages displayed unlooked-for daring," admitted the *Harper's* reporter. Almost surrounded, the cavalry fell back. Again, Albert Barnitz:

> I dashed with all speed towards the skirmish line, but before I could reach it, the men began to waver, and urged by Sergeant Hamlin to retreat, (who himself made off at all speed followed by a few of his men) the men began to turn about, and fall back in confusion . . . . I succeeded in inducing some of the most intrepid ones to again confront the enemy . . . but it was only by singling out individuals . . . and inducing each to turn and fire one or two shots, or beat back the diabolical fiends with the sabre, that I was at length enabled to check the pursuit long enough to measureably concentrate my men. Sergeant Gordon now fortunately reached us, and with his assistance . . . I was enabled to effectively check our pursuers, and drive them back beyond the hills . . . . Going meanwhile to the summit of a ridge, I took a deliberate look at the fiends, who were drawn up in fine order, upon the summit of another ridge beyond, busily engaged in reloading their arms, and preparing, as I supposed, to renew the fight. With my glass I was able to distinguish their hideous countenances, and the barbaric magnificence of their array, as they sat with

their plumed lances, their bows, and shields, and their gleaming weapons . . . . But their leading chief . . . had already . . . been killed in the fight, and . . . the Cheyennes had paid dearly in the encounter, and so they were not eager to renew the onset.[12]

The Cheyenne were not the only ones reluctant to "renew the onset." With six dead and as many wounded, Barnitz and company had learned a bloody lesson. At least one civilian spectator had been sobered as well. "The Indians . . . are more than a match for our cavalry," he wrote. "The idea industriously proclaimed by some persons East . . . 'that one white soldier is equal to fifty or one hundred Indians,' is about 'played out' with all parties at this fort."[13] Barnitz added:

All were most admirably mounted and armed; many had repeating rifles or carbines, and every Indian appeared to have at least one revolver, in addition to his powerful bow and arrows: some of the latter were shot with such force as to pierce through the hard beech wood of our saddle trees, and the two thicknesses of rawhide covering! Several of our killed were shot through with numerous arrows, besides being literally riddled with balls . . . . The ponies . . . were of remarkable size, very fleet and powerful. Our own horses were generally no match for them, either in speed or endurance.[14]

Soon after the fight with Barnitz, the north-moving raiders encountered a wagon train that Custer had sent to Fort Wallace for supplies. During the next three hours the small escort beat back waves of circling warriors. When a relief force was seen approaching, the attackers finally withdrew. In the meantime, along the Republican River, Custer was having his own problems.

It was just that uncertain period between darkness and daylight [of] the . . . morning, and I was lying in my tent . . . when the sharp, clear crack of a carbine near by brought me to my feet . . . . At the same moment my brother, [Capt. Thomas] Custer . . . rushed past my tent, halting only long enough to show his face through the opening and shout, "They are here!"

My orderly, as was his custom, on my retiring had securely tied all the fastenings to my tent . . . . Leaping from my bed, I grasped my trusty Spencer . . . and with a single dash burst open the tent and, hatless as well as shoeless, ran to the point where the attack seemed to be concentrated. It was sufficiently light to see . . . . The Indians,

> numbering hundreds, were all around the camp, evidently intending to surround us . . . . My men opened on them such a brisk fire from their carbines that they were glad to withdraw beyond range. The picket who gave the alarm was shot down at his post by the Indians, the entire party galloping over his body . . . . [S]eeing that their attempt to surprise us and to stampede our horses had failed, [they] then withdrew to a point but little over a mile from us.[15]

Curious to learn the tribe involved, Custer sent forward an interpreter. The colonel continues:

> The ordinary manner of opening communication with parties known or supposed to be hostile, is to ride toward them in a zigzag manner or to ride in a circle. The interpreter gave the proper signal, and was soon answered by a small party advancing from the main body of the Indians to within hailing distance. It was then agreed that I, with six of the officers, should come to the bank of the river . . . . To guard against treachery, I placed most of my command under arms and arranged with the officer left in command that a blast from the bugle should bring assistance to me if required . . . . Descending to the river bank, we awaited the arrival of the seven chiefs . . . . [They] soon made their appearance on its opposite bank, and, after removing their leggings, waded across to where we stood.[16]

Custer quickly saw that they were Sioux. He also saw that despite the agreement that both sides meet unarmed, everyone came "loaded down with weapons." Among the group was Pawnee Killer, a chief who, only days before on the Platte, had assured the colonel of his peaceful intent.

> Upon crossing to our side of the river Pawnee Killer and his companions at once extended their hands, and saluted us with the familiar "How." Suspicious of their intentions, I kept one hand on my revolver during the continuance of our interview. When we had about concluded our conference a young brave, completely armed . . . emerged from the willows and tall grass on the opposite bank and waded across to where we were, greeting us as the others had done. Nothing was thought of this act until a few moments after another brave did the same, and so on until four had crossed over and joined our group. I then called Pawnee Killer's attention to the conditions under which we met, and told him he was violating his part of the contract. He endeavored to turn it off by saying

> that his young men felt well disposed toward us, and came over only to shake hands and say "How." He was told, however, that no more of his men must come. The conversation was then resumed and continued until another party of the warriors was seen preparing to cross from the other side.
>
> Again reminding Pawnee Killer of the stipulations of our agreement . . . I told him that not another warrior of his should cross the river to our side. And calling his attention to the bugler, who stood at a safe distance from us, I told him that I would then instruct the bugler to watch the Indians who were upon the opposite bank, and, upon any of them making a movement as if to cross, to sound the signal which would bring my entire command to my side in a few moments . . . . He at once signalled to the Indians on the other side to remain where they were.[17]

The talks continued but little was learned and soon, unlike the dawn encounter, both sides parted in peace. A short time later, Lieutenant Lyman Kidder, along with ten troopers and a Sioux guide named Red Bead, left Fort Sedgwick with important dispatches for Custer. Learning of the mission and fearful for the safety of a mere squad moving through Indian country, Custer set out at once to locate Kidder. Riding in the colonel's column were several Delaware guides and Will Comstock, one of the best scouts on the Plains.

On July 12, Kidder's trail was finally discovered. It was quickly determined that he and his tiny command were moving leisurely toward Fort Wallace over the level prairie. When Custer asked if Kidder could reach the post without detection, Comstock only shook his head. If so, said the scout simply, "I'll lose my confidence in Indians." George Custer:

> And now that we had discovered their trail, our interest and anxiety became immeasurably increased as to their fate. The latter could not remain in doubt much longer, as two days' marching would take us to the fort . . . . How many miles we had thus passed over without incident worthy of mention, I do not now recall. The sun was high in the heavens, showing that our day's march was about half completed, when those of us who were riding at the head of the column discovered a strange-looking object lying directly in our path, and more than a mile distant . . . . Eager to determine its character, a dozen or more of our party, including Comstock and some of the Delawares, galloped in front.
>
> Before riding the full distance the question was determined. The object seen was the body of a white horse. A closer examination

showed that it had been shot within the past few days, while the brand, U.S., proved that it was a government animal . . . . When the column reached the point where the slain horse lay, a halt was ordered to enable Comstock and the Indian scouts to thoroughly examine the surrounding ground to discover, if possible, any additional evidence, such as empty cartridge shells, arrows, or articles of Indian equipment, showing that a fight had taken place.

The scouts being unable to throw any additional light upon the question, we continued our march, closely observing the ground as we passed along. Comstock noticed that instead of the trail showing that Kidder's party was moving in regular order, as when at first discovered, there were but two or three tracks to be seen in the beaten trail, the rest being found on the grass on either side.

We had marched two miles perhaps from the point where the body of the slain horse had been discovered, when we came upon a second, this one, like the first, having been killed by a bullet . . . . Comstock's quick eyes were not long in detecting pony tracks in the vicinity, and we had no longer any but the one frightful solution to offer: Kidder and his party had been discovered by the Indians . . . and against such overwhelming odds the issue could not be doubtful.

The main trail no longer showed the footprints of Kidder's party, but instead Comstock discovered the tracks of shod horses on the grass, with here and there numerous tracks of ponies, all by their appearance proving that both horses and ponies had been moving at full speed. Kidder's party must have trusted their lives temporarily to the speed of their horses—a dangerous venture when contending with Indians. However, this fearful race for life must have been most gallantly contested, because we continued our march several miles farther without discovering any evidence of the savages having gained any advantage.

We began leaving the high plateau and to descend into a valley through which at the distance of nearly two miles, meandered a small prairie stream known as Beaver Creek. The valley near the banks of this stream was covered with a dense growth of tall wild grass . . . . When within a mile of the stream I observed several large buzzards floating lazily in circles through the air . . . . This, of itself, might not have attracted my attention seriously but for the rank stench which pervaded the atmosphere.

As if impelled by one thought Comstock, the Delawares, and half-a-dozen officers detached themselves from the column and . . . instituted a search for the cause of our horrible suspicions. After riding in all directions through the rushes and willows, and when about to relinquish the search as fruitless, one of the Delawares uttered a shout which attracted the attention of the entire command . . . . Hastening . . . to his side, a sight met our gaze which . . . [made] my very blood curdle. Lying in irregular order, and within a very limited circle, were the mangled bodies of poor Kidder and his party, yet so brutally hacked and disfigured as to be beyond recognition save as human beings.

Every individual of the party had been scalped and his skull broken . . . except the Sioux chief Red Bead, whose scalp had simply been removed from his head and then thrown down by his side. This, Comstock informed us, was in accordance with a custom which prohibits an Indian from bearing off the scalp of one of his own tribe . . . . Red Bead, being less disfigured and mutilated than the others, was the only individual capable of being recognized. Even the clothes of all the party had been carried away; some of the bodies were lying in beds of ashes, with partly burned fragments of wood near them, showing that the savages had put some of them to death by the terrible tortures of fire. The sinews of the arms and legs had been cut away, the nose of every man hacked off, and the features otherwise defaced so that it would have been scarcely possible for even a relative to recognize a single one of the unfortunate vic-

The Kidder Massacre. KANSAS STATE HISTORICAL SOCIETY.

> tims . . . . Each body was pierced by from twenty to fifty arrows, and the arrows were found as the savage demons had left them, bristling in the bodies . . . . From the large number of arrows picked up . . . it was evident that a desperate struggle had ensued. . . . The ground near which the bodies . . . lay was thickly strewn with exploded metallic cartridges, showing conclusively that they had defended themselves a long time and most gallantly too, against their murderous enemies.
>
> As the officer, his men and his no less faithful Indian guide had shared their final dangers together and had met the same dreadful fate . . . it was but fitting that their remains should be consigned to one common grave. This was accordingly done. A single trench was dug near the spot . . . . Silently, mournfully, their comrades . . . consigned their mangled remains to mother earth.[18]

George Custer had discovered that, unlike in the Civil War with its prisons and paroles, there was no middle ground when fighting Indians—victory meant life and defeat meant a terrible, nightmarish death.

While the raiders continued their rampage on the High Plains, two hundred miles to the east they were no less active. "Settlers swarm about the fort for protection," a correspondent for the *Army and Navy Journal* wrote from Fort Harker, Kansas. "Dangerous to go beyond the Fort . . . . No one is permitted to go without an escort. Several dead and wounded settlers were recently brought in. The only man among the corpses not having been scalped was bald."[19]

Because most troops were fighting on the far frontier, Sioux and Cheyenne war parties found many inland communities easy prey. One settler described a typical foray along the Little Blue River in southern Nebraska.

> [T]he Indians came down the Blue to within about fifteen miles of [Big Sandy Creek], and killed two men in their house, and then set the house on fire, and burnt them up in it. Their names were Joseph Bennett and a Mr. Abernathy. They were both single men and lived together . . . . Mr. Abernathy's head and one arm was burnt entirely off. The Indians then proceeded down the Blue to within about six miles of Big Sandy, to a small German settlement . . . and then captured two of Mr. Ulbrick's children, one a boy twelve years old, and the other a girl fifteen years old, and took them away . . . . [T]his is the way our settlers are being murdered and robbed, and not a soldier within a hundred miles of us . . . . In the name of God how long is this state of things to last?[20]

Just over the state line at Haddam, Kansas, John Ferguson was asking the same question. In a letter to a friend, Ferguson described the terrible dilemma faced by farmers at harvest.

> I have been looking for the redskined Deavels in on us every day for the last month[.] the[y] have been in and killed settelars twenty miles north of me and carried of[f] gerls prisoners[.] the people here is living in constant dread of being attacted by them every day[.] the settelars cant verry well leave[.] the[y] have reased good fare crops of wheat and corn . . . and the most of them thinks as I do that we may as well stay here with what we have got and run the risk of being skalped as leave it[.] as for me I have lost over a thousand Dolars runing from Indians in the last five years and I am going to stand by what I have got now to the last minet.[21]

In the broad valley of the South Platte, Coloradans were slaughtered by the score. "Between Bishop's Ranch and Junction Cut Off," reported Henry Morton Stanley, "there are no less than ninety-three graves, twenty-seven of which contain the bodies of settlers killed within the last six weeks. Dead bodies have been seen floating down the Platte."[22]

Meanwhile, on the Smoky Hill, the besieged garrison of Fort Wallace never felt more vulnerable. As Captain Barnitz wrote to his wife in Ohio:

> [W]e keep ourselves mightily on the alert for them—especially at night. We do not intend to be caught napping . . . . Every night the command is turned out at least three or four times—the sentinels firing on wolves, or other objects which they mistake for Indians creeping up in the darkness—for we have no moon now, and the sentinels have to be doubly vigilant. It must seem very amusing to people in Ohio to be told that certain of their acquaintances are really engaged in war, in these, to them, peaceful times! I suppose they can't realize it at all!—and yet away out here, it is the serious business of our lives! Well, I sometimes laugh myself, to think of it!—and yet it is not a very laughable matter . . . to see a poor fellow every now and then with his scalp gone, and his body full of bullet holes . . . and revenge arrows, and his clothes taken off, and limbs gashed in every conceivable manner—but that is what we are compelled to witness daily here![23]

Not everyone in the West viewed the situation as seriously as Barnitz. From a relatively safe roost in Denver, at least one "poet" waxed humorous.

Noble red men of the plains
  pouncing on unguarded trains,
Where you come, and where you go,
  Sherman's scouts would like to know,
Burning here and scalping there,
  east and west and everywhere,
Prowling like the tiger cat,
  night and day along the Platte,
Stealing boldly at your will
  all along the Smoky Hill,
First you came in parties small,
  now in numbers that appall,
Spreading death and devastation,
  robbing ranches, burning stations,
Such persistent visitation,
  do not claim our admiration.
Mr. Lo, now quit your tricks,
  surely you'll get in a fix,
Now just stop those ugly capers,
  or we'll send you to the Quakers,
If our boys start on the scout,
  surely they will wipe you out,
Go bold red man of the west,
  here your stay is short at best,
Go and hunt the buffalo,
  we can spare you, Mr. Lo.[24]

While safe and secure civilians could afford to be flippant, department commander William T. Sherman was in no mood for levity. Despite the best efforts of his officers in the field, the deaths of scores of soldiers, the loss of hundreds of valuable horses, and the expenditure of millions of dollars, the campaign of 1867 had been a disaster. While the frontier had gone up in flames and the cavalry had engaged in frantic pursuits, the raiders had in almost every instance escaped unscathed. They were sure to improve upon the formula in 1868. The anger and demoralization of many, high and low, was aptly expressed by one young soldier in a simple note to his mother.

> I think as every one else with any sense at all, thinks, that Genl Sherman, Genl Hancock, Genl Custer and the balance of them have made a grand fizzle. I don't believe the whole pack of them have killed a dozzen Indians all told.[25]

6

More Tears Than Dollars

As frustrating as the war was for soldiers serving on the southern Plains, 1867 might well have proven one bloody debacle after another had it not been for the handful of men who served as the army's eyes and ears. Had Custer's wagon train north of Fort Wallace not heeded the advice of Will Comstock during one leg of the journey, it more than likely would have been ambushed. Indeed, Comstock and the other scouts and guides of the prairie were a precious resource, without which the military could not hope to win the war for the West.

"No Indian knew the country more thoroughly than did Comstock," Custer wrote. "He was perfectly familiar with every divide, water-course, and strip of timber for hundreds of miles in either direction. He knew the dress and peculiarities of every Indian tribe, and spoke the languages of many of them. Perfect in horsemanship, fearless in manner . . . as modest and unassuming as he was brave."[1]

While Comstock was certainly one of the best, Custer's praise might have applied to any number of frontier scouts. Waxed another army officer as he watched the legendary Jim Bridger and other plainsmen at work:

> Nothing escaped their vision. The dropping of a stick or breaking of a twig, the turning of the growing grass all brought knowledge to them, and they could tell who or what had done it. A single horse or Indian could not cross the trail but that they discovered it, and could tell how long since they had passed. Their methods of hunting

> game were perfect and we were never out of meat. Herbs, roots, berries, bark of trees and everything that was edible they knew. They could minister to the sick, dress wounds—in fact in all my experience I never saw . . . any obstacle they could not overcome.[2]

Though he was illiterate, Frank Grouard could "read" the wilderness like few others. Wrote one witness:

> He had orders to follow the "back trail" of the two Indians we had seen early in the evening, lead where it would. This he did through the entire night in the face of a storm that was constantly rendering the pony tracks of the two savages less distinct . . . . Over rugged bluffs and narrow valleys, through gloomy defiles and down breakneck declivities, plunged the indomitable Frank; now down on his hands and knees . . . scrutinizing the faint footprints, then, losing the trail for an instant, darting to and fro until it was found, and again following it up with the keenness of a hound.[3]

"Bill Comstock had a wonderful ability at trailing a party of Indians or a single warrior," Captain Richard Musgrove reminisced. "He could easily read all the 'signs' left by them for the information of other Indians, could interpret the meaning of one, two, or three columns of smoke used in telegraphing between different parties, and, after a party had passed could tell with remarkable accuracy, by examining the trail, how many were in the party."[4]

"These men prefer to ride at night rather than during the day," noted Theodore Davis of *Harper's Weekly* after viewing several scouts on courier call. "The Indians, they say, are not usually on watch at night, and if they are they have just as good a chance of seeing the Indians, as the Indians have of seeing them."[5]

Many scouts selected for their dangerous duty the unsightly but surefooted mule. Unlike the large army, or "American," horse, which needed constant forage, the resilient jackass could travel long distances on little more than sage and stagnant water. Additionally, the pasture-bred army horse was notorious for its fear of Indians and many a white man died because a "green" mount dashed terror-stricken toward the hostiles rather than away. On the other hand, some felt their animals' nervousness to be an asset. Explained Billy Dixon:

> A horse could be safely depended upon to give warning of the near approach of an Indian. I have had my horse run to and fro on his

> picket rope, manifesting the greatest alarm, apparently without cause, as I could see nothing. I never failed, however, to find later that an Indian had been close by.[6]

A number of old scouts, Jim Bridger and Kit Carson included, were true "sons of the wilderness," having spent most or all of their adult lives in the West. A *New York Herald* reporter noted that at least one plainsman had only the faintest notion of a world beyond the Washita River.

> Jones was a Texan, and, notwithstanding his long life on the frontiers, was a man of agreeable manners. He was one of those intensely patient individuals rarely met with . . . . He was unobtrusive, and never was so well satisfied as when let alone . . . . He seemed to little concern himself in the affairs of the world . . . . For ten years he had not left the banks of the Washita. In fact, that was the nearest he had ever been to civilization . . . . He observed, one day, that "if the brutes of savages did not lift his hair . . . he thought he would go sometime to [Fort] Riley, and see what those machines called railroads looked like."[7]

As with Jones, many newcomers marveled at the lack of sophistication and sheer simplicity of the older frontiersmen. Margaret Carrington recorded her impressions of "Big Throat" Jim Bridger.

> He cannot read, but enjoys reading. He was charmed by Shakspeare but doubted the Bible story of Samson's tying foxes by the tails, and with firebrands burning the wheat of the Philistines. At last he sent for a good copy of Shakspeare's plays, and would hear them read until midnight with unfeigned pleasure. The murder of the two princes in the Tower startled him to indignation. He desired it to be read a second and third time. Upon positive conviction that the text was properly read to him, he burned the whole set, convinced that "Shakspeare must have had a bad heart and been as devilish mean as a Sioux, to have written such scoundrelism as that."[8]

When his working days were done, Nick Janis, like so many other scouts, chose to live out his life near the scene of his adventures. Called by Bridger "the whitest man on the plains," Janis loafed his time away at the Fort Laramie sutler's store where he spun tall tales and regaled all comers with his rustic wit. As one young "pilgrim" recalled:

> In the breast pocket of my vest I carried a small Smith & Wesson twenty-two caliber pistol . . . . One day, as my vest happened to be open, the butt of the pistol was exposed. Nick saw it and asked, "What's that?" I took the little revolver out and showed it to him. The minute he got it in his hands he just roared with laughter, and exclaimed, "Oh, look at the play toy!" Then he broke open the gun, and taking out the cylinder looked through the barrel, chuckling as he did so. Finally, handing it back to me, he said, "Boy, if you shoot me with dat and I find out, I put you acrost my knee and spank hell outen you!"[9]

Unlike Janis, Bridger, and the rest, some of the best scouts were surprisingly young and relatively new to the Plains.

> By the way, I forgot to tell you about our guide—the most striking object in camp . . . lithe, active, sinewy, daring rider, dead shot with pistol and rifle, long locks, fine features and mustache, buckskin leggins, red shirt, broad-brim hat, two pistols in belt, rifle in hand—he is a picture.[10]

So wrote a visitor from Fort Kearny, Nebraska. The sketch was that of James Butler Hickok. As with this witness and thousands more to come, no one ever forgot "Wild Bill." Wherever he went following the Civil War, in which he served as spy and scout, Hickok's reputation as a plainsman and prolific mankiller preceded him. A St. Louis reporter caught up with the famous scout in 1867.

> He stands six feet one inch in his moccasins, and is as handsome a specimen of a man as could be found . . . . We were prepared, on hearing of [his] presence in the camp, to see a person who would prove a coarse, illiterate, quarrelsome, obtrusive, obstinate, bully; in fact, one of those ruffians to be found South and West, who delight in shedding blood. We confess to being agreeably disappointed when, on being introduced to him, we looked on a person who was the very reverse of all we had imagined . . . . A fine handsome face, free from any blemish, a light moustach, a thin pointed nose, bluish-grey eyes, with a calm, quiet, benignant look, yet seemingly possessing some mysterious latent power, a magnificent forehead, hair parted from the center of the forehead and hanging down behind the ears in long, wavy, silk curls. He is brave, there can be no doubt; that fact is impressed on you at once before he utters a syllable.[11]

James Butler "Wild Bill" Hickok. KANSAS STATE HISTORICAL SOCIETY.

One of the officers Hickok scouted for was Custer. From their relationship on the Plains arose a friendship that would last for the rest of their lives. Himself the object of a curious public and railroad excursionists eager to shake his hand, the colonel occasionally cajoled his famous scout to help greet the throngs.

"Bill's face was confused at the words of praise with which General Custer introduced him," remembered Libbie, "and his fearless eyes were cast down in chagrin at the torture of being gazed at by the crowd. He went through the enforced introduction for General Custer's sake, but it was a relief when the engine whistle sounded."[12]

Another scout the Custers had great affection for was Will Comstock. Comstock—a man whose livelihood was trailing and fighting Indians—was a grand-nephew of the Western laughingstock and popularizer of the "noble red man," James Fenimore Cooper.[13] Theodore Davis of *Harper's Weekly* had a chance to speak with the scout.

> Comstock is a rather reticent person and seldom talks of his exploits. A person not entirely familiar with him would be almost certain to

> regard him as a man whose early life has been blighted by misfortunes. There are few men with more kindly feelings for the human race than this man . . . . The Indians call him "Medicine Bill." The reason for this, Comstock says is the fact of his having cut off a man's finger after it had been bitten by a rattlesnake. The amputation saved the man's life and gained Comstock a great amount of respect and a title from the Arapahoes.[14]

Comstock had no way of knowing, but Davis was already aware of the nickname and how he really got it. "No Indian was ever half so superstitious as Will Comstock," the reporter laughed. "He had his 'medicine' horse, 'medicine' field-glass, 'medicine' everything, in fact. Even Will's evil-looking dog was 'medicine,' and had a 'medicine' collar."[15] Despite his foibles and ironic antecedents, Comstock was one of the best scouts on the prairie; he was, in the words of Captain Myles Keogh, "an eccentric genius."[16]

Another scout brimming with eccentricities was Moses Milner. One of those who knew "California Joe" was Custer.

> He was a man about forty years of age, perhaps older, over six feet in height, and possessing a well-proportioned frame. His head was covered with a luxuriant crop of long, almost black hair, strongly inclined to curl, and so long as to fall carelessly over his shoulders. His face, at least so much of it as was not concealed by the long, waving brown beard and mustache, was full of intelligence and pleasant to look upon . . . . On his head was generally to be seen, whether asleep or awake a huge sombrero or black slouch hat. A soldier's overcoat with its large circular cape, a pair of trousers with the legs tucked in the top of his long boots, usually constituted the outside make-up of the man.
>
> His military armament consisted of a long breech-loading Springfield musket, from which he was inseparable, and a revolver and hunting-knife, both the latter being carried in his waist-belt. His mount . . . being instead of a horse a finely-formed mule, in whose speed and endurance he had every confidence . . . . California Joe was an inveterate smoker and was rarely seen without his stubby, dingy-looking brierwood pipe in full blast. The endurance of his smoking powers was only surpassed by his loquacity. His pipe frequently became exhausted and required refilling, but California Joe seemed never to lack for material . . . to carry on a conversation.
>
> [T]here was but little of the western country from the Pacific to the Missouri River with which California Joe was not intimately acquainted. He had . . . become acquainted from time to time with

> most of the officers who had served on the Plains or on the Pacific Coast. I once inquired of him if he had ever seen General Sheridan? "What, Gineral Shuridun? Why, bless my soul, I knowed Shuridun way up in Oregon more'n fifteen years ago, an' he wuz only a second lootenant uv infantry . . . . I hed a kind of a sneakin' notion then that he'd hurt somebody ef they'd ever turn him loose. Lord, but ain't he old lightnin'?"[17]

When Milner applied for a position in an upcoming campaign, Custer recalled their first encounter.

> After [the] official portion of the interview had been completed, it seemed proper to Joe's mind that a more intimate acquaintance between us should be cultivated . . . . His first interrogatory, addressed to me . . . was frankly put as follows: "See hyar, Gineral, in order that we hev no misonderstandin', I'd jest like to ask ye a few questions." Seeing that I had somewhat of a character to deal with, I signified my perfect willingness to be interviewed by him. "Are you an ambulance man ur a hoss man?" Pretending not to discover his meaning, I requested him to explain. "I mean do you b'leve in catchin' Injuns in ambulances or on hossback?" Still assuming ignorance, I replied, "Well, Joe, I believe in catching Indians wherever we can find them, whether they are found in ambulances or on horseback." This did not satisfy him. "That ain't what I'm drivin' at. S'pose you're after Injuns and really want to hev a tussle with 'em, would ye start after 'em on hossback, or would ye climb into an ambulance and be haulded after 'em? That's the pint I'm headin' fur."[18]

Another colorful character was the "Poet Scout," Jack Crawford. "Our camp fires were lively after Captain Jack joined us," recalled one appreciative officer. "He sang his songs, told his stories, recited his poems, and kept his tireless jaw constantly wagging for our edification."[19]

Like her husband, Libbie Custer was intrigued by scouts and the mystery that seemed to surround their pasts. "Most of them," she said, "had some strange history in the States that had been the cause of their seeking the wild life of the frontier. The one whose past we would have liked best to know was ['Lonesome' Charley Reynolds,] a man most valued by my husband."

> We had no certain knowledge whether or not he had any family or friends elsewhere, for he never spoke of them. He acknowledged once, in a brief moment of confidence, that he was a gentleman by

> birth. Startled, perhaps, by the look of curiosity that even a friend's face showed, he turned the conversation, and said, "Oh, but what's the use to refer to it now?" We did not even know whether Charley Reynolds was his real name or one that he had assumed . . . . My husband had such genuine admiration for him that I soon learned to listen to everything pertaining to his life with marked interest. He was so shy that he hardly raised his eyes when I extended my hand at the general's introduction. He did not assume the picturesque dress, long hair, and belt full of weapons that are characteristic of the scout. His manner was perfectly simple and straightforward, and he could not be induced to talk of himself.[20]

Not all scouts were "silent heroes." While some considered Frank Grouard brave, at least one officer felt he was "a coward and a big liar."

> I . . . told Grouard to go ahead & find the exact location of the village. Grouard went off and remained a long time, and when he returned I noticed that he had a new horse. He had been riding an Indian pony that was thin and nearly used up. He had gone up to the herd, unsaddled, caught a fresh horse . . . & saddled it. He was acting so cowardly and hesitatingly, that I at once suspected he was getting himself in shape to get away should we get into a hot fight.[21]

Nor were all scouts honest and trustworthy. "They are," one witness wrote after viewing a new group of guides, "as sweet a lot of cut-throats as ever scuttled a ship, half-breeds, squaw men, bounty jumpers, thieves and desperadoes of different grades."[22]

Many commanders used Indians as scouts, guides, and trailers. Their natural abilities and familiarity with the land made them a favorite of some. "I always try to get Indian scouts," admitted Brigadier General George Crook, "because with them scouting is the business of their lives. They learn all the signs of the trail as a child learns the alphabet; it becomes an instinct. With a white man the knowledge is acquired in after life."[23] Indian scouts, with their acute senses of hearing, smelling, and, especially, seeing, continuously amazed all who watched. "I'd sooner trust the sharp eye of an indian," confessed Captain Frederick Benteen, "than to trust a pretty good binocular that I always carried."[24]

Many wild and semi-civilized Indian scouts joined army expeditions for the same reasons as their white counterparts—money, glory, and sheer adventure. Some tribes had added incentives, as John Finerty of the *Chicago Times* discovered during a council between General Crook and the Crow.

> The great white chief will hear his Indian brother. These are our lands by inheritance. The Great Spirit gave them to our fathers, but the Sioux stole them from us. They hunt upon our mountains. They fish in our streams. They have stolen our horses. They have murdered our squaws, our children. What white man has done these things to us? The face of the Sioux is red, but his heart is black. But the heart of the pale face has ever been red to the Crow. ("Ugh!" "Ugh!" "Hey!") The scalp of no white man hangs in our lodges. They are thick as grass in the wigwams of the Sioux. ("Ugh!") The great white chief will lead us against no other tribe of red men. Our war is with the Sioux and only them. We want back our lands. We want their women for our slaves, to work for us as our women have had to work for them. We want their horses for our young men, and their mules for our squaws. The Sioux have trampled upon our hearts. We shall spit upon their scalps. ("Ugh!" "Hey!" and terrific yelling.)[25]

The Pawnee also were eager to face their old foe, the Sioux, especially when led by the hard-riding Major Frank North. "I have never seen more obedient and better behaved troops and they have done most excellent service," praised the proud commander. "They are peculiarly qualified for service on the Plains. They are unequalled as riders, know the country thoroughly, are never sick, never desert and are careful of their horses . . . . I have never seen one under the influence of liquor."[26]

Not all whites were entirely comfortable being led by Indians against Indians. Additionally, the guides were often indifferent to discipline and impossible to manage. From Sioux country, Lieutenant James Bradley jotted in his journal what occurred one day when Crow scouts suddenly spotted some buffalo.

> [B]efore I knew what their intentions were, the Crows were chasing them at full speed firing into the herd. They killed several and the meat was acceptable enough, but the firing might have brought the Sioux down upon us. The carelessness of these fellows at times is simply amazing. One would think that the Indian's life of constant exposure to danger would make caution and precaution so much his habit that he would never lay them aside, but it is quite otherwise. In my scouts with the Crows I was compelled to watch them constantly to prevent the doing of some foolish or foolhardy thing that might have betrayed us to an enemy and brought destruction on us all.[27]

Despite the drawbacks, the advantage of using Indian scouts, often from the same tribe, was obvious. "To polish a diamond there is nothing like its own dust," said George Crook sagely. "Put upon their trail an enemy of their own blood, an enemy as tireless, as foxy, and as stealthy and familiar with the country as they themselves, and it breaks them all up."[28]

Surprisingly, the use of Indian scouts against their own was not entirely one-sided. Many times, whites joined reds to war on whites. In a sense, such "renegades" served the enemy as scouts by teaching tactics, explaining white ways, and even leading the Indians on raids and skirmishes. Some of the whites were "squaw men" who sided with their wives' people. As one newsman covering a campaign in Wyoming made note:

> In the evening two rough-looking fellows came into camp and reported that they belonged to a party which was coming from the Black Hills to the Big Horn. The main body, they said, was a day's march behind us . . . . The men went away like Arabs and only when they had gone did it strike our officers that they were squaw men from the Sioux camp, who visited us in the capacity of spies in behalf of their Indian people-in-law. It seemed stupid not to have detained the rascals as prisoners.[29]

Other "white men in war paint" were hunters and trappers who, after long stints in the wilderness, had become "more Indian than the Indian" and resented the encroachment of civilization. Though rare, soldiers occasionally "went over" to the hostiles. On more than one prairie battlefield, an expertly blown bugle coordinated Indian attacks.

Regarding "Galvanized Yankees," or those captured Confederates who chose frontier duty to Federal prison camps, Lieutenant William Drew wrote:

> Most of them made good, faithful soldiers, but some of them were exceptionally hard cases, deserting and joining the Indians, and helping them in their warfare against the whites; and what the Indians didn't know of devilment, these renegades taught them.[30]

Of all scouts, red or white, one achieved more lasting fame than any. There were better shots, better riders, better trackers, and better talkers, but none so richly captured the imagination of the public or so romantically embodied the spirit of the West as William F. "Buffalo Bill" Cody. Like Hickok, his longtime friend, Cody was handsome, dashing, and dramatic. Once seen, he was never forgotten.

> In form, as in face, he had hardly his peer on the American continent. He was dressed in full frontier costume, buckskin breeches,

> long riding boots, blue shirt, colored neckerchief and broad, white sombrero, with the usual snake band. His long, silky brown hair, with a suspicion of dark auburn glinting through it, fell over his shoulders in graceful profusion, and his dark, exceedingly expressive and handsome eyes seemed to blaze with martial ardor.[31]

In 1866, with the aid of his old Civil War friend, Hickok, the twenty-year-old Cody left his wife in Leavenworth and landed his first scouting job. Adapting to the wilderness as few others had, it was not long before Wild Bill's protege had made a name for himself—not only by hunting buffalo, for which he earned his sobriquet, but as a bold scout. In 1868, General Sheridan at Fort Hays was frantic to warn other Kansas posts that the Kiowa and Comanche were on the warpath. Several couriers already had died in the attempt. Sheridan:

> Cody, learning of the strait I was in, manfully came to the rescue, and proposed to make the trip to Dodge, though he had just finished his long and perilous ride from Larned. After four or five hours' rest he mounted a fresh horse and hastened on his journey. At Dodge he took six hours' sleep, and then continued on to his own post—Fort Larned—with more despatches. After resting twelve hours at Larned, he was again in the saddle with tidings for me at Fort Hays. Thus, in all, Cody rode about 350 miles in less than sixty hours, and such an exhibition of endurance and courage was more than enough to convince me that his services would be extremely valuable in the campaign, so I retained him at Fort Hays till the . . . Fifth Cavalry arrived, and then made him chief of scouts for that regiment.[32]

Because of such feats, Cody's star rose in the East as well as the West. Partly due to the florid, fanciful magazine articles by dime novelist Ned Buntline and partly due to his own real-life adventures, would-be plainsmen copied Cody's style. One who went a step further and actually fastened on to the scout was Charles White, "a good-natured liar," snorted an amused observer, "who played . . . Sancho Panza to Buffalo Bill's Don Quixote."[33]

"Wherever I went, no matter how dangerous the errand, my new friend went along," Cody recalled. "The first time he followed me I still remember vividly."

> I had left the Post on a five days' scout, and was particularly anxious that no one should know the direction I was to take. When I was four or five miles from the Post I looked back and saw a solitary

William F. "Buffalo Bill" Cody. BUFFALO BILL HISTORICAL CENTER.

horseman riding in my direction about a mile in my rear. When I stopped he stopped. I rode on for a little way and looked around again. He was exactly the same distance behind me, and pulled his horse up when I halted. This maneuver I repeated several times, always with the same result. Considerably disquieted by this mysterious pursuit, I decided to discover the reason for it. I whipped up my horse and when I had put a sandhill between myself and the man behind I made a quick detour through a ravine, and came abreast of him. He swung around when he heard me coming, and blushed like a girl when he saw how I had tricked him.

"Look here, White," I demanded, "what the devil are you following me in this way for?"

"Mrs. Cody said I could follow you if I wanted to," he said, "and, well, I just followed you, that's all."

That was all he would say. But I knew that he had come along to keep me from getting hurt if I was attacked, and would rather die than admit his real reason. So I told him to come along, and come along he did.[34]

"[H]e was Buffalo Bill's shadow . . . half servant, half 'pardner'," one army officer remembered. "Bill was his adoration . . . . He copied Bill's dress, his gait, his carriage, his speech—everything he could copy; he let his long yellow hair fall low upon his shoulders in wistful imitation of Bill's glossy brown curls. He took more care of Bill's guns and horses than he did of his own."[35]

During one of Cody's periodic absences, when Sheridan was searching for scouts, White entered the general's tent.

"Who the _____ are you?" asked the hard-nosed commander.
"When Cody is not here," replied White, "*I* am Buffalo Bill."
"The devil you are!" cried Sheridan. "Buffalo *Shit*, more likely."
Charley felt crushed, and the unfortunate nickname clung to him.[36]

While White labored without luck to escape the terrible new name, his hero was becoming a living legend. After winning the Medal of Honor in 1872 and after a host of Indian fights, "Buffalo Bill" became household words in America. "[We] had a genuine affection for Bill," confessed Captain Charles King of the 5th Cavalry. "He was a tried and true comrade—one who for cool daring and judgment had no superior. He was a beautiful horseman, an unrivalled shot, and as a scout unequalled. We had tried them all . . . but Bill Cody was the paragon."[37]

Scouting was not a job for a married man; Cody, California Joe, and others hardly knew their wives. Some scouts, however, managed to find a "wife" at almost every stop. "He was the most married of any man I ever saw," laughed Libbie Custer of a guide she had known, "for in every tribe he had a wife. Still this superfluity did not burden him, for the ceremony of tying a marital knot in the far West is simple, and the wives support themselves."[38]

In addition to "marriage," the philosophy of frontiersman Jack Robertson could be applied to Cody, California Joe, and most others: "There is no such thing as bad whiskey. Some is better than others, but I never saw any bad whiskey."[39]

Like their military counterparts, scouts were a hard-drinking, hard-living lot. When payday arrived Denver, Cheyenne, and Omaha were some of their favorite resorts. A Kansas editor spied one group among the railroad passengers bound for Leavenworth in 1867.

> Wild Bill, the celebrated scout, with Jack Harvey and some dozen of their companions were upon the train, having just come in from a scouting expedition under Gen. Sherman. All the party were more or less affected by frequent potations from their bottles, and Wild Bill himself was tipsy enough to be quite belligerent . . . . [T]hese wild and reckless young men . . . live in a constant state of excitement, one continual round of gambling, drinking and swearing, interspersed at brief intervals with pistol practice upon each other. At a word any of the gang draws his pistol and blazes away as freely as if all mankind were Arkansas Rebels.
>
> How long these Athletes will be able to stand such a mode of life; eating, drinking, sleeping (if they can be said to sleep) and playing cards with their pistols at half cock, remains to be seen. For ourself, we are willing to risk them in an Indian campaign for which their cruelty and utter recklessness of life particularly fit them.[40]

Although editors and their readers might assume that Hickok and company spent all of their time in drunken revelry and saloon shootouts, by far most of a scout's existence was passed alone in the snow or rain or under a broiling sun following a fading trail that often led to an early grave. While the pay of a scout was good, it was paltry considering the risks involved. And yet, after once tasting the life of perfect freedom and adventure, few men ever left the profession for good.

"Here I am," Thompson McFadden scribbled in his diary from Fort Dodge, "after an absence of five years in the states, financially broke, with the avowed intention of returning to my first love . . . . Start my wife home to her people with many more tears in her eyes than dollars in her pockets."[41] Even Cody, after gaining fame and fortune as an actor in the East, could not resist the cry of the West and returned again and again. The pull of the prairie was summed up by Billy Dixon.

> Drinking in the pure fresh air of the Plains, we rolled from our blankets every morning, clear-headed and ready for any enterprise. Just to feel one's self living in that country was a joy. We heard nothing and cared nothing about politics; it made little difference to us who was president of the United States; we worked hard, had enough money for our common needs, and were happy.[42]

Whether it was shy Charley Reynolds or loquacious Moses Milner, the scouts' lives remained shrouded in romance and mystery. Even Custer, an officer who knew the plainsmen better perhaps than any, did not pretend to know them deeply.

> Who they are, whence they come or whither they go, their names even . . . are all questions which none but themselves can answer.[43]

7

Island in the Sand

With the arrival of spring 1868, the tribes of the southern Plains resumed their raids. Though the Indians struck time and again in Texas, Colorado, and Nebraska, it was Kansas that suffered most. Along the Solomon River, the raiders burned, raped, and murdered almost with impunity. In one month alone, seventy-five settlers were slaughtered.[1]

"One poor woman," wrote a correspondent to the Boston *Banner of Light*, "was found gasping her life out but a few steps from the bodies of her babe and husband. After terrible desecration, in which a daughter twelve years of age shared, a rusty sword was thrust into the poor woman's body, and to her excruciating agony then added that of seeing her daughter bound naked to the back of a pony and carried into [a] captivity worse than death."[2]

Although small bands struck the interior of Kansas, it was the far-flung farms in the western third of the state that felt the full fury. That the settlers themselves were in part to blame for their plight was made clear by General Sherman:

> I have again and again warned the Governors and the people, that until this Indian matter was finally concluded, their people should not spread out so much. Their isolated farms, with horses and cattle, are too tempting to hungry and savage bands of Indians. If, however, they will not be restrained by motives of prudence, the people should, as they used to do in Ohio, Kentucky, Iowa and Missouri, make their settlements in groups, with block houses and a sod fort,

> so that when the savage comes they rally, and defend themselves and their stock. It is a physical impossibility for the small army . . . to guard the exposed settlements . . . . The army cannot do it, any more than we can catch all the pickpockets and thieves in our cities.[3]

What was obvious to Sherman was even more apparent to those nearest the frontier. Unlike the general, however, many Kansans felt the size of the army was not so important as the tactics it used. As one angry Kansas homesteader argued:

> Talk about regulars hunting Indians! They go out, and when night comes, they blow the bugle to let the Indians know that they are going to sleep. In the morning they blow the bugle to let the Indians know that they are going to get up. Between their bugle and their great trains, they manage to keep the redskins out of sight.[4]

Increasingly, a cry was raised for a force of frontiersmen to patrol the plains. At home in the wilderness, well versed in the ways of the Indian, a large body of such rugged, resourceful men, many felt, was bound to prevail where the army had failed. The editor of the *Leavenworth Times* summed up the sentiments of most Kansans:

> From the first alarm, up to the present moment, we have . . . urged the policy of hunting Indians by the Frontiersmen. They alone can do the work as it should be done. Regular troops are, in a great measure, the laughing stock of the Indians. Not so those bold and crafty children of the west . . . . These are the men we want to fight the red skins . . . . The border is in no humor for trifling. The howl of the savage comes too near to be musical.[5]

Because of such demands and because old methods had obviously failed, the army agreed to give the idea a try. That summer, General Sheridan ordered Major George Forsyth to enlist "fifty (50) first-class hardy, frontiersmen to be used as scouts against the hostile Indians, to be commanded by yourself."[6] Eager for independent command and tired of garrison duty, Forsyth quickly recruited his force at Fort Hays, then in early September moved to Fort Wallace. Almost immediately, the major learned of an Indian attack at nearby Sheridan in which two teamsters had been killed. Saddling up at once, the scouts soon struck a trail and followed it until dusk. Unlike in regular army campaigns, Forsyth traveled light. In addition to four pack mules, each man carried only a minimum of equipment, including a Spencer repeating rifle, a

George Forsyth.
Kansas State Historical Society.

big Colt army revolver, and a butcher knife. Second in command was Lieutenant Frederick Beecher, a veteran plainsman who was also a nephew of social reformer Henry Ward Beecher. Chief of scouts was Abner "Sharp" Grover, a grizzled frontiersman who spoke fluent Sioux.

Although most of the men were considered hard, tough scouts, Sigmund Shlesinger, a young Jewish immigrant, quickly found on the first day's march that he was not one of them.

> I was not used to the saddle, and my equipment . . . was always where it should not have been. I could not adjust all the paraphernalia so that I could be comfortable. My horse would not stay with the column, but forged ahead, being a fast walker, causing me to be ordered back into line several times. My bridle arm became stiff and lame in the effort to obey; every bone in my body began to ache; the ride and the day seemed never to end, and with every mile's travel my misery was bordering on torture. I was chafed by the saddle, and some parts became swollen to twice the normal size; my gun would never stay in place; and to add to my troubles, my clothes became wet from a drizzling rain, making the skin tender where belts attempted to hold equipment in place. At last we reached camp. I was too exhausted to enjoy my supper, and to cap the climax and fill my cup of misery to the brim, I was detailed for guard duty. But human nature could stand the strain no longer . . . . I was . . . no sooner left to myself than I dropped to the ground and fell fast asleep. So tired was I that had there been thousands of Indians around us I could not have raised my hand.[7]

Major Forsyth takes up the narrative.

> Resuming our march at early dawn, we again took the trail, but within two hours, it began to become less and less distinct; every few hundred yards it was a little less clearly apparent, and I realized that the Indians were dropping out here and there, one by one, wherever the ground hardened and their individual trail could not be easily followed. Riding together fifty yards ahead, Beecher and Grover kept their eyes fixed on the fast-diminishing trail; and knowing that either man was my superior in this especial line of plainscraft, I quietly followed on at the head of the command . . . . Within an hour they halted, and as the command overtook them, Beecher sententiously remarked, "Disappeared!"
>
> Halting and dismounting the command, we held a consultation . . . . On one point we were all agreed, and that was that the Indians had seen us, knew they were being followed, and had scattered on the trail, and it was reasonable to suppose that they would rejoin their main body sooner or later.[8]

At this point, several scouts questioned the advisability of moving deeper into hostile country. Forsyth continues:

> I . . . cut short the discussion by saying that I had determined to find and attack the Indians, no matter what the odds might be against us . . . . I thought, with fifty-one men, even if we could not defeat them, they could not annihilate us. Furthermore, it was expected that the command would fight the Indians, and I meant it should do so. Pushing on . . . and seeking for trails in every direction, on the fifth day out from Wallace . . . we ran into that of a small war party . . . . It led up to the forks of the Republican River . . . and grew steadily larger as various smaller trails from the north and south entered it, until finally it was a broad beaten road.[9]

Scout John Hurst:

> [A]s the trail kept enlarging and becoming more and more distinct, some of us became concerned as to the wisdom of following such a large party of Indians with such a small force of men. It was evident they had their families with them and could not travel as fast as a war party alone, and we realized that we would soon overtake them. We made known our anxiety to Colonel Forsyth.[10]

"I feel like we are marching right into the jaws of hell," remarked Jack Stillwell, one of Forsyth's bravest men.[11]

"We knew for two days," Louis McLoughlin added, "that we were biting off a chew that we could not get away with."[12]

"They said that if we followed the Indians to their village, we would be met with overwhelming numbers, and stood no show whatever for our lives," Forsyth recalled. "I listened to them patiently, told them that they were assuming no risk that I was not taking myself; that they had enrolled to fight Indians; and that in my opinion there was less danger to advance, and attack than there would be now to attempt to return."[13]

"That ended the discussion," shrugged John Hurst, "but all the same, it did not convince us of the wisdom of the course."[14]

In the late afternoon of September 17, just over the Colorado line, Forsyth's party camped along the Arickaree River opposite a small island in the middle of a nearly dry streambed. Horses were quickly unsaddled, meals prepared, and soon after dark most of the camp was asleep. Major Forsyth:

> [I]n my wakeful hours . . . as I paced the ground to and fro along the river-bank in front of the line of my sleeping men . . . I was somewhat apprehensive of an attack at daylight. Several times during the night I rose and visited the sentries, for I was restless, anxious, and wakeful. At early dawn, as I was standing by a sentry near one of the outposts closely scanning the sky-line . . . I suddenly caught sight of an object moving stealthily between us and the horizon. At the same moment the sentry saw it, and simultaneously cocking our rifles, we stood alert, with straining eyes and listening ears. An instant later the soft thud of unshod horses' hoofs upon the turf came to our ears, and peering just above the crest of the rising ground between us and the horizon, we caught sight of waving feathers crowning the scalp-locks of three mounted warriors.[15]

John Hurst had stood sentinel and was now deep in sleep.

> The next thing I knew was the sound of shooting and the guards shouting, "Indians! Indians!" We all grabbed our guns and were on our feet in an instant. Through the dim morning light we could discern three or four Indians driving off several of our horses that had pulled their picket pins. Colonel Forsyth gave the orders to saddle up at once, which we did, and were standing by our horses waiting for further orders, when some of the men got permission to drive off a bunch of Indians who were hiding behind rocks on the hillside

> north of us. When these men got on high ground they shouted to us to look up the creek—and such a sight! Indians by the hundred were everywhere in full view. They [sprang] . . . out of the tall weeds and bushes along the creek, from the depressions in the ground, and began swarming out over the hills.[16]

"The ground seemed to grow them," Forsyth remembered. "[T]hey broke into a gallop, and came rushing down on our camp, shouting, and beating Indians drums, and rattling dried hides, in an endeavor to stampede our horses."[17]

"I will frankly admit that I was frightened almost out of my senses," said a trembling Sigmund Shlesinger. "I felt as if I wanted to run somewhere, but every avenue of escape seemed closed . . . . I was reassured by [the major's] coolness and self possession."[18] Again, George Forsyth:

> The command was ordered to lead their horses to the little island just in front of us, to form a circle facing outwards, securely tie their horses to the bushes just outside of the circle so formed, throw themselves on the ground, and intrench themselves as rapidly as possible, two men working together, protecting each other in turn as they alternately threw up the earth to cover themselves.[19]

"[W]e all made . . . for cover like a flock of scared quail," admitted John Hurst.[20]

"[E]very man for himself," added Eli Ziegler, "with a grand rush over the embankment, across the dry creek bottom, up the bank and the island was gained in less time than it takes to tell it."[21]

"Hardly were we located on the island," noted a breathless Hurst, "before the Indians were charging through us—not in solid bodies, but singly or in groups of a few warriors."[22]

Major Forsyth:

> [T]hey made a desperate onslaught upon us, their various chiefs riding rapidly around just outside of rifle range, and impetuously urging their dismounted warriors to close in upon us on all sides. Many of the mounted Indians sprang from their horses also, and running forward they lined both banks of the river, and from the reeds and long grass poured in a steady and galling fire upon us. A few of our men had been hit, one killed, and several more badly wounded; our horses were being shot down on all sides, the poor animals plunging and rearing at their tethers, and adding their cries to the wild shouts

> of the savages and the steady crack of the rifles on every side. At the height of this crisis . . . one of the men shouted:
>
> "Don't let's stay here and be shot down like dogs. Will any man try for the opposite bank with me?"
>
> "I will," answered some one from the opposite side of the circle.
>
> "Stay where you are, men. It's our only chance," I shouted, as I stood in the centre of the command, revolver in hand. "I'll shoot down any man who attempts to leave the island."
>
> "And so will I," shouted [William] McCall.
>
> "You addle-headed fools, have you no sense?" called out Beecher, whose every shot was as carefully and cooly aimed as though he was shooting at a target.
>
> "Steady, men! steady, now! Aim low. Don't throw away a shot," was my oft-repeated command . . . . "Get down to your work, men. Don't shoot unless you can see something to hit. Don't throw away your ammunition."[23]

Forsyth's advice was followed and a rapid, well-directed fire forced the Indians back. The major continued:

> During this comparative lull in the fight the men were not idle, and with their butcher-knives to cut the sod, and their tin plates to throw up the sand, most of them had already scooped out a hole . . . . I still stood upright, walking from man to man, but from every side came appeals for me to lie down. As we were now in fairly good shape, and the men cool and determined, I did so. Scarcely had I lain down, when I received a shot in the fore part of the right thigh, the bullet ranging upward . . . . For a moment I could not speak, so intense was the agony. Several of the men, knowing I was hit called out to know if I still lived, but it was at least a full minute before I could command my voice and assure them I was not mortally hurt. In the mean time one or two Indians had crawled up on the lower end of the island, and, hidden by a few bushes, were annoying us very much. However, [Louis] Farley . . . saw the flash of one of their rifles from the centre of a little bush, and the next instant a bullet from his rifle went through the very middle of the bush and crashed into the brave's brain, and a wild half-smothered shriek told us that there was one less of our enemies to encounter.[24]

According to Hurst, not all scouts were as composed as Farley:

> [T]hree men . . . played the coward in the fight. They utterly refused to fire a shot, but kept themselves hidden . . . . One of them . . . was shaking like a man with palsy, and seemed utterly unnerved . . . . I tried to encourage him by saying, "Frenchie . . . we are in for a fight, and let us fight like men." However, it was all to no avail. He made a run for the bushes and took no part in the fighting.[25]

To the horror of those on the island, hundreds of mounted warriors massed for an attack. DeBenneville Keim spoke with survivors and described the drama.

> With faces bedaubed with war paint, bodies bare to the waist, with shields, bows, arrows, spears, rifles and pistols, flourishing in the air, they presented a fearful scene . . . . The old war-chief addressed his warriors. The "big medicine" man galloped up and down in front beating his drums and exclaiming "the white man's bullet will melt before you." The women and children gathered on the hills around to see their people scalp the pale face. Some danced and shouted, others pressed closely upon the rear of the warriors, determined to follow and share with them their bloody work.
>
> These were breathless moments on the island . . . . The savage warriors were seen upon the plain making final dispositions preparatory to an attack. It was now nine o'clock in the morning . . . . The women could be heard chanting their songs of victory. The old men narrated the deeds of their forefathers' to excite the emulation of the young. The medicine man shouted and beat his drum. The war-chief with all the dignity of command, now waved his weapons and gave the fierce war-whoop. With one responsive yell the warriors dashed across the plain.[26]

Amid wild yells and the shrill, terrifying notes of bone whistles, believed to ward off bullets, the Sioux and Cheyenne charged down on the island. "I thought we were all going to be killed and scalped or captured and held for torture," Hurst recalled. "I heard Colonel Forsyth call out and ask if anyone could pray. He said, 'We are beyond all human aid, and if God does not help us there is none for us.'"[27]

"Every trooper realized that his time had come," Ziegler added as he and his comrades opened fire in an attempt to stay the inevitable. "Volley after volley was poured into the charging foe in rapid succession . . . . Soon horses and warriors were mingled in disorganized confusion."[28]

As the Indians reached the head of the island, they passed "like a tornado" on either side, firing down on the scouts. Sharing a pit with Forsyth, who had been wounded again, was surgeon J. H. Mooers. Forsyth:

> About this time several of the mounted Indians . . . dashed up . . . and from their horses took a sort of pot-shot at us. Doctor Mooers, who had been closely watching their approach as they careered around the island . . . watched his opportunity and shot one of them through the head. As the brave fell dead from his horse he remarked, "That rascally redskin will not trouble us again." Almost immediately . . . I heard the peculiar thud that tells the breaking of bone by a bullet. Turning to the doctor, I saw him put his hand to his head, saying, "I'm hit," his head at the same time falling forward on the sand. Crawling to him, I pulled his body down into the pit and turned him upon his back, but I saw at once that there was no hope. A bullet had entered his forehead just over the eye, and the wound was mortal.[29]

After turning the furious charge, the grateful men on the island could only dig deeper and pray that the Indians had been checked. As the scouts peered up the valley, however, it quickly became evident that they had not. DeBenneville Keim:

> The chief, with a bearing of command, and in a voice of authority, addressed his people. "Young warriors, we are many and the whites are few. The white bullets are wasted. Once more and we bring the white man's scalp to our fires."
>
> The warriors yelled assent. Grover, understanding the chief's language, took an opportunity to respond to the royal savage. At the top of his voice he shouted, "Hello, old feller, got any more people to kill? This is pretty tough, ain't it?" The surprised chief involuntarily shouted back, "you speak right straight."[30]

Once again the Indians charged across the sandy streambed, but once again the repeating rifles drove them back. In the meantime, the scouts worked feverishly at the sand. John Hurst was no exception:

> While I was at work Sergeant McCall and Scout [George] Culver came in, and getting down behind [a] dead horse they went to work digging. They had been at it but a short time when some of the men

> on the inside of the circle shouted, "If you fellows on the outside don't get up and shoot, the Indians will be charging us." At this criticism both McCall and Culver arose to look for Indians. Their heads were fully exposed to the enemy, and suddenly "bang!" came the report of a rifle. The bullet grazed McCall's neck and struck Culver in the head, killing him instantly. That was the last exposure of heads during the fight.[31]

Few doubted that the Indians would try again, particularly Major Forsyth:

> We had not long to wait. A peal of the artillery bugle and at a slow trot the mounted warriors came partially into view in an apparently solid mass at the foot of the valley . . . . Closely watching the mounted warriors, I saw their chief facing his command, and by his gestures, evidently addressing them in a few impassioned words . . . . Riding up and down their line [he was] of almost gigantic stature. I was almost certain who it must be, so calling out to Grover, I asked the question, "Is not the large warrior Roman Nose?"
>
> "None other," was the reply. "There is not such another Indian on the plains."[32]

Though more than a thousand Sioux and Cheyenne warriors were in full view, all eyes were on the huge chief. "Roman Nose was the finest specimen of manhood I ever saw," said an awed Allison Pliley. "There was a natural impressiveness and dignity about him such as I have never seen in any other man."[33] Returning to Forsyth:

> His face was hideously painted in alternate lines of red and black, and his head crowned with a magnificent war bonnet, from which . . . stood up two short black buffalo horns . . . . Then waving his hand in our direction, he turned his horse's head towards us, and at the word of command they broke at once into full gallop, heading straight for the foot of the island . . . . Turning his face for an instant towards the women and children . . . who literally by thousands were watching the fight from the crest of the low bluffs . . . [Roman Nose] raised his right arm and waved his hand with a royal gesture in answer to their wild cries of rage and encouragement as he and his command swept down upon us; and again facing squarely towards where we lay, he drew his body to its full height and shook his clinched fist defiantly at us; then throwing back his head and glancing skywards, he sud-

> denly struck the palm of his hand across his mouth and gave tongue to a war-cry that I have never yet heard equalled in power and intensity. Scarcely had its echoes reached the river's bank when it was caught up by each and every one of the charging warriors . . . and answered back with blood-curdling yells of . . . vengeance by the women and children on the river's bluffs . . . . Riding about five paces in front of the centre of the line, and twirling his heavy Springfield rifle around his head as if it were a wisp of straw . . . Roman Nose recklessly led the charge with a bravery that could only be equalled but not excelled . . . . No sooner were the charging warriors fairly under way than a withering fire was suddenly poured in upon us by those of the Indians who lay in ambush around us . . . . I had expected this action, but I well knew that once their horsemen came with a certain radius their fire must cease. For eight or ten seconds it seemed to rain bullets, and then came a sudden lull. Sitting upright in my pit as well as I was able, and leaning backward on my elbows, I shouted, "Now!" and "Now!" was echoed by Beecher, McCall, and Grover. Instantly the scouts were on their knees with their rifles at their shoulders . . . and . . . sent their first of seven successive volleys into the ranks of the charging warriors.[34]

In the next few seconds a hail of lead tore into the charging Sioux and Cheyenne. Men and mounts went down in heaps. Through the smoke and the dust came the terrifying screams and shouts of not only those fighting and dying in the valley but from those viewing the tumult from above. As before, when the storm reached the island, rather than thunder straight over the white men, it split down the middle and passed by. With cheers, the emboldened scouts leaped from their holes to fire parting shots from their revolvers.

"Turning towards where my guide Grover lay," Forsyth later wrote, "I somewhat anxiously put the question, 'Can they do better than that, Grover?' "

"I have been on the plains, man and boy . . . for more than thirty years, and I never saw anything like that before," was his reply.[35]

While snipers along both banks resumed their fire, the attackers, including the mortally wounded Roman Nose, fled down the valley. Also fatally hit, young Lieutenant Beecher staggered up to Forsyth's pit, then collapsed. Forsyth continued:

> [T]he valley was resonant with the shrieks of the women and children, who, from their . . . vantage on the hills, had safely but eagerly watched the result of Roman Nose's desperate charge; and now as

The Battle of the Arickaree. KANSAS STATE HISTORICAL SOCIETY.

their fathers, sons, brothers, and lovers lay dead on the sands below them, their wild wails of . . . grief and agony fitfully rose and fell on the air in a prolonged and mournful cadence of rage and despair . . . .

[N]ow came another lull in the battle. The mounted Indians drew off to the little cañon where they had before formed for the

> charge, and for the next few hours were evidently in close consultation; but the wailing of the women and children never ceased . . . . About two o'clock, under new leaders, they essayed another charge, this time in open order, and half surrounding us as they came on. It was an abject failure, for they broke and ran before they came within a hundred yards of the island . . . .
>
> [B]etween five and six o'clock they again formed up in the little cañon, and with a rush came on en masse with wild cries for vengeance, evidently wrought up to frenzy by the wails and taunts of their women and children; but scarcely had they come within range when the scouts . . . began picking them off as cooly and deliberately as possible. It was simply death to advance, and they broke and fled just as the boldest of them had reached the foot of the island; and as they turned back and sought safety in flight I felt satisfied that it was the last attempt that would be made by mounted warriors to carry our little breastworks.[36]

Except for sporadic firing, darkness settled over the Arickaree with no further attacks. All the same, Forsyth was in a desperate strait. With half his force dead, dying, or wounded, and with almost no food or medical supplies, the major could not possibly withstand a siege. Still, he found cause for hope.

> I had an abundance of ammunition and still twenty-eight fairly sound men . . . . I knew that water within our intrenchments could be had for the digging . . . . The dead horses and mules would furnish us food for some days if we could keep the meat from putrefying . . . . Accordingly orders were given to strengthen and connect all the rifle pits; unsaddle the dead horses, and use the saddles to help build up our parapet: to dig out and fortify a place for the wounded, and dress their wounds as well as could be done . . . and to cut off a large quantity of steaks from the dead horses and mules, and to bury all the meat that we did not immediately need in the sand. The men worked with a will, and before midnight we were in very good shape.[37]

A short time later, the beleaguered officer called a quiet council. Remembered John Hurst:

> Forsyth asked . . . what the chances were of sending men through the Indian lines to Fort Wallace for reinforcements—a distance of about 125 miles. Grover said it would be impossible for a man to

> get through . . . and went on to tell what the Indians did in such an emergency, and what a close cordon they would draw all around us, so they would be able to detect any man who tried to steal through. We all stood there listening to the dark picture he was painting, and after he had finished, young Jack Stillwell . . . spoke up and said, "Colonel, if I can get some one to go with me, I'll take the risk." A scout named Pierre Trudeau replied, "I'll go with you, Jack."[38]

As Eli Ziegler noted:

> Jack was the best imitator of an Indian that I ever saw. They fixed themselves up as Indians the best they could and took off their boots and tied on some rags and blankets on their feet so that if the Indians saw their tracks next day they would think it some of their own party and not follow them . . . . At a late hour they gave us their hand and crawled out.[39]

"We listened for some time," added a tense Sigmund Shlesinger, "fully expecting every moment to hear the war whoop which would announce their discovery and capture, but not a sound followed their departure."

"I believe they got through," someone heard Forsyth whisper.

"Yes," Grover answered. "I think so too."[40]

"All night long we could hear the Indians stealthily removing the dead bodies of their slain," Forsyth continued, "and their camp resounded with the beat of drums and the death wail of the mourners."[41]

It was a sleepless, terror-filled night for the scouts. As the chill of a High Plains autumn settled over the valley, there seemed little doubt to those shivering on the island that the contest would be resumed at dawn.

"They did come early," Ziegler recalled, "just before the sun rose."

> It seemed to me there were just as many and as bad as the first day and the squaws took their places on the hills just the same as the day before. Our orders were about the same, "Hold your fire till they get close, but don't let them ride over us." We were in a good deal better position and could all be together which gave us a better show than we had the day before. [The Indians] stopped fighting and put up a white flag, but most of us were too old to be scalped alive that way and we showed no signs of a white flag so that did not last long with them. [They] soon commenced again and poured in [a fire] on us as hard as ever the rest of the day.[42]

Lying in his pit, talking to Martin Burke, George Oaks soon learned some Indian weapons could reach the island in ways a bullet could not.

> [A]n arrow came whizzing out of the sky and struck me in the hip. You ought to have heard Burke. "Haw! Haw! Haw! Lookit Oaks with a Cheyenne arrow stuck in his hind end." I'm not given much to swearing but that's one time I came pretty near shooting that goddamn Irishman. But Burke was alright [and] he grabbed the shaft and slowly worked it out. If left too long the blood-soaked sinew would loosen so badly that when the shaft was pulled out the arrowhead would stay.[43]

Throughout the long, hot day the scouts hugged their holes as snipers kept them pinned down. John Hurst:

> When night came again Colonel Forsyth deemed it wise to try and get two more scouts through the lines, not knowing, of course, if Stillwell and Trudeau were successful; I do not remember the names of the two who volunteered on the second night, but anyway they could not get through, as every avenue of escape was too closely guarded, and the two scouts soon returned.
>
> The third day was a repetition of the second—very little firing, but close watching on the part of the Indians. Evidently they were going to try and starve us out . . . . [We] had nothing to eat but the dead horses which were festering and decaying about us, and when we cut into this meat the stench was something frightful, and it had green streaks running all through it. The only way it was made at all available for eating was by sprinkling gunpowder over it while it was cooking, which partially took away the bad odor.[44]

For Sigmund Shlesinger and his neighbor, M. R. "Jim" Lane, a maggot-infested pack mule doubled as "barricade and food."

"[W]hen 'Jim' was cutting meat off the mule," Shlesinger recounted, "he must have cut deeper than he intended, for he cut an intestine and received its full contents over himself, nearly filling his pit!"[45] Returning to Hurst:

> We had no salt and our systems were crying for it. One of the men found a small piece of pork rind in his haversack and chewed it until he thought he had all the good out of it and spit it out; when another comrade took it up and chewed it for a while and spit it out; and then I took it and chewed it up and thought it tasted delicious.[46]

Once again, Shlesinger:

> Our mortally wounded were made as comfortable as possible before they died. As soon as possible we put our dead in the ground. Those that died at one end of the island were cared for by those in that vicinity, and others in their vicinity, so that one part of the island was not aware of the location of the corpses of the other part . . . . So one time, as I walked around among the pits, I noticed something red and round sticking out of the sand, like a half-buried red berry. I kicked it, but by doing so it was not dislodged; I kicked it again, but to no result. I then looked closer and discovered that it was the nose of a dead man.[47]

Though the nerve-grinding drums and chants had ceased and the Indians had seemingly pulled back, the daily horror continued. George Forsyth:

> It was very hot, our meat had become putrid, some of the wounded were delirious, and the stench from the dead horses lying close around us was almost intolerable. As the ball in my right thigh had begun to pain me excessively, I decided to extract it.
>
> I appealed to several of the men to cut [the bullet] out, but as soon as they saw how close it lay to the artery, they declined doing so, alleging that the risk was too great. However, I determined it should come out, as I feared sloughing, and then the artery would probably break in any event; so taking my razor from my saddle pocket, and getting two of the men to press the adjacent flesh back and draw it taut, I managed to cut it out myself without disturbing the artery, greatly to my almost immediate relief.[48]

After dark on the third day, Forsyth, fearful for the fate of Stillwell and Trudeau, again called on volunteers. Jack Donovan and Allison Pliley stepped forward and the two soon slipped quietly from the island and into the night.[49] "On about the fifth day . . . we began to walk about and look around," Shlesinger said.

> About fifteen or twenty feet from my pit I noticed a few of our men calling to the rest of us. I ran to the place, and there, against the edge of the island, I saw three dead Indians. Their friends evidently could not reach them to carry them off, which explained to us the persistent fighting in this direction. When I got there the Indians were

> being stripped . . . . One of them was shot in the head and his hair was clotted with blood. I took hold of one of his braids and applied my knife to the skin above the ear to secure the scalp, but my hand coming in contact with the blood, I dropped the hair in disgust.
>
> Old Jim Lane saw my hesitation, and taking up the braid, said to me: "My boy, does it make you sick?" Then inserting the point of the knife under the skin, he cut around, took up the other braid, and jerked the scalp from the head.[50]

"And now came a time of weary waiting," remembered Major Forsyth:

> We were out of food of any kind; the meat cut from the dead mules and horses had become putrid, and although we boiled it and sprinkled gunpowder upon it, it was not palatable . . . . As the days wore on the wounded became feverish, and some of them delirious, gangrene set in, and I was distressed to find the wound in my leg infested with maggots . . . . [A]t night the crests of the hills were dotted with wolves, who, attracted by the carrion . . . sat up on their haunches and howled the night through; and during the day the sun beat down upon our . . . heads.[51]

Even though the scouts could now escape their torrid rifle pits, they dared not stray far in search of food. The diary of Chauncey Whitney reveals the daily despair:

> **22d.**—No Indians to-day. Killed a coyote this morning, which was very good. Most of the horse meat gone. Found some prickly pears, which were very good. Are looking anxiously for succor from the fort.
> **23d.**—Still looking anxiously for relief. Starvation is staring us in the face; nothing but horse meat.
> **24th.**—Tried to kill some wolves last night, but failed . . . . Made some soup tonight from putrid horse meat. My God! have you deserted us?
> **25th of September, 1868.**—Arose at daylight to feel all the horrors of starvation slowly but surely approaching. Got a light breakfast of rotten meat. Some of the boys wandered away to find something to satisfy and appease their hunger.[52]

Two of those searching for food that morning of the ninth day were Fletcher Vilott and Eli Ziegler:

> We took our guns and started north across the river. When we got across . . . Fletcher said to me, "There is going to be a change today, that is why I wanted you to take a walk with me. I wanted to tell you about it." As we got nearly to the top of the hill we came to a big rock and sat down a moment to rest . . . . We sat there talking a few moments [when] my eye caught an object on the far hills to the south . . . . We jumped to our feet and walked up the hill a little farther, where we could plainly see [something] coming over the hill toward us . . . . We could not make out what it was so we hurried back to camp in case it was Indians.[53]

Nearby, a dejected John Hurst had given up a hunt for prairie dogs:

> I started back for the island empty-handed, and with the most empty stomach I ever have experienced . . . . I had not gone very far when I saw some of the men running towards me and motioning for me to hurry. The thought that it was the Indians returning for another invasion of the island took possession of me, and I started on a dead run for my comrades. I was too faint and exhausted, however, to run very far, and soon fell to the ground, all in, and scarcely caring whether it was the Indians or not, so discouraged and disheartened was I. Happening to look up, I saw three horsemen riding toward me . . . . I gazed long and earnestly at the advancing riders.[54]

On the island itself, Forsyth was still unaware of the approaching horsemen.

> [O]ne of the men near me suddenly sprang to his feet, and shading his eyes with his hand, shouted, 'There are some moving objects on the far hills!' Instantly every man who could stand was on his feet gazing intensely in the direction indicated. In a few moments a general murmur ran through the command. "By the God above us it's an ambulance!" shouts one of the men . . . and then went up a wild cheer that made the little valley ring . . . . [S]trong men grasped hands, and then flung their arms around each other, and laughed and cried, and fairly danced and shouted again in glad relief of their long-pent-up feelings.[55]

"Enfeebled as I was," Shlesinger admitted, "I jumped up and joined in a lunatics' dance that was in progress all around us."[56] Laying helplessly in the sand, expecting to be shot or speared any moment, John Hurst gazed up to see the smiling face of his old friend, Jack Donovan. "The sudden transition from despair to safety was too much for my overtaxed nerves," said the scout, "and I broke down and wept like a child."[57]

Captain Louis Carpenter, commander of the rescue party, recognized his old Civil War comrade, Forsyth, laying in a sandy hole. "He was too weak, shattered and nervous to be able to talk much," the captain noted, "but I knew that he was overjoyed that his men were relieved."[58]

"When . . . Carpenter rode up to me, as I lay half covered with sand in my rifle-pit," admitted Forsyth, "I affected to be reading an old novel that one of the men had found in a saddle pocket. It was only affectation, though, for I had all I could do to keep from breaking down."[59]

Meanwhile, the half-starved scouts, with "wolfish" faces, scrambled for anything edible. Shlesinger:

> I noticed a soldier on a white horse coming full tilt. The momentum carried him past me, but in passing I grabbed his saddle-bag and was taken off my feet, but it would have taken more than one horse to drag me from my hold. I suspected some eatables in there, and as soon as he could stop, without dismounting, he assisted me to open that bag. With both hands I dived in, and with each hand I clutched some hardtack, but only one hand could reach my mouth . . . . We ate, cried, laughed, and ate, all in a breath.[60]

Two days later, after the survivors had recovered and the seriously wounded were attended to, the soldiers and scouts rode out of the Arickaree Valley and started back toward Fort Wallace. At the end of the first day's march, September 27, the column reached the South Fork of the Republican River. Shlesinger and Ben Clark were riding a little ahead of the rest.

"Before Clark and I descended to the bottom, we looked around and saw four Indians running toward three horses," Shlesinger later wrote. "Three of them jumped on their horses and in great agitation galloped away through the water to the other side of the river and kept on to the south as fast as their ponies could carry them, leaving their companion behind. He ran after them, but of course could not overhaul them . . . . [W]e noticed two or three of our company . . . hasten down to the bottom toward the Indians."[61] One of those bearing down on the lone warrior was Jack Peate.

> Just before he came to the river he dropped a woman's white skirt and soon after a calico dress; then, as the race grew warmer (we were on the rolling ground south of the river now), he dropped his blanket. The sport, to us, was now becoming exciting. The boys shooting at the Indian whenever they could. The Indian was running

very, very fast, but we were gaining on him slowly. He would not run in a straight line; he would jump several times to the right, then back to the left, still rushing ahead . . . . [The] bullets were striking the ground all around him.

It looked as if the Indian would get to the deep cañon still a half mile away, where his comrades had passed out of sight, when a shot from a . . . rifle . . . broke the Indian's right leg above the knee . . . . After hopping a few feet he sits down and faces the foe. The few hundred feet that still separate us is soon passed over. As soon as the Indian faces us he commences to fire, being armed with a Colt's navy revolver . . . . Then something seems to be the matter with his revolver; he looks into it and throws it on the ground. Not a shot was fired by our party while advancing after the Indian discarded his revolver . . . . [H]e was a young man, perhaps twenty-five years of age . . . . He was chanting a weird song and did not offer any resistance. He knew what his fate would be and showed no fear.[62]

The next morning, Peate returned to the spot. "The wolves had held a banquet there," he noted, "and a few bones was all that remained of the warrior of yesterday."[63]

Also in the area were the graves of several Indians, including one inside a white tepee. Again, Jack Peate:

We went into the lodge and found that it was the tomb of a medicine man killed in the battle. The Indian was placed on a scaffold that was eight feet high. Fastened to the scaffold was his war bonnet and a large drum. He was wrapped in blankets and a buffalo robe and tied on the scaffold. The posts on one side of the scaffold were torn away by the boys so we could have a better look at the good Indian. The body was then rolled to the edge of the cañon and it rolled from there to the bottom.[64]

Sigmund Shlesinger also was there:

All the bodies were pulled down from their lofty perches. This may seem a wanton sacrilege, but not to those who have suffered bodily torture and mental anguish from these very cruel savages. I had no scruples in rolling one out of his blankets, that still were soaking in the blood from the wounds that evidently caused his death, and appropriating the top one that was least wet. This Indian had on a headdress composed of buckskin beautifully beaded and ornamented, with a polished buffalo horn on the frontal part and eagle feathers down the back. When I took this off, maggots were in the headpiece. I also pulled off his earrings and finger rings, which were of tin. He was so far decomposed that when I took hold of the rings the fingers came along, and these I shook out![65]

Three days later, the cavalry and its weary yet celebrated charges reached Fort Wallace. "We naturally were objects of interest," Shlesinger acknowledged. To the repeated question, "How many redskins did you dust?" Shlesinger—the boy who started the trip with saddle blisters, now suddenly a veteran Indian fighter—answered openly and honestly. And when he did, the young scout spoke perhaps for a majority of plainsmen:

> [M]y answer must truthfully be that I don't know. The conditions were such . . . that I did not consider it safe to watch the result of a shot, the Indians being all around us, shooting at anything moving above ground. At one time I threw a hatful of sand, that I scraped up in my pit, to the top of the excavation, exposing myself more

Sigmund Shlesinger, one of the survivors of Arickaree. AMERICAN JEWISH ARCHIVES.

> than usual, when a hail of bullets struck my hill of sand, almost blinding me! This will explain why I did not look for results.[66]

Thus ended the short-lived attempt to employ bands of frontiersmen against the Plains tribes. Although thirty-two Indians, according to Forsyth, were killed in the epic nine-day stand on the Arickaree, the major and his men had suffered a stunning defeat. With five dead, more than twenty wounded, and the entire command crippled physically and mentally, Forsyth's scouts had been shattered beyond repair. While the men themselves, including the four volunteers who reached Fort Wallace, had performed admirably, it was clear that only overwhelming might and continuous pressure by the army could force the defiant enemy from the warpath. Meanwhile, the forays along the frontier continued and, as General Sherman had warned, those in the scattered and isolated communities suffered the consequences.

8

A Fate Worse Than Death

> The golden sun was sinking . . . when we camped near a sandy creek bed . . . . [F]ather dug a hole one or two feet deep [and] the water arose so that he dipped a bucketful for our use. Joanna and I gathered sticks for the camp fire. Sophia opened the coop and scattered grain for her chickens. Father and Stephen milked the cows, and how we enjoyed the sweet, warm milk along with the supper mother had prepared! After supper the youngest children were soon fast asleep, but father, mother, Jane, Stephen and I sat around the camp fire talking and listening . . . . The oxen, cows and calves were allowed to feed on the green grass near the wagon; we could hear them moving about and their steady crop, crop of the grass. Crickets chirped; owls broke the silence by an occasional "Who? Who?" and the sharp bark of the coyotes in the distance was heard.[1]

Thus wrote seventeen-year-old Catherine German describing what had become for her and her family, as well as countless others, the end of a typical day's journey on the great road west. For all the reasons as those who had come before and those who came after—wealth, health, and adventure—Catherine's parents had scooped up the seven children, packed a wagon with their goods, and set out for the setting sun. During the previous two weeks, Catherine's family had passed slowly, yet steadily, through the settled regions of Kansas. When they reached the parched High Plains in the western third of the state, however, they were advised not to follow the line of the Kansas Pacific Railroad, as they had hoped. The Germans were urged to turn south instead and catch the old Smoky Hill Trail. Only on that road, they were warned, was a constant supply of water assured. Catherine's father had naturally been concerned. Since completion of the railways, the once popular Smoky Hill route had become little more than a lonely track through a treeless waste. When the Germans queried about hostiles, those who knew only laughed: None had been seen in years.

Thus, while the father and only son, Stephen, stood guard that still September night, the women and girls of Catherine's family slept soundly at their camp along the Smoky.

"With high-wrought hopes and pleasant anticipations of a romantic and delightful journey across the Plains," began Fanny Kelly's account of her eagerly awaited journey to Idaho.[2] Unlike the German family, Fanny, her husband, and their adopted child Mary, plus several others in the party, found themselves traveling through Wyoming in the heart of Indian country. And unlike the Smoky Hill route to the south, the Oregon Trail was a heavily trod road, where the dust of travellers was seldom lost to sight. Like the Germans, however, and despite the security of numbers, the Kellys were anxious about Indians. As Fanny explained:

> At the outposts and ranches, we heard nothing but ridicule . . . and at Fort Laramie, where information that should have been reliable was given us, we had renewed assurances of the safety of the road and friendliness of the Indians. At Horseshoe Creek, which we had just left, and where there was a telegraph station, our inquiries had elicited similar assurances as to the quiet and peaceful condition of the country through which we must pass. Being thus persuaded that fears were groundless, we entertained none.[3]

Other than being young, attractive white women moving west by wagon, Fanny and Catherine had something else in common—both were only moments away from hell on Earth; both were about to experience the much-dreaded "fate worse than death." Catherine:

> Soon all were up and dressed; we ate breakfast and broke camp at sunrise . . . . Father took his rifle, as was his usual custom, and walked ahead of the wagon. Stephen and I went to get our cows and calves which had wandered away and were feeding in a hollow north of the camp. We had turned the cows toward the moving wagon

> when Stephen said, "O Catherine, drive the cows; I want to see if I can get an antelope; they are so close!"
>
> I looked and saw about a dozen antelope that had crossed the road in front of our wagon. Just then I heard the most terrible yells. We looked again and saw many forms dashing down upon our wagon. Stephen exclaimed, "Indians! Indians!" I heard several dreadful groans. A great fear took possession of me. I saw Stephen running to get behind the ridge to the northeast . . . . I was terribly frightened and shook with fear, not knowing what to do. I tried to follow brother. As the savages neared me an arrow struck my thigh. A big burly Indian jumped off his horse, grabbed me and pulled out the arrow. He kicked me several times; then put me on his large bay horse and rode to our wagon. There I saw sister Jane lying dead . . . . Jane had jumped from the wagon with an axe and struck her assailant on the shoulder; then another Indian shot her . . . . [F]ather was first to fall and mother ran to his aid and was the next victim. As an Indian caught mother by the arm she was heard to exclaim, "Oh, let me get to father! Let me get to father!" Her captor cruelly murdered her and she fell near father's body.
>
> Some time passed while the Indians were parleying; they seemed to make a choice between Joanna and myself . . . . The Indians removed our bonnets to see if we had long hair . . . . My hair was short . . . . Joanna was sitting on a box that had been taken from the back of our wagon . . . . We heard the report of a rifle and when we looked again, our beloved sister, Joanna, was dead. The Indians then scalped their long-haired victims . . . . This all happened within a very short time, and before any of us could realize it, our once happy family life was forever ended.[4]

"The beauty of the sunset and the scenery around us filled our hearts with joy," recalled Fanny Kelly as she, Mary, and others joined in chorus, "Ho! for Idaho!" "We wended our way peacefully and cheerfully on."

> Without a sound . . . or a word of warning, the bluffs before us were covered with a party of about two hundred and fifty Indians . . . who soon uttered a wild war whoop and fired a signal volley of guns and revolvers into the air. This terrible and unexpected apparition came upon us with such startling swiftness that we had not time to think before the main body halted and sent out a part of their force, which circled us round . . . . Recovering from the shock, our men instantly resolved on defense, and corralled the wagons. My husband

was looked upon as leader . . . [and] I entreated him to forebear and only attempt conciliation. "If you fire one shot," I said, "I feel sure you will seal our fate, as they seem to outnumber us ten to one, and will at once massacre all of us."

My husband advanced to meet the chief . . . [and] the savage leader immediately came toward him uttering the friendly words, "How! How!" . . . He at once struck himself on his breast, saying "Good Indian, me," and while pointing to those around him, he continued, "Heap good Indian, hunt buffalo and deer." He assured us of his utmost friendship for all white people. He shook hands while others crowded around our wagons, shaking us all by the hand over and over again, until our arms ached, and grinning and nodding with demonstrations of good will . . . . My husband came to me with words of cheer and hope, but oh! what a marked look of despair was upon his face, such as I had never seen before. The Indians asked for flour, and we gave them what they wanted of provisions. Then they emptied all of it upon the ground, saving only the sack . . . . [W]e allowed them to take whatever they desired, and offered them many presents besides . . . . Our anxiety to conciliate them increased every moment, for the hope of help arriving from some quarter grew stronger as they dallied.

They grew bolder and more insolent in their advances. One of them laid hold of my husband's gun, but, being repulsed, desisted . . . . [T]hey requested that we should prepare supper, which they said they would share with us, and then go to the hills to sleep. The men of our party concluded it best to give them a feast and Mr. Kelly gave orders . . . to prepare a large meal immediately . . . . Supper, that they asked for, was in rapid progress of preparation, when suddenly . . . there was a simultaneous discharge of arms, and when the cloud of smoke cleared away, I could see the retreating form of Mr. Larimer and also the faltering motions of poor Mr. Wakefield, for he was mortally wounded. Mr. Kelly and Andy made a miraculous escape with their lives. Mr. Sharp was killed within a few feet of me. Mr. Taylor—I never can forget his face as I saw him shot through the forehead with a rifle ball. He looked at me as he fell backward to the ground, a corpse.

[T]he Indians quickly sprang into our wagons, tearing off covers, breaking, crushing, and smashing all hinderances to plunder, breaking open locks, trunks, and boxes, and distributing or destroying our goods with great rapidity, using their tomahawks to pry open boxes,

> which they split up in savage recklessness . . . . They filled the air with the fearful war whoops and hideous shouts . . . . [T]wo of the most savage-looking of the party rushed up into my wagon with tomahawks drawn in their right hands, and with their left seized me by both hands and pulled me violently to the ground, injuring my limbs very severely, almost breaking them . . . . I turned to my little Mary, who with outstretched hands, was standing in the wagon.[5]

Unlike Catherine and Fanny, Sarah Morris was not in a wagon moving west through strange country but was sitting quietly in her Colorado home surrounded by all that was familiar.

> They set the house and stables afire, and drove us into the pilgrim room. At last the doors of the pilgrim room got in flames, and we had to leave. We ran out towards the river, through the corral, hoping to make our escape. My husband said perhaps we could escape that way. When we got to the corral we found we could not. He told me to stop, that they would probably take me prisoner, and he possibly might get away. They surrounded him, and killed him and another man as they were running to the river. The Indians stood so thickly about me, I could not see him when he was killed . . . . I received five wounds from arrows and six stabs from knives. They also struck me across the head with their whips.[6]

As with these three women and others who were captured, if the victim weathered the initial attack, her chances of survival rose greatly, for Indians quickly killed or tortured to death those of no value to them. In most cases, however, the women would have gladly died rather than endure the degradation that was to come.

While her husband helplessly watched on, one woman fled to a nearby tent when Indians suddenly surrounded her uncompleted Nebraska home. The editor of a local newspaper tells what happened:

> [She] was led from her tent and every remnant of clothing torn from her body. A child that she was holding to her breast was wrenched from her arms and she was knocked to the ground. In this nude condition the demons gathered round her and while some held her down by standing on her wrists and their claws clutched in her hair, others outraged her person. Not less than thirty repeated the horrible deed! While this was going on another crew was trying to stop

> the heart-broken wailings of the child by tossing strings of beads about its face, and others were dancing about in the brush and grass, with revolvers cocked, yelping like madmen.[7]

After the murders and rapes, the Indians either continued their raids or turned homeward with the captives. In their stunned condition, few women failed to follow. Five Colorado captives who did refuse had their hair plaited onto horses' tails and were dragged helplessly along.[8]

"We sisters were taken on the ponies behind those who chose us," said Catherine German. Julia, age seven, and Addie, five, were chosen by a squaw and her husband while "an average-sized buck" claimed twelve-year-old Sophia.

> I, Catherine was taken by . . . a hard-hearted, brutal and cruel savage . . . . Later, they found a few horses so Sophia and I were each put on one with old pack saddles, which were better than none at all. We were not allowed to sit sidewise on the horses and for several days some one led them. I wondered if they feared we might escape. How glad we would have been to do so but there was no opportunity.[9]

Like the German girls, Fanny Kelly found herself on a horse bound for an Indian village. Captured at sundown, however, Fanny soon saw that chance to escape that Catherine had not.

> I rode on in my helpless condition with my child clinging to me . . . . In the darkness of our ride I conceived a plan for the escape of little Mary. I whispered in her childish ear, "Mary, we are only a few miles from our camp . . . . Drop gently down and lie on the ground for a little while to avoid being seen; then retrace your steps, and may God in mercy go with you. If I can, I will follow you later." . . . Watching for an opportunity, I dropped her gently, carefully, and unobserved to the ground, and she lay there while the Indians pursued their way . . . . To portray my own feelings upon this separation would be impossible. The agony I suffered was indescribable . . . . I continued to think of it so deeply that at last I grew desperate, and resolved to follow her at every risk. Accordingly, watching for an opportunity, I too, slipped to the ground under the friendly cover of night, and the horse went on without its rider.
>
> My plan was not successful. My flight was soon discovered and the Indians wheeled around and rode back in my pursuit. Crouching in the undergrowth I might have escaped in the darkness were it not for their cunning. Forming a line of forty or fifty abreast, they

> actually covered the entire ground as they rode toward me. The horses . . . betrayed me when they were frightened at my crouching form. They stopped and reared, thus revealing my hiding place . . . . The Indians used great violence toward me, assuring me that if any further attempts were made to escape, my punishment would be accordingly. They then promised to send a party out in search of the child when it became light. Poor little Mary! alone in the wilderness, a little, helpless child; who can portray her terror![10]

Nearly insane over the fate of her husband and Mary, desperate for want of water, Fanny again stood at death's door on the third night of captivity when she accidentally broke her captor's "peace" pipe.

> The sun began to sink, and the chief was so enraged against me that he told me by signs that I should behold it rise no more. Grinding his teeth with wrathful anger he made me understand that I was not to be trusted; had once tried to escape; had made them suffer the loss of my child, and that my life would be the forfeit. A large fire had been built and they all danced around it. Night had begun to darken heavily over me and I stood trembling and horror-struck not knowing that the flame, which the savages capered about, was destined to consume my tortured form . . . . An untamed horse was brought and they told me I would be placed on it as a target for their deadliest arrows, and the animal might then run at will, carrying my body where it would.
>
> Helpless and almost dying with terror at my situation, I sank on a rocky seat in their midst. They were all armed and anxiously awaited the signal. They had pistols, bows, and spears; and I noticed that some were ready to raise blazing firebrands to frighten the pawing beast that was to bear me to death . . . . In an instant a lifetime of thought condensed itself into my mind. I could see my old home and hear my mother's voice; and the contrast between the love I had been so ruthlessly torn from, and the hundreds of savage faces, gleaming with ferocity and excitement around me, seemed like the lights and shadow of some weird picture . . . .
>
> In what I almost felt to be my final breath . . . and remembering a purse of money which was in my pocket . . . I drew it out and divided it among them . . . . One hundred and twenty dollars in notes I gave them, telling them its value as I did so, when, to my astonishment, a change came over their faces. They laid their weapons upon the ground, seemingly pleased, and very anxious to

> understand; then asking me to explain the worth of each note clearly by holding up my fingers. Eagerly I tried to obey . . . but my cold hands fell powerless by my side, my tongue refused to utter a sound, and . . . I sank to the ground.[11]

A short time later Fanny again faced death when an enraged Indian tried to shoot her with an arrow. Finally, the weary woman's suffering was assuaged somewhat when she was allowed water at a campsite, whereupon she quickly dropped down in sleep. But even then, Fanny's nightmare continued.

"I was aroused by a whistling sound, and, gathering myself up, looked fearfully around me," said the startled woman. "Two flaming eyes seemed to pierce the darkness like a sword. I shuddered and held my breath, as a long lithe serpent wound past me, trailing it's shining length through the damp sand and moving slowly out of sight among the dripping vines. After that I slept no more."[12] Catherine German fared no better:

> The large squaw, whom I called Big Squaw, seemed delighted to see us tortured or frightened. Once when I was roasting a piece of liver over the camp fire, Big Squaw snatched it from the stick which held it and ate it just before I had finished cooking it. Another day, a buck tried to make us eat raw meat and because we would not do so, he threw firebrands at us and would not let me come near to cook our meat. These Redskins often tried to frighten me by saying they were going to kill me. Sometimes I heard the threat and felt the muzzle of the gun against my back but I stood very still for I felt that death would be better than living a miserable life with them. I was very despondent and did not care really what happened to me.[13]

When they finally neared the village, Catherine's captors stopped, donned their finest dress, including feathered bonnets, then smeared on war paint.

> When all were ready, they mounted their bare-backed ponies. The savage Indian who captured me, considered me his personal trophy, so he took me on behind himself and made me understand that I must cling to him. Thus adorned as the leader, he was nearly ready to start. I saw Sophia mounted behind a young Indian buck. She seemed uneasy, wondering what they meant to do. An intense sadness came over me as I noticed they had divided dear mother's and sister Jane's scalp locks into five pieces to represent the number of persons they had killed in our family. These long-haired scalp locks were fastened to the ends of rifles and swung to the breeze . . . .

Catherine German. KANSAS STATE HISTORICAL SOCIETY.

When all were ready the Indians mounted and set out at full speed, my captor and myself as leaders. On, on, we dashed for several miles and soon our ponies were a lather of sweat. Still onward we sped and it seemed that they must drop from exhaustion. We must have raced on for four or five miles until we entered an Indian village; without slacking speed, they raced through it yelling and firing revolvers into the air. Men, women and children, also barking dogs, took after us. The Indians grabbed at me from all side as we passed them. I wondered if they intended to tear me into pieces. They did tear my dress skirt into strips . . . .

Strange Indians gathered around until I was the center of a large crowd . . . . [M]y face was dirty, hair disheveled and my gingham dress had been torn from my body . . . . Every way I turned, I saw many pairs of black eyes fixed upon me.[14]

Terrible as captivity had been thus far, once the victim reached the village, bondage began in earnest. Fanny Kelly:

I had read of . . . all the characters of romance and history, wherein the nature of the red man is enshrined in poetic beauty. The untutored nobility of soul, the brave generosity, the simple dignity untrammeled by the hollow conventionalities of civilized life, all rose mockingly before me, and the heroes of my youthful imagination

> passed through my mind in strange contrast with the flesh and blood realities . . . . The stately Logan, the fearless Philip, the bold Black Hawk, the gentle Pocahontas; how unlike the greedy, cunning, and cruel savages who had so ruthlessly torn me from my friends![15]

Almost immediately, the coveted white women were claimed by chiefs. "He forced me, by the most terrible threats and menaces, to yield my person to him," Lucinda Eubanks revealed. In a few weeks, when the chief grew tired of the young Nebraskan, he sold her to another named Two Face.

> He did not treat me as a wife, but forced me to do all menial labor done by squaws, and he beat me terribly. Two Face traded me to Black Foot who treated me as his wife, and because I resisted him his squaws abused and ill-used me. Black Foot also beat me unmercifully, and the Indians generally treated me as though I was a dog.[16]

Simply because they were claimed by one Indian did not necessarily shield a captive from others. Catherine German was compelled by her master to serve as tribal prostitute and the frail young woman quaked each time she was forced to fetch wood or water, for she was often raped as many as six times on a single trip.[17] Additionally, jealous squaws bitter over the attention captives received often beat them mercilessly and forced them into back-breaking labor. Although a white woman was considered a prized piece of property, her child was not. Unlike their mothers, who could be used as laborers or sexual slaves, small children had no immediate value. As Sarah Morris declared of her owner:

> He . . . did not like my little boy . . . [who] was afraid of him and would cry. One day he took him by the neck and threw him down, and stamped on him. The child then took sick, and died in about three weeks. They wanted to bury him before he was fairly dead. I had hard work to keep them from doing it. He sunk away, and I knew he was not entirely dead. After his death they put him in a coffee sack, and laid him in a hole in the ravine, hardly covering him over. I wanted them to dig the grave deeper, but they would not.[18]

Seen as little more than a burden, the two youngest German girls were set adrift on the prairie and left to die. After wandering for weeks, living on grass and berries, the starving children were eventually recaptured by the

Indians and brought to camp.[19] Meanwhile, uncertain of Mary's fate since the night she escaped, Fanny Kelly could only pray the child had somehow reached safety.

> One day as I was pursuing what seemed to me an endless journey, an Indian rode up beside me, whom I did not remember to have seen before. At his saddle hung a bright and well-known little shawl, and onto the other side was suspended a child's scalp of long, fair hair.
>
> As my eyes rested on the frightful sight, I trembled in my saddle and grasped the air for support. A blood-red cloud seemed to come between me and the outer world . . . . I dropped from the saddle as if dead and rolled upon the ground at the horse's feet.[20]

Perhaps more terrible than the continuous physical abuse was the mental torture. Although instances of warmth and kindness did occur and Indians could display considerable compassion, many captors delighted in tormenting their victims at every turn. "I found them frequently kind and nearly always agreeable in their quiet family life," recalled Catherine German, "but toward the white race they were revengeful and cruel in the extreme."[21]

"The Indians were killing the whites all the time and running off their stock," Lucinda Eubanks added. "They would bring in the scalps of the whites and show them to me and laugh about it."[22]

One of the most horrifying moments of Fanny Kelly's captivity was not a beating, burning, or rape:

> [W]hile the savages lingered in camp about the banks of the Yellowstone River . . . a large Mackinaw, or flatboat, was seen coming down the river. From their hiding places they watched its progress like a tiger waiting for his prey. At sundown, the unsuspecting travelers pushed their boat toward the shore to camp for the night. The party consisted of about twenty men, women, and children. Suspecting no danger, they left their arms in the boat.
>
> With a vicious yell, the savages set upon them, dealing death and destruction in rapid strokes. The defenseless emigrants made an attempt to rush to the boat for arms, but were cut off, and their bleeding bodies dashed into the river as fast as they were slain. Then followed the torture of the women and children.[23]

The captives were lost in a trackless waste and surrounded by a mounted foe who knew every foot of ground. For them to even consider escape seemed madness; yet, driven to desperation, some women did try. Anna Belle Morgan and Sarah White tried to reach the Arkansas River, somewhere to the north, where Fort Dodge beckoned. According to a man who later heard their story:

> Near midnight they stealthily arose and slipped away, and at dawn they had reached the sand hills south of that stream and could see the fort. With their hopes high risen they chanced to look back and saw the Indians trailing after them and near at hand. In despair they were soon in the hands of the savages, who forced them to walk back to camp, and when the journey was complete they could scarcely stand upon their feet. This effort brought with it harsher treatment for quite a while thereafter.[24]

Because of the terrible beating she received after her first escape attempt, Fanny Kelly began writing pathetic pleas for help that were then placed where she prayed whites would pass. Likewise, while her captors were encamped along the headwaters of the Brazos in Texas, Catherine German corked a message tightly inside a bottle and tossed it into the trickle of water.

When all else was taken from them—their children, their virtue, their dignity—the captives had little else to cling to but hope. Fanny had her notes, Catherine her bottle, and other tortured souls slept with visions of heavenly release. Though most no doubt prayed for the sweet sounds of blaring bugles as the U.S. Cavalry rode to the rescue, such a liberation would almost certainly have ended in tragedy. Time and again, Indians murdered their prisoners at the first sign of trouble. Consequently, when the army learned of a captive's presence in a village, it normally moved with extreme caution. Some women were rescued after long, delicate negotiations. Others were surrendered by frightened or peacefully inclined chiefs. In the case of the Box sisters, seventeen-year-old Josephine and fourteen-year-old Margaret, freedom was gained after a young officer paid their Kiowa captors a huge ransom.

As for Fanny Kelly, nothing came easy. When the haggard woman heard that the red men were finally willing to exchange her for goods from Fort Sully, Dakota Territory, joy turned into horror upon learning the Indians planned to massacre the garrison as soon as the gates were opened. Smuggling a message to the fort, Fanny courageously alerted the commander. When she finally was brought into the post, the gates were quickly closed behind her and Fanny at last was free.

"The day that Mrs. Kelly was brought into the fort was one of the coldest I ever experienced," remembered an officer, "and she was very poorly clad, having scarcely anything to protect her person. Her limbs, hands and face were terribly frozen, and she was put in the hospital . . . where she remained for a long time."[25] Fanny Kelly:

> During all this time no tidings had been received by me concerning my husband. But one day, great commotion was occasioned in the fort by the announcement that the mail ambulance was on the way to the fort and would reach it in a few moments. An instant after, a soldier approached me saying: "Mrs. Kelly, I have news for you. Your husband is in the ambulance."
>
> No person can have even a faint idea of the uncontrollable emotions which swept over me . . . . Mechanically, I moved around, awaiting the presence of my beloved and was soon folded onto his breast, where he held me with a grasp as if fearful of my being torn from him again . . . . For seven long months we had not beheld each other; the last time being on the terrible field of slaughter and death. His personal appearance, oh! how changed! His face was very pale and his brown hair was sprinkled with gray. His voice was alone unchanged. Then he called my name and it never sounded so sweet.[26]

In spite of the abuse she had endured, Fanny tried to piece together her life. To a degree, she succeeded. Unfortunately, not all freed captives had Fanny's inner strength. From Fort Harker, Alice Baldwin recalled:

> One evening my husband and I were talking before our cheerful fire . . . . It was shortly before midnight when we heard the rattle of wheels outside. Some vehicle stopped in front of our house, shortly followed by a sharp, vigorous knock on our door. It proved to be Lieutenant G. A. Hesselberger . . . . In the ambulance at the door were two white women whom the lieutenant had rescued from the Indians, and he was taking them to their eastern homes. They had been captured, and for months had been living in revolting captivity. Now, after a long, perilous journey, the lieutenant had reached Fort Harker with his hapless charges, and sought shelter for the night . . . . Everything possible was done for the pitiful creatures. They were two young women, sisters, who had met this awful fate. The elder girl, about twenty years of age, was in an indescribable plight—starved, beaten and abused, her sufferings culminated in making her a raving maniac. The other sister had not lost her mentality, and could give us—especially myself—an indescribable history of their life in captivity.

> That night was one I shall never forget. Nearly all night the wretched maniac shrieked and raved over the awful sufferings she had endured, living over her terrible experiences. At one time she would appeal to us to save her and besought God to take care of her. The hospital steward, with the post surgeon, came and remained all night, and at length after sedatives had been repeatedly given the poor exhausted girl, she slept for hours undisturbed.[27]

Upon release, one woman wanted nothing greater from life than to blot out all traces of her Indian captivity. As a friend later wrote, "She thought it a terrible disgrace and any reference to it only added to the infamy." Yet, the woman soon learned that her wish was never to be.

> A few months after she . . . was recovered from the Indians a baby boy was born . . . . He was a strong, healthy little fellow and certainly resembled the Indians both in features and disposition. [Her] brother . . . like her, considered the life among the Indians a disgrace, and requested his sister to give into his keeping this little boy after he had attained a certain age so that he could take him and go to the haunts of the Indians, shoot and kill all savages sighted as long as both or either lived and thus gain a partial revenge for the crime committed.[28]

Like this vengeance-minded brother, others whose sisters, wives, and mothers had been captured or butchered, devoted their lives to revenge. After witnessing the rape and murder of his entire family, young George Porter wandered the West on a one-man mission. A reporter for an Iowa newspaper spoke with him.

> He carries with him a piece of cane brake, about twelve inches in length, and whenever he killed an Indian, he would make a notch in this. One hundred and eight notches are now to be counted . . . . By night and by day he has followed them, through the trackless forests, over desert wastes, by the mountain side, and in the lonely glen has he pursued his victims, until the crack of the rifle and the death yell proclaimed that another red-skin had been sent to his final account . . . . Porter has not passed through all these perilous scenes unscathed. His body has been riddled by eleven bullets, and slashed in thirty-three places by the knife. But he has withstood all, come out victorious, and now exhibits with pride the trophy of his prowess. Truly, his parents and relatives have been deeply, terribly avenged.[29]

As they crossed the Plains, other vengeful relatives left pieces of strychnine-laced hardtack where hostiles were sure to pass. In one case alone, more than a score of Indians were poisoned like wolves.[30]

Vengeance was not limited to husbands, brothers, and sons. Those who knew the Indians best, those who first witnessed the emaciated and broken frames of the freed women, those who heard from the victims' own lips the terrible tales of rape and abuse, also sought revenge. Years after Fanny Kelly's release, Lieutenant James Bradley happened upon a Sioux burial scaffold.

> It proved to be the remains of a warrior of fifty-odd years of age . . . . His effects had been buried with him, and among them was a small package of letters, a soldier's hymn book, and a picture history of his life . . . . There was also a paper signed "Fannie Kelly, captive white woman," whose reading touched us all to the heart and made us wish the savage was again alive that we might wreak upon him some of the indignation we felt. I cannot remember its entire contents, but it concluded by saying: "I am compelled to do their bidding." "To do their bidding!" Alas, how many poor captive women have suffered this to them worse fate than death! May the end of such atrocities be near at hand! May the military operations that are now in progress result in so complete an overthrow of the hell-hounds . . . that never again shall poor women be made the victims of such barbarity at their hands![31]

Meanwhile, as her tiny bottle drifted slowly down a shallow stream in Texas, Catherine German, as well as other captives, continued to dream of deliverance.

> One night I dreamed that I had a visitor, but I did not seem to know him. He told me how sorry he was for me, and that I must keep up my courage, for surely I would be rescued some time. As he was departing I saw dear brother Stephen—oh, so plainly . . . I tried to follow him, and was really crying . . . . I passed an uneventful day, but I kept thinking of the encouraging dream and my depressed spirit was somewhat revived and cheered by the hope that rescuers might soon come.
>
> That night I dreamed again and my dream was similar to that of the previous night. There seemed to be a kindred and a living presence near me. I felt a warm kiss and heard these words so very distinctly, "Catherine, do the very best you can." I then saw my own

dear mother and tried to go to her but she was beyond my reach and vanished. After these dreams I felt very much encouraged. I could not explain why, but I felt confident that sometime I would be reclaimed . . . . [T]hose comforting words, "Catherine, do the very best you can," have been an inspiration to me.[32]

9

Old Men Laugh

Throughout the summer of 1868 the tribes on the southern frontier continued their rampage. After one brutal raid along the Solomon River in which scores of settlers were killed, Gov. Samuel Crawford of Kansas went to see for himself if the reports were as bad as stated. What he stumbled upon was staggering:

> Men, women and children were murdered indiscriminately. Many of them were scalped, and their bodies mutilated. Women, after receiving mortal wounds, were outraged and otherwise inhumanly treated in the presence of their dying husbands and children. Two young ladies and two little girls were carried away by the red-handed assassins . . . . The settlements, covering a space sixty miles wide . . . were driven in, the country laid in ashes and the soil drenched in blood.[1]

As in the past, depredations diminished with the approach of autumn, as the Cheyenne, Arapahoe, Kiowa, and Comanche drifted toward their Indian Territory reservations. The paradox of government agents distributing annuities of food, clothing, supplies, and even guns to "friendlies" during the winter months while the army chased hostiles in the summer angered Westerners. None was more incensed than a still-shaken Samuel Crawford. Horrified by what he had seen and heard in western Kansas, outraged by Washington's inept handling of Indian affairs, in a letter to President Andrew Johnson, the governor split no hairs.

> If the Government cannot protect its own citizens let the fact be made known, that the people may endeavor to protect themselves . . . . The Peace Commission is a mockery and their policy a disgrace to the nation. I trust, therefore, that you will keep the Commissioners at home, and stop issuing arms, ammunition and supplies to hostile Indians while they are robbing, murdering and outraging defenseless people . . . . The savage devils have become intolerable, and must and shall be driven out of this State.[2]

The Department of the Missouri commander, Major General Phil Sheridan, was equally angered at the atrocities committed in Kansas. He assured Crawford that the army would do its duty. "I will at once order the Cheyennes, Arapahoes and Kiowas out of your state and into their reservations and will compel them to go by force," Sheridan said. "We will not cease our efforts until the perpetrators of the Solomon massacre are delivered up for punishment. It may take until the cold weather to catch them, but we will not cease until it is accomplished."[3]

Unappeased, Crawford authorized the creation of the 19th Kansas Volunteer Cavalry. In a final flourish, the governor resigned, freeing himself to lead the regiment. "My people's blood is crying to me from the ground," he announced. "I must go."[4] With a frenzied public screaming for extermination of the Indians, "a la Chivington," the unit was ready to ride in less than a month. Shocked by the flaming Western rhetoric, Eastern humanitarians excoriated Crawford and loudly demanded patience, peace, and mercy.

But Westerners would have none of it. "Wives and sisters disfigured after death and babes brained upon doorsteps, are not conducive to the growth of mercy," raged one Kansan to a Boston newspaper.

> Their hands dripping with the blood of our settlers, their saddles hung with scalps, their whole path one agonizing scene of desolation, the savages are still hovering upon our borders. But yesterday there were here in our streets, begging for sustenance, the widows of men recently murdered on the Solomon. Outraged by a whole band, stripped naked, abandoned in a cold storm, these poor women were left desecrated and broken wrecks of humanity, to die, or what was more cruel still, live . . . . Supposing bands of cruel savages should sweep suddenly down upon your own beautiful town, and under the morning sun your desolated hearthstones should be but bloody mockeries of the spots lately so dear.[5]

With pressure mounting, the army was forced to act. As he had hinted to Crawford, Sheridan was already considering something new.

> Unless the Indians are crushed out, and made to obey the authority of the government, there will be a total paralysis of some of the best interests of this section of country. All confidence is destroyed . . . . Not less than eight hundred persons had been murdered, the Indians escaping from the troops by traveling at night when their trail could not be followed, thus gaining enough time and distance to render pursuit, in most cases, fruitless. This wholesale marauding would be maintained during the seasons when the Indians ponies could subsist upon the grass, and then in the winter, the savages would hide away, with their villages, in remote and isolated places, to live upon their plunder, glory in the scalps taken, and in the horrible debasement of unfortunate women whom they held as prisoners. The experience of many years of this character of depredations, with perfect immunity to themselves and their families, had made the Indians very bold. To disabuse their minds of the idea that they were secure from punishment, and to strike them at a period when they were helpless to move their stock and villages, a winter campaign was projected against large bands hiding away in the Indian Territory.[6]

Old frontiersmen, such as Jim Bridger, strongly advised Sheridan against a winter expedition. When word leaked to the Indians that the army would march on their stronghold, there was not a stir. "Old, gray-headed men here laugh when told the government will punish, and say they have been told that since they were children," remarked one observer from the Territory.[7]

To spearhead the drive, Sheridan chose Custer and the 7th Cavalry. "I rely on you in everything," confided the general, "and shall send you on this expedition without orders, leaving you to act entirely on your own judgement . . . . [S]eek the winter hide-out of the hostiles, and administer such punishment for past depredations as . . . able to."[8]

Excited as Custer was by the vision of active duty, some of his officers, Albert Barnitz included, were dubious. "I hope that the campaign may be prosecuted vigorously . . . and that we may keep on until we really accomplish something," the young captain wrote to his wife, Jennie. "It is whispered . . . that we will not be expected to accomplish much against our red brethren further than, by keeping them constantly on the move, to wear down their ponies, until March, and that then we will proceed against them in earnest!"[9]

Albert and Jennie Barnitz. LITTLE BIGHORN BATTLEFIELD NATIONAL MONUMENT.

Custer felt otherwise, as a letter to Libbie made clear.

> Some of the officers think this may be a campaign on paper—but I know Genl. Sheridan better. We are going to the heart of the Indian country where white troops have never been before . . . . Yesterday my twelve Osage guides joined me, a splendid set of warriors, headed by a Chief, Little Beaver. They are painted and dressed for the war-path, and well-armed with Springfield breech-loading guns. All are superb horsemen.[10]

In November, after some initial sparring with hostiles, the column struck south from Fort Dodge and entered the Indian Territory. At the confluence of Beaver and Wolf creeks, the troops halted and built an advanced outpost, Camp Supply. While Custer settled in to await Crawford's 19th Kansas, the commander of the campaign left Fort Hays on November 15 and headed south in person. Sheridan:

> The first night out a blizzard struck us and carried away our tents; and, as the gale was so violent that they could not be put up again, the rain and snow drenched us to the skin. Shivering from the wet and cold, I took refuge under a wagon, and there spent such a miserable night that, when at last morning came, the gloomy predictions of Old Man Bridger and others rose up before me with greatly increased force . . . . The evening of November 21st we arrived at the Camp Supply depot, having traveled all day in another snow storm.[11]

Wasting no time, Sheridan ordered his eager subaltern to move the following day. Lieutenant Colonel Custer:

> It snowed all night, and when reveille wakened us at four we found the ground covered to the depth of one foot, and the storm still raging. Little grooming did the shivering horses get from the equally uncomfortable troopers. While they were saddling I galloped across the narrow plain to the tents of Genl. Sheridan who was awake and had been listening attentively to our preparations. His first greeting was to enquire what I thought about the storm. All the better for our purpose, I told him, for we could move in it while the Indians could not.[12]

Outside, officers and men, Lt. Edward Godfrey included, were making sure all was secure.

> The darkness and heavy snowfall made the packing of the wagons very difficult, but at dawn the wagons were assembled in the train and daylight found us on the march, the band playing, "The Girl I Left Behind Me," but there was no woman there to interpret its significance. The snow was falling so heavily that vision was limited to a few rods. All landmarks were invisible and the trails were lost. "We didn't know where we were going, but we were on the way." Then General Custer, with compass in hand, took the lead and became our guide.
>
> As the day wore on the weather became warmer and I have never seen the snowflakes as large or fall so lazily as those that fell that day. Fortunately there was no wind to drift the snow to add to our discomfort. They melted on the clothing so that every living thing was wet to the skin. The snow balled on the feet of our shod animals causing much floundering adding to the fatigue of travel. About two o'clock we came to Wolf Creek . . . and continued to march till we came to a clump of fallen timbers and there went into camp.[13]

That night the snow ceased and the next day, November 24, the command moved out under clear skies. Although balled snow continued to plague the mounts, as it did the numerous hounds that tagged along, "the travelin' was good over head," as one of the scouts in the column, California Joe, phrased it. Two days later, while ranging on Custer's flank, Major Joel Elliott stumbled upon the trail of a large war party leading south toward the Washita River. According to Lieutenant Godfrey:

> Officer's call was sounded and when assembled we were told the news and ordered to be prepared to move as soon as possible . . . . Each trooper was ordered to carry one hundred rounds of ammunition on his person . . . . The main train guarded by about eighty men under the command of the officer of the day was to follow as rapidly as possible. For this guard men with weak horses were selected. Captain Louis M. Hamilton, a grandson of Alexander Hamilton, was officer of the day. He was greatly distressed because this duty fell to him and begged to go along to command his squadron, but was refused unless he could get some officer to exchange with him. Lieutenant E. G. Mathey, who was snowblind, agreed to take his place.[14]

Cutting free from the supply train, the excited column picked up the pace. Custer:

> Soon after dark we reached the [Washita] valley whose timbered surface we had caught faint glimpses of hours before. Down this valley and through this sparse timber the trail led us. Hour after hour we struggled on . . . . I conferred with our Indian allies, all of whom were firmly convinced that our enemy's village was probably not far away, and most likely was in the valley in which we then were . . . . To prevent the possibility of the command coming precipitately upon our enemies . . . two scouts were directed to keep three or four hundred yards in advance of all others; then came, in single file, the remainder of our Osage guides and the white scouts—among the rest California Joe. With these I rode, that I might be as near the advance guard as possible. The cavalry followed in rear at the distance of a quarter or half a mile; this precaution was necessary from the fact that the snow, which had thawed slightly during the day, was then freezing, forming a crust which, broken by the tread of so many hundreds of feet, produced a noise capable of being heard at a long distance.
>
> Orders were given prohibiting even a word being uttered above a whisper. No one was permitted to strike a match or light a pipe . . . . In this silent manner we rode mile after mile. Occasionally an officer would ride by my side and whisper some inquiry or suggestion, but aside from this our march was unbroken by sound or deed. At last we discovered that our two guides in front had halted and were awaiting my arrival . . . . One of them could speak broken English and in answer to my question as to "What is the matter?" he replied: "Me don't know, but me smell fire" . . . .
>
> Silently we advanced, I mounted, they on foot, keeping at the head of my horse. Upon nearing the crest of each hill . . . one of the guides would hasten a few steps in advance and peer cautiously over the hill. Accustomed to this, I was not struck by observing it until . . . one . . . advanced cautiously to the crest and looked carefully into the valley beyond. I saw him place his hand above his eyes as if looking intently at some object, then crouch down and come creeping back to where I waited for him. "What is it?" I inquired as soon as he reached my horse's side. "Heap Injuns down there."[15]

In the column far to the rear was Captain Albert Barnitz.

> About 2 or 3 o'clock in the morning . . . Lieut. [Myles] Moylan . . . rode back and stated that Genl. Custer directed that I should halt my command, and . . . report at the head of the column . . . . A

rapid gallop of a few minutes took me [there] where I found the other officers already assembled . . . and as soon as all were collected, Genl. Custer stated that the scouts had reported that the valley in advance was filled with ponies, and that the tinkling of a little bell could be distinctly heard; that he wished us to leave our horses, and go quietly, with him, on foot, to the crest of a ridge in front, and carefully study the topography of the country, and see what we could make out . . . . So we all crept very quietly and slowly to the top of the ridge, removing our hats, or caps as we neared the summit, and I could not help thinking that we very much resembled a pack of wolves . . . .

Having gained the crest of the ridge, we could see . . . the course of the Washita . . . but the herds of ponies, and teepes [*sic*] were not visible although the tinkling of a little bell could be distinctly heard at times, and some of the officers who looked through a night glass were of the opinion that they could discern herds of ponies. Having made our observations, we returned to the point where our horses were left.[16]

With orders for absolute quiet, battalion commanders were directed to deploy around the village and charge at dawn. Assigned to Major Elliott's unit was Albert Barnitz.

The plan of attack having been announced, the columns were ordered to move at once to their respective positions, as only about an hour remained until daybreak. As Major Elliott[']s column moved out a number of dogs, belonging to the command, followed, and as it was feared that they would alarm the Indians, prematurely, some of the men were directed to catch them and strangle (or muzzle) them, with lariat ropes, and dispatch them with knives . . . .

[T]he night was so dark that we could see nothing except the dark outline of the timber along the stream . . . but as the barking of a multitude of dogs could be heard in the woods, we conjectured that there, without doubt, was the village . . . . [W]e pressed forward . . . toward the village . . . [and] found a large number of ponies, tethered with lariats, in a grove of second growth white oak trees, to which the dry leaves still clung, and these were diligently pawing through the snow to obtain the grass beneath it, and paid not the slightest attention, at our approach, as they were evidently famished for food. We here expected, confidently, to be fired upon by Indians who might be in charge of the herd, but to our surprise moved for-

> ward unchallenged, and at length reached the stream, below the village, at a ford, the approach to which was much trampled by ponies. We were halted, without crossing, and facing up the stream dismounted to fight on foot.[17]

Despite the "furious barking of the dogs" and "the whinnying of multitudes of ponies," the Cheyenne camp was not aroused. At dawn, Custer led his main column forward at a walk.

> [W]e began to descend the slope leading down to the village . . . [and] soon reached the outskirts of the herd of ponies. The latter seemed to recognize us as hostile parties and moved quickly away. The light of day was each minute growing stronger and we feared discovery before we could approach near enough to charge the village. The movement of our horses over the crusted snow produced considerable noise and would doubtless have led to our detection but for the fact that the Indians . . . presumed it was occasioned by their herd of ponies . . . .
>
> Immediately in rear of my horse came the band, all mounted and each with his instrument in readiness to begin playing the moment . . . [they] should receive the signal . . . . We had approached near enough to the village now to plainly catch a view here and there of the tall white lodges as they stood in irregular order among the trees.[18]

Meanwhile, downstream, Major Elliott set his force in motion. Captain Barnitz:

> As we moved forward, we soon came to ponies and mules, tied beneath cottonwood trees, with piles of branches piled in front of them, and which they were eating with evident relish. An Indian wrapped in a red blanket, presently sprang up from among the animals, and ran rapidly in the direction of the camp. Others quickly followed him, until we appeared to have started a numerous covey. Some of the men raised their carbines to fire upon them, but wishing to prevent alarming the camp until the last moment, I forbade them to fire, and we pressed forward with increased speed. We had just reached the edge of a shallow ravine beyond which we could see the clustered tepees . . . when a shot was fired in the village.[19]

"I was about to turn in my saddle and direct the signal for attack to be given," Custer recounted, "when a single rifle shot rang sharp and clear on the far side of the village."

> Quickly turning to the band leader, I directed him to give us Garry Owen. At once . . . that familiar marching and fighting air sounded forth through the valley and in a moment were reechoed back from the opposite sides by the loud and continued cheers of the men . . . . The bugles sounded the charge and the entire command dashed rapidly into the village. The Indians . . . quickly overcame their first surprise and in an instant seized their rifles, bows, and arrows, and sprang behind the nearest trees, while some leaped into the stream, nearly waist deep, and using the bank as a rifle-pit began a vigorous and determined defense.[20]

Returning to Albert Barnitz:

> [The] Indian village rang with unearthly war-whoops, the quick discharge of fire-arms, the clamorous barking of dogs, the cries of infants and the wailing of women . . . . It was surprizing [*sic*] to see how soon, when once the action had commenced, how all the hills were alive with mounted warriors, armed and equipped with their shields, and war bonnets . . . . I observed a large body of Indians running off towards the left. I at once dashed in among them, passing through a large drove of Squaws and children who were screaming and very much frightened. I came upon the warriors who were ahead and striking out as hard as they could run for their ponies. Riding up close along side of the first I shot him through the heart. He threw up his arms, by the same movement drawing his bow from the scabbard let fly an arrow at me. This was the last act of his existence. I passed on to the second and shot him in the same manner. There was yet another close to me. He was armed with a large Lancaster rifle . . . . He took aim, while I was closing upon him and about to fire, but was several times disconcerted by my acting as if I were about to fire upon him myself, until finally I had some doubt if his rifle was loaded. When however I got quite close to him to fire, he returned my fire at the same instant, both shots taking effect. Mine I believe must have passed through his heart, as he threw up his hands frantically and . . . died almost immediately.
>
> I rode back toward the village, being now unable to manage my horse, and the pain of my wound being almost unbearable. I

> dismounted and lay down in such a way that I would not bleed internally.[21]

Among the Indian guides, at least one thirsted for revenge. Some months before, a Cheyenne war party had raided an Osage village and, in the ensuing carnage, the man's wife was slain. Soon after the charge on the Washita began, the Osage, according to newsman DeBenneville Keim, "disappeared in the thickest of the fray."

> A few moments after, the same warrior was seen standing over the lifeless form of a Cheyenne warrior. He had discovered the murderer of his squaw. Stooping, knife in hand, he was about to take the scalp, when he discovered it was gone. Such an expression of fiendish disappointment was probably never exceeded. Frantically gesticulating, he fell upon the body with the ferocity of a beast of prey, and severed the throat from ear to ear. Again he stood erect, his whole frame quivering with rage. Once more he fell upon the lifeless form. Completely severing the head from the trunk, he took his knife between his teeth, clutched the gory object in both hands, and raising it high above him, dashed it upon the ground at his feet.[22]

In the village, the troops pressed ahead. "The lodges and all their contents were in our possession within ten minutes after the charge was ordered," Custer revealed, "but the real fighting . . . began when attempting to clear out or kill the warriors posted in ravines or underbrush; charge after charge was made, and most gallantly, too, but the Indians had resolved to sell their lives as dearly as possible."[23] Custer continued:

> [T]he command was at once ordered to fight on foot, and the men were instructed to take advantage of the trees and other natural means of cover and fight the Indians in their own style . . . . Slowly but steadily the Indians were driven from behind the trees, and those who escaped . . . posted themselves with their companions who were already firing from the banks. One party of troopers came upon a squaw endeavoring to make her escape, leading by the hand a little white boy . . . . [T]he squaw, finding herself and prisoner about to be surrounded by the troops and her escape cut off, determined, with savage malignity, that the triumph of the latter should not embrace the rescue of the white boy. Casting her eyes quickly in all directions to convince herself that escape was impossible, she drew

from beneath her blanket a huge knife and plunged it into the almost naked body of her captive. The next moment retributive justice reached her in the shape of a well-directed bullet.[24]

Lieutenant Edward Godfrey:

> While the fighting was going on, Major Elliot seeing a group of dismounted Indians escaping down the valley called for volunteers to make pursuit. Nineteen men . . . responded. As his detachment moved away, he turned . . . [and] waved his hand and said: "here goes for a brevet or a coffin."
>
> After passing through the village, I went in pursuit of pony herds and found them scattered in groups about a mile below the village . . . . While the roundup was progressing, I observed a group of dismounted Indians escaping down the opposite side of the valley. Completing the roundup, and starting them toward the village, I turned . . . to take . . . my platoon and go in pursuit of the group I had seen escaping down the valley. Taking the trail . . . and following it about a couple of miles, I discovered a lone tepee, and soon after two Indians circling their ponies. A high promontory and ridge projected into the valley and shut off the view of the valley below the lone tepee. I knew the circling of the warriors meant an alarm and rally, but I wanted to see what was in the valley beyond them . . . . Arriving at and peering over the ridge, I was amazed to find that as far as I could see down the well wooded, tortuous valley there were tepees—tepees. Not only could I see tepees, but mounted warriors scurrying in our direction. I hurried back to the platoon and returned at the trot . . . .
>
> On reaching the village I . . . at once reported to General Custer what I had done and seen. When I mentioned the "big village," he exclaimed, "What's that?" and put me through a lot of rapid fire questions.[25]

By mid-afternoon, the last defenders had been wiped out and the 7th held the camp and immediate area. Most Cheyenne had escaped the dawn attack, but many had not. Among the more than one hundred Indians slain was the luckless peace chief, Black Kettle, whose admitted inability to curb his band had first brought him to grief at Sand Creek in 1864 and now on the banks of the Washita four years later. A number of women and children were dead. Custer:

> Before engaging in the fight orders had been given to prevent the killing of any but the fighting strength of the village; but in a struggle of this character it is impossible at all times to discriminate, particularly when . . . the squaws are as dangerous adversaries as the warriors, while Indian boys between ten and fifteen years of age were found as expert and determined in the use of the pistol and bow and arrow as the older warriors. Of these facts we had numerous illustrations.[26]

Several soldiers were also killed in the fighting, including Louis Hamilton. A similar fate was feared for Major Elliott and his missing squad, which so rashly pursued the Indians at dawn. Among the wounded were the colonel's brother, Lieutenant Tom Custer, and Albert Barnitz, whose wound in the stomach was believed to be mortal. "Oh, hell!" cursed the tough captain. "They think because my extremities are cold I am going to die, but if I could get warm I'm sure I'll be all right. These blankets and robes are so heavy I can hardly breathe."[27]

Nervous over the report of Indian villages stretching for miles down the Washita, Custer ordered the captives rounded up and the camp destroyed. Edward Godfrey:

> I allowed the prisoners to get what they wanted. As I watched them, they only went to their own tepees. I began the destruction at the upper end of the village, tearing down tepees and piling several together on the tepee poles, set fire to them . . . . As the fires made headway, all articles of personal property—buffalo robes, blankets, food, rifles, pistols, bows and arrows, lead and caps, bullet molds, etc.—were thrown in the fires and destroyed . . . .
>
> While this destruction was going on, warriors began to assemble on the hill slopes on the left side of the valley facing the village, as if to make an attack. Two squadrons formed near the left bank of the stream and started on the "Charge" when the warriors scattered and fled. Later, a few groups were seen on the hill tops but they made no hostile demonstrations.
>
> As the last of the tepees and property was on fire, the General ordered me to kill all the ponies except those authorized to be used by the prisoners and given to scouts. We tried to rope them and cut their throats, but the ponies were frantic at the approach of a white man and fought viciously. My men were getting very tired so I called for reinforcements and details from other organizations were sent to complete the destruction of about eight hundred ponies.[28]

Returning to Custer:

> Accessions to our opponents kept arriving, mounted warriors in full war-panoply, with floating lance-pennants . . . Cheyennes, Arapahoes, Kiowas, Comanches, and some Apaches, hostile tribes from some twelve miles off . . . . From being the surrounding party we now found ourselves surrounded . . . . It was about three in the afternoon . . . . I knew that the officers in charge of the train and eighty men would be following us on the trail, and feared that the Indians, reconnoitering from hill-tops, might discover this helpless detachment, and annihilate them, at the same time leaving the command in mid-winter, in the heart of enemy country, destitute of provision for horse and man . . . . I could look in nearly all directions and see the warriors at a distance collected in groups on the tops of the highest hills, apparently waiting and watching our next move . . . . To guide my command safely out of the difficulties which seemed just then to beset them I again had recourse to that maxim in war which teaches a commander to do that which his enemy neither expects nor desires him to do . . . . I now determined to take the offensive.[29]

With band blaring and flags flying, Custer moved down the Washita toward the hostile camps. Stunned by the sight, hundreds of warriors lurking in the area lashed their ponies along the river to warn others of the attack. His strategy successful, the colonel quietly retraced his steps after dark and struck north. Meanwhile, at Camp Supply, Sheridan anxiously awaited word from the south. On the morning of November 29, California Joe rode up to headquarters. Reporter DeBenneville Keim was on hand.

> Joe's manner, upon making his appearance before the General's tent, indicated that he had some agreeable intelligence to communicate. His two diminutive blue orbs flashing on either side of a prodigious nasal formation, confirmed the belief.
>
> "Well, Joe, what brings you back so soon; running away?" said the General.
>
> Joe replied somewhat indignantly in manner at the suggestion of running away. "I've just made that ole critter of mine out thar get up and dust, for the last thirty-six hours. I tell yer it's a big thing, and we just made those red devils git."
>
> "So you have had a fight," said the General.
>
> "Weel, we've had suthin; you may call it fittin, but I call it wipin

out the varmints; yes, and sich a one as they wont have agin, I tell you."[30]

Two days later, according to Keim, "[a] courier arrived at the camp with the announcement that Custer's column would be in that morning."

Every one was anxious to greet the victors of the Washita, and it was with considerable impatience the appearance of the column was looked for. Shortly after the sun had passed meridian, a cluster of dark objects appearing upon the crest of a hill, about a mile distant, accompanied with shouts and the firing of musketry, announced their approach. The mules and horses, grazing in the valleys near by, hearing these unusual sounds, stampeded in great alarm from all directions towards camp. On the summit of the hill the head of the column halted for a few moments. Meanwhile, Sheridan accompanied by his staff and a number of officers of the garrison, took position in the valley. All the officers and soldiers, not on duty, assembled in the vicinity of the fort to witness the warlike pageant.

The troopers now resumed their march, and as they descended the hill, the flashing of sabres and carbines, and the shouts of the men, were in wild counterpart of the dreary surroundings of their departure a week before . . . . The Indians whooped, the band reiterated the stirring tones of "Garry Owen," and the troopers cheered. In response, rounds of huzzas from the troops of the fort shouted welcome and congratulation. In the advance were the Osage Indian trailers . . . . Their faces were fantastically painted, and about their persons dangled the trophies which they had captured in battle. Spears, upon which were fastened the scalps of their fallen foe, were slung upon their shoulders. From their own plaited scalp-locks were suspended long trains of silver ornaments and feathers. Over their shoulders hung shields, and bows, and quivers full of arrows, while in their hands they held their trusty rifle. Even the animals, which the Osages bestrode, were decorated with scalps and strips of red and blue blankets. At the head of the band rode Little Beaver, the chief, with a countenance as fixed as stone, yet in his bearing showing . . . an inward self-glorification, which . . . kept stirring and swelling higher and higher by discharged fire-arms and wild notes of the war-songs.[31]

"Next came the white scouts riding four abreast," recorded Private David Spotts of the recently arrived 19th Kansas, "led by their chief, California Joe, on his mule and his pipe in his mouth."[32] Trailing the guides came Custer, whom Spotts and his fellow Kansans failed to recognize because "he was dressed like a scout." Directly behind the colonel "followed the living evidences of the victory," Keim noted, "over fifty squaws and their children, surrounded by a suitable guard, to prevent escape. These were mounted on their own ponies . . . their persons wrapped in skins and blankets, even their heads and faces being covered, leaving nothing visible but the eyes."[33]

"The prisoners were awed and silent," Lieutenant Godfrey added, "till the band began playing . . . when they awakened to conversation."[34]

Bringing up the rear were the troopers with drawn sabers and the wagon train with the wounded. "The scene, during the remainder of the day, was that of joyous holiday," Keim concluded.[35] But at least one man was not experiencing a "joyous holiday." While the Osage held a thunderous scalp dance that lasted all night, Albert Barnitz rolled on his cot in agony. Wrote Lieutenant Godfrey to Jennie Barnitz:

> After the battle was over the Drs. gave him up and delegated me to inform him. I very reluctantly did it in as delicate terms as possible. He received it with some emotion and gave me messages for you . . . . "Tell Mrs. B. that I don't regret the wound so much as I do leaving her. It has been so long since we met, that the expectations of the happiness we would enjoy upon our reunion is more than I can bear. I am glad she is not here to see my suffering as she could do me no good. Tell her not to grieve for me, that I love her."[36]

One week later, while Sheridan, Custer, and a large column moved south to follow up the Washita victory, doctors went to work on Barnitz. The result was a complete success. "The ball entered just in front of the short ribs," the relieved soldier explained to his wife, "and passed out below the ribs, and just above the hip bone, and nearer to the spine than where it entered, a mass of tissues about the size of a man's fist protruded from the anterior wound and looked exactly like one of the sausage balls which are sometimes exposed at Butcher's stalls; this the surgeon . . . removed, by operation."[37]

Barnitz was through with riding and fighting, however. After rejoining his beloved Jennie at Fort Dodge, the two returned to Ohio on leave of absence. Recalled the captain:

> [T]he word went forward, as usual, that I was dead again, and so my old friend, Murat Halstead, of the Cincinnati Commercial, wrote up my obituary in good style, and for the third time, recounting how I had written poetry in my youth, and had corresponded for his paper

> during the war, and how I had distinguished myself as poet, journalist and warrior. He may even have shed a tear or two, as a parting tribute. Then when a few weeks later I surprised him by calling upon him to pay my respects, as I passed through Cincinnati . . . I thought he appeared a little disgusted to be again confronted by . . . one whom he had so often glorified as dead! At all events, he said, on parting, "Barnitz, the next time you are killed, I am just going to say, 'Barnitz is dead.' I am tired of writing obituaries of you—and all to no purpose."[38]

In the meantime, the 7th Cavalry, bolstered by the 19th Kansas, reached the Washita and the scene of the late fight. DeBenneville Keim:

> As we moved closer to the immediate site of the village, our approach . . . alarmed . . . innumerable beasts and birds of prey. Suddenly lifting from the ground could be seen thousands of ravens and crows, disturbed in their carrion feast. The dense black mass, evidently gorged, rose heavily, and passing overhead . . . set up the greatest confusion of noises. The cowardly wolves started from their abundant repast on human flesh, reluctantly left the spot, and while slowly getting out of reach of danger often stopped to take a wishful look behind. Retiring to the summit of the nearest hills, they seated themselves on their haunches and watched every movement of the intruders.[39]

After scanning the battlefield, Sheridan, Custer, Keim, and a small escort went in search of Major Elliott and his men. Crossing to the south shore, the party had not gone far before the first victim was spotted. Once again, reporter Keim:

> [T]he body of a white man was found, perfectly naked, and covered with arrow and bullet holes. The head presented the appearance of having been beaten with a war-club. The top of the skull was broken into a number of pieces, and the brain was lying partly in the skull and partly on the ground . . . . Marking the spot where his body was found, we continued moving down stream. Crossing, with some difficulty, a small ravine . . . objects were seen lying in the grass, and were supposed to be bodies. Our attention attracted in this direction, we rode to the spot at a gallop. A scene was now witnessed sufficient to appall the bravest heart. Within an area of not more than fifteen yards, lay sixteen human bodies . . . . The winter air swept across the plain, and its cold blasts had added to the ghastliness of death the

> additional spectacle of sixteen naked corpses frozen as solidly as stone. There was not a single body that did not exhibit evidences of fearful mutilation. They were all lying with their faces down, and in close proximity to each other. Bullet and arrow wounds covered the back of each; the throats of a number were cut, and several were beheaded . . . . All the bodies were carefully examined, but it was with great difficulty that any of them were recognized owing to the terrible atrocities to which they had been subjected.[40]

"In addition to the wounds," Custer noted, "I saw a portion of the stock of a 'Lancaster rifle' protruding from the side of one of the men. The stock had been broken off near the barrel, and the butt of it, probably 12 inches in length, had been driven into the man's side a distance of eight inches."[41]

After burying the bodies, the command moved down the river the following day. Custer:

> The forest along the banks of the Washita from the battleground [to] a distance of twelve miles was found to have been one continuous Indian village. Black Kettle's band of Cheyennes was above; then came other hostile tribes camped in the following order: Arapahoes under Little Raven; Kiowas under Satanta and Lone Wolf; the remaining bands of Cheyennes, Comanches, and Apaches. Nothing could exceed the disorder and haste with which these tribes had fled from their camping grounds. They had abandoned thousands of lodge poles, some of which were still standing as when last used. Immense numbers of camp kettles, cooking utensils, coffee-mills, axes, and several hundred buffalo robes were found.[42]

Accompanying the soldiers as guides and go-betweens were several Cheyenne women captured during the fight. "The Kiowas and Arrapahoes [*sic*], our friends, run like dogs," spit one squaw upon viewing the abandoned villages. "They were worse cowards than women. Black Kettle was killed because they were afraid of the white man . . . . If the white man fights the Kiowas and Arrapahoes, I want a knife and will fight too, and kill all their papooses."[43] Amid the clutter and confusion, Custer made another grisly find.

> In the deserted camp lately occupied by Satanta with the Kiowas my men discovered the bodies of a young white woman and child, the former apparently about twenty-three years of age, the latter probably eighteen months old. They were evidently mother and child and had not long been in captivity, as the woman still

> retained several articles of her wardrobe about her person, among others a pair of cloth gaiters but little worn . . . . [U]pon our attacking and routing Black Kettle's camp her captors . . . had deliberately murdered her and her child in cold blood. The woman had received a shot in the forehead, her entire scalp had been removed, and her skull horribly crushed. The child also bore numerous marks of violence.[44]

In an effort to force the tribes back to their reservations, Sheridan pressed slowly down the Washita toward Fort Cobb, driving the Indians ahead. According to Custer:

> [O]n the morning of the 17th of December . . . my Osage scouts came galloping back . . . and reported a party of Indians in our front bearing a flag of truce . . . . Taking a small party with me I proceeded beyond our lines to meet [them]. I was met by several of the leading chiefs of the Kiowas . . . . Large parties of their warriors could be seen posted in the neighboring ravines and upon the surrounding hill tops. All were painted and plumed for war, and nearly all were armed with one rifle, two revolvers, bows and arrows and lance. Their bows were strung. Their whole appearance and conduct plainly indicated that they had come for war.[45]

No fight developed, however, for the commanding general and his large main force quickly hove into view. "I hesitated to attack them," Sheridan said, "but directed them to proceed with their families to Fort Cobb. This they assented to, and nearly all the warriors came over and accompanied the column, for the purpose of deceiving me while their families were being hurried towards the [Wichita] mountain . . . . As they commenced slipping away one by one, I arrested the head chiefs, Lone Wolf and Satanta, and on my arrival at Fort Cobb, as I suspected, there was not a Kiowa."[46] Returning to Custer:

> Then it was that I announced to Lone Wolf and Satanta the decision which had been arrived at regarding them. I gave them until sunrise the following morning to cause their people to come in, or to give satisfactory evidence that they were hastening to come in. If no such evidence appeared, both these chiefs were to be hung at sunrise to the nearest tree . . . . This produced the desired effect. By sunrise several of the leading Kiowas came to my camp and reported the entire village on the move, hastening to place themselves under our control.[47]

Satanta. Kansas State Historical Society.

"I will take some of the starch out of them before I get through," clapped an elated Sheridan. "The Indians for the first time begin to realize that winter will not compel us to make a truce with them."[48]

Despite Sheridan's optimism, however, the Southern Cheyenne and Arapahoe did not meekly submit as he and Custer had hoped. And if these two tribes suddenly realized that winter no longer afforded security, Sheridan also came to understand that there was still plenty of "starch" left in them. Finally, in March 1869, the general decided to act. Learning that two white women captured in Kansas were held by the Cheyenne, Sheridan ordered Custer to take the 7th Cavalry and the 19th Kansas and bring the Indians to bay.

After a fruitless search through Indian Territory, the colonel and several scouts finally spotted the Cheyenne camp on Sweetwater Creek, Texas. In a bold move, Custer and a single orderly approached the village.

> I knew that the first shot fired on either side would be the signal for the murder of the two white girls . . . . Desiring to establish a truce with the Indians before the troops should arrive, I began making signals inviting a conference . . . . Immediately there appeared on the bluffs about twenty mounted Indians; from this group three advanced toward me at a gallop, soon followed by the other of the party. I cast my eyes behind me to see if the troops were near, but the head of the column was still a mile or more in the rear . . . . Directing the orderly to remain stationary, I advanced toward the Indians a few paces, and as soon as they were sufficiently near made signs to them to halt, and then for but one of their number to advance midway and meet me. This was assented to, and I advanced with my revolver in my left hand, while my right hand was held aloft as token that I was inclined to be friendly.[49]

Despite his warning, Custer quickly found himself surrounded by a score of braves, including a principal chief, Medicine Arrow.

> By this time [Lt. William] Cooke had again joined me . . . and taking . . . Cooke with me I started with Medicine Arrow and a considerable party of his warriors to the village, Medicine Arrow urging us to put our horses to the gallop . . . . I knew, before accepting the proposal of the chief to enter his village, that he and every member of his band felt it to be to their interest not only to protect me from harm, but to treat me with every consideration, as the near approach of the troops and the formidable number of the latter would deter the Indians from any act of hostility . . . . A brisk gallop soon

> brought us to the village . . . [and] Medicine Arrow hurried me to his lodge, which was located almost in the center of the village . . . .
>
> By Medicine Arrow's direction the village crier in a loud tone of voice began calling the chiefs together in council. No delay occurred in their assembling.[50]

Meanwhile, the vengeful 19th Kansas had reached the bluff overlooking the village. "There, almost at the feet of the Nineteenth, were teepees [*sic*] representing from 1200 to 1500 Cheyennes," remembered Sgt. James Hadley.

> [O]ne picture . . . loomed before all else and eclipsed all else in the heart of every man in that long, ragged, faded line from Kansas; the mother lying dead on an army blanket, and in her arms a pretty little boy but two years old; the blue spot in the forehead of the one and the crushed head of the other telling how they died at the hands of the people in yonder camp—butchered out of malice that was more than devilish . . . . Every officer and man thought of that picture as they saw it in the deep snows of the Washita. "Now is the time and this is the place!" They could hardly believe their good luck.[51]

Another looking down from the bluff was Private David Spotts.

> [T]he Indian camp . . . was alive with Indians all greatly excited . . . . [E]very pony had a rider and some had several women and children. They were ready to leave and we received no orders to stop them. Now was our chance for a real Indian fight, but no orders came. Gen. Custer was still in their midst, and all the time they were getting ready to make a break for escape. Suddenly they all made a dash down the creek and not a gun was fired. We were not to fire until we had the order, and when they had gotten away all the Kansas men were disgusted for this was the only opportunity we had to punish the Indians who had killed so many of the Kansas settlers. Gen. Custer was then branded by some who had lost relatives or friends, as a coward and traitor to our regiment.[52]

"The men of the Nineteenth . . . were angry," Sergeant Hadley continued. "It looked, at one time, like they could not be restrained. The line officers argued, begged and cursed."[53] No one watched the drama below with more anxiety than Dan Brewster, a young civilian teamster. "Ever since his sister's capture," Spotts revealed, "Brewster has been at forts and with troops, trying to find some trace of her and now he has great hopes that one of the women is she."[54]

After being compelled to smoke the peace pipe until he was nearly sick, Custer, without mentioning the captives, told the chiefs he and his men had come in friendship. When the brief council ended the relieved officer returned to his command and set up camp less than a mile from the Indians. "I felt confident that as soon as it was dark the entire village would probably steal away and leave us in the lurch," he admitted, "but I proposed to make my demand for the surrender of the captives long before darkness should aid the Indians in eluding us."[55]

Later that day, several dozen warriors and chiefs, including Medicine Water, Big Head, and Dull Knife, visited Custer's campfire. In a few minutes, braves with musical instruments rode up to provide entertainment. Custer:

> Before their arrival, however, my lookouts reported unusual commotion and activity in the Indian village. The herd of the latter had been called in, and officers sent by me to investigate this matter confirmed the report and added that everything indicated a contemplated flight on the part of the Indians. I began then to comprehend the object of the proposed serenade; it was to occupy our attention while the village could pack up and take flight. Pretending ignorance of what was transpiring in the village, I continued to converse . . . with the chiefs, until the arrival of the Indian musicians . . . .
>
> During all this time reports continued to come in leaving no room to doubt that the entire village was preparing to decamp. To have opposed this movement . . . would have only precipitated a terrible conflict . . . . I determined to seize the principal chiefs then present, permit the village to depart if necessary, and hold the captured chiefs as hostages for the surrender of the white girls . . . . This was a move requiring not only promptness but most delicate and careful handling in order to avoid bloodshed. Quietly passing the word to a few of the officers who sat near me around the camp fire, I directed them to leave the group one by one and in such manner as not to attract the attention of the Indians proceed to their companies and select quickly some of their most reliable men, instructing the latter to assemble around and near my camp fire, well armed, as if merely attracted there by the Indian serenade. The men thus selected were to come singly, appear as unconcerned as possible, and be in readiness to act promptly, but to do nothing without orders from me. In this manner about one hundred of my men were in an inconceivably short space of time mingled with the Indians . . . .
>
> I then rose from my seat near the fire and unbuckling my revolver from my waist asked the Indians to observe that I threw my weapons upon the ground as an evidence that in what I was about to

> do I did not desire or propose to shed blood unless forced to do so. I then asked the chiefs to look about them and count the armed men whom I had posted among and around them . . . . Upon the first intimation from me regarding the armed men . . . every Indian who was dismounted sprang instantly to his feet, while those mounted gathered the reins of their ponies; all drew their revolvers or strung their bows; and for a few moments it seemed as if nothing could avert a collision . . . . All this time the Indians were gesticulating and talking in the most excited manner; the boys and young men counselling resistance, the older men and chiefs urging prudence . . . .
>
> Near me stood a tall, gray-haired chief, who, while entreating his people to be discreet, kept his cocked revolver in his hand ready for use . . . . Near him stood another, a most powerful and forbidding-looking warrior, who was without firearms, but who was armed with a bow already strung and a quiver full of iron-pointed arrows . . . . He stood apparently unaffected by the excitement about him . . . . Holding his bow in one hand, with the other he continued to draw from his quiver arrow after arrow. Each one he would examine as cooly as if he expected to engage in target practice . . . .
>
> The noise of voices and the excitement increased until a movement began on the part of the Indians who were mounted, principally the young men and boys. If the latter could be allowed to escape and the chiefs be retained, the desired object would be gained. Suddenly a rush was made . . . . I, as well as the other officers near me, called upon the men not to fire. The result was that all but four broke through the lines and made their escape. The four detained, however were those desired, being chiefs and warriors of prominence.[56]

When the dust settled, Custer selected one of the captives, loaded him with gifts, then returned his pony.

> I . . . intrusted him with verbal messages to his tribe, the substance of which was as follows: First, I demanded the unconditional surrender of the two white girls held captive in the village . . . . Second, I required the Cheyenne village . . . to proceed at once to their reservation . . . . Third, I sent a friendly message to Little Robe, inviting him to visit me with a view to the speedy settlement of the question at issue.[57]

Little Robe, wise and peacefully inclined, accepted the offer to mediate. Over the next several days of tense talk, however, the Indian demand was always the same. "[T]he Cheyennes desired us to release the three chiefs . . ." said Custer, "after which they would be prepared to consider the question of the release of the two white girls."[58]

Because of the stalled situation, rations among the soldiers began to run low. Few seemed to mind, though. "We hear no complaints about hunger for everybody is anxious and excited, hoping to see the prisoners brought in," David Spotts recorded in his journal. "We are living on excitement now and our stomachs are getting so used to being empty that they have shrunk to fit the occasion."[59] Returning to Custer:

> Finally, after I had almost exhausted the patience of the troops, particularly of the Kansas regiment . . . I determined to force matters to an issue . . . . I sent for a delegation of chiefs from the Cheyenne village to receive my ultimatum . . . . I stated that I had but one other message to send to the village . . . . Further delay would not be submitted to on our part. We knew they had two of our race captives in the village . . . . I then informed them that if by sunset the following day the two white girls were not restored to our hands unharmed the lives of the three chiefs would be forfeited and the troops would resume active hostilities.[60]

"[H]e will hang Big Head and Dull Knife to a large overhanging tree," Spotts wrote. "He took them and showed the limb and explained it so they understood just what he meant . . . . The Indian chiefs are sullen and occasionally mutter something to each other. Evidently they do not like to see the lariats hanging from the . . . limb."[61]

When the following day passed without note, a terrible foreboding gripped the soldiers, including Custer.

> Three o'clock arrived, and no tidings from the village. By this time the officers and men of the command had assembled near headquarters . . . eagerly watching the horizon in the direction of the village . . . . Even the three chiefs became despondent as the sun slowly but surely approached the horizon, and no tidings from the village reached them . . . .
>
> The sun was perhaps an hour high when the dim outlines of about twenty mounted figures were discerned against the horizon . . . . Instantly all eyes were directed to the party, but the distance was too great to enable any of us to clearly define either the number or character of the group. The eyes of the three chiefs perceptibly brightened with hope. Securing my field glass, I carefully

> scanned the party on the hill . . . . Gradually . . . I was able to make out the figures in sight. I could only determine at first that the group was . . . composed of Indians, and began counting them audibly, when I discovered two figures mounted upon the same pony. As soon as this was announced several of my companions at once exclaimed: "Can they be the girls?" . . . I saw the two figures descend from the pony and . . . advance toward us on foot. All this I reported to the anxious bystanders . . . . I began describing the appearance of the two as well as I could with the aid of the glass: "One seems to have a short, heavy figure: the other is considerably taller and more slender." Young Brewster, who stood at my side, immediately responded, "The last one must be my sister; she is quite tall. Let me go and meet them; this anxiety is more than I can endure." But this I declined, fearing that should one of the two now approaching us prove to be his sister, seeing her in the forlorn condition in which she must be might provoke young Brewster . . . to obtain revenge.[62]

In a gesture of good will, Custer allowed the three senior officers of the Kansas regiment to advance and receive the women.

> They had passed one-fourth of the distance, perhaps, when young Brewster, whom I had detained at my side with difficulty, bounded away and the next moment was running at full speed to greet his long-lost sister. Dashing past the three officers, he clasped in his arms the taller of the two girls. This told us all we had hoped for . . . . Men whom I have seen face death without quailing found their eyes filled with tears, unable to restrain the deep emotion produced by this joyful event. The appearance of the two girls was sufficient to excite our deepest sympathy.[63]

As David Spotts observed:

> They did not even smile when they were brought in . . . . The larger one appeared to be 50 years old, although she was less than 25. She was stooped, pale and haggard, looking as if she had been compelled to do more than she was able . . . . Her clothes were made of three or four kinds of material, pieces of tents and blankets, all worn out and sewed together with strings. The other . . . also was pale and dressed pretty much the same.[64]

"Besides indignities and insults far more terrible than death itself," Custer added, "the physical suffering to which the two girls were subjected was too great almost to be believed."[65]

"Heavy burdens had been carried on their bare shoulders till the skin was as hard and callous as the palm of a laborer's hand," noted James Hadley. "The jealous squaws, with their barbaric rawhides, had covered their backs with scars. Some of the more recent lashings left unhealed gashes as wide as a man's finger. At first they had been sold back and forth among the bucks for fifteen ponies each, but their last owners only paid two."[66]

The following day the camp learned more of the cruel captivity, including the fact that both women were pregnant. "The recital of the many brutalities to which these poor women were subjected," wrote an outraged correspondent to a Kansas newspaper, "should inspire every one with a desire for the condign punishment of the savages, and nothing less than death is at all appropriate or adequate to their desserts."[67]

"Dan Brewster has sworn vengeance on the Indians for the rough treatment of his sister," Private Spotts revealed, adding that when the woman suddenly caught sight of Big Head, she tried to snatch a revolver from an officer, screaming that the chief was "the worst Indian in the whole tribe."[68]

Despite the growing mood to murder the captives and wipe out the village, Custer held firm. "The three chiefs begged to be released, upon the ground that their people had delivered up the two girls," the colonel later wrote, "but this I told them was but one of the two conditions imposed; the other required the tribe to return to their reservation and until this was done they need not hope for freedom."[69]

The following morning, the soldiers broke camp and prepared for their return journey. David Spotts:

> We were all ready to march . . . when a troop of Indians came bearing a white flag and wanted one more talk with the "White Chief." It was the last effort to secure the release of their chiefs. They made all kinds of promises and were willing to give any security they had if Custer would set them at liberty. They were told that it was an impossibility, but if the tribe would go on a reservation and be peaceable they would be set free and also the women and children captured at the fight on [the Washita].[70]

The Cheyenne did indeed return to their reservation, but even as he was gaining the freedom of the white women and the surrender of an entire tribe without a shot being fired, George Custer was being skewered by peace advocates for what was seen as butchery on the Washita. Ignoring the women and children taken prisoner and their later release, Easterners accused the colonel of wholesale massacre. "One or two church papers were exceedingly bitter," commented Sergeant Hadley of the 19th Kansas. "[T]hey demanded the 'punishment' of Custer and all the officers and men of the Seventh Cavalry for 'deliberate, premeditated and brutal murder of inoffensive and peaceful people.'"[71]

"Surely you do not believe the current rumors that Autie and others are cruel in their treatment of Indians?" Libbie Custer asked a questioning aunt. "Autie and others only do what they are ordered to do. And if those who criticize these orders could only see for themselves . . . the brutalities of the men, the venom of the squaws . . . . People in civilized conditions cannot imagine it. But we who have seen it know."[72]

Some critics claimed the attack took place on the Cheyenne reservation, when in fact it had been nearly a hundred miles to the west. Sheridan:

> It is also alleged the band was friendly. No one could make such an assertion who had any regard for truth. The young men of this band commenced the war; I can give their names. Some of Black Kettle's young men were out depredating at Dodge when the village was wiped out. Mules taken from trains, matter carried by our murdered couriers, photographs stolen from the scenes of outrages on the Solomon and Saline, were found in the captured camp, and, in addition, I have their own illustrated history, found in their . . . camp, showing the different fights or murders in which this tribe was engaged; the trains attacked; the hay parties attacked about Fort Wallace; the women, citizens, and soldiers killed.[73]

"In his talk with me some five or six days before he was killed," another officer from Fort Cobb revealed, "Black Kettle stated that many of his men were then on the war path, and that their people did not want peace with the people above the Arkansas."[74]

In the meantime, Custer carried on with his job and appeared supremely indifferent to the debate swirling around his name. Though he fought the Indian as he had the Rebel—with every ounce of energy he possessed—few soldiers had more respect and, ultimately, more genuine sympathy for the plight of the Indian than George Armstrong Custer. Realizing that their time was short, the colonel and a handful of others were determined to learn all they could about these mysterious people of the Plains before they vanished from the face of the earth forever.

10

If I Were an Indian . . .

Following the Civil War, the tribes of the High Plains fought furiously with the army for well over a decade. There were moments of peace, however, and during these interludes, white men—and occasionally white women—visited their recent enemy to try and learn more of their ways. Among these intrepid souls was New York *Herald* reporter DeBenneville Keim, who stopped one day at a Comanche village.

> Our advent was duly announced by a drove of snarling, snapping curs, of all sizes, colors and conditions. Two great clubs with which we had provided ourselves beforehand alone prevented a complete rout . . . . Our movements, however, were most cautiously performed by backing in the direction we wished to proceed and thus preventing a dash on our heels. The noise of our approach as developed by the dogs, started a few old squaws who came out of their lodges, and by giving vent to a few gutterals completely silenced the growling storm, and we continued to the lodge of . . . Essahavit, the war-chief of the band. This exalted hero of the savage community heard of our coming and was ready to greet us. He politely waved us an invitation to enter. We complied by crowding through an aperture . . . about three feet in height, and covered with a piece of buffalo hide dried, and as stiff as a board.
>
> Upon entering the lodge we were invited to a seat on a fine buffalo robe spread upon the ground, for the accommodation of visitors

A Plains tepee. KANSAS STATE HISTORICAL SOCIETY.

. . . . The war-chief was a man of about forty-five years of age, heavy muscular frame, and a broad face. The latter was specially illuminated with a coating of vermillion. He wore a brown shirt, and about his waist a broad belt supporting a breech-clout, his lower limbs were bare, with the exception of a pair of beautifully worked moccasins on his feet. Both ears were fearfully disfigured by large incisions which had been made in them for . . . earrings.

Like most men of deeds, Essahavit soon began to narrate his warlike performances against the Utes and Navajoes, the ancient and mortal enemies of the [Comanche] . . . . His fierce black eyes . . . soon flashed up, indicating the chief's fire of temper and no ordinary intelligence. He was reclining, his coarse raven hair streaming over his shoulders . . . . Near the couch, and within arms length, stood a forked stick, upon which were suspended the chief's trappings for war and the chase, his head gear and ornaments, and shell and silver breast decorations . . . . Opposite the chief on our right lay several very fine robes and parfleshes finely painted. On our left, lay the rude cooking utensils of the lodge. In the centre, a hole sunk about six inches, contained a small fire burning brightly, and emitting a pleasant heat.

At the head of the couch, lay a squaw incorrigibly ugly and emaciated. We were early informed by herself that she was sick "a heap." . . . At the foot of the couch sat the favorite squaw, young,

> pretty, and unusually cleanly in appearance. During our entire presence this one of the female members of the family was busily occupied in finishing a beautiful buffalo robe which she had just tanned. Occasionally from her work in response to some words from the chief, she would lift a pair of fine black eyes, and with a pleasantness of expression respond in striking contrast, with the old hag cuddled up in the corner.[1]

Thomas Battey also shared his impressions of an Indian camp, one of the Plains Apache.

> After making our way through the midst of hundreds of dogs, every-one of which appeared to exert his vocal and explosive powers to the utmost, filling the air with . . . the most horrid din of snaps, snarls, yelps, growls, and howls . . . we found a convenient place for lariating our ponies and mule . . . . We then proceeded to the lodge of Pacer, the head chief of the Apaches, being escorted by most if not all the dogs in the community, still continuing their deafening clamor, and crowding upon us to the degree that we had to keep them off with clubs . . . .
>
> The lodge, like nearly all belonging to the wild Indians, was built in the form of a conical tent . . . . The internal arrangements are very simple. A round hole is dug in the centre for the fire, three sides are occupied by the beds, while the side in which is the entrance is used as kitchen, pantry, and general storeroom. The beds are elevated above the ground, perhaps from four to six inches, and serve for seats and lounges in the daytime . . . . They are . . . but for the vermin, a comfortable bed.
>
> A large kettle was boiling over the fire, the contents of which were stirred from time to time with the broad rib of a buffalo . . . . In due time supper was announced, consisting of boiled beef . . . coffee, and very good biscuits or short-cakes, baked in an old-fashioned bake-kettle, or Dutch oven. After we had partaken all that was desirable, and pushed the dishes back, our host and his two wives finished what was left. A basin of water was then passed around to drink, and to wash our fingers, which is usually done by filling the mouth with water, and spurting it upon the hands, afterwards wiping them upon a dirty cloth.[2]

Other than both being assailed by swarms of "snarling, snapping curs," the lesson gained by Keim, Battey, and dozens of other whites was that no matter how hostile an Indian could be when at war, within a chief's tepee even enemies were treated as friends. "Though he may be barbarous in the extreme, no stranger seeking repose or refreshment in his lodge will be turned away unsheltered or unfed," Battey noted. "In his lodge an enemy is a brother, warmed by his fire and sharing his food, and for whose defence even his own life would be risked."[3]

Some of the customs of the lodge seemed strange: "No matter how pressing or momentous the occasion, an Indian invariably declines to engage in council until he has filled his pipe and gone through with the important ceremony of a smoke."[4]

And some of the food was startling: "In the centre of [our] circle were three dogs, the hair merely scorched, which had been roasted entire, intestines and all. Over this Indian delicacy was poured the gravy, dog's grease."[5]

While off duty, David Spotts and several comrades of the 19th Kansas toured a Kiowa camp near Fort Cobb.

> We soon came to a group of boys who were playing a game with arrows. They had two stakes about thirty feet apart. They stood at one stake and threw their arrows with the hand, sticking them in the ground around the other stake. It was very much like the white man pitches horseshoes. They would put the arrows quite close . . . . After a lot of Indian talk they would then pitch them back to the other stake. While we were watching the game some dogs chased a squirrel up a tree a short distance away and began to bark . . . . We could see the squirrel lying flat on the top of a large limb about forty feet from the ground. Several boys were soon there with the bows and arrows. One of them who seemed to be a good shot, sent an arrow so close that the squirrel jumped higher on the limb and laid closer than before. The same boy shot again and the arrow plowed through the hair on his back. He ran out on a small limb and jumped into space. He no sooner struck the ground when one of the dogs seized him and ended the sport.
>
> We next visited a kind of work shop, where two or three old men were making bridles, lariats, leggins and some other things out of colored leather . . . . The work was well done for the kind of tools used. They did not notice us or speak to us and when we spoke to them they sometimes gave a grunt, but said nothing that we could understand . . . .
>
> There were no men to be seen except a few old ones, and they all seemed to be busy. An old squaw came up to us and offered to sell us a pair of nicely beaded moccasins. She could not understand us, nor could she tell us the price. She finally started off and motioned for us

to follow, which we did. She led us to a nice tent some distance, where the lodges were quite thick, and there we met a very intelligent looking squaw who could talk English. She was engaged in making fancy work of scenery, buds and flowers, on cloth and leather, and showed us some very gaudy clothing, trimmed with many colored beads . . . . We visited another tent where two squaws were engaged in painting pictures. They had the walls of their tent covered with skins of various sizes and on each was a painting of some kind . . . . The two women occasionally spoke to each other, but said nothing to us and we went on to the next people we saw. An old squaw and two old men were making a frame of wicker work for an addition to their tepee. The frame was in the shape of a "prairie schooner" made of willows . . . . Another one near was finished and covered with buffalo skins. This was to be the bedroom to their home.

Then we returned and found the boys still near where we left them but they had bows and arrows and showed us some good marksmanship . . . . When they tell you an Indian is lazy, we beg to dispute it, for we did not see one idle in all that camp. All were doing something, even the little youngsters.[6]

On his stroll around the village, newsman Keim cast a more scientific eye.

The plains warrior exhibits less muscular development than those of his race occupying the mountain districts . . . . He is tall, but his limbs are small and badly shaped, showing more sinew than muscle. His chest, however, is deep and square. His bearing is erect, with legs considerably bowed, the effect of constant use of the saddle. His hair is long and black, and worn at full length, streaming over his shoulders. The scalp-lock . . . is artistically plaited. His beard, moustache, and eyebrows he plucks out . . . . The practice has a tendency to produce a feminine appearance.

In physiognomy we find in the plains Indians a greater diversity than would be supposed. Some have features perfectly Caucasian . . . with the different shades of color, from a dark reddish brown to a perfect olive . . . . Specimens are often seen bearing close resemblance to the subjects of several European nations. We have seen one band, except in color, perfect Italians, a few resembling the Germans and quite a number the Jews of to-day . . . .

The women about the village were occupied in most of the daily out-door employments of their sex. Some were driving in the herds of ponies, others fleshing buffalo hides, others carrying water and

> fire wood. In this last occupation I was amazed at the wonderful strength of the women. I saw one old squaw, not less than sixty years of age, with an enormous bundle of wood on her back held together by strips of raw hide. What she carried at the time could not have weighed less than three hundred pounds, and I was even told that for a short distance it was not uncommon for squaws to carry six hundred pounds in the same manner . . . . The women of the plains tribes, though smaller in stature, show a much more perfect development. The relations between the sexes is the same in nearly all cases—that is, they are the servants or slaves.[7]

"She is beaten, abused, reviled, driven like any other beast of burden," Lieutenant James Steele observed. "She is bought and sold; wife, mother, and pack animal, joined in one hideous and hopeless whole."[8] Returning to Keim:

> All the labor performed in an Indian village, taking down or setting up the lodges, packing for transportation, saddling the ponies, cooking, tanning robes, making moccasins, doing bead-work, providing covering for the body out of the skins brought in by the warrior, and the raising of children, fall to the lot of the women. The sphere of the men is to hunt and to supply the lodge with game and skins, and to take scalps from their enemies wherever they find them.
>
> The general characteristics of the sexes are in the men a boasting spirit, no moral and little animal courage, consummate indolence . . . and intolerable pride, and a fiendish thirst for blood. In the women we find patience, a degree of tenderness, industry, devotion, and ingenuity. They are particularly timid, and frequently set off in a regular stampede from some imaginary or real cause. On these occasions it is useless for the men to attempt to use their authority. The usual argument administered towards refractory squaws, such as kicks, cuffs, and violent floggings, are at such times perfectly powerless . . . . Condemned to a sphere of drudgery and domestic oppression, it would naturally be supposed that the women would be gross and hideous. Although beauty in its higher sense is rare, many winning faces will be seen in the Indian village. The children are uncommonly good looking. The old women are perfect frights.[9]

Like Keim, Libbie Custer noted the arrested muscular development among Plains warriors.

> The legs and arms of Indians are almost invariably thin. None of them ever do any manual labor to produce muscle, and their bones are decidedly conspicuous . . . . I never knew but one Indian who worked. He was an object of interest to me, though he kept [to] himself . . . and skulked around the fire when he cooked. This was the occupation forced upon him by the others. He had lacked the courage to endure the torture of the sun-dance; for when strips of flexible wood had been drawn through the gashes in his back, and he was hung up by these, the poor creature had fainted. On reviving he begged to be cut down, and ever after was an object of scorn. He was condemned to wear squaw's clothing from that time on. They mocked and taunted him, and he led as separate an existence as if he were in a desert alone. The squaws disdained to notice him, except to heap work upon his already burdened shoulders.[10]

Of all the Indians' customs, begging was the most loathsome to whites. "To beg is the one thing of which an Indian is never ashamed," wrote Captain Charles King. "[T]o hang around camp for an entire day, and when they had coaxed us out of our last plug of tobacco, our only remaining match, and our old clothes, instead of going home satisfied they would turn to with reviving energy and beg for the things of all others for which they had not the faintest use—soap and writing paper."[11]

Love of liquor, or "crazy water," was another Indian characteristic noted by many. When white whiskey peddlers or Mexican traders did not supply the insatiable demand the Kaw in Kansas, the Caddo in Indian Territory, and other "semi-civilized" tribes did. Nothing was more shattering to their culture than the abuse of liquor. "Whisky . . . will, in some form or another, prostitute the fairest virtue of the Indian maiden," complained an agent for the Kiowa and Comanche tribes, "and next to this is the association formed at military posts, not alone with the enlisted men, but, I say it with pain, with very many of the commissioned officers."[12]

When whiskey and young soldiers didn't debauch Indian girls, their own husbands, brothers, and fathers did. Confided Captain Albert Barnitz to his journal:

> Last night . . . an Arrapahoe Indian brought me a young squaw, which he assured me was 'heap good' and which he desired to present to me as a companion for the evening! I showed him Jennie's picture, and explained to him that <u>she</u> was my squaw, and that one squaw was amply sufficient and two squaws "<u>no</u> <u>wano</u>!" whereupon

he begged a candle, and disappeared . . . . (She was very elegantly ornamented with vermillion, and seemed to have been especially gotten up for the occasion!)[13]

One of the features that distinguished the Plains tribes from those farther west or east was the multitude of horses at each camp. "No warrior or chief is of any importance or distinction who is not the owner of a herd of ponies numbering from twenty to many hundreds," George Custer explained.[14] DeBenneville Keim added:

> The herd is always divided into two classes of animals, war and squaw-ponies, the latter being also used for carrying burdens. The war-pony is selected from the best stock, is fearless, quick in his movements, and of great strength and endurance . . . . A warrior usually has several of these selected animals, one of which, even in time of peace, is always lariated near his lodge, ready to be mounted at a moment's notice. These war-ponies are really fine animals, and frequently are very fleet. In action they exhibit remarkable courage, and manoeuvre either to the voice or gesture.[15]

After marvelling at the movements of man and mount during a buffalo hunt, Thomas Battey was also on hand when Kiowas lassoed a mustang.

> Notwithstanding his rearing and plunging, kicking, lashing, and biting, he was soon made fast to a tree, and gradually drawn up to it, until he had but very little play room, but used what he had to the greatest possible advantage. He manifested his wildness and strength by the most furious striking and kicking, whenever approached. An old blanket was repeatedly thrown upon him, which would soon be under his feet . . . .
>
> Though foiled and brought up on every occasion, he would not give up, while his merciless tormentors took a barbarous delight in punching him with poles, and striking him with long sticks. After continuing this cruel sport for about an hour, during which time, in his mad plungings, he had thrown himself several times upon the ground, he at length fell exhausted, and lay quiet and docile as a lamb. Thereupon, after some patting and manifestations of kindness, the lariat was removed, we saddled up, and started on; the pony, rendered manageable by exhaustion, was driven by one of the party.[16]

From such brutal beginnings a prized pony could become a pampered pet. "When Indians kill game on the hunt they cut out the tongue, liver and heart, and unless very hungry leave the carcass to rot upon the prairie," observed John Finerty of the Chicago *Times*. "They don't want to load their horses much unless when near their villages."[17]

At war, atop his mount, the Plains Indian was a sight to behold. In Custer's words:

> The Indian warrior is capable of assuming positions on his pony . . . at full speed, which no one but an Indian could maintain for a single moment without being thrown to the ground. The pony . . . is perfectly trained, and seems possessed of the spirit of his rider . . . .
>
> Once a warrior was seen to dash out from the rest in the peculiar act of "circling" which was simply to dash along in front of the line of troopers, receiving their fire and firing in return. Suddenly his pony while at full speed was seen to fall to the ground . . . . The warrior was thrown over and beyond the pony's head and his capture by the cavalry seemed a sure and easy matter . . . . The troop advanced rapidly, but the comrades of the fallen Indian had also witnessed his mishap and were rushing to his rescue. He was on his feet in a moment, and . . . another warrior mounted on the fleetest of ponies was at his side, and with one leap the dismounted warrior placed himself astride the pony of his companion; and thus doubly burdened the gallant little steed, with his no less gallant riders, galloped lightly away, with about eighty cavalrymen, mounted on strong domestic horses, in full cry after them.
>
> There is no doubt but that by all the laws of chance the cavalry should have been able to soon overhaul and capture the Indians in so unequal a race; but . . . the pony, doubly weighted as he was, distanced his pursuers and landed his burden in a place of safety. Although chagrined at the failure of the pursuing party to accomplish the capture of the Indians I could not wholly suppress a feeling of satisfaction, if not gladness, that for once the Indian had eluded the white man.[18]

Because of such life-and-death situations, the warrior naturally put much stock in a good pony. Custer continued:

> Indians are extremely fond of bartering . . . . They will sign treaties relinquishing their lands and agree to forsake the burial ground of

> their fore-fathers; they will part . . . with their bow and arrows and their accompanying quiver, handsomely wrought in dressed furs; their lodges even may be purchased at not an unfair valuation, and it is not an unusual thing for a chief or warrior to offer to exchange his wife or daughter for some article which may have taken his fancy . . . . [B]ut no Indian of the Plains has ever been known to trade, sell, or barter away his favorite war pony . . . . Neither love nor money can induce him to part with it.[19]

Even during periods of peace, war seldom strayed far from the collective heart and soul of the Plains tribes. "War with somebody is . . . the natural state of an Indian people," observed Colonel William O. Collins. "Every tribe has some hereditary enemies with whom it is always at war and against whom it makes regular expeditions to get scalps and steal ponies . . . . To heal these difficulties perfectly is impossible, as there is always some wrong unavenged. It is by war that they obtain wealth, position, and influence with the tribe. The young men especially look up to and follow the successful warrior rather than the wise and prudent chiefs."[20]

Against the ever-encroaching white man, there was always a ready reason for war. As one Sioux chief orated:

> The palefaces, our eternal persecutors, pursue and harass us without intermission, forcing us to abandon to them, one by one, our best hunting grounds, and we are compelled to seek a refuge in the depths of these Bad Lands like timid deer. Many of them even dare to come into the prairies which belong to us, to trap beaver and hunt elk and buffalo, which are our property. These undesirable creatures, the outcasts of their own people, rob and kill us when they can. Is it just that we should suffer these wrongs without complaining? Shall we allow ourselves to be massacred . . . without seeking to avenge ourselves? Does not the law . . . say, "Justice to our own nation and death to all palefaces?"[21]

Once a tribe opted for war, a grand demonstration of unity and will was in order. When the Crow of Montana sided with whites to punish their old foe, the Sioux, John Finerty watched in stunned silence as the warriors "made night hideous with a war-dance and barbaric music."

> They imitated in succession every beast and bird of the North American forests. Now they roared like a bison bull. Then they

A Comanche warrior. Kansas State Historical Society.

mimicked a wildcat. All at once they broke out with the near, fierce howling of a pack of wolves; gradually the sound would die away until you might imagine that the animals were miles off, when all of a sudden the howling would rise within a few yards, and in the darkness you would try to discern the foul coyotes . . . .

All night long . . . the savages continued their infernal orgies. Their music is fitter for hell than for earth . . . [and] I fell asleep dreaming of roistering devils and lakes of brimstone.[22]

During times of peace, white traders and even the U.S. government supplied the Plains tribes with the most advanced firearms, ostensibly for hunting. But when war erupted, the Indians quickly turned the weapons on their benefactors. In the warriors' hands, though, the rifle and pistol were not as lethal as might be imagined.

"Compared with the white hunter of the plains," declared Colonel Richard Dodge, "the Indian is a wretched shot. He is about equal to the United States soldier, being deficient for the same reason—lack of practice. The Government and the Indian are each too poor to afford to waste more than ten cartridges a month on drill, and no man ever became an expert marksman on that allowance. The Indian is really much more dangerous with the bow than with the pistol; but the latter gives a longer range and the Indian does not like close fighting any better than other people."[23]

Highly accurate with bow and arrow, the Indian occasionally developed his own brand of technology. During attacks along the Smoky Hill, Albert Barnitz was astonished that the raiders had tried to burn stage stations with "torpedo arrows." The devices were "made by placing a percussion cap on the point of the arrow blade, and encasing the same in a little cotton sack, containing about a thimble full of gun-powder!"[24]

As *Harper's Magazine* reported, Indians also manufactured poison arrows.

A rattlesnake is caught and penned. He is made angry by being poked with sticks, when a piece of deer liver is held towards him on the end of a stick. Into this he strikes his fangs. The liver is then withdrawn and a piece of dogwood about four inches long carefully sharpened is thrust into the incision made by the fangs. The stick is permitted to dry for a short time, when it is dipped into a glutinous solution, which, drying hermetically seals the poison, which would otherwise decompose. This piece of dogwood is used at the head of the arrow.[25]

With faith in his mount, his bow, and his ability to use both, a warrior nevertheless invoked supernatural powers to protect him in battle should any of the first three fail. "To-day I saw an Indian with a little bunch of feathers, buffaloes hair &c, made up into something resembling a doll baby," Barnitz wrote in his journal. "[I] learned from him that it was a charm, and that he considered himself impervious to bullets while he wore that, and he would not be persuaded otherwise, but insisted that bullets would glance from him, and that he could remain unharmed, and invulnerable!"[26]

Whites communicated with flags, flashing mirrors, and telegraph; Indians also had highly effective ways of relaying information. Recorded DeBenneville Keim:

> [T]he savages use a code of signals, which enables them to communicate with each other at long distances. The waving of a buffalo robe, or a quiver, communicates certain actions of the enemy . . . . Smoke by day and fires by night are more intricate and tedious methods resorted to, but with almost equal detail and success. The color of the smoke, either light or heavy, its volume, the diameter of the column, from a thin thread to a broad dense black mass, are all intelligible to the warrior.[27]

Custer watched in awe one day as two Indians performed a simple yet efficient act of long-range communication.

> First gathering an armful of dried grass and weeds, this was carried and placed upon the highest point of the peak, where, everything being in readiness, the match was applied close to the ground; but the blaze was no sooner well lighted and about to envelop the entire amount of grass collected than Little Robe began smothering it with the unlighted portion . . . . [H]e now took his scarlet blanket from his shoulders and with a graceful wave threw it so as to cover the smouldering grass, when, assisted by Yellow Bear, he held the corners and sides so closely to the ground as to almost completely confine and cut off the column of smoke. Waiting but for a few moments, and until he saw the smoke beginning to escape from beneath, he suddenly threw the blanket aside and a beautiful balloon shaped column puffed upwards . . . . Again casting the blanket on the pile of grass the column was interrupted as before, and again in due time released, so that a succession of elongated, egg-shaped puffs of smoke kept ascending toward the sky in the most regular manner.

> This beadlike column of smoke . . . was visible from points on the level plain fifty miles distant.[28]

"The secret of these signals is jealously guarded by every tribe," Keim added, "that the knowledge of their meaning may not escape, and thus be used against them."[29]

Once the warrior had chosen his battleground, there was no mystery about what he would do next. According to Richard Dodge:

> His tactics are always the same; never to receive a charge, but by constantly breaking, to separate the enemy into detached fragments; then suddenly concentrating to overwhelm them in detail. Having no trains or impediments of any kind, he is always able to avoid battle if the ground or opportunity does not suit him. The heavier slowly-moving troops, encumbered with trains of supplies, must attack when they can, and therefore almost always at disadvantage . . . . I know of no single instance where troops have gained any signal advantage over Indians in open fight, and this for the reason that the moment they gain even a slight advantage, the Indians disappear with a celerity that defies pursuit. On the other hand, if the Indians gain the advantage, they press it with a most masterful vigor, and there results a massacre.[30]

From afar, many credited such tactics to cowardice. Those who fought "Lo" knew otherwise. "No man," Dodge acknowledged, "possesses more of that quality of brute courage [than the Indian] . . . . No man can more gallantly dash into danger . . . . No man can take more chances when . . . risking his life to carry off unscalped his dead and wounded comrades."[31] An incredibly brave man himself, Custer felt the same.

> Surely no race of men . . . could display more wonderful skill . . . than the Indian warrior on his native plains, mounted on his well-trained war pony, voluntarily running the gantlet of his foes, drawing and receiving the fire of hundreds of rifles and in return sending back a perfect shower of arrows.[32]

Such bravery was instilled from birth. "The Indians who approached nearest the Post the other day," wrote a stunned Albert Barnitz from Fort Dodge, "were all little boys—only 8 to 10 years of age it appears!—A large band of warriors, however, was collected in the hills, in rear of the Post, watching them, and ready to make a descent if they had been closely pursued."[33] At the Battle of the Washita—where the surprised Southern Cheyenne quickly recovered and, in Custer's words, "fought with a desperation and courage which no . . . men could surpass"—the colonel witnessed another example of youthful heroism.

> Major [Frederick] Benteen . . . encountered an Indian boy scarcely fourteen years of age; he was well mounted and was endeavoring to make his way through the lines . . . . This boy rode boldly toward the Major, seeming to invite a contest. His youthful bearing . . . induced Major Benteen to endeavor to save him by making peace signs . . . but the young savage desired and would accept no such friendly concessions . . . . With revolver in hand he dashed at the Major . . . . Levelling his weapon as he rode, he fired, but . . . the shot whistled harmlessly by Major Benteen's head. Another followed in quick succession, but with no better effect. All this time the dusky little chieftain boldly advanced, to lessen the distance between himself and his adversary. A third bullet was sped . . . and this time to some purpose, as it passed through the neck of the Major's horse close to the shoulder. Making a final but ineffectual appeal to him to surrender and seeing him still preparing to fire again, the Major was forced in self-defense to level his revolver and despatch him . . . . He regarded himself as a warrior and the son of a warrior and as such he purposed to do a warrior's part.[34]

As masters of guerrilla warfare, the Indians' hit-and-run tactics were designed to create confusion, inflict damage, steal horses, and escape with as little loss as possible. When cornered, however, the Indian fought to the death. Following a descent on the Union Pacific by the Sioux, Luther North, part-Indian Baptiste Behale, and other scouts finally overhauled one of the raiders. According to North:

> [A]fter his horse had been shot he started to run on foot, shooting his arrows at us until they were all gone, when Baptiste . . . shot him with an arrow. It struck him under the right shoulder, went clear through his body and came out low down on the left side. He stopped, took hold of the spike end of the arrow, pulled it through himself, fitted it on to his bow, shot it back at Baptiste and fell over dead. Baptiste threw himself flat down over his horse's neck and the arrow whizzed over his neck about two inches too high.[35]

Despite the cautious tactics, war among Plains tribes could be unbelievably bloody. North:

> I was at the Pawnee Reservation the day when Crooked Hand killed six Sioux with his own hand and three horses were shot under him; and personally saw him on his return to the village that evening. He was covered with blood, and a Sioux arrow had been driven through his neck from the front . . . . It had gone into his throat on one side of the windpipe, and about half the length of the arrow protruded from the back of his neck.[36]

Like the Pawnee, the Crow were another ally of the whites eager to kill Sioux. When a large body of Indians approached Fort C. F. Smith in Montana, the garrison turned out to watch. Wrote a witness:

> Colonel [N. C.] Kinney examined them attentively through a field glass, and then permitted Iron Bull to do likewise; the chief instantly pronounced them to be hostile Sioux, and requested permission from Colonel Kinney to allow him to go out and fight them, which the Colonel cordially granted. The little band of Crows hastily mounted and rode out within arrow shot, and then began a parley; a war of words and abuse followed . . . . The Indians shouted and gesticulated in an amusing manner for some little time; at length each band, in a twinkling, arranged themselves in a circle, riding furiously, one following another in an endless chain, looking like two large moving wheels with their edges together, the warriors of each band lying along their horses, on the opposite side from his enemy . . . . As soon as the order of battle was arranged, the arrows began to fill the air, each warrior being careful not to hit the horse of his enemy—for they understood that it would be useless to either side after the battle.
>
> This spectacle had endured some ten or fifteen minutes when Iron Bull, arising to a bold, upright position upon his pony, rode bravely at the Sioux chieftain, and with lasso in hand skilfully threw the noose of it over the head and tightened it around the neck of his foe; then suddenly wheeling, rode for the fort, dragging the unlucky Sioux over the ground at the heels of his horse in a rapid rate. This practically ended the battle, and the Sioux retired, in a demoralized condition.[37]

The Scalp Dance. KANSAS STATE HISTORICAL SOCIETY.

Despite Kinney's protests, the Crow hauled their captive into camp and tortured him to death.

White warriors had medals to prove their bravery; red men had scalps. The scalp dance was a grand celebration of victory and valor, as a white witness in a Sioux village later described:

> The performance is only gone through at night and by the light of torches . . . . The braves came vauntingly forth with the most extravagant boast of their wonderful prowess and courage in war, at the same time brandishing weapons in their hands with the most fearful contortions and threatenings. A number of young women came with them, carrying the trophies . . . which they held up high as the warriors jumped in a circle, while brandishing their weapons and whooping and yelling . . . . All were jumping upon both feet at the same time with simultaneous stamping and motions . . . while keeping exact time. Their gestures looked as if they were actually cutting and carving each other to pieces as they uttered their fearful, sharp yell. They became furious as they grew more excited, their faces becoming distorted to the utmost; their glaring eyes protruded with a fiendish, indescribable appearance while they grind their teeth and attempt to imitate the hissing, gurgling sound of death in battle. Furious and faster grows the stamping . . . .

> No description can fully convey the terrible sight in all its fearful barbarity, as the bloody trophies of their victory are brandished aloft in the light of the flickering blaze and their distorted forms were half concealed by darkness.[38]

Because a typical Indian's world was limited to his prairie hunting ground, most refused to believe that the white traders, hunters, and soldiers they met were but the van of millions more beyond the Missouri River. Major Andrew Burt recalled a conversation he had one day with a Crow named Bearstooth.

> I liked old Bearstooth very much. He was neat and clean and never begged . . . . On this occasion when he came into my office I saw he was very much excited about something. I nodded to him. He replied with a grunted "How." . . . I did not speak . . . [but] quietly walked to the window and stood looking out of it. Squatted on the floor he lighted his pipe and began smoking. After some minutes of silence, having finished his smoke he arose gathering his blanket about his hips. Thus stripped to the waist he advanced to me and said "Poomacatee (my Indian name), you are the only white man who never lied to me. Now, I want you to tell me something. When a delegation goes to Washington the chiefs and warriors, all of them come back here and tell big lies of what they have seen and the biggest lie is how many big villages full of warriors they have seen. They say they are plentiful as leaves on the trees. The party just back are as crazy as the others. I picked out to go with them a young man who I had known all his life. I gave him two bundles of sticks, long and short ones; great big bundles. I told him to throw away a little stick when he passed a small village and a long one when he came to a great big village. Now he comes back and tells me he threw away all the short sticks before he came to the Big Muddy, and when he had travelled on chee-chee wagon, two sleeps on the other side of the river, all the long sticks were gone. So he's a big heap liar all same as the others. Now Poomacatee you tell me the truth. You won't lie to me, Bearstooth, your brother."
>
> Taking his hand and looking him straight in the eyes I said with all the earnestness I could put into my voice, "My brother, you have said that I am the only white man who never lied to you. I will not lie to you now. You cannot collect enough sticks in one moon to count the white men. Way back from the chee-chee wagon there are

> many, many villages your young man never saw and the white men are more numerous than the leaves on the tree."
>
> The old warrior's head slowly sank down. He turned dejectedly and strode out of the room. He never came into my room again.[39]

When the truth finally dawned on holdouts like Bearstooth, the result was at once devastating and utterly demoralizing, as Thomas Battey made clear.

> As a body, the Indians . . . believe that their own people who have been east have been duped by some kind of sorcery, or, as they would say, "medicine." . . . Consequently, my exhibiting [photographs of] towns, buildings, rural scenes, and soldiers, has had a most convincing effect . . . .
>
> One middle-aged man, who has always treated these reports with the utmost scepticism, was particularly struck with them. He could not sufficiently express his surprise, but beat upon his mouth in utter astonishment. Sun Boy, who had often told him what he saw in the east, would say to him in Kiowa, "What you think now? You think all lie now? You think all chiefs who have been to Washington fools now?" Again and again would he look them over, with his hand upon his mouth, dumb with amazement. After he had looked them over several times, being a war-chief, he called in his warriors, and exhibited the pictures to them, talking to them all the time. I could understand but a part, yet would gather such expressions as these: "Look! see what a mighty powerful people they are! . . . We are fools! We don't know anything! We just like wolves running wild on the plains."[40]

If the same images could be shown to other tribes, the war in the West would soon end, Battey believed. But even if some, like the awed Kiowa chief, were sobered into submission, others, even in the certain knowledge that they were mere hundreds facing millions, would have still chosen war as the only true path of a warrior. Whites made good each loss with ease; when a brave died, there were none to take his place. After one costly skirmish with soldiers, a witness described the agony of a Sioux camp.

> [A] scene of terrible mourning over those killed ensued among the women. Their cries are terribly wild and distressing on such occasions, and the near relations of the deceased indulge in frantic expressions of grief . . . . Sometimes the practice of cutting the flesh is carried to a horrible . . . extent. They inflict gashes on their bodies

> and limbs an inch in length. Some cut off all their hair, blacken their faces, and march through the village in procession, torturing their bodies to add vigor to their lamentations.[41]

John Finerty painted a similar picture among another ally of the whites, the Shoshoni, or Snakes.

> During the night a melancholy wailing arose from the Snake camp down by the creek. They were "waking" the young warrior killed by the Cheyennes that morning, and calling upon the Great Spirit for vengeance. I never heard anything equal to the despairing cadence of the wail, so savage and so dismal . . . . I had been led to believe that Indians never yielded to the weakness of tears, but . . . the experience of that mourning convinced me of my error. The men of middle age alone restrained their grief, but the tears of the young men and of the squaws rolled down their cheeks as copiously as if the mourners had been of the Caucasian race. I afterward learned that the sorrow would not have been so intense if the boy had not been scalped.[42]

As their numbers dwindled and the end of an age neared, fallen warriors at least had the satisfaction of knowing they were bound for the Great Beyond.

> [W]hen Kiowas die, the spirit travels a great way towards the sunset, and crossing a high mountain ridge, it comes at length to a wide water, which it has to cross. Upon arriving at the opposite shore, it is met by former loved friends, who have gone before to this happy land, and who now rejoice to meet it again. There the game is always fat and plenty, the grass is always green, the horses large, swift, and beautiful. The inhabitants are never sick, nor feel pain. Parting and tears are unknown—joy fills every heart.[43]

Few pursued the Indian more relentlessly and few had a greater role in crushing his culture than George Armstrong Custer. And yet, few more clearly understood or truly identified with the plight of the Plains Indian than this strange white warrior called Long Hair.

> In studying the Indian character, while shocked and disgusted by many of his traits and customs, I find much to be admired . . . . Grant that some of its pages are frightful, and if possible to be avoided, yet the attraction is none the weaker. Study him, fight him,

civilize him if you can, he still remains the object of your curiosity, a type of man peculiar and undefined, subjecting himself to no law of civilization, contending determinedly against all effort to win him from his chosen mode of life. He stands in the group of races solitary and reserved, seeking alliance with none, distrusting all. Civilization may do much for him, but he can never be civilized. Nature intended him for a savage; every instinct, every impulse of his soul inclines to it. The white race might fall into a barbarous state, and afterwards be reclaimed and prosper. Not so the Indian. He can not be himself and be civilized . . . .

If I were an Indian, I . . . would greatly prefer to cast my lot among those of my people adhered to the free open plains rather than submit to the confined limits of a reservation.[44]

11

A Lease on Hell

Although the winter campaign on the Washita forced the Southern Cheyenne, Arapahoe, Kiowa, Comanche, and Plains Apache back onto their reservations, raids on the southern Plains did not cease entirely. In May 1869, the Dog Soldiers, a splinter group of Cheyenne warriors led by Tall Bull, carried out a bloody sweep along the Solomon and Saline rivers in Kansas. After murdering several unsuspecting settlers, including George Weichell, they captured the man's attractive wife, Maria, just arrived from Germany. Later that day, the raiders surrounded Susanna Alderdice, shot her three children full of bullets and arrows, then carried the pregnant mother and her infant into captivity. Because of its continual crying, the Cheyenne soon dispatched the baby and left the tiny corpse for the wolves.

In response, Major Eugene Carr and the 5th Cavalry, guided by William F. Cody, set off in pursuit. Throughout June, the column, which included a large party of Pawnee led by Frank and Luther North, trailed the hostiles up the sandy Republican River and into Colorado. "[W]herever they had encamped we found the print of a woman's shoe," Cody recalled.[1]

By July 10, fresh signs indicated that the Cheyenne were not far ahead. Cutting clear from his supply train the following day, Carr and 250 men moved to the attack. At three that afternoon, the column neared the South Platte River. Major Carr:

> When we reached the breaks of the Platte Bluffs the Pawnees reported seeing two horsemen, and recommended taking the whole command into the ravine which was done . . . .
>
> We galloped about an hour through low sand hills and loose sand and saw no sign of Indians, and I began to think the whole [affair] was a humbug . . . when some Pawnees beckoned me to come to them . . . . [They] pointed out a herd of animals about four miles off in the hills . . . . I thought it were possible it might be Buffalo but of course determined to go and see.
>
> The Pawnee stripped themselves for the fight, taking off their saddles and as much of their clothing as could be dispensed with and still have something to distinguish them from the hostiles . . . . When concealment was no longer possible, I placed the three leading companies in parallel columns of two's . . . and sounded the charge. We were over a mile from the village and still undiscovered. The leading companies with the Pawnees on their left put their horses at speed while the rest followed at a fast gallop.[2]

Luther North takes up the narrative:

> About half a mile from the village . . . a Cheyenne boy was herding horses. He was about fifteen years old and we were very close to him before he saw us. He jumped on his horse, gathered up his herd, and drove them into the village ahead of our men, who were shooting at him. He was mounted on a very good horse and could easily have gotten away if he had left his herd, but he took them all in ahead of him, then at the edge of the village he turned and joined a band of warriors that were trying to hold us back, while the women and children were getting away, and there he died like a warrior. No braver man ever lived than that fifteen year old boy.[3]

As the cavalry thundered down, the weight of the charge carried the men into the village and fighting became fierce. Again, Luther North:

> About this time a woman came crawling out of the lodge, and running to Capt. [Sylanus] Cushing fell on her knees and threw her hands about his legs. We now saw that she was a white woman. She was bleeding from a bullet wound through her breast. She . . . could not talk English, and . . . [w]e finally made her understand that she was safe and that she should stay where she was . . . . Before we started across the village . . . I came to a dead woman, and upon

examination found she was white. She [Susanna Alderdice] had been killed with a tomahawk . . . .

We had been moving slowly up to this time, as the Indians were putting up a fight, but now the soldiers were firing volleys into the camp farther up the creek, and the Indians were running away as fast as they could. We started up the hill out of the village on the west side. My brother and I were a little ahead and to the left of our men when an Indian that was hidden in a ravine stuck his head up and fired at my brother. At first I thought he was hit, as he threw his hand up to his face and stopped his horse. He jumped off his horse and handed me his bridle reins and said, "Ride away and he will stick his head up again."

I started the horses off on a lope and the Indian raised his head to look, but did not get it very high, as my brother was ready for him and shot him in the forehead . . . .

[W]e went up toward the head of the canyon where our men were all dismounted. The canyon was about twenty feet deep there, and very narrow, with perpendicular sides, and a lot of Cheyenne warriors had run up there. They were armed with bows and arrows and whenever we came near to the edge of the canyon they would let fly with their arrows, and then we would run up to the canyon, stick our guns over the edge, shoot and jump back. After keeping this up for some time and there were no more arrows coming, we looked down into the canyon and found there thirteen dead warriors, and between there and the mouth of the canyon were six or seven more, and in the village were about twenty.[4]

When the smoke and dust cleared, fifty-two Indians lay dead, including Tall Bull, shot from his pony by Buffalo Bill. "One of the squaws among the prisoners suddenly began crying in a pitiful and hysterical manner at the sight of this horse," said Cody, who had claimed the chief's mount, "and upon inquiry I found she was Tall Bull's wife." Further questioning revealed that the same woman was responsible for the murder of one captive and the wounding of the other.[5]

The devastating charge at Summit Springs broke the back of the Cheyenne Dog Soldiers. Never again would they be a force on the frontier.

During the early 1870's, the tribes of the southern Plains lived an uneasy existence on their reservations. Although there were sporadic raids and isolated atrocities, the region was largely spared the horror of a general war. By the spring of 1874, however, the signs of an outbreak were everywhere. One cause of unrest was an insufficient supply of promised government rations.

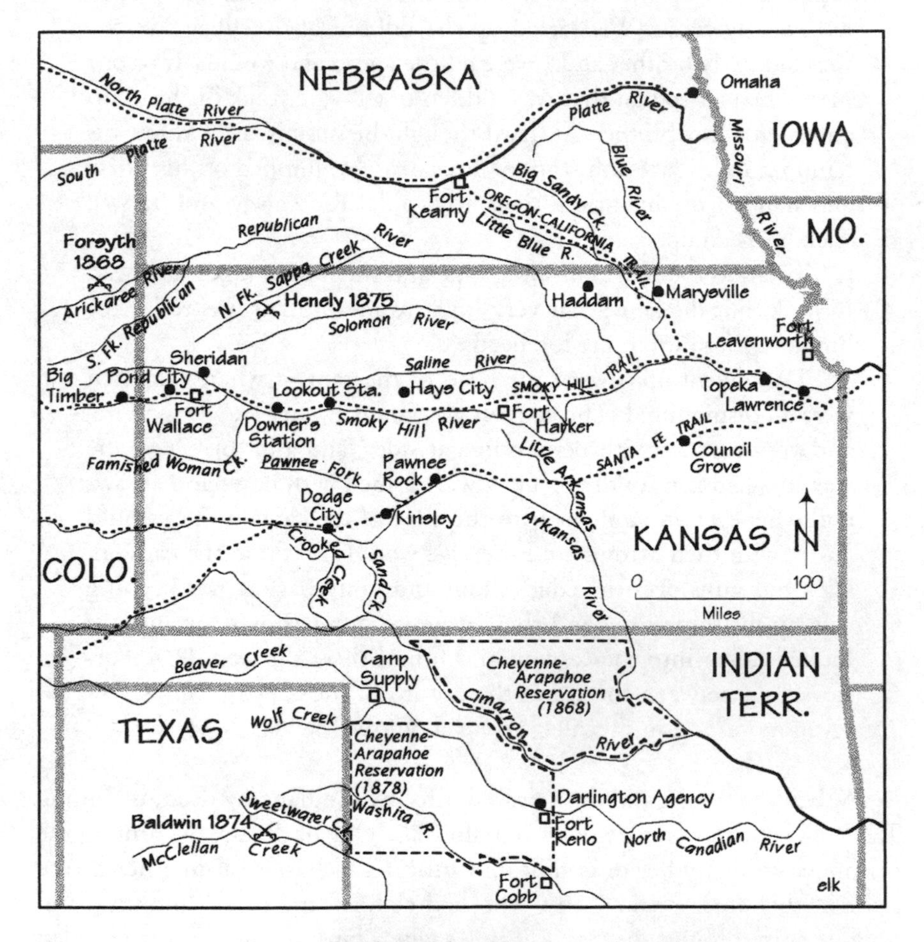

Southern battleground.

Another reason for anger was the repeated invasion of the reservations by white horse thieves and desperadoes. Attempts by authorities to punish the culprits, though sincere, were largely ineffectual.

"This . . . tends to make horse-thieves, whisky-peddlers, buffalo-hunters, and law-breakers generally bold and defiant," warned the hard-pressed agent of the Cheyenne and Arapahoe. "I was threatened with mob-law by a prominent paper in southern Kansas, for having a party of buffalo-hunters removed from the reservation."[6]

As the agent suggested, another cause of Indian outrage was the decimation of the once-great buffalo herds. Although the Indian often was no more economical of the buffalo than the white—sometimes killing for sport and often slaughtering vast numbers to obtain the succulent tongue—the increasing flood of whites and their more efficient killing methods were deeply resented. A glimpse at the carnage was given by a passenger on the Kansas Pacific, who saw herds of buffalo trying to cross the track.

> During these races the car-windows are opened and numerous breech-loaders fling hundreds of bullets among the densely crowded and flying masses. Many of the poor animals fall, and more go off to die in the ravines. The train speeds on, and the scene is repeated every few miles until Buffalo Land is passed . . . .
>
> All over the plains, lying in disgusting masses of putrefaction along valley and hill, are strewn immense carcasses of wantonly slain buffalo. They line the Kansas Pacific Railroad for two hundred miles.[7]

Each year, fewer and fewer of the great beasts made the migration to Indian Territory.

Yet another reason for restlessness on the reservation was the very nature of the Indians. Although readily acknowledging the other factors, Colonel Nelson Miles attributed much of their discontent to their own war-like attitude and an innate love of adventure.

"The Indians," he wrote, "accustomed from childhood to the wild excitement of the chase, or conflict with some other hostile tribe, taught that murder is noble and labor degrading, can not be expected to suddenly change their natures and become peaceful agriculturists."[8]

Thus it was that in May 1874, the disgruntled tribes bolted from their reservations and took to the warpath. "I propose now, if let alone," snapped an exasperated and determined General Sheridan, "to settle the Indian matter in the Southwest forever."

Since the small force at hand could not corner the raiders in such country, the strategy was simple: Keep them moving "until the cold weather and starvation force them in." Nevertheless, the favorite haunt of the tribes, the headwaters of the Red River in Texas, contained some of the most forbidding terrain on the Plains, and merely trailing the Indians would prove difficult. That Sheridan clearly understood the job at hand was evident when the Dallas *Herald* quoted him as saying, "If he owned hell and Texas, he would rent out the latter and move to hell."[9]

In June, a band of Comanche, Kiowa, and Cheyenne swooped down on a camp of white buffalo hunters at Adobe Walls in Texas. After a furious fight and siege, the enraged attackers drew off with heavy loss. Other unsuspecting hunters and traders were killed or driven out. Although dubbed the Red River War, the attacks were not confined to the panhandles of Texas and Indian Territory but occurred as far north as the Smoky Hill Trail in Kansas. There, a Cheyenne war party butchered five members of an immigrant family and carried Catherine German and her three sisters into captivity. On the banks of Crooked Creek in southern Kansas, six surveyors were slaughtered; two of the victims were brained by their own heavy transit.

While the Indians carried out small raids, they wisely avoided the army columns that scoured the region. Increasingly, the Red River campaign became a game of cat and mouse in which scouts on both sides played leading roles. As the diary of scout Thompson McFadden reveals, the road was hard.

> **August 30th:** After a miserable night of thirst and lying in the sand burrs, we are in the saddle at daylight and follow the trail through a very rough cedar canyon country . . . . While riding up a ravine . . . I came across a beautiful little spring of water bubbling out from under the roots of a cedar tree and sinking into the sandy soil within a few feet of its source . . . . Springing from my saddle, I laid aside my sombrero and, flopping flat on my belly with a "Thank God" for the blessing, I gulped down about a gallon of water which was quite cold. I only desisted when out of breath, when horror upon horrors, I found it more salty than the stream upon which we had camped, with the addition of something as bitter as quinine and puckering my mouth like green persimmon . . . . I don't think I've uttered another prayer today . . . .
>
> We have not as yet caught sight of a single Indian, but the indications are that they are not far ahead of us, and so it proved; for upon nearing the hill (the scouts being about two miles in advance of the troops) we were charged upon with no previous warning by about two hundred fifty of the Red Devils, who came swooping over the hill like a Kansas cyclone, with the evident intention of riding us down and killing us all before the soldiers could reach us . . . .

Myself and a Delaware Indian being the farthest out, they aimed to cut us off . . . . They came so close . . . that they hurled a spear at my companion; but slightly missing its aim, the staff of the spear . . . knocked him senseless from his horse . . . . I dismounted hastily and commenced firing into them . . . . My Delaware friend soon scrambled to his feet and looked around in a dazed sort of a way, looking for his horse and wondering no doubt how it all happened . . . . [W]e regained the little band of scouts who had dismounted and were pouring a galling fire into their ranks . . . .

The troops in our rear . . . came to our relief and we charged the hill in our front and dislodged the braves . . . . The Indians . . . made a grand display as they formed their lines with their chiefs riding to and fro giving orders . . . while from a clump of trees . . . came the sound of a tom-tom or Indian drum, this presumably being done by their medicine man for luck. But his medicine was no good, for when our gatling guns were brought into play, it seemed to demoralize them, and after a few faint efforts to charge us, they began to waver, and we, following upon every advantage, soon had them in full retreat. A running fight followed which brought us to the banks of Red River . . . .

August 31st: The cavalry move at daylight . . . . We . . . lie down and sleep sweetly among the tarantulas and centipedes which abound here . . . .

September 2nd: [O]ne man and myself are ordered to report to General [Nelson] Miles, where we learn we are to be sent to Camp Supply, a distance of nearly 200 miles, with dispatches . . . . We were advised to keep a sharp lookout . . . but the general was of the opinion that the Indians were all in our front. After a handshake and adios, we start on our lonesome and perilous trip, on horses so jaded, being hardly able to raise a hard gallop . . . .

September 3rd: [M]aking about sixty miles . . . . We supped on hard tack and water, laid down to sleep with one eye open, built no fire for precaution sake.

September 4th: At the first break of dawn in the east, we are in the saddle . . . . We take a northeast course towards Sweetwater Creek. Upon reaching higher ground, I perceived unmistakeable signs which betoken us no good . . . .

We had by this time crossed the divide and were nearing Sweetwater Creek, where sure enough right in front in the valley, we saw six horsemen not more than a mile distant and, upon looking up the valley . . . we saw a large outfit of something raising a big dust . . . . Hoping that we would escape notice under cover of [a] ravine, we reached the creek, watered our horses, and quickly filled our canteens. We crossed over . . . [and] reach the higher ground in safety and are about to congratulate ourselves in not having been discovered, when lo—here they come—five of them—with a yell and worse than all the sixth one off up the creek in the direction of the main body. All is explained in an instant. Those five will engage us until that devil can come with reinforcements and then they will have a picnic. 'Tis no use to run, our horses are nearly worn out and the country in our front is sand hills. We halt, dismount and, in sheer desperation, I take off my hat and wave it over my head, answering back their menace as though as eager for a scrap as they. This proved to be the best that could have been done for it cooled their ardor and caused them to change their minds as to riding us down and killing us like turkeys; for after an interchange of shots . . . they went to cover under the hill we occupied . . . .

"Now," said I, "this is our chance for escape. We have . . . bluffed them out. It is now nearly night and, if we can elude that other party for two hours more, we're all right."

Mounting our horses we move off northeast through the sand hills as fast as our poor horses could admit of. We manage to keep under cover for about four miles . . . . Looking back, we saw a party of at least fifty coming up out of the Sweetwater Valley. These were the reinforcements that the low devil had gone after, but they are too late, for we are four miles away and the sun is down . . . .

September 6th: Start as soon as we can see. We travel on Wolf Creek . . . [and] met here . . . two scouts . . . . [They] were in a sorrowful plight; had . . . been harassed by savages night and day for almost a fortnight, having been driven hither and thither in all directions. They said it seemed as though the entire country was full of Indians and they would no sooner elude one band until they would encounter another; they had ridden their horses until completely broken down and were compelled to abandon them . . . . They were nearly starved; feet blistered, and worn to the quick . . . .

> [W]e proceed to Camp Supply . . . . We had made the trip of about 240 miles on jaded horses, through a country swarming with hostile savages, in four days and nights, and have not lost a hair.
>
> **September 7th:** We start on our return to the command . . . through a drenching rain . . . .
>
> **September 8th:** [U]pon rounding a point in the little valley, we came suddenly upon a band of about thirty Indians who were dismounted on a hillside west of the trail, but hidden from it, with one of their number lying flat on top of the hill watching the trail . . . . They saw us about as soon as we did them, however, and immediately gave chase. We had about a quarter of a mile head start, and being fairly well mounted, we made our escape, but 'twas an exciting race for they tried their best to cut off our retreat in the direction of Wolf Creek, where we knew that the train we had met a few hours before had camped for the night. When almost dark, we sighted the camp and they abandoned the chase.[10]

Returning from dispatch duty to actual scouting, McFadden had the task two months later of locating a good campsite for a patrol he was leading.

> About a mile in our front is a nice clump of timber and we see something moving that looks like horses and upon rounding a little range of sandhills and looking up a ravine, we discover an Indian lodge. We at once conclude that we have struck a camp as it is fair to presume that there are more lodges farther up the ravine. The sergeant and men said to me, "Guide, what shall we do?" I said first drop back a few yards out of sight, now secure the pack horses and detail three or four men to take care of them and we will charge the camp for 'tis evident 'tis a very small party or else 'tis a squaw camp . . . . If they are squaws and children we will capture them and hold as hostages for our own safety. If warriors we will surprise them so badly that we will whip them at the first dash . . . .
>
> So with strained nerve and revolvers in hand, at a signal we drove the spurs into our horses' flanks and charged over the hill . . . . We found but one lodge and but one Indian and he had been dead at least a fortnight. The riddle was now solved. The lodge had been erected over some big brave who had been killed in a recent engagement and the horses we had seen were buffalo with some Texas cat-

> tle that were running wild with the buffalo. The soldiers wanted to drag the dead Indian down off of his platform and carry off the trinkets deposited with him, but I objected, telling them that this was probably the only "Good Indian" we would encounter on our trip.[11]

Few scouts displayed McFadden's scruples. While searching for water, Lem Wilson discovered an unattended campfire and investigated.

> I'd just got two or three feet from th' fire when a big, fine lookin' Indian comes into sight just a few feet away. He had been sittin' behind a big stump whettin' a long butcher knife, and I suppose came out to take a look at th' roast . . . . Just as soon as he saw me, he made a jump forward raisin' his knife and lettin' th' whetstone fall from his other hand. And I let him have it, th' bullet hittin' him just above th' chin and comin' out th' back of his head. He dropped in his tracks, never knowin' what struck him. He only kicked once or twice . . . . I took his knife and scalped him, takin' a much bigger hunk of his scalp than Indians usually took, makin' it almost big enough for a wig. It was th' happiest moment of my life . . . . I was like a wild man. I was wavin' th' bloody scalp in one hand and th' Indian's knife in th' other. All th' hatred I had for them cusses that had been tryin' to kill me for years was turned loose inside of me and outside.
>
> Th' lieutenant was pretty mad when he saw what I'd done. He was afraid I might start a general attack . . . . When he was through ravin' I says: "Lieutenant, I don't give a damn what you think about it! You can talk all you please about orders! I ain't in th' army! But if I was it wouldn't change me . . . . Whenever I sees a wild Indian I'm goin' to shoot him. . . . And if I can I'm goin' to scalp him, too—don't you forget that, lieutenant!" . . .
>
> [W]hile we was chewin' th' rag th' friendly Indians . . . were cuttin' off th' fingers of th' dead buck to get th' brass and silver rings he was wearin'. That boiled me all over. I made a run for them and pushed and kicked 'em away from th' corpse.
>
> "Get the hell outta here!" I yelled. "This is my Indian!"[12]

As intended, Sheridan's strategy kept the Indians moving, wearing them down mentally and physically. In September, Colonel Ranald Mackenzie surprised a large village in Palo Duro Canyon. Although most of the warriors escaped, a thousand indispensable ponies were captured and killed.[13]

On the morning of November 8, 1874, advance scouts spotted tepees on the prairie above McClellan Creek in Texas. Soon after receiving the news, a small force led by Lieutenant Frank Baldwin immediately attacked. The surprise was complete and while some pursued the fleeing Cheyenne, others rummaged through the camp. According to Baldwin, the soldiers had just begun their looting when they were startled by a strange sight.

> [A]ttention was centered on a warrior returning on horseback. Silently they scrutinized his every move and wondered what his object in returning alone might be. They saw him raise his revolver, so they aimed at him, but the savage fired first, then one of the soldiers shot him.
>
> The Indian had fired at a pile of buffalo robes and blankets which were near a fallen lodge. The soldiers saw the robe move so they investigated. Cautiously they lifted the robe with the end of a rifle, thinking perhaps an Indian might be hiding there, but no, they found one of the white girl captives. She was sick and very weak, dirty and half-starved . . . .
>
> "What is your name, dear little girl?" they asked her.
>
> She replied, "My name is Julia German, and Addie and Sophia were here awhile ago."
>
> Soon they found Addie in a near-by lodge, trying to place a few sticks on the fire, so as to keep warm. She was so weak that she fell to the ground every few steps . . . . Sergeant Mahoney was so moved with compassion . . . that he wept . . . . He gently lifted frail little Addie, and held her close for a time. After he released her she sat alone on the ground, watching with large, sad blue eyes, all that went on about her. Some soldiers spoke to her and she said, "What kind of Indians are you?"[14]

Despite the army's best efforts, however, there was no swift, dramatic rescue of the girls' older sisters, Catherine and Sophia.

Hounded relentlessly, the Indians were ultimately forced to seek refuge on the bleak, wind-swept plains of Texas and New Mexico, where the harsh winter caused much pain and suffering. Admitting defeat, most of the errant bands had slipped back to their reservations by February 1875. On March 1, some of the last Cheyenne holdouts limped in to their agency at Darlington. Catherine German recalled:

> Just before the sun set we came to the soldier's camp. They stood at the side of the trail cheering. We stopped, but I could hardly say

Addie and Julia German. KANSAS STATE HISTORICAL SOCIETY.

> anything, and when I think of it now a lump rises in my throat. Oh, I was so glad. I thought I had never seen such white people . . . . [T]hey seemed so white and pretty . . . . We cried and cried for joy as we rode into safety among our people.
>
> "Safe at last! Safe at last!" were the words that repeated themselves in my mind.[15]

Outraged by the brutal treatment of the two girls and angered at the other crimes and massacres, the authorities sentenced seventy-two of the main instigators of the uprising to exile at Fort Marion, Florida. "I think this finishes the war," wrote a buoyant Lt. Col. Thomas Neill.[16]

"[T]hey have been almost constantly harassed, hunted down and whipped in every engagement of importance," added his commander, Nelson Miles, "until the powerful tribes that a few months ago went forth confident in the possession of abundant weapons of war, their thousands of ponies, and their own prowess, have been thoroughly subjugated, humbled and impoverished.[17]

Unfortunately, both assessments were premature. One month after the release of the German girls, a large band of Southern Cheyenne dug up a cache of weapons and set off to join their northern brethren in Montana. Although a number of them soon returned under a promise of amnesty, many continued their trek north. Ironically, the bloodiest engagement of the war would take place on a tiny creek in Kansas, hundreds of miles from the Red River.

After trailing them for several days, at dawn on April 23, Lieutenant Austin Henely and a company of cavalry discovered a Cheyenne camp on the north fork of Sappa Creek. As Henely later reported:

> I intended to intrude myself between the Indians and their herd and attack them if they did not surrender . . . . As we charged down the side of the bluff I could see about ten or twelve Indians running rapidly up the bluff to a small herd of ponies—others escaped down the creek to another herd, while the remainder, the last to be awakened probably, seeing that they could not escape, prepared for a desperate defense . . . . I formed my men rapidly into line and motioned the Indians to come in . . . . One Indian, who appeared to be a chief, made some rapid gesticulation, which I at first thought was for a parley but soon discovered it was directed to those in rear. I gave the command to fight on foot . . . .
>
> As the men dismounted, the Indians fired, but excitedly, as fortunately no one was hit. I then ordered my men to fire and posted them around the crest in skirmish line.[18]

With the Indians fighting from holes dug in the sand, the struggle soon turned fierce. Two troopers were killed within twenty feet of the pits. "The lieutenant had some trouble in getting his men to lie down," said Homer Wheeler, a scout with the troopers. "They fought like madmen. Their whole desire seemed to be to charge the Indians and drive them out." Wheeler continues:

> Finally, we got down to business, and whenever an Indian showed his head we would shoot at it. It seemed as if we never would drive them out. Some of them hid behind the creek bank and the men could only see them when they raised their heads to shoot.
>
> I went around to the rear, unnoticed by them, but to do this had to crawl some distance on my hands and knees through the grass. From my new position I could see the Indians lying along the bank, and I soon drove them from this position. As soon as they had discovered me they all commenced firing on me and made it mighty uncomfortable, and I was not slow to leave my dangerous position. I had to run the gauntlet for some fifty yards in order to reach a place

> of safety. I ran in a zigzag manner, falling down two or three times, which no doubt saved me, as the bullets whistled around me as thick as bees when swarming . . . .
>
> While I was in that position, a large Indian dog came running toward me. I was somewhat frightened and was about to shoot it. When about five yards from me the animal turned and ran in a different direction, evidently having just discovered me.[19]

Returning to Henely:

> After firing about twenty minutes and the Indians having ceased firing, I withdrew my men and their horses for the purpose of pursuing the Indians who had escaped. Hardly had we mounted when the Indians ran up to the two bodies which had been carried some distance up the ridge. I immediately detached three or four men at a gallop to charge them and the Indians retreated, accomplishing nothing. Just then an Indian, gaudily decked, jumped from a hole and with peculiar side-long leaps attempted to escape, which he did not. I then posted my men at the two ends of the crest . . . . [T]he Indians return[ed] the fire from their holes . . . for some time when the firing again ceased and I concluded all were dead.[20]

When yet another shot rang out from the pits and struck a horse, the angry lieutenant at last decided to make a "sure finish" and ordered the charge. Within minutes, all opposition ceased. "Nineteen dead warriors were counted," Henely concluded, "[and] eight (8) squaws and children were unavoidably killed by shots intended for the warriors. From the war bonnets and rich ornaments, I judge two were chiefs and one whose bonnet was surmounted by two horns to be a medicine man . . . . I then burned all their lodges and threw some of the arms into the fire, destroying also a quantity of ammunition."[21]

"[W]hat was supposed to be a roll of plunder was carelessly tossed into a roaring fire of tepees and tepee poles," remembered one trooper, "when an outcry told them that the roll contained a living human being, a little Indian papoose."[22]

On that sad note, the Red River War ended and all Indian resistance on the southern Plains ceased. "This campaign was not only comprehensive, but it was the most successful of any Indian campaign in this country since its settlement by the whites," praised a much elated commander, Philip Sheridan.[23]

In the meantime, Catherine German and her sisters were trying to piece their lives back together. Unknown to Catherine, throughout her captivity, during all the rapes and beatings, during the freezing nights and terrifying days, the little bottle of hope that she had secretly tossed into a trickle of water in northern Texas had, despite snags and shoals, continued its journey down a muddy prairie river. Four months after Catherine's rescue, a Kansas newspaper reported:

> Strange to say, after having traveled eight hundred or one thousand miles along the devious windings and changing current . . . a bottle . . . was picked up on the beach of the Gulf of Mexico near the mouth of the Brazos River, in which upon examination, was a written account of the capture of . . . .[24]

12

The Girl I Left Behind Me

On a bright summer day in 1873, Libbie Custer, her husband George, and a fellow officer, steered their horses gently through the tall cottonwoods that fringed the Missouri River. On the highlands far to the rear rumbled the 7th Cavalry, bound for its new home in Dakota Territory, Fort Abraham Lincoln. Since their marriage during the Civil War, Libbie and the colonel had become all but inseparable. No matter how remote the assignment, she had somehow found a way to join her mate. As to the risks of following a soldier over the untamed prairie, the pretty young woman well understood.

> During the five years I had been with the regiment in Kansas I had marched many hundred miles. Sometimes I had to join my husband going across a dangerous country, and the exposure from Indians all those years had been constant. I had been a subject of conversation among the officers, being the only woman who, as a rule, followed the regiment, and, without discussing it much in my presence, the universal understanding was that any one having me in charge in an emergency where there was imminent danger of my capture should shoot me instantly. While I knew that I was defended by strong hands and brave hearts, the thought of the double danger always flashed into my mind when we were in jeopardy.[1]

Despite her years in the wilderness and her understandable fears, Libbie had never been in any real peril. So, on this sunny, cheerful day in Dakota, as the trio moved quietly through the woods, danger was never further from her mind.

Suddenly, a deer bolted from the brush. Ever the hunter, Custer dashed away in pursuit. Libbie and her amused escort watched briefly but soon resumed their leisurely ride. After only a short distance, however, the woman's horse grew nervous and balked. Then, for no apparent reason, the beast reared wildly. At that moment, Libbie saw a sight that made her heart stop.

> Without the least warning, in the dead stillness of that desolate spot, we suddenly came upon a group of young Indian warriors seated . . . in the underbrush. I became perfectly cold and numb with terror . . . . If time could have been measured by sensations, a cycle seemed to have passed in those few seconds. The Indians snatched up their guns, leaped upon their ponies, and prepared for attack. The officer with me was perfectly calm, spoke to them cooly without a change of voice, and rode quickly beside me, telling me to advance. My horse . . . started to run. Gladly would I have put him to his mettle then, except for the instinct of obedience . . . . I managed to check my horse and did not scream . . . .
>
> Whether because of the coolness of the officer, or because the warriors knew of the size of the advancing column, we were allowed to proceed unharmed. How interminable the distance seemed to where the general awaited us, unconscious of what we had encountered! I was lifted out of the saddle a very limp and unconscious thing.[2]

Few women on the frontier ever had such an experience but an encounter like this was never far from their thoughts. All the same, in spite of the risks and hardships, scores of women insisted on joining their soldier husbands in the West. Some wives, like Libbie, roamed the Plains from motives of love or, again like Libbie, were drawn by a simple spirit of adventure. Because an officer's pay was low, other women found it impossible to maintain two homes—one in the East and one in the West. In addition, envy may have prompted some army wives to journey west, as a letter from Alice Baldwin to her husband, Frank, seems to imply.

> It is so easy for you to tell me to not be so discouraged & blue & to not feel uneasy but with you how different from me. You are living a life fraught with peril & excitement . . . you are living the Life you love—that's everything and besides all this you are a Man! Now look

> at me—I am a woman with all the love & anxiety of a wife for the man she loves. I have no stirring scenes to pass thro—there are no eventful episodes in my existence. I am not living the life I love. All I have . . . are a few paltry insignificant duties to perform & that makes up my daily life.[3]

After a woman finally made up her mind to go, the jolt to those remaining could be severe, as Elizabeth Burt discovered.

> When we announced this decision to our families a great outcry was raised together with urgent protests against this rash resolution. The idea of our taking our two-year-old baby out on the frontier . . . was preposterous. Pictures of the trials of soldier life were given us from all quarters—principally of wild Indians, tent life, in the snow and again in burning sands, all painted in vivid colors.[4]

Before the advent of railroads, the trek across the Plains was a vastly more daunting endeavor for the wives. Not only was the journey painfully slow, but for most "she-soldiers" it could be terribly tedious. "We . . . found nothing but stage stations to relieve the monotony," Mrs. Burt continued. "They afforded nothing to interest us except the chance of receiving news from the passengers as they passed east and west each day, and occasionally left a precious newspaper . . . . One day was much like another day."[5]

Monotonous as most miles were, the trail west could at any moment display surprising peril. Though Indian attacks were certainly the most dreaded of dangers, it was the mundane but equally menacing hazards that most often greeted the wives. At a temporary camp in Dakota, Libbie Custer was overcome by heat one day and forced to her cot. "In my indolent, weak condition," she recalled, "hearing a peculiar sound, I looked down and saw a huge rattlesnake gliding towards me. I had long ago learned to suppress shrieks, but I forgot all such self-control then . . . . The snake was soon despatched."[6]

There also were diseases, storms, and other natural calamities on the trail. When she reached a ferry on the North Platte in Wyoming, Mrs. Burt and her party found a torrent.

> After waiting a few days hoping for a fall in the river, the perilous trip began . . . . Mrs. McClintock, my sister and I sat with our two babies on the shore watching the progress with great interest. The Headquarters ambulance was over with safety; then came Mrs. McClintock's turn in her ambulance with her baby and nurse. All was safe thus far. Then came our ambulance with my husband's

assurance that all would be well; he crossed with us in safety and then returned to bring his company over.

It was not long before a crash came. In a second we saw the boat overturned in the stream; the white wagon top was carried down; mules quickly disappeared and alas, also the three men who were with the wagon. All vanished like a flash. The wagon proved to be one belonging to Company F, and with it was Sergeant St. John, one of my husband's most reliable non-commissioned officers, and two good men of the company. The sergeant's wife and two children were sitting near us on the bank. The suspense was agonizing while we waited a long time before it was known who were the unfortunate victims.[7]

The completion of the railroads relieved much of the tedium and most of the terror of a trip across the Plains. All the same, many forts lay well beyond the tracks and could be reached only by wagon, coach, or mount.

"[M]y heart sank within me," admitted Ada Vogdes after stepping from the cars only to discover that Fort Laramie was still several days away. "I thought of all the miles to be gone over with only mule power, and no rail road to call upon in case of necessity. Oh! It was a fearful feeling for me, in the midst of an Indian country, and far from home."[8]

In most cases, first encounters with the Indians Ada so feared were with "friendlies." "While we were waiting for the boat to be repaired," Elizabeth Burt later wrote, referring to the ferry disaster, "a startling episode occurred."

A large number of Indians appeared among us, with professions of friendship . . . . Dressed in bright blankets and buckskin shirts and leggins, with necklaces and trimmings of elk teeth and beads, with their hair decorated in feathers, and ornamented moccasins on their feet, their appearance was very picturesque. Evidently they were in their gala attire for our benefit for they never travel in their "best clothes.". . . At night when their camp fires lighted the bluffs, where their tepees were pitched, the scene was extremely picturesque. Their weird songs added interest to the novel sight. However, there was great rejoicing when they stole quietly away in the early dawn.[9]

Other Indians frequented frontier trails to buy, sell, trade, or simply visit. Remembered Libbie Custer:

These visitors grew to be great trials, for they were inveterate beggars. One day an old Indian . . . came riding in, elaborately decorated and on a shapely pony. He demanded to see the chief. The general appeared, assisted him to dismount, and seated him in my camp-chair. The savage leaned back in a grand sort of manner and calmly surveyed us all. I was soon in agonies of anxiety, for Colonel Tom [Custer] and the young officers lounging near entered the tent. They bowed low, took the hand of the old fellow with profound deference, and, smiling benignly, addressed him. In just as suave a voice as if their words had been genuine flattery, they said, "You confounded old galoot, why are you here begging and thieving, when your wretched old hands are hardly dry from some murder, and your miserable mouth still red from eating the heart of your enemy?" Each one saluted him, and each vied with the other in pouring forth a tirade of forcible expletives, to which he bowed in acknowledgment and shook hands. My terror was that he might understand, for we often found these people as cunning as foxes, sitting stolid and stupid, pretending not to know a word, while they understood the gist of much that was said.[10]

On more than one occasion, the worst fears of a mother seemed close to reality. Elizabeth Burt:

One of the chiefs made an astounding proposition to buy our dear baby boy. It took time for us to realize his offer was made in earnest. "Ten ponies?"—"No, indeed." "Twenty?" Then we began to feel he really meant this as a bona fide proposition. The monstrous idea! "Thirty ponies?" "No—no—no," and our dear boy was tightly clasped in my arms and carried into the tent. After this, when an Indian appeared, a terrible fear seized me that our boy might be stolen and we held a closer watch over him than ever.[11]

Once the women and their party reached hostile territory, there was no mistaking the matter. Libbie Custer's first hint of trouble came when she saw strips of red cloth fastened to stakes. "[W]e came upon another premonitory warning from the Indians," noted the anxious woman. "A pole was found stuck in the trail before us, with a red flag, to which were fastened locks of hair. It was a challenge, and when interpreted meant, that if we persisted in advancing, the hostiles were ready to meet the soldiers and fight them. The officers paid little attention to this, but my heart was like lead for days afterwards."[12]

On their way to Colorado, Colonel Andrew and Eveline Alexander encountered an even more graphic warning. According to Eveline:

> On top of the highest butte was a pole with something hanging from it and waving in the wind which, exciting our attention, Andrew sent a man up after it. He succeeded in scaling the butte and returned a human scalp, dried and stretched within a small reed hoop! It was fastened securely to the pole by thongs of buckskin. It was evidently, from the color and texture of the hair, a white woman's scalp . . . . We had the guides up, and from what they said came to the conclusion it was the scalp of a little girl about twelve years old.[13]

It was relatively rare, but sometimes army wives came under attack. At an evening camp on Crazy Woman's Fork in Wyoming, Elizabeth Burt recorded:

> [W]e were all startled by the sudden rush of the herd following the bell mare into the corral on the run. The Indians were on us. Some of them were even among the herd waving buffalo robes endeavoring to bring a stampede. Their wild whoops pierced our ears and then bang, bang, bang went the rifles of our men . . . . My boy, my boy! was my first thought, for he slept outside the corral in his father's tent among those of the other officers and men. My anguish was greatly relieved when Dr. Frantz appeared at the door with our dear boy in his arms . . . . The shots still continued, however, so my sister and I and Christina lay flat on the mattress trying to present as small a target as possible. Trembling with fear and uncertainty, with both children held closely in my arms, we waited to know the result. At last the firing ceased but our anxiety and fears in the stillness were only relieved when my husband opened the door saying: "It is all over, no one is hurt and the herd safe in the corral. There is no danger of another attack."
>
> Tears of thankfulness were mingled with our prayers and my husband added: "Those were sure enough war whoops—how did you like them?"[14]

Unlike Elizabeth Burt, Libbie Custer, and Eveline Alexander, not all wives ventured west surrounded by soldiers. Some, from necessity or impulse, set out via any conveyance at hand. While rumbling through Nebraska, one woman discovered the stage she was on had abruptly entered hostile land.

> [S]uddenly twenty-five Indians emerged from the bluffs and commenced firing at the coach. They aimed first to kill the horses and prevent the further progress of the coach, but in this cruel design they utterly failed . . . . While the horses were running at full speed,

Willie and the two other gentlemen got on top of the coach and kept up a continuous fire. One Indian was killed, which feat Willie accomplished with his heavy rifle.

After the first fire . . . I became so excited that I could not keep my eyes off of them. It was the most beautiful fighting I had ever seen. Such drilled men—it seemed that every foot of ground over which they rode had been measured off. Such bravery on the part of the Indians is thought unequaled. In the midst of all none of us were hurt, and consequently we kept up our running and fighting until we reached camp . . . .

Now that it is all over, and we got so safely out of it, I do not regret or wish it had not been, but it is the last fight I ever want to have a hand in. I would not take the trip again for the world.[15]

After an arduous trek across the Plains, most army wives found small solace at the end of the trail. "When at last we drove up to my 'future home,'" remembered Alice Baldwin, "I found it to be merely another dug-out."

I exclaimed, "Why, where is our house?" and before my husband could reply, the sole occupant of the dug-out . . . came bustling up the few steps. He apologized and explained that he hadn't started a fire because the Indians had attacked the wood-train the day before, killing two soldiers, and they were "shy" of wood . . . .

When I first entered my new abode I gazed with disgusted disappointment around the bare, squalid room. Its conveniences were limited to one camp chair, two empty candle boxes and a huge box stove, red with rust and grime . . . . The sordid interior filled me with gloom, scarcely lessened by the four-pane glass window, dirty, dim and curtainless.

Exploring the "inner regions" I found the kitchen scarcely big enough to contain a stove, and such an array of cooking utensils as I had never before beheld lay on the dirt floor and on a packing box, which served duty as a kitchen table! The walls of the kitchen were stayed and supported by logs, while the ceiling was of the same material and covered with dirt. The logs had not been trimmed or cut off, and obliged one to bend low when passing underneath.

The "drawing room," as my soldier-husband facetiously called it, had a board floor, unplaned and full of slivers. Canvas covered the ceiling and dirt sides. It sagged slightly in the center and trembled under the scampering feet of pack-rats and prairie mice. The canvas cover not quite extending on one end, the pack-rats would perch on

Frank and Alice Baldwin. THE HUNTINGTON LIBRARY.

the beams, rear up on their hind legs, with their bushy tails hanging below, and survey me with their beady eyes.[16]

From Montana, Elizabeth Burt could commiserate with Alice Baldwin. "The floor was of dirt beaten hard and covered with gunny sacks," she recalled. "At night, beds were made on the floor in the front room . . . . [E]ach morning they were piled in the back room and the table was prepared for breakfast. After this repast, we made ourselves as comfortable as possible in these two rooms."[17]

For women raised in the East, life in the West could be one trial after another. When a false alarm of an Indian attack was sounded one night at Fort Hays, it ignited an incredible series of entries in Jennie Barnitz's journal, in which all man and nature seemed determined to destroy her.

> **June 5.** The camp was aroused, guns were fired, bugles sounded, & after a great deal of excitement . . . [we] found all safe. Gen Gibbs was so intoxicated he could not give an order, scarcely walk. Oh! it is dreadful . . . . The guns were fired so at random & in every direction that we were really in great danger of being shot. Some fell down in the grass, or went into ravines to escape the balls, but at last everything was quiet . . . .
>
> **June 6.** To night we were invited to Gen Gibbs. The Gen. was drunk, as usual! It is lightning to night & looks like a storm. Oh I am afraid of storms here, but we will hope for the best.
>
> **June 7.** Oh! what a night I passed. Such a storm I had hardly conceived of . . . . The lightning was chain & burst like rockets, & some said [it] fairly hissed & fell like stars. The whole air was filled with electricity. The thunder I cannot describe. Much heavier than cannonading, & so very near us. It was terrific . . . . The rain fell in torrents, and the wind blew fearfully . . . . At about 3 O'C a m Gen Smith came to our tent & screamed, "For God's sake Barnitz get up, we are under water." . . . With one shoe & one of Alberts boots . . . [I] took my watch jewelry & money & went out never expecting to see my things again. The sight was fearful. The creek upon which we were encamped & which had been very shallow the previous day, now was a mighty rushing river, & I think I never saw so strong a current. A few feet back of us, where before had been dry land, was another river madly rushing along, so we were entirely surrounded on a little spot of land, & the water constantly rising . . . . The ladies were out half dressed, with hair over their shoulders, & to add to the terror of the scene, drowning men went floating past us shrieking for help, & we could not save them. Oh I can never forget those cries for help, never never . . . . The water was rising as rapidly as a man could step back to keep from it.[18]

Miraculously, the torrent soon crested then rapidly receded. Jennie continued:

> During the day the water was so low we could possibly have crossed, & how strange we did not, but drunken Generals thought it would rain no more & we stayed.
>
> **June 8.** About midnight . . . [i]t was raining harder than I ever heard it . . . . Almost a water spout & the wind blew even harder than the night before. I dressed myself again & went with Albert to Mrs Gen Custers in that fearful storm. They sent men out who came back and reported that the stream could not be crossed, that we had better risk our lives where we were. Once more we gave up. Mrs Custer says, "Well, we will all go down together. I am glad the Gen doesn't know of it."
>
> **June 9.** Daylight came again, & the water again commenced falling, & this time we moved & are now on the crest of a hill where we feel safe, comparatively. What an experience! May I never have to pass through such another![19]

In addition to storms and floods, the women suffered through scorching heat and dust. The frontier had many ways of breaking a strong spirit and of snuffing even the simplest of pleasures. The fate of a tiny canary, one of the few rays of sunshine in a lonely wife's otherwise gloomy life, was reported by a correspondent from rattlesnake-infested Camp Supply.

> The bird was in a cage, hanging near the eaves of [the] house . . . . Missing the sound of the canary Mrs. Hastings went to the cage to inquire into the silence. Gently lowering the cage, something was heard to drop, followed by a scream and running of footsteps to and fro . . . . [B]y some means a snake managed to get into the cage and swallowed the bird.[20]

Certainly, not every woman loathed life in the West. Libbie Custer flourished there. The same trials that so shattered Jennie Barnitz seemed little more than trifling adventures to young Mrs. Custer. "Our tents have been charmingly situated as regards shade and cool air," Libbie wrote from Fort Hays, "and with the exception of several freshets and some most terrific winds, nothing has troubled us . . . . One finds that a bedouin life in open air constantly gives such perfect health that such things as freshets and winds are quite small matters and forgotten as soon as over."[21]

Just as friendlies were usually the first Indians encountered on the trail, so too were "hangs-around-the-forts" the first met at frontier posts. While most were viewed as squalid, stupid brutes, there were exceptions. At Fort Bridger, Wyoming, Elizabeth Burt's husband, Andrew, and the Shoshoni chief Washakie became genuine friends. Major Burt:

> I had talked so much to my wife about Washakie, she became desirous of seeing him and asked me to invite him to our quarters. I invited him one day to call on Mrs. Burt and bring his squaw. At first he declined and when asked why he replied: "I got two squaws. You have only one. Your wife won't want to see one chief and two squaws. I bring one squaw other squaw get mad. I will have to lick 'em both make peace."
>
> At the appointed hour . . . Washakie . . . rang the bell of the front door . . . . I received the Chief, shook hands with him and went through the ceremony of presentation to Mrs. Burt. With extra elaborate politeness Washakie advanced, took her hand and said, "How. I like your man. Glad to see his wife."
>
> Mrs. Burt, Washakie and myself sat in the parlor chatting until dinner was announced. Upon acquainting Washakie with this fact, he arose in a dignified manner, turned and pulled his blanket around his shoulders . . . . He stood at complete ease until Mrs. Burt preceded us into the dining room, and upon a sign from me followed as if accustomed to such actions every day. In the dining room Mrs. Burt pointed out the seat he was to occupy and he stalked up to his chair but, to my utter amazement, he remained standing until Mrs. Burt took her seat at the head of the table and sat down. He remained perfectly passive awaiting Mrs. Burt's next move. She removed the bread from her napkin and placed it across her lap. He immediately did the same thing. Soup was served and I was anxious to see what he would do, for Indians have no regard for the silver . . . but again he did the right thing, picked up the soup spoon and ate as delicately as if he had been accustomed to it all his life. The same thing happened with his knife and fork as the turkey and other courses were served, and his dessert spoon came into use at the proper time. He took his after dinner coffee, used his finger bowl with a nicety and after Mrs. Burt had left the table joined me in a smoke and chat.[22]

Washakie. DENVER PUBLIC LIBRARY, WESTERN HISTORY DEPARTMENT.

After the successful defense of his High Plains hunting grounds in the late 1860s, an aging Red Cloud became a celebrity at forts in the region. Like Elizabeth Burt, Ada Vogdes opened her home on numerous occasions to the famous Sioux chief. One day Red Cloud discovered a photograph of his hostess. "After looking at it a moment, in the most affectionate manner," Ada wrote, "he kissed it, and said I was a 'washta squaw.'. . . He is really very polite, and dignified in all respects, and when he smiles I never saw a sweeter."[23]

Many humorous moments occurred during these visits. From Fort Lincoln, Libbie Custer recalled an incident when Running Antelope and several other warriors were in her home.

> While he spoke, lifting his graceful hands towards Heaven in appeal, one of my husband's birds that was uncaged floated down and alighted on the venerable warrior's head. It had been so petted, no ordinary movement startled the little thing. It maintained its poise, spreading its wings to keep its balance, as the Indian moved his head in gesture. The orator saw that the faces of the Indians showed signs of humor, but he was ignorant of what amused them. His inquiring

eyes saw no solution in the general's, for, fearing to disconcert him, General Custer controlled every muscle in his face. Finally the bird whirled up to his favorite resting-place on the horn of the buffalo head, and the warrior understood the unusual sight of a smile from his people.[24]

Not all women were so gracious and sensitive. During a peace council with the Kiowa and Southern Cheyenne at Fort Larned, several westering wives decided to get a closer look. According to Alice Baldwin:

> These Indians . . . all sat in a circle, silently smoking, with the interpreter, a half-breed woman, Celestia Adams. She was a good-looking woman, with her white blood predominating in her features and general appearance . . . . [S]everal officers . . . [were] seated in the circle. One of the women from among the traveling caravans seated herself next to Celestia, in spite of the latter's whispered remonstrances, and when the pipe of peace was passed around to each individual in the circle, she took a whiff herself, to the surprised consternation of her husband and the indignant chiefs. But it was done, and after asking Celestia to tell them to "come again," she withdrew from the circle.[25]

The head chief, Alice noted, "was insulted, and frowned with a malignant eye at the fun-loving white squaw."[26] The playful woman's antics were doubly mortifying to the Indian males because of their well-known attitude toward females. Elizabeth Burt recorded after warriors visited her home, "Women are such very inferior creatures in the estimation of an Indian, that . . . I engrossed little of their attention,"[27]

> My first impression of domestic life among the Indians was intensely disagreeable and prejudiced me greatly against the lordly chiefs. I saw one of them walking in front of a squaw, whose back was bent under a heavy sack of something, probably flour, while he, with his tall strong body wrapped in a gayly colored blanket, carried nothing but a stick. We stopped to watch them. Did he offer to help her carry the load? Not he indeed; but on the contrary would use the stick to poke her in the back, to urge her on when . . . he found her falling back with her heavy load. The brute![28]

Because of chronic overwork and the beatings many received, squaws aged rapidly. "Repulsive in appearance, their faces were full of deep lines, showing the hardships they must have endured," one shocked lady noted after viewing Cheyenne women.[29] Naturally, a degree of sympathy arose among white women. When the wife of a captain at Fort Arbuckle, Indian Territory, noticed a "most miserable and repulsive" Kiowa approach her home and suddenly pick up the couple's baby, she angrily snatched back her child.

> The poor miserable woman looked at me in the most pitiful manner, then gathering up the corner of her blanket she held it as one would hold a sick infant, at the same time crooning a mournful cry, she made a sign that her baby had died, and to tell how great her grief, she showed she had cut off her little finger at the second joint . . . . [M]y sympathies were so moved that almost unconsciously I replaced our baby in her arms. Tenderly and carefully, the bereaved Indian mother handled her as she passed her hands over the plump little limbs. After some moments she handed her back with a grateful look and with a hearty handshake she departed.[30]

The following week, the woman returned. Wrote the kind-hearted officer's wife, "this time . . . this sorrowing Indian mother was no longer repulsive."[31] To her surprise, Alice Baldwin also found that some sentiments were universal.

> I went around in the encampment and tents of the women. They were filled with wonder as to my attire, and urged by their innocent, and I must confess, feminine curiosity, I consented to undress and let them see for themselves. They crowded around me. Crinoline and corsets they marveled at, but did not admire. Through the interpreter, Mary . . . they said they did not see how I could wear so many clothes, and wished to know if I did not suffer from the heat and exhaustion when the weather was hot . . . . My hair . . . they were delighted with, and insisted that I take it down so they could see how much of it was mine. One ancient Crow woman, taking a strand in her hand, examined it carefully, and said she thought I had a scalp in my tresses.[32]

For many army wives, however, no amount of familiarity with friendlies could quell their fear of Indians. Some, like Ada Vogdes, were terrified by the world beyond Fort Laramie. "I am frightened nearly to death every evening, when the sun goes down, until it comes again," she confessed. "I [am] so afraid of Indians all the time."[33] Similarly, the log palisades of Fort C. F. Smith were cold comfort to Elizabeth Burt.

> The back part of our kitchen and dining room formed part of the stockade and, in spite of the unceasing vigilance of the sentinels, I thought how easy it would be for the Sioux to climb those logs and be upon us. The Major's chiding words, "Don't worry, the Indians will never attack us," could not entirely dispel my fears.[34]

A number of women, like Libbie Custer, discovered firsthand that their fears were amply justified. Riding a short distance from Fort Lincoln with her husband one day, a deer bounded into view and the couple gave chase.

> Scarcely any time elapsed before an officer and a detachment of men riding over the ground where we had started the deer . . . came to a horrible sight. The body of a white man was staked out on the ground and disembowelled. There yet remained the embers of the smouldering fire that consumed him . . . . The horror and fright this gave us women . . . rendered unnecessary the continued warnings of our husbands about walking outside the line of the pickets.[35]

As the weeks and months passed, however, the women realized that, except for raids on tempting horse herds, hostile Indians rarely came within rifle range of the forts and almost never assailed them directly. Thus, desperate to escape their self-imposed prisons, some wives found the allure of the countryside irresistible. Elizabeth Burt learned of a beautiful spring gurgling through a carpet of flowers just beyond the bleak walls of Fort C. F. Smith.

> The temptation to gather those flowers and to see the spring was great. Upon consultation with Kate and Mrs. Miller we yielded to the voice of the tempter and walked out of the gate, past the sentinel, very foolishly taking [my] four-year old . . . with us.
>
> The picture had not been overdrawn. The clear tiny spring flowed from the foot of the hill amid a bed of violets which we at once began to gather, together with several varieties of ferns. The pleasure of the outing was such that we unconsciously lengthened our stay beside the stream until to our consternation, we heard a shot fired by the bastion sentinel and the cry of "Indians, Indians" shouted by many voices within the stockade. For a moment we stood paralyzed with horror, then sister Kate screamed, "Run, run for your lives!"
>
> This cry broke the spell. My sister and I each grabbed a hand of the boy and gathering up our skirts ran as I believe no women ever

> ran before. We rushed into the stockade to see the officers and soldiers double-timing through the gates to meet the raiders . . . . As the troops arrived on the scene in a few minutes the Indians galloped off without doing any damage. I, of course, was waiting in fear and trembling to see my husband return. He greeted me with a reassuring smile saying, "My dear, you are pale and trembling . . . ."
>
> [H]enceforth our walks were limited to within a few feet of the gate of the stockade.[36]

"It seemed, sometimes, as if we must get outside of our prescribed limits," Libbie Custer wrote from Fort Hays. "The rolling bluffs beyond, tinged with green and beginning to have prairie flowers, looked so tempting. One evening we beguiled an officer . . . to take us for a little walk." As Libbie and her friends soon discovered, danger had many faces.

> At last our escort saw the dark coming on so fast he insisted upon going home, and we reluctantly turned. As we came toward the post, the shadows were deepening in the twilight, and the figures of the sentinels were not visible. A flash, followed by a sound past our ears . . . was the warning that we three were taken for Indians and fired upon by the sentinel. Another flash, but we stood rooted to the spot, stunned by surprise. The whiz and zip of the bullet seemed to be only a few inches from my ear. Still we were dazed, and had not the officer gained his senses our fate would have been then and there decided. The recruit, probably himself terrified, kept on sending those deadly little missives, with the terrible sound cutting the air around us. Our escort shouted, but it was too far for his voice to carry. Then he told us to run for our lives to a slight depression in the ground, and throw ourselves on our faces. I was coward enough to burrow mine in the prairie-grass . . . . [A]s I lay there quaking with terror, my body seemed to rise above the earth in such a monstrous heap that the dullest marksman . . . might easily perforate me with bullets. What ages it seemed while we waited in this prostrate position, commanded by our escort not to move! The rain of bullets at last ceased, and blessed quiet came.[37]

Lonely in the best of times, when the women watched their husbands prepare for long and dangerous Indian campaigns, the true meaning of the word became apparent. "Such partings are a torture that it is difficult even to refer to," Libbie Custer confessed. "My husband added another struggle to my lot by imploring me not to let him see the tears that he knew, for his sake, I could keep back until he was out of sight."[38]

"Our family farewells were always made in quarters behind closed doors," echoed Elizabeth Burt. "Then he to his duty and I in a back room to my tears and prayers. I would choose a back room to shut out the tune . . . 'The Girl I Left Behind Me.' To this day when I hear that air tears come to my eyes."[39]

"No expedition goes out with shout and song, if loving, weeping women are left behind," Libbie concluded. "There was silence as the column left the garrison . . . . [T]he closed houses they left were as still as if death had set its seal upon the door; no sound but the sobbing and moans of women's breaking hearts."[40]

13

Red is the Rosebud

In the fall of 1874, the first confirmation of gold in the Black Hills of Dakota reached the outside world. This cool, green oasis set down amid a burning waste, then a part of the Sioux Reserve, had remained a favorite resort of the Plains tribes from time immemorial and its secrets were jealously guarded. As one army officer recalled:

> Not infrequently they would pay traders for supplies in gold nuggets, but never would they tell where these nuggets were found. Whenever attempts were made to "pump" the Indians about the Black Hills country they would maintain a mysterious silence; naturally this mystery excited great curiosity. Stories and traditions of fabulous wealth there hidden were bandied about among the frontiersmen, but none had dared to go there.[1]

As word spread, the hysteria of sudden wealth swept the Plains. "In Cheyenne we could see and hear nothing but Black Hills," Lieutenant John Bourke wrote in his journal. "Everything is bound for the Black Hills. Cheyenne is full of people and the merchants and the saloon keepers are doing a rushing business."[2]

Duty-bound to defend not only citizens from hostile Indians but also to protect the reservations from rapacious whites, the government warned that it would arrest all invaders of the Black Hills. For the most part, the edict was ignored as gold-seekers poured in. As Annie Tallent and the party of prospectors she travelled with moved stealthily across the Sioux Reserve, Indians were only one of the perils they kept a sharp lookout for. "We were in constant expectation," she said, "of seeing a troop of cavalry come upon us from the rear, seize our train, burn our wagons and supplies, march us back in disgrace, and possibly place us in durance vile."[3]

Like Annie and her companions, many were indeed overtaken by cavalry and forced from "the Hills." But also like the young woman and her party, when the culprits were released, many simply re-equipped for another try. Unable to halt the gold rush, the government desperately sought a solution. When an offer to buy the Black Hills was made, the Indians were split between those who sensed the inevitable and sought peace and those who preferred war to any further loss of land. After it was later learned that Washington also wanted to purchase the Powder River country, some of the last and best hunting grounds, most Indians were furious. In the summer of 1875, a group of government representatives sought out the northern tribes to discuss the sale. Many of the non-reservation Sioux, including militant leaders Sitting Bull and Crazy Horse, refused to attend.

"Are you the Great God that made me?" Sitting Bull replied defiantly to the summons. "If he asks me to come see him, I will go, but the Big Chief of the white men must come see me. I will not go to the reservation. I have no land to sell . . . . We don't want any white men here."[4]

On September 23, near Camp Robinson, Nebraska, thirteen Federal commissioners, 120 cavalrymen, and a group of Indian reservation police pitched tents in anticipation of the council. By noon, with thousands of Sioux and Cheyenne already gathered, two hundred mounted warriors suddenly appeared. According to one writer who spoke with witnesses:

> They swept down toward the commission's tent in a column, then whipped their ponies into a run and began circling madly around the seated white men in a whirl of dust, whooping and firing their rifles. Presently they drew off and formed a line facing the commission; then their chief dismounted, walked forward, and sat down facing the white men. A signal was given, and another band of warriors emerged from the hills and repeated the performance of the first band. Band by band the Sioux rode proudly out of the hills, until at length seven thousand warriors were drawn up in a great circle surrounding the commission and its little guard of cavalry and Indian soldiers.[5]

After the commissioners had stated the government's view, Red Cloud and Spotted Tail delivered impassioned speeches, followed by the Sioux orator Red Dog. "He had scarcely finished," remembered another man, "when an excited commotion was observed among the thousands there assembled."

> Riding naked to the front on an iron gray horse, and brandishing a grim weapon in [the] air, Little-Big-Man proclaimed: "My heart is bad. I have come from Sitting Bull to kill a white man." Rapidly the ponies disappeared from the hills. Wrinkled squaws and soft-eyed maidens hurried to their camp. As the painted and armed [Indians] seized the contiguous knoll, the martial tones of Captain [James] Egan . . . rang out loud and firm, "Stand to Horse—Mount." Impelled by the command, each trooper, grasping carbine, vaulted into saddle.[6]

With thousands of enraged warriors circling the camp and bumping the cavalry horses to provoke their riders, a fight seemed certain. "It looks like hell will break out here in a few minutes," a frightened interpreter warned the commissioners. "The Indians are all mad, and when they start shooting we'll be the first to catch it."[7]

At this critical moment, a bold leader of the reservation bands, fearing the terrible judgment a massacre would bring down upon all Indians, strode forward and ordered Little-Big-Man to leave or be killed. The tumult did abate "but," added an astute observer, "Sitting Bull's work was done. The council was at an end, and no treaty was accomplished."[8]

Not only had the commission failed to resolve the issue of the Black Hills, but when hundreds of Indians suddenly abandoned their reservations and joined the hostiles, a virtual state of war arose between the U.S. government and the tribes of the north. Unlike other campaigns on the High Plains, an all-out contest with the powerful and undefeated Sioux loomed as the most formidable challenge faced by the army since the Civil War. Those who knew them best paid the greatest respect. William F. Cody:

> Of all the Indians I encountered in my years on the Plains the most resourceful and intelligent, as well as the most dangerous, were the Sioux . . . . They were a strong race of men, the braves tall, with finely shaped heads and handsome features. They had poise and dignity and a great deal of pride, and they seldom forgot either a friend or an enemy . . . . They had the courage of dare-devils combined with real strategy. They mastered the white man's tactics as soon as they had an opportunity to observe them.[9]

In short, Cody concluded, "The Sioux fought to win." Not only were they perhaps the best mounted fighters in the world but, as one Crow scout put it, "They are numerous as grass."

"The Indians, known to be scattered over [this] vast extent . . . would number at least 18,000 or 20,000, and could muster nearly 4,000 warriors," reported one newsman after talking to another scout. "[T]hat they would fight he considered there would be no reasonable doubt, as he witnessed their prowess in that line on more than one occasion when there was not as much to arouse them as at present." Not included in this estimate were the hundreds, perhaps thousands, of young Sioux, Cheyenne, and Arapahoe who annually visited their brothers in the summer to hunt.[10]

Many soldiers, sobered by the task, felt betrayed. "We are now on the eve of the bloodiest Indian war the Government has ever been called upon to wage," Lieutenant John Bourke confided to his diary. "The war with a tribe that has waxed fat and insolent on Govt. bounty and has been armed and equipped with the most improved weapons by the commissioners or the carelessness of the Indian agent."[11]

The opening act of the Great Sioux War occurred on March 1, 1876, when a column under Brigadier General George Crook left Fort Fetterman, Wyoming, and marched up the old Bozeman Trail. With Custer's Washita campaign in mind, Crook hoped to catch the Sioux snug in their winter camps. That such a surprise would be difficult, if not impossible, was made clear on day two of the march. Reported Robert Strahorn of the Denver *Rocky Mountain News*:

> At about two o'clock this morning, when the entire camp was wrapped in deepest slumber, and when all but the sentinels and herders were sleeping in as fancied security as though yet at Fetterman, we went through the novel sensation of a modern Indian stampede. There were a number of unearthly yells as if from a man surprised, several rifle shots in quick succession, an Indian whoop, a cloud of dust, and a man was dangerously wounded, a herd of fifty cattle and a horse vanished, and that is what we know of a stampede . . . . [A]ll this, too, within thirty-two miles of the fort.[12]

For those who swore Indians would never attack at night, the raid was another reminder that the Sioux were unpredictable. As the column continued north, there was further proof that the hostile villages were on the alert. "Indian signs were numerous and fresh in almost every direction," Strahorn continued, "and that they—the savages—are watching our every movement in spite of all precaution, is indisputable."[13]

"Indian signal smokes were to be seen all day away off on our right," added Lieutenant Bourke, "and once or twice our guards noticed signals flashed across country. These signals are made by the reflection of the sun from the small round looking glasses Indians wear about their necks."[14]

On the evening of March 16, a small track was discovered leading toward the Powder River in Montana. Detaching a battalion of three hundred men, Crook ordered Colonel Joseph Reynolds to follow the trail and find its source. Early next morning, after struggling all night through a snowstorm, Reynolds at last came upon a large Indian village. "Not the slightest mistrust or alarm was apparent in this forest home," wrote an incredulous Robert Strahorn, "and it was undoubtedly as clear a case of surprise as there is on record. Arms were hastily inspected, belts filled with cartridges, and overcoats and other impediments to hasty movements strapped to the saddles."[15]

Dividing his already outnumbered command, Reynolds directed Captain James Egan, with fewer than fifty men, to engage the camp. According to Lieutenant Bourke:

> Egan ordered us to keep at a walk until we had entered the village or been discovered by the enemy. Then to charge at a slow trot (our animals being too tired and cold to do more) and upon approaching closely to fire our pistols and storm the village . . . . Moving in this order, we were soon in among the herds of the ponies, which trotted off to the right and left at our approach.
>
> An Indian boy herding his ponies, was standing within 10 feet of me. I covered him with my revolver. I could have killed him; Egan said, "Let him alone, John." The youngster betrayed great stoicism maintaining silence until we passed and then shouting the war whoop to clear the village.[16]

Riding with Egan, Strahorn continued:

> "Charge, my boys!" came like an electric flash from the dauntless leader, and, giving their magnificent gray steeds rein and spur and yelling like so many demons, the gallant 47 men bounded into the village with the speed and force of a hurricane. With the savages swarming out of their tepees and scattering almost under our feet, we fired right and left at their retreating forms. Our horses meanwhile worked into such a frenzy by the din of whoops and yells and discharging arms that they fairly flew over the ground . . . .
>
> In charging into one of the tepees a man received a bullet through his cap. It just grazed his head, and as himself and a comrade or two rushed in to wreak their vengeance on the redskin who had fired, what was their astonishment at seeing 3 or 4 squaws, armed with revolvers, in the act of slipping through the opposite side of the wigwam by the way of a hole they had just carved with butcher knives.[17]

Returning to John Bourke:

> [T]he Indians who at first were greatly frightened now threw themselves behind the brush and opened upon us a lively fire which was returned with apparently good effect from our pistols as the Indians abandoned the first line of trees and took refuge further to the rear . . . . The Indians, seeing the paucity of our numbers, regained confidence and rushed forward to cut us off but we dismounted and formed a line on foot so rapidly in the undergrowth whence we opened up on them such an unpleasant fire from our carbines that the Sioux were only too glad to retire and leave us in possession of that end of the village.[18]

As the Indians gained in boldness, however, Reynolds decided to burn the camp and retreat. Strahorn:

> In the more than one hundred large tepees totally destroyed were beds of furs and robes, that, to a soldier, looked simply fit for savage Gods; war bonnets and squaw dresses regal in the construction and decoration, requiring months for making, and worth from five to ten ponies each; cooking utensils that an ordinary housewife would not need to be ashamed of; tons of dried and fresh meats, and occasionally dried fruits; every tepee an arsenal within itself with its kegs and canisters of powder; its large supply of bar lead, caps, and fixed ammunition . . . . With the exception of a few robes and other trinkets removed by the troops, these vast stores, in many instances the accumulation of a life time, were piled upon the dismantled tepees, and the whole reduced to ashes . . . .
>
> Among the domestic animals about the village, we noticed several broods of chickens and a number of fine dogs. The conduct of several of the latter seemed particularly strange. Lying by the side of their master's tepees when we arrived, they would not change their position one iota, as its domicile was torn down and with its effects set on fire. The great faithful fellow would still remain motionless as a statue, heedless of coaxing, gazing wistfully without a growl at the bands of the destroyers.[19]

Rounding up some 700 ponies, Reynolds fell back precipitously toward Crook and the main column. A short time later the Sioux and Cheyenne roared down on the retreating soldiers and recaptured all but 180 of their mounts. When Reynolds at last reached Crook and safety, and the Indians did not pull back as expected, the general responded. Bourke:

To remove all excuse of their presence Crook ordered that the throats of the captured ponies be cut, and this was done . . . . [F]irst, some fifty being knocked in the head with axes, or having their throats cut with the sharp knives of the scouts, and again, another "bunch" of fifty being shot before sun-down. The throat-cutting was determined upon when the enemy began firing in upon camp, and was the only means of killing the ponies without danger to our own people. It was pathetic to hear the dismal trumpeting (I can find no other word to express my meaning) of the dying creatures, as the breath of life rushed through severed windpipes. The Indians in the bluffs recognized the cry, and were aware of what we were doing, because with one yell of defiance and a parting volley, they left us alone for the rest of the night.[20]

Although he had routed the village and destroyed much property, Reynolds and his expedition had proven, as one officer termed it, a "lamentable failure."[21] Despite complete and almost unbelievable surprise, only one Indian was killed. Additionally, in his race to escape the enraged warriors, Reynolds had allowed several of his own dead and dying to fall into hostile hands. Concluded William T. Sherman when reviewing Crook's overall campaign:

This expedition was not conclusive or satisfactory. Therefore, General Sheridan determined to proceed more systematically by concentric movements, similar to those which in 1874–75 had proved so successful at the south against the hostile Comanches, Kiowas, and Cheyennes. He ordered three distinct columns to be prepared to move to a common center, where the hostiles were supposed to be, from Montana, from Dakota, and from the Platte. The two former fell under the command of the Department Commander, General [Alfred] Terry, and the latter under General Crook. These movements were to be simultaneous, so that Indians avoiding one column might be encountered by another.[22]

In April 1876, a brief thrust into Sioux country had scouted a branch of the Bighorn River without results. While there, however, a Crow guide could not resist the temptation to draw pictures on an old bread box and then stuff grass into its cracks. When the column moved off, the box remained behind as a warning to all Sioux that the Crow and whites were on their track and would clean them out that summer.[23]

By June, Sheridan's grand strategy to subdue the Sioux was in full swing. Moving to the east, Colonel John Gibbon led a column of 500 men from

Fort Ellis, Montana. Revived and re-equipped, Crook rumbled north out of Fort Fetterman once again with a force of nearly 1,000. Marching westward from Fort Abraham Lincoln, Brigadier General Terry commanded an additional 900 men, including the regiment under George Custer. Libbie Custer recorded the emotional farewell of the famous 7th Cavalry.

> The morning for the start came only too soon. My husband was to take . . . me out for the first day's march, so I rode beside him . . . .
>
> As we rode at the head of the column, we were the first to enter the confines of the garrison. About the Indian quarters, which we were obliged to pass, stood the squaws, the old men, and the children singing, or rather moaning, a minor tune that has been uttered on the going out of Indian warriors since time immemorial. Some of the squaws crouched on the ground, too burdened with their trouble to hold up their heads; others restrained the restless children who, discerning their fathers, sought to follow them. The Indian scouts themselves beat their drums and kept up their peculiar monotonous tune . . . .
>
> After we had passed the Indian quarters we came near Laundress Row, and there my heart entirely failed me. The wives and children of the soldiers lined the road. Mothers, with streaming eyes, held their little ones out at arm's-length for one last look at the departing father. The toddlers among the children, unnoticed by their elders, had made a mimic column of their own. With their handkerchiefs tied to sticks in lieu of flags, and beating old tin pans for drums, they strode lustily back and forth in imitation of the advancing soldiers. They were fortunately too young to realize why the mothers wailed out their farewells . . . .
>
> It was a relief to escape from them . . . and yet, when our band struck up "The Girl I Left Behind Me," the most despairing hour seemed to have come. All the sad-faced wives of the officers who had forced themselves to their doors to try and wave a courageous farewell, and smile bravely to keep the ones they loved from knowing the anguish of their breaking hearts, gave up the struggle at the sound of the music. The first notes made them disappear to fight out alone their trouble.[24]

Riding from the fort by her husband's side, Libbie continued.

> As the sun broke through the mist a mirage appeared, which took up about half of the line of cavalry, and thenceforth for a little distance it

> marched, equally plain to the sight on the earth and in the sky. The future . . . seemed to be revealed, and already there seemed a premonition . . . as their forms were reflected from the opaque mist of the early dawn. The sun, mounting higher and higher as we advanced, took every little bit of burnished steel on the arms and equipments along the line of horsemen, and turned them into glittering flashes of radiating light . . . . At every bend of the road, as the column wound its way round and round the low hills, my husband glanced back to admire his men, and could not refrain from constantly calling my attention to their grand appearance . . . . They were so accustomed to the march the line hardly diverged from the trail. There was a unity of movement about them that made the column at a distance seem like a broad dark ribbon stretched smoothly over the plains . . . . The soldiers, inured to many years of hardship, were the perfection of physical manhood. Their brawny limbs and lithe, well-poised bodies gave proof of the training their out-door life had given. Their resolute faces, brave and confident, inspired one with a feeling that they were going out aware of the momentous hours awaiting them, but inwardly assured of their capability to meet them.
>
> The general could scarcely restrain his recurring joy at being . . . with his regiment . . . . His buoyant spirits at the prospect of the activity and field-life that he so loved made him like a boy . . . . He was sanguine that but a few weeks would elapse before we would be reunited, and used this argument to animate me with courage to meet our separation.[25]

When the first day's march was done and camp was made, the colonel and his wife shared a final night on the Plains they so loved.

> In the morning the farewell was said . . . . With my husband's departure my last happy days in garrison were ended, as a premonition of disaster that I had never known before weighed me down. I could not shake off the baleful influence of depressing thoughts. This presentiment and suspense, such as I had never known, made me selfish, and I shut into my heart the most uncontrollable anxiety, and could lighten no one else's burden.[26]

In the meantime, Crook's column approached Rosebud Creek in southern Montana, where large numbers of Sioux were thought to be camped. On June 15, the general's force was augmented by 250 Indian allies. Although Sitting Bull had warned Crook that he "need not procure scouts to find him," the "Gray Fox" was determined to employ his new arrivals to the utmost. After a war dance and all-night feast, the Crow, led by their chief, Old Crow, and the Shoshoni under Washakie, fell in with the north-moving column.[27] Wrote Reuben Davenport, a reporter for the New York *Herald*:

> [T]he Snakes . . . are divided into two companies, regularly disciplined in imitation of the white soldiers . . . . They march sometimes in column, and nearly every Soshonee [*sic*], in going to war, carries a long white wand ornamented with pennants or streamers of fur, hair and red cloth. They wear parti-colored blankets, and ride usually either white or spotted ponies, whose tails and manes they daub with red or orange paint. Nothing could be more bright and picturesque than the whole body of friendly Indians as they galloped by the long column of the expedition early in the . . . morning.[28]

Later that day, Crook learned from scouts that a large trail had been discovered. The Crow and Shoshoni immediately painted their faces, broke into a war dance, then raced their ponies back and forth until man and beast were in a frenzy. Startled by the demonstration when no enemy was in sight, newsman Robert Strahorn asked a scout what it all meant. "Oh, they are only making brave," he replied quietly. "That all stops when we get into a fight."[29]

Despite the excitement, the advance continued and little occurred that day save a brief cold shower in which the whites quickly donned raincoats. Strahorn:

> While my arms were helplessly entangled in the garment, the flapping of its ample folds scared my horse and he bucked me off ingloriously . . . with one foot, however, still clinging to the stirrup. Then, with increasing fright, he started to run, bucking and kicking, dragging me face downward through a patch of thickly growing prickly pear and cactus. General Crook and the others . . . finally surrounded and rescued us. When I was picked up it was found that my face and arms, which were dragged over the prickly pear, were as full of the sharp barbed thorns as the quills on the fretful porcupine.[30]

Early next morning, June 17, Crook broke camp and formed up for the advance on the village, believed to be somewhere down the Rosebud. Another newsman with the column, John Finerty, noted:

> The Indians, having digested their buffalo hump banquet of the previous night, were quite alert, but prepared to go on with another

> feast. The General, however, sent his half-breed scouts to inform them that they must hurry up and go forward. The Snakes, to their credit . . . obeyed with some degree of martial alacrity, but the Crows seemed to act very reluctantly. It was evident that both tribes had a very wholesome respect for Sioux prowess. I noticed, among other things, that the singing had ceased, and it was quite apparent that the gentle savages began to view the coming conflict with feelings the reverse of hilarious.[31]

"About half-past seven an advance of ten miles had been made," wrote Reuben Davenport, "when, suddenly, the Old Crow appeared on a hill near the stream, and gave a signal. Soon other scouts dashed into the valley. Meanwhile the Crows were catching their war ponies, stripping off their superfluous garments, and some of them had formed in line and were singing their war song. A halt had been made at the first signal of the scouts."[32]

Because of the rumors and alarms of the past two days, John Finerty felt no special anxiety about the most recent.

> The sun became intensely hot in that close valley, so I threw myself upon the ground, resting my head upon my saddle . . . . At 8:30 o'clock, without any warning, we heard a few shots from behind the bluffs to the north. "They are shooting buffaloes over there," said [an officer]. Very soon we began to know, by the alternate rise and fall of the reports, that the shots were not all fired in one direction. Hardly had we reached this conclusion when a score or two of our Indian scouts appeared upon the northern crest and rode down the slopes with incredible speed. "Saddle up, there—saddle up, there, quick!" shouted [Captain Anson] Mills, and immediately all the cavalry within sight . . . were mounted and ready for action. General Crook, who appreciated the situation, had already ordered the companies of . . . [i]nfantry, posted at the foot of the northern slopes, to deploy as skirmishers, leaving their mules with the holders.
>
> Hardly had this precaution been taken when the flying Crow and Snake scouts, utterly panic stricken, came into camp shouting at the top of their voices: "Heap Sioux! heap Sioux!" gesticulating wildly in the direction of the bluffs, which they had abandoned in such haste. All looked in that direction, and there, sure enough, were the Sioux.[33]

"All the Indians in the world seemed gathered right there," said one terrified soldier.[34] Crook was equally surprised. With Indians, friend and foe alike, screaming "at the tops of their lungs [and] giving the war whoop that caused the hair to raise on end," the general was momentarily stunned. "I ran up on a bluff, not far from where we halted, to take in the situation."[35]

What Crook saw made his blood run cold—perhaps 2,500 Sioux and Northern Cheyenne warriors, either on the bluffs facing him or racing over the prairie to reach him. Detaching much of his cavalry, the general ordered Captain Mills to charge up the bluff toward the massing Indians. Reporter John Finerty leaped into his saddle.

> Mills immediately swung his fine battalion . . . by the right into line, and rising in his stirrups shouted, "Charge!" Forward we went at our best pace to reach the crest occupied by the enemy, who, meanwhile, were not idle, for men and horses rolled over pretty rapidly as we began the ascent . . . . We went like a storm, and the Indians waited for us until we were within fifty paces. We were going too rapidly to use our carbines, but several of the men fired their revolvers . . . . [O]ur men broke into a mad cheer.[36]

Anson Mills:

> We met the Indians . . . and charged right in and through them, driving them back to the top of the ridge. These Indians were most hideous, every one being painted in . . . colors and designs, stark naked, except their moccasins, breech clouts and head gear . . . . [T]he Indians proved then and there that they were the best cavalry soldiers on earth. In charging up towards us they exposed little of their person, hanging on with one arm around the neck and one leg over the horse, firing and lancing from underneath the horses' necks, so that there was no part of the Indian at which we could aim. Their shouting and personal appearance was so hideous that it terrified the horses more than our men and rendered them almost uncontrollable . . . . [W]e dismounted and placed them behind the rocks. The Indians came not in a line but in flocks or herds like the buffalo, and they piled in upon us until I think there must have been one thousand or fifteen hundred in our immediate front, but they refused to fight when they found us secured behind the rocks.[37]

When flanking warriors threatened to overrun his infantry in the valley, Crook ordered a second cavalry battalion to charge in that direction. But more Indians were pouring in from elsewhere. "Right, left, front and rear alike were faced by the incoming braves," recalled Robert Strahorn who, despite his tender hands and arms, was blazing away for his life. "[I]t seemed as though the whole surface of the country for miles around was one vast skirmish line."[38]

As bullets and arrows whizzed by, Captain Andrew Burt paused briefly beside his commander. "General, many say that they get so hardened to this sort of thing that they don't mind it, and I often wonder whether you feel like I do in a position of this kind."

"Well," asked Crook, "how do *you* feel?"

"Why, just as though, if you were not in sight, I'd be running like hell!"

"Well," the general replied calmly, "I feel exactly that way myself."[39]

At length, because of the accurate fire of troopers forced to fight on foot, the Indians fell back a short distance. Finerty:

> The Sioux, having rallied on the second line of heights, became bold and impudent again. They rode up and down rapidly, sometimes wheeling in circles, slapping an indelicate portion of their persons at us and beckoning us to come on. One chief, probably . . . Crazy Horse, directed their movements by signals made with a pocket mirror or some other reflector. Under Crook's orders our whole line remounted, and after another rapid charge we became masters of the second crest. When we got there, another just like it rose on the other side of the valley. There, too, were the savages, as fresh, apparently, as ever. We dismounted, accordingly, and the firing began again. It was now evident that the weight of the fighting was shifting from our front.[40]

The Sioux and Cheyenne were indeed probing other points of the line. One section of the cavalry charge was halted abruptly by a furious countercharge. Reuben Davenport:

> [T]hey dashed forward on the right and left, and in an instant nearly every point of vantage . . . was covered with savages wildly circling their ponies and charging hither and thither, while they fired from their seats with wonderful rapidity and accuracy. At this moment the loss to the troops commenced . . . . Still the troops on the right did not advance, and the suspense grew terrible as the position was every moment more perilous as the Sioux appeared at intervals on the left flank, charging on their ponies and each time further toward the rear. In the meantime they swept down into the valley where the command had halted in the morning at the first alarm . . . and, killing a Snake, captured a small herd of ponies which he was guarding.[41]

George Crook. Paul L. Hedren Collection.

With the Sioux threatening to break the line and split the entire command, those in Davenport's area began to waver and fall back for the valley.

> At this juncture the soldiers felt great discouragement, but preserved their coolness, although death had just begun his work among them, a murderous enfilading fire causing them to drop every moment . . . . I dismounted at several points during our retreat and fired with the skirmishers . . . . The tide of retreat now grew more excited and turbulent, and I was pressed back . . . . A swarm of Sioux were within 1,000 yards of me in front and I heard their shots in the rear as they murdered the poor soldiers of the rear guard of the retreat . . . . [A]s I galloped up the slope opposite the one I had left I heard the yells of the savages close behind, and the reports of their rifles . . . . Looking behind I saw a dozen Sioux surrounding a group of soldiers who had straggled behind the retreat. Six were killed at one spot. A recruit surrendered his carbine to a

> painted warrior, who flung it to the ground, and cleft his head with a stroke of the tomahawk . . . . The Sioux rode so close to their victims that they shot them in the face with revolvers . . . .
>
> [J]ust after my escape the Snake Indians, gallantly led by their chief . . . dashed with thrilling shouts into the hollow, among the Sioux who were on the rear of the cavalry, and drove them back. Captain [Guy] Henry, weak from the bleeding of his wound, had been unable to keep up with the retreat and had sunk on the ground. [Washakie] put himself astride the body and for five minutes kept the Sioux off, when some soldiers of his company rushed back and rescued him.[42]

Like Davenport, John Finerty witnessed the bloody drama in the hollow as contending red men renewed their age-old ritual.

> The two bodies of savages . . . came together in the trough of the valley, the Sioux having descended to meet our allies with right good will . . . . Then began a most exciting encounter. The wild foemen, covering themselves with their horses while going at full speed, blazed away rapidly. Our regulars did not fire because it would have been sure death to some of the friendly Indians, who were barely distinguishable by a red badge which they carried. Horses fell dead by the score . . . . The whooping was persistent . . . .
>
> Finally the Sioux on the right, hearing the yelping and firing of the rival tribes, came up in great numbers and our Indians, carefully picking up their wounded and making their uninjured horses carry double, began to draw off in good order. Sergeant [John] Van Moll was left alone on foot. A dozen Sioux dashed at him. Major [George] Randall and Lieutenant Bourke . . . turned their horses to rush to his rescue. They called on the Indians to follow them. One small, misshapen Crow warrior mounted on a fleet pony outstripped all others. He dashed boldly in among the Sioux against whom Van Moll was dauntlessly defending himself, seized the big Sergeant by the shoulders and motioned him to jump up behind. The Sioux were too astonished to realize what had been done until they saw the long-legged Sergeant, mounted behind the little Crow, known as Humpy, dash toward our lines like the wind. Then they opened fire, but we opened also and compelled them to seek higher ground. The whole line of our battalion cheered Humpy and Van Moll as they passed us on the home stretch. There were no insects on them, either.[43]

The Battle of the Rosebud. Kansas State Historical Society.

For the next several hours Crook and Crazy Horse fought viciously among the breaks of the Rosebud, while scores of men fell on both sides. Amid the tumult, John Finerty noted many gruesome scenes.

> One man . . . was in the act of firing when a bullet from the Indians passed along the barrel of his carbine, glanced around his left shoulder, traversed the neck under the skin, and finally lodged in the point of his lower jaw. The shock laid him low for a moment, but, picking himself up, he had the nerve to reach for his weapon, which had fallen from his hand, and bore it with him off the ground . . . . [Captain] Henry . . . was struck by a bullet which passed through both cheek bones, broke the bridge of his nose and destroyed the optic nerve in one eye . . . . [He was] temporarily blinded . . . and throwing blood from his mouth by the handful [as he] sat his horse.[44]

"As the day advanced," Finerty continued, "General Crook became tired of the indecisiveness of the action and resolved to bring matters to a crisis."

> He rode up to where the officers of Mills' battalion were standing or sitting behind their men, who were prone on the skirmish line, and said, in effect: "It is time to stop this skirmishing, Colonel. You must

> take your battalion and go for their village away down the cañon." "All right, sir," replied Mills, and the order to retire and remount was given. The Indians, thinking we were retreating, became audacious and fairly hailed bullets after us, wounding several soldiers.[45]

The column under Mills moved down the Rosebud into Dead Canyon, "a dark, narrow and winding defile" more than twelve miles long. The closed nature of the valley, an "elongated trap," Finerty thought, caused immediate misgivings among the soldiers. Should an ambush occur few could doubt the outcome. Fortunately, a courier soon overtook Mills and ordered him to return and help beat back yet another attack.[46] Once more at the scene of action, John Finerty resumes the narrative:

> There was very heavy firing and the Sioux were evidently preparing to make an attack in force, as they were riding in by the score . . . . Suddenly the Sioux lookouts observed our unexpected approach and gave the alarm to their friends. We dashed forward at a wild gallop, cheering as we went . . . but the cunning savages did not wait for us. They picked up their wounded, all but thirteen of their dead, and broke away to the northwest on their fleet ponies, leaving us only the thirteen scalps, 150 dead horses and ponies and a few old blankets and war bonnets as trophies of the fray.[47]

With that, the Battle of the Rosebud ended. It was only then, when the screams and shouts had ceased and the soldiers finally could see through the lifting smoke, that they truly appreciated what had occurred. "We then all realized for the first time," a stunned Anson Mills said as he stared at the litter of dead and wounded comrades, "that while we were lucky not to have been entirely vanquished, we had been most humiliatingly defeated."[48]

Accustomed as he was to relatively easy victories in the desert Southwest against Apaches, George Crook was shattered by his check on the northern Plains. "[I] never saw a man more dejected," Mills wrote later.[49] There was no question of continuing the advance. When, despite all that had passed, Crook once more muttered something about heading for the Sioux village, the exhausted Crow allies dismissed the words as the ravings of a lunatic. "[T]he force you have been fighting is only a little war party," one warrior warned. "If you go to village you will find as many Indians as the grass. If you go down there you can never get out of the trap; you will all be killed." With that, the Crow rubbed his palms together as if grinding a clod of dirt to dust.[50]

Crook wisely retreated the following day. In doing so, he in effect cleared his command from the board. Ironically, even as one column fell back, another force, much smaller than Crook's, was preparing to advance. Unaware of defeat on the Rosebud, this column, within days, would march right in to that huge camp that the Crow so feared. And when it did, it rode right through the gates of hell . . . and into glory.

14

Garry Owen . . . in Glory

On the evening of June 21, 1876, the steamboat *Far West* lay docked along the normally placid Yellowstone River of Montana. All about the makeshift landing was noise and movement as soldiers and sailors unloaded supplies in preparation for the big scout, set to depart the following day. Spirits were high among officers of the 7th Cavalry. Winfield Scott Edgerly sat chatting and joking with others outside headquarters. "Soon the General came out of his tent," Lieutenant Edgerly recalled, "and I said 'General, won't we step high if we get those fellows!' He replied, 'Won't we!' adding, 'It all depends on you young officers. We can't get Indians without hard riding and plenty of it!'"[1]

George Custer's optimism in locating the normally elusive Indian was based not only on his pride and trust in his beloved 7th, but on the latest reports as well. While scouting the upper Rosebud, Major Marcus Reno had struck a large trail crossing the divide toward the Little Bighorn. Along the banks of that obscure and often misnamed stream, Custer felt he would find 1,000 to 1,500 warriors of the allied tribes, perhaps fewer, but certainly no more. All the same, his 600 men could expect to be outnumbered by two to one. Still, the colonel was not troubled by the odds, nor did he doubt the outcome of the pending engagement.

Custer's confidence was well-founded. After the 7th's victories on the southern Plains in the 1860s and after besting Crazy Horse on the Yellowstone in 1873, his faith in the unit bordered on invincibility and in his heart he felt the regiment could go wherever he cared to lead it. When an additional battalion was offered by General Terry as a precaution, the proud colonel politely refused. Far from fearing an encounter, Custer hoped to keep the Indians from scattering, as they tended to do. Consequently, not only did he opt for pack mules over the slower supply wagons, he also chose to leave a battery of Gatling guns parked at the *Far West*.[2]

Not everyone was so confident of finding Indians; James DeWolf, for one, was dubious. Dr. DeWolf—only just returned from Reno's scout—was taking time this night to pen a last letter to his wife: "We found no Indians, not one. All old trails. They seem to be moving west and are driving the buffalo. I think it is very clear that we shall not see an Indian this summer."[3]

Frederick Benteen agreed. "Many of us are of the opinion," the captain wrote to his wife, "that we shall have no opportunities of exhibiting our prowess on redskins—& I am one of these."[4] Among the more knowledgeable, however, among those whose life on the Plains had developed in them almost a sixth sense, something strange and sinister was in the air. Many, like Custer's chief of scouts, Charley Reynolds, felt the coming campaign would witness "the greatest Indian battle ever fought on this continent."[5] And the colonel's friend and favorite guide, Bloody Knife, already had a terrible vision of what he would find beside the clear and sparkling waters of the "Little Horn."

Whether it was a "fight or foot race," most troopers, like bugler Henry Dose, realized their job would not end until Sitting Bull had been forced onto the reservation: "I wish for mine part we would meet him tomorrow. Sergt. Botzer and me come to the conclusion, it is better anyhow to be home baking flapjacks. When we get home we will pay up for this, and bake flapjacks all the time."[6]

As the only newsman with the 7th, Mark Kellogg was working far into the night, finishing up a long dispatch to the New York *Herald*, describing the events of the past few days and what was likely to come. "And now," he scribbled, "a word for the most peculiar genius in the army."

> [A] man of strong impulses, of great hearted friendships and bitter enmities, of quick, nervous temperament, undaunted courage, will and determination; a man possessing electrical mental capacity and of iron frame and constitution; a brave, faithful, gallant soldier, who has warm friends and bitter enemies; the hardest rider, the greatest pusher, with the most untiring vigilance, overcoming seeming impossibilities, and with an ambition to succeed in all things he undertakes; a man to do right, as he construes the right, in every case; one respected and beloved by his followers, who would freely follow him into the "jaws of hell." Of Lieutenant Colonel G. A.

> Custer I am now writing. Do not think I am over-drawing the picture. The pen picture is true to life, and is drawn not only from actual observation, but from an experience that cannot mislead me.[7]

Near midnight, as the dark, swirling Yellowstone slid by and made soothing sounds "like that of a soft wind rustling in the tall grass," Kellogg signed off with a final note to his boss back in Bismarck.

> We leave [up] the Rosebud to-morrow, and by the time this reaches you we will have met and fought the red devils, with what results remains to be seen. I go with Custer and will be at the death.[8]

Next morning, amid a flurry of last-minute activity, General Terry gave Custer his parting instructions. Unlike normal directives, Terry's words were suggestions, not commands, for, as the general explained, "The Department Commander places too much confidence in your zeal, energy, and ability to wish to impose upon you precise orders which might hamper your action."[9]

As the regiment prepared to mount, Custer advised his Crow and Ree guides that a fight was looming and they should sing their death songs. "Custer had a heart like an Indian," one of the scouts said. "If we ever left out one thing in our ceremonies he always suggested it to us. We got on our horses and rode around, singing the songs. Then we fell in behind Custer."[10] Lieutenant Edward Godfrey:

> At twelve o'clock, noon, on the 22nd of June, the "Forward" was sounded, and the regiment marched out of camp, each troop followed by its pack mules. Generals Terry, Gibbon and Custer stationed themselves near our line of march and reviewed the regiment. General Terry had a pleasant word for each officer as he returned the salute.[11]

Like the famous commander they so proudly paraded past, the veteran rank and file exuded self-confidence. Private Charles Windolph:

> You felt like you were somebody when you were on a good horse, with a carbine dangling . . . and a Colt army revolver strapped on your hip . . . . You were a cavalryman of the Seventh Regiment. You were part of a proud outfit that had a fighting reputation, and you were ready for a fight or a frolic.[12]

"[C]olumn of fours, guidons flying, trumpets sounding . . . . We started out in 'Grand Galore,'" wrote Captain Benteen.[13]

As the buoyant colonel rejoined his regiment and steered it up the Rosebud, 300 miles away a lonely woman was at her desk penning a last letter to the only man she had ever loved.

> My own darling—I dreamed of you as I knew I should . . . . Oh, Autie how I feel about your going away so long without our hearing. . . . Your safety is ever in my mind. My thoughts, my dreams, my prayers, are all for you. God bless and keep my darling.
>
> Ever your own Libbie[14]

Despite his normally unshakable spirit and the joy surrounding the onset, by the end of the first day's ride a gloom had settled over George Custer. The feeling, in turn, filtered down to the entire command. Again, Lieutenant Godfrey:

> About sunset "officer's call" was sounded, and we assembled at General Custer's bivouac and squatted in groups about the General's bed. It was not a cheerful assemblage; everybody seemed to be in a serious mood, and the little conversation carried on, before all had arrived, was in undertones. When all had assembled, the General said that until further orders, trumpet calls would not be sounded except in an emergency; the marches would begin at 5 A.M. sharp; the troop commanders were all experienced officers, and knew well enough what to do . . . . He took particular pain to impress upon the officers his reliance upon their judgment, discretion, and loyalty . . . . All officers were requested to make to him any suggestions they thought fit.
>
> This "talk" of his . . . was considered at the time as something extraordinary for General Custer, for it was not his habit to unbosom himself to his officers . . . . [T]here was an indefinable something that was not Custer. His manner and tone, usually brusque and aggressive, or somewhat curt, was on this occasion conciliating and subdued. There was something akin to an appeal, as if depressed, that made a deep impression on all present. We compared watches to get the official time, and separated to attend to our various duties. Lieutenants [Donald] McIntosh, [George] Wallace and myself walked to our bivouac, for some distance in silence, when Wallace remarked: "Godfrey, I believe General Custer is going to be killed." "Why, Wallace?" I replied, "What makes you think so?" "Because," said he, "I have never heard Custer talk in that way before."[15]

Edward Godfrey. LITTLE BIGHORN BATTLEFIELD NATIONAL MONUMENT.

After a word with his men and a check of the animals, Godfrey entered the camp of the Indian scouts.

> "Mitch" Bouyer, Bloody Knife, Half-Yellow-Face, and others were having a "talk." I observed them for a few minutes, when Bouyer turned toward me . . . and said, "Have you ever fought against these Sioux?" "Yes," I replied. Then he asked, "Well, how many do you expect to find?" I answered, "It is said we may find between one thousand and fifteen hundred." "Well, do you think we can whip that many?" "Oh, yes, I guess so." After he had interpreted our conversation, he said to me with a good deal of emphasis, "Well, I can tell you we are going to have a damned big fight."[16]

Godfrey continues:

> At five o'clock sharp, on the morning of the 23rd, General Custer mounted and started up the Rosebud, followed by two sergeants, one carrying the regimental standard, and the other his personal or headquarters flag . . . . This was the signal for the command to mount and take up the march. Eight miles out we came to the first of the Indian camping-places. It certainly indicated a large village and numerous population . . . . During the day we passed through three

> of these camping-places and made halts at each one. Everybody was busy studying the age of the pony droppings and tracks and lodge trails, and endeavoring to determine the number of lodges. These points were all-absorbing topics of conversation. We went into camp about five o'clock, having marched about thirty-three miles.
>
> June 24th we passed a great many camping places, all appearing to be of nearly the same strength . . . . We passed through one much larger than any of the others. The grass for a considerable distance around it had been cropped close, indicating that large herds had been grazed there. The frame of a large "Sun-Dance" lodge was standing, and in it we found the scalp of a white man . . . . The command halted here and the "officers' call" was sounded. Upon assembling we were informed that our Crow scouts . . . had discovered fresh signs, the tracks of three or four ponies and one Indian on foot. At this point a stiff southerly breeze was blowing; as we were about to separate, the General's headquarters' flag was blown down, falling toward our rear. Being near the flag I picked it up and stuck the staff in the ground, but it again fell to the rear . . . . Lieutenant Wallace . . . had observed [this], and regarded the fact of it falling to the rear as a bad omen, and felt sure we would suffer a defeat.
>
> The march during the day was tedious. We made many long halts, so as not to get ahead of the scouts, who seemed to be doing their work thoroughly . . . . The valley was heavily marked with lodge-pole trails and pony tracks, showing that immense herds of ponies had been driven over it. About sundown we went into camp under the cover of a bluff, so as to hide the command as much as possible. We had marched about twenty-eight miles.[17]

"[W]e camped . . . on abandoned Indian camp," a Ree scout recalled, "and found a stone with two bulls drawn on it. On one bull was drawn a bullet and on the other a lance. The two bulls were charging toward each other. Custer asked Bloody Knife to translate it, and Bloody Knife said it meant a hard battle would occur if an enemy came that way."[18]

As the scouts gathered that evening to eat, they discussed the track discovered that day, "a trail," remarked young Billy Jackson, "all of three hundred yards wide."

> All agreed that at least fifteen hundred lodges of the enemy had made that broad trail. Said Bloody Knife: "My friends, this big trail proves what we heard, that the . . . Sioux have left their agencies to join Sitting Bull and Crazy Horse; but I am sure that even this trail

does not account for all that have left their agencies. There surely are other trails of them; and trails, too, of Cheyennes and Arapahoes . . . . It is as I have told Long Hair: this gathering of the enemy tribes is too many for us. But he will not believe me. He is bound to lead us against them. They are not far away; just over this ridge, they are all encamped and waiting for us. Crazy Horse and Sitting Bull are not men-without-sense; they have their scouts out, and some of them surely have their eyes upon us. Well, to-morrow we are going to have a big fight, a losing fight. Myself, I know what is to happen to me; my sacred helper has given me warning that I am not to see the set of to-morrow's sun."

Sad words, those. They chilled us. I saw Charlie Reynolds nod agreement to them, and was chilled again when he said in a low voice: "I feel as he does: tomorrow will be the end for me, too. Any one who wants my little outfit of stuff . . . can have it right now." He opened it, began passing out tobacco; a sewing-kit; several shirts and so on. Many refused the presents; those who accepted them did so with evident reluctance.

We had little appetite for our coffee and hardtack, and the meat that we were broiling.[19]

Later, with the camp wrapped in sleep, Custer ordered all officers to his tent. Edward Godfrey:

So we gave up our much-needed rest and groped our way through horse herds, over sleeping men, and through thickets of bushes trying to find headquarters. No one could tell us, and as all fires and lights were out we could not keep our bearings. We finally espied a solitary candle-light, toward which we traveled and found most of the officers assembled at the General's bivouac. The General said that the trail led over the divide to the Little Big Horn; the march would be taken up at once, as he was anxious to get as near the divide as possible before daylight.[20]

After a dusty ride of ten miles, the column halted at 2 A.M. on Sunday, June 25, to await morning light. Billy Jackson:

At dawn . . . [w]hile we were eating, several of the packers rode swiftly up through the command to General Custer . . . . [W]e soon learned that they had lost a box of hardtack off one of the mules, and, on going back, had found some Indians around it, stuffing the contents into their clothing. None could now doubt that the enemy had all along kept watch of our advance. With a grim laugh, Charlie Reynolds said to me: "I knew well enough that they had scouts ahead of us, but I didn't think that others would be trailing along to pick up stuff dropped by our careless packers."

Convinced at last that we could not possibly surprise the enemy, General Custer ordered a quick advance, with the scouts and himself in the lead. We had not gone far when Bloody Knife and his two Rees joined us, and reported that on the other side of the ridge they had found the day-old trail of many more of the enemy going toward the valley of the Little Bighorn.[21]

Again, Lieutenant Godfrey:

We . . . marched uninterruptedly until 10:30 A.M. when we halted in a ravine and were ordered to preserve quiet, keep concealed, and not do anything that would be likely to reveal our presence to the enemy . . . . Our officers had generally collected in groups and discussed the situation. Some sought solitude and sleep, or meditation. The Ree scouts . . . were together and their "medicine man" was anointing them and invoking the Great Spirit to protect them from the Sioux.[22]

Meanwhile, Custer and several scouts had climbed to a high point in hope of gaining a glimpse of the village. From such a great distance nothing was definite but above the Little Bighorn Valley, an ominous haze stretched for miles. Soon the colonel returned to his command. "At 12m . . . we crossed the divide between the Rosebud and the Little Big Horn," Lieutenant Wallace remembered. "From the divide could be seen the valley . . . and about 15 or 20 miles to the northwest could be seen a light blue cloud, and to the practised eyes showed that our game was near."[23] Returning to Billy Jackson:

On we went over the divide. We soon met [Mitch Bouyer] and his two Crows. They were excited, and Bruyer [*sic*] said to Custer: "General, we have discovered the camp, down there on the Little Horn. It is a big one! Too big for you to tackle! Why, there are thousands and thousands of Sioux and Cheyennes down there."

For a moment the general stared at him, angrily, I thought, and then sternly replied: "I shall attack them! If you are afraid, Bruyer—"

"I guess I can go wherever you do," Bruyer quickly answered; and at that, the general turned back to the command, we following him. He had the bugler sound the officers' call . . . and Custer gave his orders for the attack upon the camp.

> None of the scouts had been far in the lead, and they all came in . . . . [W]e were a gathering of solemn faces. Speaking in English, and the sign language, too, so that all would understand, Bruyer described the enemy camp. It was, he said, all of three miles long, and made up of hundreds and hundreds of lodges. Above it and below and west of it were thousands and thousands of horses that were being close-herded. With his few riders, Long Hair had decided to attack the camp, and we were going to have a terrible fight; we should all take courage, fight hard, make our every shot a killer. He finished, and none spoke. But after a minute or two, Bloody Knife looked up and signed to [the] Sun: "I shall not see you go down behind the mountains to-night."[24]

Detaching a battalion under Captain Benteen to veer left and prevent the Sioux from escaping up the river, Custer led the rest down toward the Little Bighorn. When two miles from the valley, Major Reno, with more than 100 troopers and scouts, was to push ahead, ford the river, and strike the village from the south. With the remainder of the regiment, roughly 230 men, Custer would hug the bluffs and charge the camp from the north.

As Custer moved off to the right, Reno's small force moved rapidly down a draw toward the river. "[W]e could see a big dust over the valley of the Little Bighorn, there being a north wind," said interpreter Fred Girard, "and this gave the impression that the Indians were fleeing north."[25] Another man riding with Reno was Sergeant John Ryan.

> [We] started down [to] the valley, first on a trot, and then at a gallop, marching in columns of twos. Lieutenant [Charles] Varnum, a very brave young officer in command of the scouts, rode ahead of Reno's battalion. He swung his hat around in the air, and sung out to the men, "Thirty days' furlough to the man who gets the first scalp.". . .
>
> We arrived at the bank of the Little Big Horn river and waded to the other side, and here there was a very strong current, and there was quick-sand about three feet deep. On the other side of the river we made a short halt, dismounted, tightened our saddle girths, and then swung into our saddles . . . . We were then in the valley . . . and facing down stream. We started down on a trot and then on a slow gallop . . . . We advanced . . . [toward] a heavy piece of timber. Before we arrived at the timber, there was one shot fired away ahead of us . . . . That was the first shot that I heard.[26]

In a few moments Sioux began to race up the valley. "Our horses were scenting danger," noted Private William Slaper, "and several . . . became unmanageable and started straight for the open among the Indians, carrying their helpless riders with them."[27]

"When we got to the timber we rode down an embankment and . . . dismounted in haste," Sergeant Ryan continued, "number four of each set of four holding the horses. We came up onto higher ground . . . facing down stream in the direction of the Indian camp. This was our first view of the Indian camp."[28] Also in the woods with Reno was Billy Jackson.

> Within two minutes from the time that we left our horses, and climbed up the bank from them, we had a line of defense in the brush and out across toward the west bluff of the valley. Then came the rush of the enemy, all of five hundred well-mounted riders . . . eager to get at us. Their shots, their war-cries, the thunder of their horses feet were deafening.
>
> It was the intention of the enemy to charge straight through the center of our line, but, by the time they had come within fifty yards, we had shot so many of them that they swung out and went streaming past the outer end of our line, lying low upon their horses and firing rapidly. The dust that their swift charge raised . . . almost choked us: it drifted upon us like a thick fog, and obscured the sun . . . . Several hundred of the enemy went thundering past that outer end of our line, and, swinging in, began [an] attack upon our rear, and more and more arrivals from the camp swarmed in front of us.[29]

The pressure was too great. The scattered men to the west, terrified by the screaming Indians and the sight of hundreds more streaming in, wavered, then ran. Others along the line also bolted; in a few moments, all had fled "pell mell" back to the trees.

"I . . . soon saw that I was being drawn into some trap," Reno said. "I could not see Custer or any other support, and at the same time the very earth seemed to grow Indians. They were running toward me in swarms and from all directions. I saw I must defend myself and give up the attack . . . . This I did."[30] Remembered Fred Girard:

> As Major Reno left the line and passed into the timber, I saw him put a bottle of whisky to his mouth and drink the whole contents . . . . In the timber all was confusion . . . . The Sioux had closed in and were firing into the timber more or less at random from the south and the northwest . . . . Reno, however, seeing no support from the rear, lost his head . . . and suddenly decided to run the gauntlet of the Sioux.[31]

Marcus Reno. KANSAS STATE HISTORICAL SOCIETY.

Sergeant John Ryan:

> As we mounted I looked to the rear in the direction of the river and saw the Indians completing the circle, riding through the brush and lying flat on their ponies . . . . Just at that moment one of those Indians fired and Private George Lorentz . . . was shot, the bullet striking him in the back of his neck and coming out of his mouth. He fell forward on his saddle and dropped to the ground. Just at that moment the Indians fired into us from all sides.[32]

Returning to Billy Jackson:

> I saw Major Reno, hatless, a handkerchief tied around his head, getting up on his plunging horse. Waving his six-shooter, he shouted something that I couldn't hear, and led swiftly off, up out of the depression that we were in. We all swarmed after him, and headed back up the way that we had come, our intention being to recross the river and get up onto the bluffs, where we could make a stand. By this time hundreds more of the enemy had come up from the camp, and all together they swarmed in on us and a hand-to-hand fight with

> them began. I saw numbers of our men dropping from their horses, saw horses falling, heard their awful neighs of fright and pain. Close ahead of me, Bloody Knife, and then Charlie Reynolds, went down.[33]

With much of his head blown away, Bloody Knife had indeed fulfilled his vision. Amid the smoke and dust, however, the quiet man called "Lonesome" regained his feet. "I saw Charlie . . . dismounted and wounded with pistol standing still and showing fight," one witness recalled as he and the others flew by.[34] Soon, Reynolds was engulfed by the howling storm and vanished. Like everyone else, Billy Jackson was lashing his horse for safety.

> A big heavy-set Indian brushed up against me, tried to pull me out of the saddle, and I shot him. Then, right in front, a soldier's horse was shot from under him, and as I came up, he grasped my right stirrup and ran beside me. I had to check my horse so that he could keep up, and so began to lag behind. Numbers of Indians were passing on both sides of us, eager to get at the main body of the retreat. At last one of the passing Indians made a close shot at the soldier and killed him, and as I gave my horse loose rein, [Fred] Girard came up on my left, and we rode on side by side. Ahead, there was now a solid body of Indians between us and the retreating, hard-pressed soldiers, and Girard shouted to me: "We can't go through them! Let's turn back!" . . .
>
> [W]e finally got into thick, high brush, dismounted and tied our horses. Just then we saw some one coming toward us, and were about to fire at him when we discovered that he was Lieutenant [Charles] DeRudio. He told us that his horse had run away from him. As we stood there, listening to the heavy firing up on the river, we were joined by [Private] Thomas O'Neil . . . also horseless.[35]

In the meantime, among the bluffs, the battalion under Benteen was approaching the valley. Lieutenant Edward Godfrey rode with it.

> We now heard firing, first straggling shots, and as we advanced, the engagements became more and more pronounced and appeared to be coming toward us. The column took the gallop with pistols drawn, expecting to meet the enemy which we thought Custer was driving before him . . . . We were forming in line to meet our supposed enemy, when we came in full view of the valley of the Little Big Horn. The valley was full of horsemen riding to and fro in

clouds of dust and smoke, for the grass had been fired by the Indians to drive the troops out and cover their own movements.[36]

"I saw an immense number of indians on the plain . . . charging down on some dismounted men of Reno's command," added a stunned Frederick Benteen. "[T]he balance of R's command were mounted and flying off for dear life to the bluffs on the same side of the river I was."[37] One of those "flying for dear life" was Private William Morris.

> I made for the river . . . and jumped my horse off the bank—which was at least ten feet high—landing in the center of the river which proved to be deep. I thought I was a goner, but we . . . crossed to the opposite side and made for the cut or pony trail which led up to the bluff. When I arrived there, Lieutenant [Benjamin] Hodgson . . . was in the river grabbing for a trooper's stirrup, who refused to help him. I then saw that the water was crimson around his legs and thighs . . . . I rode up . . . and Hodgson reached out and said to me: "For God's sake, don't leave me here, I am shot through both legs." I said: "All right, grab hold." I gave him my right stirrup which he grabbed with both hands, and I grabbed him by the collar . . . . I had a firm grip on him and he was safe until the second plunge of the horse which took us halfway up the cut. On the third plunge he let go, and all his weight fell upon me and almost pulled me apart. He was probably hit again. At any rate, he fell to the ground.[38]

"The Indians . . . were now riding into the stream," said one soldier, "shooting into the ranks of the stampeding troopers and actually pulling many of them from their horses right there in the river."[39] Another trooper struggling through the churning red current was Henry Petring.

> [W]hen part way across [I] saw four or five Indians on the bank ahead of me and very near. One Indian . . . drew up his gun as if to fire, and I . . . drew up my carbine without taking aim and fired, and both the pony and the Indian dropped. Then I . . . jumped down off my horse and started downstream as fast as I could in water waist deep and deeper. I did not look back until I had gone some little distance, and when I did I saw two of the Indians carrying off the one I had shot, and the pony still lay there as if dead. I was then several hundred yards away and back on the same side of the river from which I had started to cross. I immediately went

> under a stump and . . . wondered if, after all, the best thing I could do would not be to shoot myself.[40]

Cut off in front and rear, many, like Private Petring, were left to their fate. According to witnesses:

> Some distance from the timber, Lieutenant McIntosh was trying to make his way. He was singled out by himself, and he was trying to urge his horse along but he was not succeeding well. His lariat was dragging, which seemed to bother his horse. McIntosh was surrounded by 20 or 30 Indians who were circling about him, apparently determined to get him . . . . [H]e was overtaken, pulled from his horse and plugged with pistol shots while lying at the feet of his murderers.[41]

Once across the river, the terror-stricken survivors found only a narrow cut leading up the bluffs, barely wide enough for a single rider. As the soldiers scrambled up, the Indians shot them down. William Morris:

> I got off . . . and adjusted my saddle girth, jumped on again and pushed on. Two-thirds of the way up the bluff I overtook Privates Dave Gordon and Bill Meyer . . . . I said to them: "That was pretty hot down there." . . . The next second all three of us were hit . . . . Bill was hit in the eye, and Dave Gordon was shot through the neck, cutting his windpipe. All three horses were hit, and I was shot through the left breast.[42]

"After we gained the bluffs," Sergeant Ryan noted, "we could look back upon the plains where the Indians were, and could see them stripping and scalping our men, and mutilating their bodies in a horrible manner."[43]

"Hordes of squaws and old, gray-haired Indians were roaming over the battlefield, howling like mad," another witness recalled. "The squaws had stone mallets and mashed in the skulls of the dead and wounded."[44]

Soon after the breathless troopers reached the top of the bluffs, Benteen's battalion arrived. "For God's sake, Benteen," gasped Major Reno, "halt your command and help me. I've lost half my men."[45] Benteen was none too soon. "[T]he Indians commenced to swarm around us like devils," Lieutenant Frank Gibson remembered, "thousands of them, all with modern rifles, while we were using old carbines."[46] One who arrived with Benteen was Edward Godfrey.

Benteen's battalion was ordered to dismount and deploy as skirmishers on the edge of the bluffs overlooking the valley. Very soon after this the Indians withdrew from the attack. Lieutenant [Luther] Hare came to where I was standing and, grasping my hand heartily, said with a good deal of emphasis: "We've had a big fight in the bottom, got whipped, and I am———glad to see you.". . . I had already suspected that something was wrong, but was not quite prepared for such startling information . . . .

A number of officers collected on the edge of the bluff overlooking the valley and were discussing the situation. At this time there were a large number of horsemen, Indians, in the valley. Suddenly they all started down the valley, and in a few minutes scarcely a horseman was to be seen. Heavy firing was heard down the river. During this time the questions were being asked: "What's the matter with Custer, that he don't send word what we shall do?". . . thus showing some uneasiness, but still no one seemed to show great anxiety, nor do I know that any one felt any serious apprehension but that Custer could and would take care of himself. Some of Reno's men had seen Custer's headquarters party, including Custer himself, on the bluffs about the time the Indians began to develop in Reno's front. This party was heard to cheer, and seen to wave their hats as if to give encouragement, and then they disappeared behind the hills . . . .

During a long time after the junction of Reno and Benteen we heard firing down the river in the direction of Custer's command. We were satisfied that Custer was fighting the Indians somewhere, and the conviction was expressed that "our command ought to be doing something or Custer would be after Reno with a sharp stick." We heard two distinct volleys which excited some surprise, and . . . brought out the remark from some one that "Custer was giving it to them for all he is worth.". . . About five o'clock the command moved down toward Custer's supposed whereabouts, intending to join him. The advance went as far as the high bluffs . . . . The air was full of dust. We could see stationary groups of horsemen, and individual horsemen moving about. From their grouping and the manner in which they sat their horses we knew they were Indians.[47]

"We saw a good many . . . galloping up and down and firing at objects on the ground," added Lieutenant Edgerly.[48] Returning to Godfrey:

Looking toward Custer's field, on a hill two miles away, we saw a large assemblage. At first our command did not appear to attract their attention, although there was some commotion observable among those near to our position. We heard occasional shots, most of which seemed to be a great distance off, beyond the large groups on the hill. While watching this group, the conclusion was arrived at that Custer had been repulsed, and the firing we heard was the parting shots of the rear guard. The firing ceased, the groups dispersed, clouds of dust arose from all parts of the field, and the horsemen converged toward our position . . . . The Indians almost immediately followed [us] to the top of the bluff, and commenced firing into the retreating troops, killing one man, wounding others and several horses. They then started down the hillside in pursuit. I at once made up my mind that such a retreat and close pursuit would throw the whole command into confusion, and, perhaps, prove disastrous. I dismounted my men to fight on foot, deploying as rapidly as possible . . . .

Our fire in a short time compelled the Indians to halt and take cover, but before this was accomplished a second order came for me to fall back as quickly as possible to the main command. Having checked the pursuit we began our retreat, slowly at first, but kept up our firing. After proceeding some distance the men began to group together, and to move a little faster and faster, and our fire slackened. This was pretty good evidence that they were getting demoralized. The Indians were being heavily reinforced and began to come from their cover, but kept up a heavy fire. I halted the line, made the men take their intervals, and again drove the Indians to cover; then once more began the retreat. The firing of the Indians was heavy. The bullets struck the ground all about us; but the "ping-ping" of the bullets overhead seemed to have a more terrifying influence than the "swish-thud" of the bullets that struck the ground immediately about us. When we got to the ridge in front of Reno's position I observed some Indians making all haste to get possession of a hill to the right. I could see the rest of the command, and I knew that that hill would command Reno's position . . . . It was now about seven o'clock.[49]

"We dismounted in haste," John Ryan recounted, "putting the wounded in a low depression on the bluffs and put packs from the mules around them to shelter them from the fire of the Indians. We then formed a circle of our pack mules and horses, forming a skirmish line all around the hole, and then lay down and waited for the Indians."[50] The sergeant continued:

We had been in this position but a short time when they advanced in great numbers from the direction in which we came. They made

> several charges upon us and we repulsed them every time. Finally they surrounded us. Soon the firing became general all along the line, very rapid and at close range. The company on the right of my company had a number of men killed in a few minutes. There was a ridge on the right . . . and one Indian in particular . . . [was] a good shot. While we were lying in this line he fired a shot and killed the fourth man on my right. Soon afterward he fired again and shot the third man. His third shot wounded the man on my right, who jumped back from the line, and down among the wounded. I thought my turn was coming next. I jumped up, with Captain [Thomas] French, and some half a dozen members of my company, and, instead of firing straight to the front, as we had been doing up to the time of this incident, we wheeled to our right and put in a deadly volley, and I think we put an end to that Indian, as there were no more men killed at that particular spot.[51]

"Everybody . . . lay down and spread himself out as thin as possible," recalled Lieutenant Godfrey. "After lying there a few minutes I was horrified to find myself wondering if a small sagebrush, about as thick as my finger, would turn a bullet."[52] For the remainder of the day Sioux and Cheyenne snipers kept the soldiers pinned down. By dusk, however, the firing ceased and the relieved whites began to stir. "Of course, everybody was wondering about Custer—why he did not communicate by courier or signal," Godfrey continued. "But the general opinion seemed to prevail that he had been defeated and driven down the river, where he would probably join General Terry, and with whom he would return to our relief. Quite frequently, too, the question, 'What's the matter with Custer?' would evoke an impatient reply."[53]

"We felt terribly alone on that dangerous hilltop," recalled Private Windolph. "We were a million miles from nowhere. And death was all around us."[54]

As Edward Godfrey revealed, such forlorn feelings coupled with the strain of the past several hours had a devastating effect on the besieged.

> Soon after all firing had ceased the wildest confusion prevailed. Men imagined they could see a column of troops over on the hills or ridges, that they could hear the tramp of the horses, the command of officers or even the trumpet-calls . . . . [S]hots were fired by some of our men, and familiar trumpet-calls were sounded by our trumpeter immediately after, to let the supposed marching column know that we were friends. Every favorable expression or opinion was received with credulity, and then ratified with a cheer. Somebody suggested that General Crook might be coming, so some one . . .

> mounted a horse, and galloping along the line yelled: "Don't be discouraged, boys, Crook is coming." But they gradually realized that the much-wished-for reinforcements were but the phantasma of their imaginations.[55]

That evening, Sergeant Ryan remembered, "[w]e went to work with what tools we had, consisting of two spades, our knives and tin cups, and, in fact, we used pieces of hard tack boxes for spades, and commenced throwing up temporary works. We also formed breastworks from boxes of hard bread, sacks of bacon, sacks of corn and oats, blankets, and in fact everything that we could get hold of."[56] Though the fighting had mercifully ceased, the nightmare had not. Godfrey:

> The long twilight was prolonged by numerous bonfires, located throughout their village. The long shadows of the hills and the refracted light gave a supernatural aspect to the surrounding country . . . . Their camp was a veritable pandemonium. All night long they continued their frantic revels: beating tom-toms, dancing, whooping, yelling with demoniacal screams, and discharging firearms. We knew they were having a scalp dance.[57]

Terrible as the situation seemed to those atop the bluffs, it was far worse for the men still trapped below. After cowering all day in the brush along the river and after witnessing Indians skin alive their wounded comrades, one group of four decided at dark to make their break. Billy Jackson:

> Girard and I were to ride our horses, the others walking close at our side. Then, if we were discovered, De Rudio and O'Neil were to drop down flat upon the ground, and we were to ride away, drawing the enemy after us. We were no sooner out of the brush than we began to pass the bodies of the men and horses that had been killed along the line of Reno's retreat. The men had all been stripped of their clothing, and were . . . badly cut up . . . .
>
> We went on to the river, coming to a halt at the edge of a bank dropping straight down to the water; on the other side, a high, black, and very steep bank faced us . . . . O'Neil jumped in to ascertain the depth, went in almost to his neck and would have been carried downstream had he not seized some overhanging brush and drawn himself to footing closer in. He filled his hat with water and passed it up to De Rudio, who handed it to me. I drank every drop it contained and wanted more . . . . We went on up the shore, looking for a place to cross . . . .

> Ahead of us was black darkness, heavy silence. As we went on, our hearts became more and more heavy; we feared that all of the troops had been killed. We came to a place where the river was rippling and murmuring, as water does over a shallow stony bed . . . . "Take hold of my horse's tail, I will lead in," Girard replied. In we went, slowly, feeling our way. Nowhere across was the water up to our horses' knees![58]

In the words of Lieutenant DeRudio:

> [W]e forded the stream but found it was at a bend and that we would have to ford it again. When we recrossed the river, we ran full into a band of eight savages. The two mounted men ran for their lives, the soldier and myself jumped into the bushes near us. I cocked my revolver and in a kneeling position was ready to fire at the savages if they should approach me. They evidently thought, from the precipitate retreat of the two mounted men, that all of us had decamped; and began to talk among themselves . . . . We then saw that all the fords were well guarded by the savages, and it would be very dangerous to attempt to cross any part of the river.[59]

Though these four were forced to hunt new holes, others, including Private Petring, somehow managed to rejoin their comrades on the hill. Sergeant Ryan:

> During the night ammunition and the rations reached us where we were entrenched in the lines, but we suffered severely from lack of water. Although the river was only three or four hundred yards away, we were unable to get any water, as the Indians held the approach to it. During the night several men made attempts to get water, but they were killed or driven back.
>
> About the middle of the night we heard a trumpet call, and the men commenced to cheer, thinking it was Custer's men who were coming to our assistance. Major Reno ordered one of our trumpeters to sound a call, but it was not repeated, so we made up our minds that it was a decoy on the part of the Indians to get us out of our works.
>
> The next morning, being the 26th, two shots were fired just before daylight by the Indians, in rapid succession . . . . This began the engagement of another day. In a few moments the battle raged in earnest, the Indians advancing in large numbers and trying to cut through.[60]

After driving back the attackers, both sides engaged in heavy firing. "Of course it was their policy to draw our fire as much as possible to exhaust our ammunition," Godfrey noted. "The Indians amused themselves by standing erect, in full view for an instant, then dropping down again before a bullet could reach them . . . . Then they resorted to the old ruse of raising a hat and blouse, or a blanket, on a stick to draw our fire."[61]

Whatever contempt a soldier may have had for Indian marksmanship before June 26 quickly dissolved after that day. Charles Windolph:

> My buddy . . . was lying alongside of me . . . . Together we had scooped out a wide, shallow trench and we piled up the dirt to make a little breastwork in front of us. It was plumb light now, and the Indian sharpshooters on the knob of the hill south of us and perhaps a thousand yards away, were taking pot shots at us. Jones said something about taking off his overcoat, and he started to roll on his side so that he could get his arms and shoulders out without exposing himself to fire. Suddenly I heard him cry out. He had been shot straight through the heart.[62]

After a comrade next to him received a mortal stomach wound, Jacob Adams saw another trooper nearby double up when a "ball struck him in the breast . . . and came out of his back just above the hip."[63] Regarding a civilian packer, another soldier said: "He was aiming a carbine over a breastwork

Charles Windolph. LITTLE BIGHORN BATTLEFIELD NATIONAL MONUMENT.

about 3 ft. high, and after he had been observed in this position about 20 min., some one made [a] remark that 'something must be wrong with the packer.' Upon going up he was found stone dead, having been hit in the temple and killed so quick that he did not move from [the] position [of] sighting his gun."[64]

As the fighting intensified and the circle tightened, one man boldly took control. "Benteen was on his feet all day," remembered Private George Glenn, "and, it being hot, his shirt tail worked out of his pants and hung down, and he went around that way encouraging the men. He would say 'Men, this is a groundhog case; it is live or die with us. We must fight it out with them.'"[65]

"The bullets were flying very fast and I don't see why . . . Benteen was not riddled," added an amazed Lieutenant Edgerly.[66]

"He was perfectly cool," Godfrey recalled. "There was a smile on his face . . . . I shouted at him that he better come away from the place where he was, that there was a real danger of him being shot. He replied something to the effect that the bullet had not been molded yet that would shoot him."[67]

"Lieutenant Gibson was trying to get out of sight in a pit too shallow and was acting so cowardly that he was in the way of men passing back and forth," revealed Private Glenn. "Benteen got ashamed of him and told the men to run over him if he persisted in lying there."[68]

"[A]n Indian had shot one of Gibson's men," Godfrey continued, "then rushed up and touched the body with his 'coup-stick,' and started back to cover, but he was killed."

> This boldness determined Benteen to make a charge . . . . The firing almost ceased for a while, and then it recommenced with greater fury . . . . Benteen came back to where Reno was, and said if something was not done pretty soon the Indians would run into our lines. Waiting a short time, and no action being taken on his suggestion, he said rather impatiently: "you've got to do something here on the north side pretty quick; this won't do, you must drive them back." Reno then directed us to get ready for a charge, and told Benteen to give the word. Benteen called out, "All ready now, men. Now's the time. Give them hell. Hip, hip, here we go!" And away we went with a hurrah, every man . . . but one, who lay in his pit crying like a child. The Indians fired more rapidly than before from their whole line. Our men left the pits with their carbines loaded, and they began firing without orders soon after we started. A large body of Indians had assembled at the foot of one of the hills on the north intending probably to make a charge, as Benteen had divined, but they broke as soon as our line started.[69]

"[T]o say that 'twas a surprise to them, is mild form," Benteen laughed, "for they somersaulted and vaulted as so many trained acrobats, having no order in getting down those ravines, but quickly getting!"[70]

Returning to Godfrey:

> When we had advanced 70 to 100 yards, Reno called out "Get back, men, back," and back the whole line came. A most singular fact of this sortie was that not a man who had advanced with the lines was hit; but directly after everyone had gotten into the pits again, the one man who did not go out was shot in the head and killed instantly. The poor fellow had a premonition that he would be killed, and had so told one of his comrades.[71]

Driven to delirium by heat, thirst, and the crushing pressure, some soldiers snapped. One man "went insane," a witness said, "and . . . we had to tie him fast."[72] Private Peter Thompson recorded the fate of another crazed comrade.

> His name was Pat Golden, a young man of striking appearance, with dark hair, black mustache, tall, straight as an arrow and nimble as a cat . . . . [S]hooting from the shelter of a rifle pit was not suitable to him, and to get a better view of the enemy he sprang out of the pit and commenced to fire at anything that appeared to him like an Indian. He was urged by his comrades to come under cover as it was too dangerous to expose himself that way. Heedless of the danger, he held his position amid a shower of lead, both a challenge and a target to the fire of the Indians. It was not long before he was hit by a ball, but he still kept his place. Again he was struck but he still kept his feet, firing when the opportunity presented itself, apparently paying no attention to the entreaties of his comrades to come under shelter. He called out as another bullet struck him, "Boys, that is number three, but I'm still here. Number four," he shouted as another bullet struck him, and he still kept his feet and fired his gun. Every man of his company admired his pluck, but they could not help but see that he was throwing his life away. Finally, a ball went crashing through his brain and his lifeless body rolled into a rifle pit which became his grave.[73]

As the morning wore on, the cry for water increased, especially among the wounded. "Some of the enlisted men would propose that some . . . should volunteer to get to the river for this purpose," Stanislas Roy recounted. "This talk went around, and finally the officers said if any of the

Stanislas Roy. LITTLE BIGHORN BATTLEFIELD NATIONAL MONUMENT.

men wanted to volunteer they might do so."[74] Eventually, a dozen men, including Corporal Roy, crawled from the line.

> In going down . . . we had to run across an open space about 100 yards wide to get to [the] head of [the] ravine. From here to [the] river we were concealed from [the] Sioux. We got down to [the] mouth of [the] ravine and could see Indians in [the] brush on [the] opposite bank . . . but we did not want to shoot, to bring an engagement [on]. . . . I was [the] fifth man to dash for water . . . . [W]e numbered ourselves off and said that as each man's name was called off he could go or not as he would choose. The first man, whose name I do not remember, came back with a kettle full and we all took a drink, the first in 36 hours. I think Wilber was fourth, and he was wounded. After Madden was hit, he crawled back and we gave him water and nursed him and there was then an intermission of about one-half hour before anyone went again. Altogether we were there in the ravine about an hour getting water. We would rush and fill the kettle from the river and then fill canteens from the kettles.
>
> In about one and one-half hours after starting we got back to the top of [the] hill.[75]

Heroic as the act had been, the water was but a fraction of what was needed and most was reserved for the wounded. Even then, Roy admitted, "there was not enough to give them all they craved for."[76]

As the heat of the day approached, the stench of decomposition became hideous. "My horse was killed, and he was one of the dead horses piled up on [the] line," said scout George Herendeen. "I lay behind him . . . and he was bloated up with gas, and two or three times when the body was struck, I could hear the hiss of escaping gas."[77] The sniping along the bluffs continued until about 3 P.M., when it abruptly abated. A relieved, yet perplexed, Edward Godfrey:

> Late in the afternoon we saw a few horsemen in the bottom apparently to observe us, and then fire was set to the grass in the valley. About 7 p.m. we saw emerge from behind this screen of smoke an immense moving mass crossing the plateau, going toward the Big Horn Mountains. This moving mass was distant about five or six miles, but looked much nearer, and almost directly between us and the setting sun, now darkened by the smoke and dust ladened atmosphere . . . . A fervent "Thank God" that they had at last given up the contest was soon followed by grave doubts as to their motive for moving. Perhaps Custer had met Terry, and was coming to our relief; perhaps they were short of ammunition and were moving their village to a safe distance before making a final desperate effort to overwhelm us; perhaps it was only a ruse to get us on the move and then clean us out, were the conjectures.[78]

From their coverts along the river, Billy Jackson and Fred Girard also watched the exodus. "The great horde of warriors and ponies and squaws and children passed so near to us," Girard recalled, "that we could plainly see wounded warriors on travois and dead warriors thrown across and tied to the backs of horses. Above all the noise and rattle and the hum of voices and cries of children we could hear the . . . chanting of the squaws."[79]

"They were happy, they were singing victory songs," noted a confused Billy Jackson. "I could not understand that. Where was victory for them when the fight was not ended?"[80] Grateful for the Indians' departure, even if temporary, the soldiers atop the hill moved quickly to improve their lot. "The stench from the dead men and horses was now exceedingly offensive, and it was decided to take up a new position nearer the river," Godfrey explained. "[T]he men were put to work digging pits with the expectation of a renewal of the attack. Our loss on the hill had been eighteen killed and fifty-two wounded."[81]

That night, volunteers brought up more water for the thirst-crazed men. To everyone's surprise, Billy Jackson and the three companions, who had been cowering amid thousands of Indians for nearly two days, finally slipped across the line to safety. The following morning, with no enemy in sight, the troopers felt bold enough to lead the surviving mounts down the hill. "It was a pitiful sight," recalled one soldier, "to see the poor animals plunge their heads in the water up to their eyes and drink."[82] Sergeant John Ryan:

> [A]t daylight we could look from the bluffs over the timber to where the Indian camp was, and we saw that it was deserted, with the exception of the lodge poles, which remained standing. On the other side, a long way off from the Indian camp, we noticed a large cloud of dust arising, and a body of either Indians or troops coming towards the Indian camp, but at the time we could not distinguish which they were. Some of the officers turned their field glasses on, and thought they were troops. Reno immediately dispatched a couple of his scouts.[83]

First word of the June 25 fight had reached Alfred Terry when Crow scouts from Custer's column found him along the Little Bighorn the following day.[84] Though the general had no reason to doubt an engagement had occurred, neither he nor his staff gave any credence to the Crow claim that the 7th Cavalry had been wiped out. According to plan, Terry, John Gibbon, and their combined cavalry and infantry force continued up the valley toward the battlefield. Colonel Gibbon:

> [W]e caught sight, through the scattered timber, of a couple of Indian tepees standing in the open valley . . . . At length we reached the tepees, found them occupied by dead Indians laid out in state, and surrounded in every direction with the remnants and various odds and ends of a hastily abandoned camp. Tepee poles, skins, robes, pots, kettles, and pans lay scattered in every direction. But we had little time or inclination to comment on these sights, for every thought was now bent upon the possible fate of our fellow-soldiers, and the desire was intense to solve as soon as possible the dread doubt which now began to fill our minds. For, in searching about amongst the rubbish, someone had picked up a pair of bloody drawers, upon which was plainly written the words, "Sturgis—7th Cavalry," whilst a buckskin shirt recognized as belonging to Lieutenant [James] Porter, was discovered with a bullet-hole passing through it.[85]

Summoning a company of mounted infantry, Terry ordered the men to comb the hills east of the campground. Gibbon:

> Looking up the valley I caught sight of something on the top of a hill . . . which at once attracted my attention . . . . I sprang from my horse, and with a field glass looked long and anxiously at a number of dark objects which might be either animals or stubby cedar trees . . . . One of General Terry's staff officers took the glass and seating himself on the ground peered long and anxiously at the spots.[86]

"On returning to headquarters I found my friends turning their field glasses on the hills in every direction," noticed Lieutenant Edward McClernand, who had been sifting through the abandoned camp. "The fate of Custer was now more puzzling than ever. Our chief, General Terry, was calm but serious. He evidently was weighing the situation."[87] Returning to John Gibbon:

> Whilst watching . . . and wondering . . . the officer in charge of the mounted infantry party . . . rode up to where General Terry and I sat upon our horses, and his voice trembled as he said, "I have a very sad report to make. I have counted one hundred and ninety-seven dead bodies lying in the hills!" "White men?" was the first question asked. "Yes, white men." A look of horror was upon every face, and for a moment no one spoke.[88]

McClernand:

> Now two horsemen were seen dashing toward us from up the valley . . . . As the hurrying riders drew nearer we discovered they were riding bare-back, then that they were white men, and finally two lieutenants, Wallace and Hare, sent by Reno . . . .
>
> "Where is Custer?" they were asked. Wallace replied, "The last we saw of him he was going along that high bluff . . . toward the lower end of the village. He took off his hat and waved to us. We do not know where he is now."
>
> "We have found him," said General Terry, his eyes filling with tears . . . .
>
> Reno's messengers sat their horses aghast at the information given them, and seemed slow to grasp the fact that their detachment had not played the major role in the drama that had been enacted.
>
> Leaving Custer and his companions in death on the hills where we had found them, we placed ourselves under the guidance of Wallace and Hare to be taken to those of our comrades who had survived

the catastrophe. They led us along the valley for some three and a half or four miles, where the village had stood the day before.[89]

Again, Colonel Gibbon:

> Nearly the whole valley was black and smoking with the fire which had swept over it . . . . Except the fire, the ground presented but few evidences of the conflict which had taken place. Now and then a dead horse was seen; but as I approached a bend of the creek just below the hill occupied by the troops, I came upon the body of a soldier lying on his face near a dead horse. He was stripped, his scalp gone, his head beaten in, and his body filled with bullet-holes and arrows . . . . More bodies of both men and horses were found close by, and it was noted that the bodies of men and horses laid almost always in pairs, and . . . the inference was drawn that in the run, the horses must have been killed first, and the riders after they fell.
>
> The command was placed in camp here, and details at once set to work to haul away the dead horses and bury the men, both of which were already becoming offensive. Then mounting my horse, I proceeded to visit . . . Reno's command. As I rode a few hundred yards up the river towards the ford, bodies of men and horses were seen scattered along at intervals, and in the river itself dead horses were lying.[90]

Amid cheers and tears, Reno's beleaguered command greeted Terry and his deliverers. As Godfrey noted, however, "The grave countenance of the General awed the men to silence."[91] When it was revealed what had occurred just down the ridge a scant four miles away, there was only stunned disbelief.

While the seriously wounded were either tended to on the spot or carried carefully down to the camp, the recovery of bodies along the river continued. Some of the first corpses, including that of Doctor DeWolf, were discovered in the cuts of the bluffs where the victims had been mowed down during the Sunday rout. In the Little Bighorn itself, George Herendeen remembered another find.

> [W]e found a dead horse in the middle of the river, just below where Reno had crossed in retreat. This horse lay in water too shallow to float him off. The horse was much bloated, and upon investigation we found a dead soldier under him. Whether he had been drowned by being caught under the horse . . . or whether he had been killed simultaneously with the horse, I do not know.[92]

In the valley itself, the grass was littered with dead men and mounts. "They were covered with swarms of flies," said a horrified Marcus Reno, "and the odor from decomposing bodies under the blazing sun was intolerable."[93]

After only a glance, the hideous mutilation and torture were obvious. One body was found with "a stick rammed down the throat."[94]

"Another man," Herendeen observed, "had strips of his skin cut out of his body . . . . Many bodies were gashed with knives, and some had their noses and other members cut off."[95] The wounds of interpreter Isaiah Dorman, the only black man with Custer, displayed a savagery reserved for only the most despised of enemies. Wrote a witness:

> Isaiah lay with his breast full of arrows and an iron picket pin thrusted through his testicles into the ground, pinning him down . . . . Dorman's penis was cut off and stuffed in his mouth, which was regarded among the Indians as the deepest insult possible . . . . [H]e had small pistol balls in his legs from the knees down . . . . [His] body had been ripped open, and a coffee pot and cup which he carried with him were filled with his blood. What devilish purpose the Indians had in catching his blood I do not know.[96]

If possible, the village exhibited scenes even more revolting. Reno:

> One ghastly find was near the center of the field where three teepee poles were standing upright in the ground in the form of a triangle. On top of each were inverted camp kettles, while below them on the grass were the heads of three men . . . . The heads had been severed from the trunks by some very sharp instrument, as the flesh was cut smoothly. The three heads had been placed within the triangle, facing each other in a horrible, sightless stare.[97]

"We found the ashes and debris of a large fire," Private Theodore Goldin added, "and near it, in the trodden grass, one of our party found two human heads which were so charred and burned as to be beyond recognition."[98] Another private kicked over a camp kettle and found the head of a red-haired soldier staring back at him.

The following day the troops turned to Custer's slaughtered command. "The morning was bright," recalled Edward Godfrey, "and from the high bluffs we had a clear view of Custer's battle-field. We saw a large number of objects that looked like white boulders scattered over the field. Glasses were brought into requisition, and it was announced that these objects were the dead bodies. Captain [Thomas] Weir exclaimed: 'Oh, how white they look!'"[99]

"The scene . . . was beyond description," Reno wrote, "and it filled us with horror and anguish."

> The dead had been . . . scattered in the wildest confusion over the ground, in groups of two or three, or piled in an indiscriminate mass of men and horses. They had lain thus for nearly three days under the fierce heat of the sun, exposed to swarms of flies and flesh-eating crows, and the scene was rendered even more desolute by the deep silence which seemed to hang like a weird mystery over the battlefield.[100]

"It was a horrible sight," said another soldier. "There the bodies lay, mostly naked, and scattered over a field maybe a half mile square. We went among them to see how many we could recognize."[101] Although the corpses were bloated and discolored, many faces maintained a "pained, almost terrified expression."[102] Private Jacob Adams:

> The men . . . were . . . scalped and horribly mutilated. Some . . . were decapitated, while many bodies were lacking feet . . . . As I walked over the field I saw many unfortunate dead who had been propped into a sitting position and used as targets by bowmen who had proceeded to stick them full of steel-headed arrows . . . . Some bodies were set up on their knees and elbows and their hind parts had been shot full of arrows.[103]

"Many of their skulls had been crushed in, eyes had been torn from their sockets, and hands . . . arms, legs and noses had been wrenched off," Reno noted. "Many had their flesh cut in strips the entire length of their bodies, and there were others whose limbs were closely perforated with bullets, showing that the torture had been inflicted while the wretched victims were still alive."[104]

"The eyes of surviving comrades were filled with tears, and throats were choked with grief unspeakable," remembered Fred Girard as he moved amid the carnage.[105] "It made me sick," another trooper confessed, "to see my fellow comrades . . . lying on the hillside, disemboweled, with stakes driven through their chests."[106]

George Glenn came to a body and soon realized it was that of his former "bunky," Tom Tweed. "His crotch had been split up with an ax and one of his legs thrown up over his shoulder," Glenn recalled. "He was shot with arrows in both eyes. A wounded horse lay near him groaning, and we knocked him in the head with a bloody ax that lay near by."[107]

Moving up the ridge, past scores of bodies, including those of trumpeter Henry Dose and newsman Mark Kellogg, the soldiers finally came to the scene of the last stand. Here, according to a witness, the corpses lay thick. Lieutenant Godfrey came upon one butchered body, that of his old friend, Tom Custer.

> It was lying downward, all the scalp was removed, leaving only tufts of his hair on the nape of his neck. The skull was smashed in and a number of arrows had been shot into the back of the head and in the body. I remarked that I believed it was Tom as he and I had often gone in swimming together and the form seemed familiar. We rolled the body over; the features where they had touched the ground were pressed out of shape and were somewhat decomposed. In turning the body, one arm which had been shot and broken, remained under the body; this was pulled out and on it we saw [a tattoo] "T.W.C." and the goddess of liberty and flag . . . . His belly had been cut open and his entrails protruded.[108]

Nearby lay the older brother, the commander of the regiment. Jacob Adams:

> General Custer was stripped with the exception of his sox. He had a gunshot wound in his head and another in his side, and in his left thigh there was a gash about eleven inches long that exposed the bone. Custer was not scalped . . . and I am sure he did not commit suicide . . . . There were no powder burns on [his] face and . . . it would have been next to impossible for a man to hold a gun far enough away from his face to escape such burns when committing suicide.[109]

"When I arrived there," Godfrey later wrote, "General Custer's body had been laid out . . . . [Girard] . . . informed me that he preceded the troops there. He found the naked bodies of two soldiers, one across the other and Custer's naked body in a sitting posture between and leaning against them, his upper right arm along and on the topmost body, his right forearm and hand supporting his head in an inclining posture like one resting or asleep."[110] Girard and Godfrey also saw something more—an arrow shaft had been rammed up the lieutenant colonel's penis.[111]

With as much speed as possible, the troopers began to bury the dead. "[T]he stench was so great that my men began to vomit," one officer admitted.[112] "Many times," another soldier added, "in taking hold of a body to lift it into the grave, the skin would slip from the wrist, or the shoulders would become dislocated."[113]

"As we had but few spades, the burial of the dead was more of a pretense than reality," Edward McClernand confessed. "A number were simply covered with sage brush."[114] After the grim task, when most of the men had returned to the valley and were preparing to break camp, McClernand paused. Standing on the ridge, surveying the location of the last stand, the young officer replayed in his mind the dramatic, final moments of George Armstrong Custer.

> He was dismounted, and doubtless many of his men also, the enemy was pressing, and here was a position on which they could stand and strike back—probably without hope of victory, but at least with the possibility of holding on until Reno or Benteen came, or that relief of dying like brave men. I think no thoughtful and unprejudiced man could have examined the last positions held by Custer, as marked by the dead, without being convinced that he was thinking clearly, fast and courageously. I said to myself, as did others doubtless, here a hero died. That his was the spirit of battle seemed clear from those who chose to die on the knoll with him.[115]

Later that day, June 28, Alfred Terry quickly formed his command and with Reno, Benteen, and their numerous wounded in tow, the general led away toward the Bighorn River, where news of the disaster would soon spread to the outside world. As he moved along with the column, Edward McClernand recalled earlier that spring when the Crow scout had left his defiant message on the old bread box. "It is a little strange," reflected the lieutenant, "considering the hundreds of miles we have marched over, that this taunt should have been left almost on the very spot where the one desperate fight of the campaign took place."[116]

Early on July 6, 1876, the steamboat *Far West* docked near Fort Abraham Lincoln. During the previous two days, dark currents had swirled mysteriously around the anxious garrison. In the words of one young officer:

> There was whispering and excitement among the Indian police. There were rumors of a great battle. Those who saw the Indians and witnessed their movements knew that something unusual must have happened. But what? Who would not give worlds to know just why all this excitement among the Indians? Fleet-footed warriors, mounted on still fleeter animals, aided perhaps by signals, had brought the news even before the *Far West* came, but no white man knew. That it brought joy to them was reason enough why it should have brought depression to the whites . . . .

Men and women moved anxiously, nervously, straining their eyes for the expected messenger, listening as footsteps fell . . . .

The news came to us about 2 A.M. Captain William S. McCaskey . . . summoned all the officers to his quarters at once, and there read to them the communication he had just received . . . . After we had recovered from the shock, Captain McCaskey requested us to assist him in breaking the news to the widows. It fell to my lot to accompany Captain McCaskey . . . to the quarters of Mrs. Custer . . . . We started on our sad errand a little before 7 o'clock on that . . . morning. I went to the rear of the Custer house, woke up Maria, Mrs. Custer's housemaid, and requested her to rap on Mrs. Custer's door . . . . On my way through the hall . . . I heard the opening of the door of Mrs. Custer's room. She had been awakened by the footsteps in the hall. She called me by name and asked me the cause of my early visit.[117]

15 Death Song

As shocking, horrifying, and unbelievable as the news from Montana was to a nation celebrating its centennial, the near annihilation of America's most celebrated cavalry regiment was a staggering blow to frontier regulars. For those accustomed to victory after victory over the Indians, it was a time for serious reexamination.

"There is no use trying to conceal the fact," wrote James O'Kelly of the New York *Herald*, "that the victory of the Sioux, so terrible in its completeness, has lowered the morale of our troops; not much, perhaps; but if one listens to the soldiers as they discuss among themselves the campaign the conviction is forced that they no longer look upon victory as certain."[1]

While troops faced the coming campaign on the northern Plains with grim foreboding, the federal government, determined to hammer home its resolve, rushed forward thousands of reinforcements.

Ironically, although his camp was barely fifty miles from the scene of the massacre, George Crook was one of the last men in America to learn of Custer's fate. After his stinging rebuff on the Rosebud, the shaken general had withdrawn to the base of the Bighorn Mountains and bivouacked along the headwaters of the Tongue River. Although he had premonitions of disaster to the north, it was not until July 10 that Crook heard the incredible details.

"Grief, Revenge, Sorrow and Fear stalked among us," Lieutenant John Bourke noted in his diary. Bitter as defeat on the Rosebud had been, Bourke and his comrades suddenly realized just how much worse it could have been. Another young officer who quietly counted his blessings was Frederick Sib-

Tribune--Extra.

BISMARCK, D.T., JULY 6, 11:30 A.M.

MASSACRED

GEN. CUSTER AND 261 MEN THE VICTIMS

NO OFFICER OR MAN OF 5 COMPANIES LEFT TO TELL THE TALE

3 Days Desperate Fighting by Maj. Reno and the Remainder of the Seventh

Full Details of the Battle.

LIST OF KILLED AND WOUNDED

THE BISMARCK TRIBUNE'S SPECIAL CORRESPONDENT SLAIN.

ley. Four days before news arrived from the Little Bighorn, Crook had ordered the lieutenant to scout that river for Sioux. Besides a squad of twenty-five picked men, veteran guides Frank Grouard and Baptiste "Big Bat" Pourier were assigned to Sibley. Additionally, newsman John Finerty asked Crook for permission to ride along.

"The General seemed somewhat surprised at my request and hesitated about letting me go," Finerty remarked. "He finally consented, but warned me that I might get into more trouble than, perhaps, I anticipated. Lieutenant Bourke asked me what kind of an epitaph I would like him to write for me."[2]

On the move for most of the night, Sibley's tiny command pulled up within a few miles of the Little Bighorn. Finerty:

> Early [in] the morning . . . we were again in the saddle, pressing on cautiously toward where the scouts believed the Indian village to be. When we had reached a point several miles from our late bivouac and close to the Little Big Horn River, Gruard [*sic*], motioning us to halt, ascended a rocky mound directly in our front, leaving his horse slightly below the crest . . . . Scarcely had the scout taken a first cautious look from the crest of the ridge when a peculiar motion of his hand summoned Baptiste Pourier to his side. Baptiste dismounted also, leaving his pony below the crest.
>
> He joined Gruard and both scouts keenly observed the country . . . through their glasses. Their observations finished, they mounted their ponies and came galloping back to us in hot haste. "Be quick, and follow me for your lives," cried Gruard. We mounted immediately and . . . reached a bluff of sufficient size to conceal our horses on its westerly side . . . . Sibley, Gruard, Pourier and myself—went up into the rocks and waited to see what was coming.
>
> "What did you see, Frank?" asked Sibley of the scout, after we had settled down to make our observations.
>
> "Only Sitting Bull's war party," Frank replied. "I knew they would be here around the Little Big Horn without coming at all."
>
> We did not have long to wait for confirmation of his words. Almost as he spoke, groups of mounted savages appeared on the bluffs north and east of us. Every moment increased their numbers . . . .
>
> "They appear not to have seen us yet," observed Gruard. "Unless some of them hit upon our trail of this morning, we are comparatively safe." Gradually the right wing of the war party approached the ground over which we had so recently ridden. We watched their movements, as may be supposed, with breathless interest. Suddenly an Indian attired in a red blanket halted, looked for a moment at the

ground, and then began to ride around in a circle. "Now we had better look out," said Gruard. "That fellow has found our trail, sure, and they will be after us in five minutes."[3]

Realizing that they could not outrun the warriors, Grouard led Sibley straight into the rugged Bighorns. After a rigorous ride among rock and pine, the Sioux seemingly gave up the chase and the troops halted to rest their mounts. Finerty continued:

> [W]e again saddled up and pushed forward, feeling much invigorated . . . . We were riding in single file, the scouts leading . . . . Suddenly John Becker, the packer, and a soldier who had lingered somewhat in the rear rode up to the Lieutenant, exclaiming: "The Indians! the Indians!" Gruard and the rest of us looked over our right shoulders and saw a party of the red fiends in their war bonnets riding rapidly along that flank at no great distance . . . . Scarcely was the warning uttered when from the rocks and trees upon our right . . . came a ringing volley . . . . "Fall back on the woods!" cried the scout, and every horse was wheeled toward the timber on the left. My horse stumbled from the shock of [a] bullet, but recovered its feet almost immediately and bore me in safety to the edge of the timber, under the rapid Indian fire . . . .
>
> There was no need to urge our horses to cover because they were badly stampeded by the firing . . . and we were soon dismounted in the edge of the woods. Lieutenant Sibley, before we tied the animals, made some of the soldiers fire upon the Indians, which had the effect of confining them to the rocks. The savages . . . succeeded in injuring several other horses by their subsequent volleys, some fatally . . . . Lieutenant Sibley formed us into a semi-circular skirmish line, and matters soon became exceedingly hot in our front. The trees and fallen timber, particularly the latter, served us admirably for breastworks and we blazed away for some time with right good will. The Lieutenant warned us not to waste our lead, and we slackened fire somewhat. We could see, occasionally, the Indian leader, dressed in what appeared to be white buckskin and wearing a gorgeous war bonnet, directing the movements of his warriors . . . .
>
> The Indians lay low among the tall rocks and pine trees and kept up an almost incessant fire upon our position, filling the trees around us with their lead. I could hear their bullets rattling against the pine tree trunks like hail-stones on the roof of a barn . . . . Not a man of our party expected to leave that spot with life, because all well knew that the noise of the firing would bring to the attack every

John Finerty. KANSAS STATE HISTORICAL SOCIETY.

Sioux and Cheyenne within reach, while we were fully fifty miles from any hope of re-inforcement. The savages evidently aimed at our horses, thinking that by killing them all means of retreat would be cut off from us.

Meanwhile, their numbers continued to increase and they seemed to swarm on the open slopes of the hills within the range of our vision. We could distinctly hear their savage, encouraging yells to each other . . . all of whom appeared to be in great glee at the prospect of a scalping entertainment at our expense. They had evidently recognized Gruard, whom they heartily hated . . . and one savage shouted to him: "Do you think there are no men but yours in this country?"[4]

With torture and death staring Finerty in the face, the beauty surrounding him did not go unnoticed. "[I]n one of the intervals of the firing," the reporter recalled, "I picked a few specimens of the mountain crocus and forget-me-not growing within my reach and placed them between the leaves of my notebook . . . . Life seemed particularly sweet throughout that eventful day."[5]

With more and more Indians arriving and with rescue out of the question, Grouard warned Sibley that their only hope of escape was up and over the towering Bighorns. Again, Finerty:

> [T]he eternal shadows seemed to be fast closing around us. The Indian bullets were hitting nearer every moment and the Indian yell was growing stronger and fiercer when a hand was laid on my shoulder and Rufus, a soldier who was my neighbor on the skirmish line, said: "The rest are retiring. Lieutenant Sibley tells us to do the same." As I passed by Sibley, who wanted to see every man under his command in the line of retreat before he stirred himself, the young officer said: "Go to your saddle bags, with caution, and take all your ammunition. We are going to abandon our remaining horses." I did as directed, but felt a pang at leaving my noble animal, which was bleeding from a wound in the right side. We dared not shoot our surviving horses for that would have discovered our movement to the enemy . . . .
>
> A couple of scattering volleys and some random shots were fired to make the savages believe that we were still in position. As we had frequently reserved our fire during the fight, our silence would not be noticed immediately. We then retired in Indian file through the trees . . . . We retreated for perhaps a mile . . . and gained the slippery rocks of the great mountain range, where no mounted Indians, who are as lazy on foot as they are active on horseback, could pursue us. Then, as we paused to catch our breath, we heard in the distance five or six ringing volleys in succession. It was most likely the final fire delivered by the Indians before they charged our late position . . . . [W]e had escaped one danger only to encounter another.[6]

With fifty miles of sheer-faced mountains ahead, with no food and only light clothing, the task that greeted Sibley's men was daunting yet vastly more attractive than the fate left behind. With Grouard leading, the desperate troopers eagerly hiked up and away. Returning to Finerty:

> [A]bout midnight . . . absolute fatigue compelled us to make a halt . . . . [W]e bivouaced under the projections of an immense pile of rocks on the very summit of some unknown mountain peak, and there witnessed one of the most terrible wind and hail storms that can be imagined. The trees seemed to fall by the hundred, and their noise as they broke off and fell, or were uptorn by the roots, resembled rapid discharges of field artillery. To add to our discomfort, the

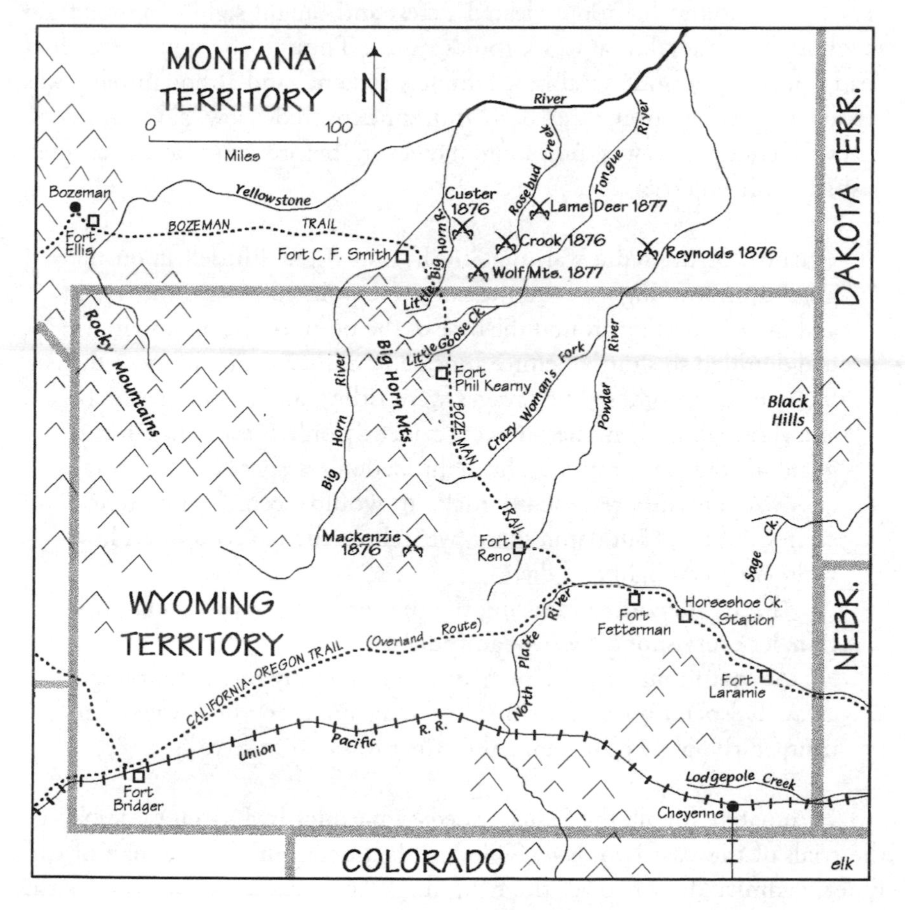

Northern battleground.

thermometer suddenly fell several degrees and being attired in summer campaign costume only we suffered greatly from the cold.[7]

After a sleepless night the trek was resumed before dawn. Throughout much of the day, Sibley's squad slipped and stumbled over the rocky wilderness. At one point, the troops cleared a crest and caught sight of a mountain at whose base they knew was Crook's camp. Though the men were "half dead from fatigue and . . . almost famine stricken," and although relief was yet twenty miles away, the beautiful, unexpected view gave everyone renewed energy.[8] It was not long, however, before hope again seemed dashed. John Finerty:

Gruard . . . uttered a warning "hush" and threw himself upon the ground, motioning us to do the same. He pointed toward the north and there, wheeling around the base of the point of the mountain we had doubled so shortly before, appeared another strong party of the Sioux in open order. The savages were riding along quite leisurely, and although fairly numerous were evidently only the advance or rear guard of some larger party. This sight made us desperate . . . .

"We are in pretty hard luck, it would seem," said Sibley, addressing me, "but damn them, we'll show the red scoundrels how white men can fight and die."

"Men," he said, addressing the soldiers, "we have a good position; let every shot dispose of an Indian!"

At that moment not a man among us felt any inclination to get away. Desperation and a thirst for vengeance on the savages had usurped the place of the animal instinct to save our lives.[9]

Fortunately for all, the Sioux passed by harmlessly. Driven to despair by the trials of the past two days, Sibley made a decision. "Not a man of us," Finerty admitted, "whatever the risk, Sioux or no Sioux, could endure the mountain route longer, so we took our wearied, jaded lives into our hands and struck out for Crook's camp across the plains."[10]

We judged that our main camp must still be some dozen miles away on Little Goose Creek, but every step . . . became laborious. . . . The rocks had broken our boots and skinned our feet, while starvation had weakened our frames. Only a comparatively few were vigorous enough to maintain a decently rapid pace. About 5 o'clock we saw some more Indians toward the east, but at some distance. We took

> no pains, whatever, to conceal ourselves, which, indeed, would have been a vain task on the nearly naked plain . . . . At about 6:30 o'clock we saw two horses grazing on a little knoll, and the carbines glittering in their boots on the saddles proclaimed the riders to be cavalry-men . . . . [W]e hailed them and they recognized us . . . . Lieutenant Sibley sent them into camp for horses and some rations . . . . Most of [the] men threw themselves on the ground, unable to move farther, and awaited the arrival of the horses . . . . It was 10 o'clock Sunday morning, July 9, 1876, when we rode in among the tents, amid congratulations from officers and men alike.[11]

As Finerty and the others regaled the camp with tales of hair-breadth escapes, Crook waited anxiously for reinforcements and news from Terry to the north. The following day, July 10, came first word of the Custer disaster. "With it," Finerty added, "came a characteristic dispatch from General Sheridan to Crook, in which the former said, referring to the Rosebud fight: 'Hit them again, and hit them harder!' Crook smiled grimly when he read the telegram, and remarked: 'I wish Sheridan would come out here himself and show us how to do it. It is rather difficult to surround three Indians with one soldier!'"[12]

While Crook found himself hard-pressed and on the defensive in one corner of Wyoming, the army was taking the offensive in another corner of the territory. In an effort to draw fire from the Yellowstone campaign, Colonel Wesley Merritt and the 5th Cavalry set out to patrol the Wyoming/Nebraska boundary and prevent Indians on the Dakota reservations from reinforcing Sitting Bull and Crazy Horse. And when the 5th moved, the most famous frontiersman in America moved with it.

Despite a glittering career on the Eastern stage, the call of his beloved High Plains was too much for Bill Cody. When Merritt requested his services, the dashing scout swiftly complied. "All the old boys in the regiment," one grateful trooper wrote, "expressed themselves to the effect that with such a leader and scout they could get away with all the Sitting Bulls and Crazy Horses, in the Sioux tribe."[13] Joining Cody was his faithful follower, Charley "Buffalo Shit" White, or, as writers more delicately dubbed him for their readers, "Buffalo Chips."

On the morning of July 7, while bivouacked along Sage Creek, the 5th received the first dramatic news from the north. Captain Charles King:

> Towards ten o'clock . . . while the camp was principally occupied in fighting flies, a party of the junior officers were returning from a

> refreshing bath in a deep pool of the stream, when Buffalo Bill came hurriedly towards them from the General's tent. His handsome face wore a look of deep trouble, and he brought us to a halt in stunned, awe-stricken silence with the announcement, "Custer and five companies of the Seventh wiped out of existence. It's no rumor—General Merritt's got the official despatch."[14]

With the question of whether it would reinforce Crook settled once and for all, the 5th began the long march north. King:

> At reveille on the 14th . . . a rumor ran through the camp that Merritt had received despatches during the night indicating that there was a grand outbreak among the Indians at the reservation. Of course we knew that they would be vastly excited and encouraged by the intelligence of the Custer massacre. Furthermore, it was well known that there were nearly a thousand of the Cheyennes.[15]

Two days later, while the regiment was camped along Warbonnet Creek in Nebraska, Cody galloped in at dawn to warn Merritt that a large band of Cheyenne was nearby. When they were finally spotted moving in his direction, Merritt prepared an ambush. The plans were thwarted, however, when a military wagon train suddenly rumbled onto the scene. While Merritt, Cody, King, and the others watched from behind a hill, two couriers with the train rode out to meet the cavalry. At the same time, a small party of warriors spied the messengers and whipped their horses down a ravine to surprise them. Charles King:

> Only a mile away come our couriers; only a mile and a half up the ravine [the] Cheyennes lash their excited ponies into eager gallop, and down they come towards us.
>
> "By Jove! General," says Buffalo Bill, sliding backwards down the hill, "Now's our chance. Let our party mount here out of sight, and we'll cut those fellows off."
>
> "Up with you, then!" is the answer. "Stay where you are, King. Watch them till they are close under you; then give the word. Come down, every other man of you!"
>
> I am alone on the little mound. Glancing behind me, I see Cody, [Ed] Tait, and Chips with five cavalrymen, eagerly bending forward in their saddles, grasping carbine and rifle, every eye bent upon me in breathless silence, watching for the signal . . . . Not a horse or man of us visible to the Indians. Only my hatless head and

> the double fieldglass peer over the grassy mound. Half a mile away are our couriers, now rapidly approaching.[16]

With the Indians pounding closer to the unwary whites, King found the tension almost unbearable. At last, Merritt calmly gave the go-ahead: "All ready, King. Give the word when you like."

"Now!" yelled the impatient captain to those below.[17] Setting spurs to their mounts, Buffalo Bill and the rest raced up the ravine. "Cody was riding a little in advance of his party and one of the Indians was preceding his group," recalled a private perched atop a butte peering through a telescope. "From the manner in which both parties acted [when they met] it was certain that both were surprised. Cody and the leading Indian appeared to be the only ones who did not become excited."[18] In the scout's words:

> Both of us rode at full speed. When we were only thirty yards apart I raised my rifle and fired. His horse dropped dead under him, and he rolled over on the ground to clear himself of the carcass. Almost at the same instant my own horse stepped into a hole and fell heavily. The fall hurt me but little .... The chief and I were now both on our feet, not twenty paces apart. We fired at each other at the same instant .... His bullet whizzed harmlessly past my head, while mine struck him full in the breast. He reeled and fell, but I took no chances. He had barely touched the ground, when I was upon him, knife in hand, and ... drove the steel into his heart.[19]

Reveling in his victory over the Cheyenne chief, Yellow Hair—so named for the scalp of a white woman he carried—Cody bent over the foe and, according to the private with the telescope, "neatly removed his scalp." Galloping back to Merritt with a wide-eyed Charley White at his side, the plainsman raised his grisly trophy in triumph. "Here is one for Custer!" he shouted.[20]

While Cody dashed off after more Indians, "White accordingly dismounted and we all surrounded him," one witness remembered. "He related the whole of Buffalo Bill's exploit with great glee, and made us think that the days of Achilles and Hector had been renewed . . . on War Bonnet Creek. Poor fellow! Buffalo Bill seemed to him a bigger man than all the generals of the United States Army."[21]

Meanwhile, Merritt had ordered a charge on the startled Cheyenne. Captain King:

> We gain the crest only to find the Indians scattering like chaff before us, utterly confounded at their unexpected encounter. Then comes

> the pursuit—a lively gallop over rolling prairie, the Indians dropping blankets, rations, everything weighty they could spare except their guns and ammunition. Right and left, far and near, they scatter into small bands and go tearing homeward. Once within the limits of the reservation they are safe, and we strain every nerve to catch them; but when the sun is high in the heavens and noon has come, the Cheyennes are back under the sheltering wing of the Indian Bureau, and not one of them can we lay hands on.[22]

The following day, King and his companions rode onto the reservation.

> [T]here came to see us . . . quite a number of Cheyennes . . . . Shrouded in their dark blue blankets and washed clean of their lurid war paint, they were by no means imposing. One and all they wanted to see Buffalo Bill, and wherever he moved they followed him with awe-filled eyes. He wore the same dress in which he had burst upon them in yesterday's fight, a Mexican costume of black velvet, slashed with scarlet and trimmed with silver buttons and lace—one of his theatrical garbs, in which he had done much execution before the footlights in the States.[23]

Though a minor affair at best, Merritt's action on War Bonnet Creek prevented hundreds of Cheyenne from joining Sitting Bull's Sioux farther north. When the 5th finally found Crook, the combined force set off for the Yellowstone country in search of Terry. Even with 2,000 men, few in the column felt secure. As Reuben Davenport of the New York *Herald* reported: "The soldiers, on the eve of seeking another battle, with the terrible fate of Custer and his men so fresh in their memories, are by no means as gay as they were when they last started toward the Yellowstone."[24]

On August 8, with an equally strong force and equally strong trepidation, Alfred Terry's column moved up the Rosebud. Wrote Lieutenant Edward McClernand:

> Two days later . . . such of our Indian scouts as were in advance came rushing back crying, "Sioux—Sioux," and pointing to a large cloud of dust seen rising behind a hill a few miles up the valley. That the Crow scouts thought the time had come at last to meet their hated enemy in fair battle, was evident from their excited words and actions. They sprang from their ponies and began stripping for the fight, and daubing their faces with paint. The squaws, even more excited than the braves, went hurriedly to work saddling

> the war ponies, and all the time screaming and gesticulating in the wildest manner . . . .
>
> [T]he expected fight . . . however, was not to be, for soon the appearance of the famous Buffalo Bill, riding toward us with a few companions, put an end to our warlike demonstrations.[25]

Curiously, while the Sioux and Northern Cheyenne were scattering into smaller, swifter bands following their smashing success in Montana, the army, fearing a repeat of the disaster, was becoming larger and slower. At least one scout was not fooled by the tremulous tactic. "If they want to find Indians," Cody complained to John Finerty, "let them send a battalion, which I am willing to guide, and I'll engage we'll have our fill of fighting . . . . The hostiles will never face this outfit unless they get it in some kind of a hole."[26]

After sniffing out fresh trails that were passed off as "old," after locating bands of Sioux that were for some reason or another never pursued, it became clear to Cody that "no one . . . with the army had lost any Indians, and consequently they were not going to hunt any."[27] Resigning in disgust, the plainsman promptly caught a downriver packet and steamed east. At the same time, many Indian scouts, bored with inaction, dropped from the column and rode home as well.

Finally, in late August 1876, after groping about the Yellowstone for days, Crook decided to strike off with his 2,000 men and fight Indians.[28] Foregoing his wagon train for speed, Crook set out with a minimum of supplies.

"The general idea was to follow the trail to the Little Missouri and then nobody knew where," John Finerty wrote. "The Snake and Crow Indians, appalled by the hardships which they clearly saw in store for them, abandoned the column the moment we faced up the Powder River." From the outset, the heavens let loose and seldom thereafter did a day pass without a deluge. Finerty:

> The horses sank in the mud to their knee-joints, and soldiers' shoes were pulled off in trying to drag their feet through the sticky slime. "Can hell be much worse than this?" said an officer to me next morning. He was cleaning about twenty pounds of wet clay from his boots with a butcher knife. His clothes were dripping, his teeth chattering, and his nose a cross between purple and indigo.[29]

Mile after mile, day after day, the ill-fated expedition slogged through the mud. "Not a stick of wood had we seen for eighty-six miles," Finerty continued, "and this, added to the cold, ever-falling rain, made life almost unendurable. There was hardly any coffee left, and this could not be cooked, while the poor remains of sugar and salt were absolutely washed out of the pack saddles by the falling flood."[30]

The rain, mud, and diminishing diet quickly weakened the men mentally and physically. Many, Lieutenant Walter Schuyler noted, had "become so exhausted that they were actually insane . . . . I saw men who were very plucky sit down and cry like children because they could not hold out."[31]

Perhaps the only man on the march never heard to complain was the commander himself. "The worse it gets, the better," muttered the raw-boned George Crook. "[A]lways hunt Indians in bad weather."[32] Ran one newspaper account of the general:

> The fact is, Crook is nothing but an Indian . . . . I mean that his mind, physiognomy and education are all Indian. Look at his face . . . and his manners—stolid, separate, averse to talk. He can take his gun and cross the desert, subsisting on the way where you or I would starve. Perfectly self-reliant for any venture, delighted with lonely travel and personal hazard, carrying nothing but his arms, he will walk after a trail all day and when night comes, no matter how cold, he wraps himself in an Indian blanket, humped up, Indian fashion, and pitches himself into a sage brush, there to be perfectly easy till morning. He will follow an antelope for three days. He requires nothing to drink or smoke, and very little to eat . . . . [U]tterly ignorant of fear, and yet stealthy as a cat.[33]

By September 5, Crook had crossed the Little Missouri and reached the Heart River without engaging a single enemy. With only a few days' rations remaining and with man and beast ready to drop, the general announced he would turn south and strike for the gold camps of the Black Hills. Finerty:

> I looked at him in some amazement, and could not help saying: "you will march 200 miles in the wilderness, with used-up horses and tired infantry on two and one-half days' half rations!"
>
> "I know it looks hard," was his reply, "but we've got to do it, and it shall be done . . . . If necessary," he added, "we can eat our horses."
>
> This suggestion fell upon me like a splash of ice water. I could hardly believe . . . that such an alternative would present itself . . . . We were encamped in a bleak and dreary spot. Everybody appeared to be gloomy, and even old Lieutenant [Joseph] Lawson admitted that he had never seen such hard times . . . . "As for eating a horse," said he, after I had told him of General Crook's remarks, "I'd as soon think of eating my brother!"[34]

As the command moved south, every step suddenly became a challenge. "Men very weak and despondent," one soldier scratched in his diary. "Many of them unable to stand on their feet, and some droping to sleep on the . . . wet ground without any covering of any kind."[35] As always, the mounts suffered most. Finerty recalled:

> Our horses played out by the score and between two and three hundred dismounted cavalrymen were marching in the rear . . . . Every little while the report of a pistol or carbine would announce that a soldier had shot his horse, rather than leave it behind with a chance of being picked up by straggling Indians. Some of the poor beasts fell dead from the effects of fatigue and want of proper forage, but a majority simply lay down and refused to budge an inch farther.[36]

Well aware of his plight, on September 7, Crook detached a battalion under Anson Mills to "make a dash" for the Black Hills and return with food. With the captain went scouts Frank Grouard, Baptiste Pourier, Jack Crawford, and Charley White. The following day, Crook and the main column resumed their nightmarish march. Once again, Finerty:

> Hard tack had disappeared, and nothing remained on September 8th but to eat one another or our animals. While trudging along through the mire on the morning of that day, leading our worn-out steeds, Lieutenant Lawson and I observed a small group of soldiers by the side of the trail busily engaged in skinning a dead horse and appropriating steaks from its hinder parts. This was the beginning of our horse rations. The men were too hungry to be longer controlled and the General wisely ordered that as many horses as would be necessary to feed the men be selected by the officers and slaughtered day by day. It was a tough experience, but there was no help for it, and anything outside of actual cannibalism was preferable to starving slowly to death.[37]

"To us who have to depend on them so much," Lieutenant Schuyler agonized, "it seems like murder to kill horses."[38] Later that day, as Crook's column staggered south, Mills' detachment stumbled upon a camp of Sioux at Slim Buttes. Despite the lesson of the Little Bighorn and prodded by hunger, Mills never considered retreat.

> As the commanding general had instructed me to lose no opportunity to strike a village, the command was rapidly put out of sight . . . [to wait] and attack at daylight. The night was one of the ugliest I ever

passed—dark, cold, rainy, and muddy in the extreme. At 2 a.m. we moved to within a mile of the village, where I left the pack-train . . . with twenty-five men to hold them . . . . [A]bout day-break . . . when we were within a hundred yards of the lower end of the village . . . a small herd of loose ponies stampeded and ran through the village. Gruard informed me that all chance for a total surprise was lost, when I ordered the charge sounded.[39]

"When the herd stampeded," Mills continued, "[Lieutenant Frederick] Schwatka followed them right into the village, riding through it and firing with pistols into the lodges. He chased the herd through it, knocking down and trampling over some of the lodges, and then turning the herd [he] came back with it to us."[40] Mills went on:

Immediately, the dismounted detachments closed on the south side and commenced firing on the Indians, who, finding themselves laced in their lodges, the leather drawn tight as a drum by the rain, had quickly cut themselves out with their knives and returned our fire, the squaws carrying the dead, wounded, and children up the opposite bluffs . . . . The Indians, as soon as they had their squaws and children in security, returned to the contest, and soon completely encompassed us with a skirmish-line . . . . The Indians were constantly creeping to points near enough to annoy our wounded.[41]

Although most of the Sioux soon fled, one group, which included many women and children, defiantly fought on from a ravine. When Crook arrived at Slim Buttes later that morning, the impatient general ordered an assault. Charles King:

Lieutenant [William] Clark . . . sprang into the entrance, carbine in hand, and a score of cavalrymen followed, while the scouts and others went cautiously along either bank, peering warily into the cave-like darkness at the head. A squad of newspaper correspondents . . . came tearing over, pencil in hand, all eagerness for items, just as a second volley came from the concealed foe, and three more of their assailants dropped, bleeding, in their tracks. Now our people were fairly aroused, and officers and men by dozens hurried to the scene.[42]

"It was a wonder to me," reflected John Bourke, "that the shots of the beleaguered did not kill them by the half-dozen."[43] Returning to King:

Just at this moment, as I was running over from the western side, I caught sight of "Chips" on the opposite crest. All alone, he was cautiously making his way, on hands and knees, towards the head of the ravine, where he could look down upon the Indians beneath. As yet he was protected from their fire by the bank itself—his lean form distinctly outlined against the eastern sky. He reached a stunted tree that grew on the very edge of the gorge, and there he halted, brought his rifle close under his shoulder in readiness to aim, and then raised himself slowly to his feet, lifted his head higher, higher, as he peered over. Suddenly a quick, eager light shone in his face, a sharp movement of his rifle, as though he were about to raise it to the shoulder, when, bang!—a puff of white smoke floated up from the head of the ravine, "Chips" sprang convulsively in the air, clasping his hands to his breast, and with one startled, agonizing cry, "Oh, my God, boys!" plunged heavily forward, on his face, down the slope.[44]

Despite White's death, Pourier was determined to claim a trophy. "[He] fought his way into the cavern," an astonished Finerty later wrote, "and succeeded in killing one of the male Indians, ingeniously using a captive squaw as a living barricade between himself and the fire of the other warriors. He took the scalp of the fallen brave in a manner that displayed perfect workmanship."[45] Finerty continued:

The shower of close-range bullets . . . terrified the . . . squaws and they began singing the awful Indian death chant. The papooses wailed so loudly and so piteously that even the hot firing could not quell their voices, and General Crook ordered the men to suspend operations immediately. Then Frank Gruard and Baptiste Pourier . . . by order of General Crook approached the abrupt western bank . . . and offered the women and children quarter. This was accepted by the besieged and Crook in person went to the mouth of the cavern and handed out one tall, fine-looking woman, who had an infant strapped to her back. She trembled all over and refused to liberate the General's hand. Eleven other squaws and six papooses were then taken out, but the few surviving warriors refused to surrender and savagely recommenced the fight.

Then our troops re-opened with a very rain of hell upon the . . . braves, who, nevertheless, fought it out with Spartan courage against such desperate odds for nearly two hours. Such matchless bravery electrified even our enraged soldiers into a spirit of chivalry and General Crook, recognizing the fact that the unfortunate savages had fought like fiends in defense of wives and children, ordered another suspension of hostilities and called upon the dusky heroes to surrender.

After a few minutes' deliberation the chief, American Horse, a fine looking, broad-chested Sioux, with a handsome face and a neck like a bull, showed himself at the mouth of the cave, presenting the butt end of his rifle toward the General. He had just been shot in the abdomen and said . . . that he would yield if the lives of the warriors who fought with him were spared. Some of the soldiers, who had lost comrades in the skirmish, shouted "No quarter!" but not a man was base enough to attempt shooting down the disabled chief. Crook hesitated for a minute and then said . . . "Tell the Chief . . . that neither he nor his young men will be harmed further."

This message having been interpreted to American Horse, he beckoned to his surviving followers . . . [who] followed him out of the gully. The Chieftain's intestines protruded from his wound, but a squaw . . . tied her shawl around the injured part and then the poor, fearless savage, never uttering a complaint, walked slowly to a little camp fire occupied by his people, about 20 yards away, and sat down among the women and children . . . .

Several soldiers jumped at once into the ravine and bore out the corpses.[46]

Reported a correspondent for the *New York Times*:

I was standing directly upon the place where the [Indians] had come from, and heard the shouts of the men who were groping in the hole of the bank underneath, that "there were more of them." "Bring them out—drag them out!" yelled the crowd. "There's a white man," was next heard in excited and half-smothered tones from below. At this the mass of men above seemed to go wild. "A white man!" was repeated from mouth to mouth, and then rose a wild chorus of yells, oaths, and execrations. "Drag him out!" "Cut him to pieces!" "We'll burn him alive!" "Show him to us." There was no white man, however. When the body was dragged into light, it proved to be that of a squaw whitened by death. She was frightfully shot. A bullet had torn her neck away, three had gone through her breast and shoulder, and two through each limb. Her body and clothing were one mass of mud and coagulated blood . . . . Then followed the half-naked body of the old Indian Big Bat had killed. It was very unceremoniously hauled up by what hair remained and a leather belt around the middle. The fatal shot had struck him under the ear, and shattered the whole base of the

> skull . . . . The body had stiffened in death in the posture of a man holding a gun, which was the way he was shot. He was an old man, and his features wore a look of grim determination. After this came still another squaw, also shot in several places. It seemed that the bodies of the women had been used by the survivors as defences.[47]

Another who examined the corpses as they were laid out was John Finerty.

> The skull of one poor squaw was blown, literally, to atoms, revealing the ridge of the palate and presenting a most ghastly and revolting spectacle. Another of the dead females, a middle-aged woman, was so riddled by bullets that there appeared to be no unwounded part of her person . . . . Ute John, the solitary friendly Indian who did not desert the column, scalped all the dead . . . and I regret to be compelled to state a few—a very few—brutalized soldiers followed his savage example. Each took only a portion of the scalp, but the exhibition of human depravity was nauseating . . . . [A] slaughtered Indian papoose, only about two months old, lay in a small basket, where a humane soldier had placed the tiny body. Had the hair of the poor little creature been long enough, Ute John, I believe, would have scalped it also.[48]

With a child he had captured and befriended in the village earlier, Captain Mills also viewed the dead.

> As soon as the little girl saw these she began to cry, and all of a sudden, ran up to one of the bodies and fell upon it and threw her arms around it. The corpse was that of her mother, who was shot several times through the body. In clasping the dead body the face and arms and hands of the little girl had become smeared with her mother's blood, and the sight was enough to touch the heart of the strongest man.[49]

"With all this group of mutilated mortality before them and with the groans of the wounded soldiers from the hospital tepee ringing in their ears," noted John Finerty, "the hungry troopers and infantry tore the dried Indian meat they had captured into eatable pieces and marched away as unconcernedly as if they were attending a holiday picnic. It was, indeed, a ghastly, charnel-house group."[50]

In addition to food, much else was found in the camp. "Among the trophies," Anson Mills revealed, "was a guidon of the Seventh Cavalry, a pair of gloves marked Colonel Keogh, 3 Seventh Cavalry horses, and many other articles recognized to have belonged to General Custer's command."[51]

As Frank Grouard feared and as he had warned Mills earlier, there was indeed another Indian camp near Slim Buttes. Later that day, the Sioux made a furious attack on Crook's command. Finerty:

> They kept up perpetual motion, apparently encouraged by a warrior, doubtless Crazy Horse himself, who, mounted on a fleet white horse, galloped around the array and seemed to possess the power of ubiquity. Failing to break into that formidable circle, the Indians, after firing several volleys . . . and recognizing the folly of fighting such an outnumbering force any longer, glided away from our front with all possible speed. As the shadows came down into the valley, the last shots were fired and the affair of Slim Buttes was over.[52]

Concluded Captain King:

> They have lost their village; lost three hundred tiptop ponies. A dozen of their warriors and squaws are in our hands, and a dozen more are dead and dying in the attempt to recapture them; and the big white chief Crook has managed to gain all this with starving men and skeleton horses . . . . Our own dead are fortunately few, and they are buried deep in the ravine before we move southward in the morning—not only buried deep, but a thousand horses, in column of twos, tramp over the new-made graves and obliterate the trace.[53]

The food from Slim Buttes helped Crook's ragged command to reach the Black Hills and safety a short time later. But the nightmare was not quite over. Greeting these men, and others just returned to "civilization" from hard campaigns, was a ghastly phenomenon. The reaction of one gaunt soldier when he and his comrades spotted a sentry at a long-sought camp was typical:

> [T]hat sentinel, personally, was a monstrosity. His body appeared to be swollen, his cheeks were puffed, his eyes bulged, his face was white, his lips were large, loose and covered his teeth altogether, while his clothes were a gaudy blue. He had a sickly, bloated and dropsical look generally. I was astonished to see that all the men at . . . [the] camp had the same peculiarities, and it was some time before I understood that this was the normal man. We didn't realize that it was our appearance that had changed. It had come about gradually, and as all were alike there was no contrast to attract attention.[54]

Although disaster had been averted, the failure of Crook's campaign was apparent. As one newspaper correspondent later stated:

> [T]he general impression in this command is that we have not much to boast of in the way of killing Indians. They kept out of the way so effectually that the only band which was struck was struck by accident, and when, by the subsequent attack upon us, it was discovered that another and much larger village was not far off, the command was in too crippled and broken down a condition from starvation and overmarching to turn the information to any account.[55]

Whatever, among those who had risked their lives seeking gold, Crook and his "starving scare-crows" received a hero's welcome for saving the mines and breaking the "siege" of the Black Hills. Incredibly, like gold-crazed prospectors who found their way to and from Dakota, miners, merchants, missionaries, and others continued to roam the land between the Missouri and the Rockies, seemingly oblivious to danger. Wrote one dumbfounded officer, Colonel Richard Dodge:

> They are brave to imbecility or stupid beyond expression. A few men, possibly comparative strangers to each other, band together and agree to go to this place or that place. Without apparently the slightest concern, they plunge into unknown wilderness, and through countries swarming with treacherous and deadly Indians. They travel without order and without care. If while hunting one should discover Indians, he rushes back to his party, which flies if it can, or fights with courage and tenacity if necessary. Arrived at a camping place they turn out their stock, get supper and go to bed, unconcerned as if no danger were around them . . . . I once when travelling with a train and troops . . . on the high wide prairie [came] suddenly on the form of a man, lying on his stomach and sleeping profoundly. He was at least 30 miles from any road and in a very dangerous country. I called to him loudly. He sat up and gazed stupidly for a moment or two then smiled and seemed relieved. "Where do you belong?" I asked. "I come from Iowa," he answered. "What are you doing here?" I demanded very peremptorily. "Oh, I am looking for work," he said genially. I thought at first that he was a lunatic, but further questioning satisfied me that he was only an ordinary plain lunatic, that is, one who feared no danger because he saw none.[56]

Peddlers, lured by profits from soldiers afield, were some of the most daring "lunatics." One entrepreneur from the Montana mining district sailed a flatboat down the Yellowstone through Sioux territory in 1876 to hawk wares among Colonel Gibbon's troops. "The luxuries he brought found ready sale and gave great satisfaction," a happy officer exclaimed. "Not the least acceptable article was a keg of beer."[57]

During the height of Red Cloud's War in 1868, Elizabeth Burt and others at Fort C. F. Smith in Montana had been stunned one day by a sight that seemed impossible.

> Field glasses showed a wagon coming from the north on the Bozeman Trail. No one but Indians ever came from that direction which, whenever I thought of it, gave me the feeling of being at the very end of civilization . . . . Anxiously we watched the approach of this strange vehicle. To our astonishment it proved to be filled with potatoes, onions and a scant supply of butter, brought by two men from the Bozeman country . . . . In spite of high prices the wagon was soon emptied and the men returned to Bozeman with their purses well filled.[58]

To the south, when soldiers at besieged Fort Phil Kearny began turning up drunk, officers investigated. Recalled Private Alson Ostrander:

> A tough-looking citizen between fifty and sixty years of age, and wearing an old-style peg leg, had planted himself in a convenient spot out of sight of the fort. With a mule and cart, upon which were fastened two barrels of liquor, he had made his way through those miles of dangerous territory and had encountered neither Indians nor outfits to interfere with him . . . . [T]he liquor dispensed by the man was rank poison, consisting chiefly of strychnine, capsicum, alcohol, and water.[59]

Though many individuals, through more luck than skill, did indeed negotiate the Plains, the odds often overtook others. From Dakota, Lieutenant Luther North:

> Just after we were settled in camp a party of seven miners from Deadwood passed through our camp on their way to the Big Horn Mountains to prospect for gold. They had a wagon and several saddle horses, and were pretty well armed. Frank advised them to give up their trip, as the country was full of hostile Indians, but they said they could take care of themselves, and went on up the river.

About four o'clock the next morning one of the men came into our camp half naked and pretty badly frozen. He said the Indians had attacked their camp, and he didn't know where the rest of the party were. The poor fellow was about half crazy, and was suffering terribly with his frozen feet.[60]

Unlike these men, many a lonely sojourner who tempted fate had no one to tell when his luck ran out. Captain Charles King:

I was attracted by a shout and the gathering of a knot of soldiers around some fallen timber. Joining them, and stepping over the low barrier of logs, I came upon the body of a white man, unscalped, who had evidently made a desperate fight for life, as the ground was covered with the shells of his cartridges . . . . [A] bullet through the brain had finally laid him low, and his savage foeman had left him as he fell, probably a year before we came upon the spot.[61]

While Crook rested and refitted in Dakota for another go at the hostiles, Colonel Nelson Miles and the 5th Infantry were pressing Sitting Bull in Montana. Ironically, Miles and his tenacious "walk-a-heaps" were succeeding against the fleet Sioux where thousands of cavalrymen had failed. After a series of scouts and skirmishes along the Yellowstone in October, Sitting Bull suddenly turned on his tormentor. One of those on hand was Lieutenant James Pope.

[T]wo [Indians] were seen coming over a hill bearing a white flag . . . . [T]hey stated that Sitting Bull wished a council . . . . Gen. Miles decided at once to grant the council and so notified the flag bearers. Between two and three hundred Indians soon appeared over a ridge . . . and drew up in a line . . . . Gen. Miles with his staff and orderlies rode out to the centre and twelve chiefs, dismounted, walked out in line to meet him. The command was drawn up in line on a ridge parallel to that of the Sioux . . . . A long consultation was then held, some of the chiefs being inclined to yield, but Sitting Bull obstinately demanding the cessation of the passing trains and the withdrawal of the troops along the Yellowstone . . . .

Sitting Bull appeared a stern, unyielding savage, with an intelligent, rather brutal face, and a powerful frame. He was . . . speaking but little though bearing great authority . . . . Nothing was effected, however, and the council quietly dissolved with the understanding that it should be renewed the next day . . . .

> Early next morning, Oct. 21, the command took up the march northward, whither the Indians had gone the previous day, and had only proceeded a few miles when Indians showed themselves on a high knoll . . . . The white flag having again been displayed, the line was halted . . . . Here Indians and soldiers freely mingled, the former having become reassured by the previous council. Sitting Bull still retained his suspicions and made difficulties, especially fearing the Rodman gun planted on the knoll . . . . The council lasted until the afternoon, many of the more tractable chiefs being decidedly disposed to yield, one actually offering himself as hostage for his band. This indication of yielding angered the stern old chief.[62]

According to Col. Miles, Sitting Bull acidly announced that "the white man never lived who loved an Indian, and that no true Indian ever lived that did not hate the white man. He declared that God Almighty made him an Indian and did not make him an agency Indian either."[63] Returning to Pope:

> Gen. Miles had given a parting message to Sitting Bull repeating his demand that he yield himself and followers to the orders of Government, to send his reply quickly or he would open with his guns . . . . The command after moving forward in line a few hundred yards opened out in beautiful order into skirmishers . . . . There had not yet been a shot fired, Gen. Miles desiring not to be first to break the late armistice . . . . As the long, undulating line of skirmishers moved up the hill as before described, the Sioux commenced their first hostile demonstration by riding in rapid circles, hanging over the sides of their ponies . . . . Still there was no firing. Some Indians were observed firing the prairie; an order to stop which caused the first firing.[64]

Throughout the afternoon and following day, the sides sparred amid smoke and flame, with Miles ever pressing the Sioux back. Another truce was reached several days later when chiefs representing a large number of warriors appeared. After a brief council, the Indians agreed to return to their agency. Thus, in one stroke, perhaps half of all hostile bands had been swept from the northern Plains. "[T]he Indians fought as well as they could," reported one who had talked with them, "but [they] had never seen so many men on foot or that shot so well; that Sitting Bull had entirely lost his prestige and influence with the other chiefs, and had only his own fifty or seventy lodges with him."[65]

A great victory had been won, but the Sioux War went on. With the smashing success of the Washita Campaign ever in mind, the army had no

Sitting Bull. LITTLE BIGHORN BATTLEFIELD NATIONAL MONUMENT.

intention of pausing and allowing the Indians to winter in peace, no matter how severe the weather. By mid-November 1876, Crook was again on the move. Learning that a large band of Cheyenne were camped in the Bighorns, the general ordered Colonel Ranald Mackenzie, with a battalion of cavalry and Indian auxiliaries, to investigate.

"This was about the hardest march that we ever had," recalled Luther North. "We climbed up and up, it seemed for miles, then over a ridge, and down again. In many places the trail was so narrow along the side of the mountain that we could march only in single file, and the command was strung out for perhaps a couple of miles; then if the valley or canyon spread out, we would trot our horses and close up the ranks. The night was very dark and it was quite cold."[66] By dawn, November 25, Mackenzie was within earshot of the village. "[W]e soon heard . . . the thump! thump! of war drums, and the jingling of their rattles sounding the measure of a war-dance," Lieutenant John Bourke recorded in his diary.[67]

Another man listening to the ominous sounds and ruing his earlier indiscretion was William Earl Smith. Before Mackenzie split from the main column, the private had begged so persistently to go along that his request was granted. "It was now I thought of [the] Custer Mascree and began to think what I was about to go into," admitted Smith as the drums throbbed in his ears.[68] At last, Mackenzie nodded to his bugler. Lieutenant Henry Bellas:

> Replying to the clear notes of the bugle, as it rang out the charge—echoed and reechoed from the walls of the canyon—was the music furnished by one of the Pawnees, who sounded a wild humming tune on a pipe that rose above all other sounds and somewhat resembled the prolonged shriek of a steam whistle. Added to this were now the shouts and cries of our foremost line of scouts, who dashed into the herds of ponies to stampede them. Then quickly followed . . . the loud cheer of our troopers and the thundering roar of more than 1,200 horsemen of the rushing column resounding from the sides of the narrow canyon.[69]

William Earl Smith:

> We had not gone far when I looked up and saw an Indin on top of a big rock. He firred one shot and that was a signal that the Ball had opend. He was there as a sentinnal for the camp, I suppose. He mounted his poney and lit out. It was now that our Indins set up the war hoop. This was the first time i had ever hird it in earnest. Then I was wild with excitement.[70]

Returning to Bellas:

> [M]any of the Cheyennes fled as they saw us entering at the opposite end . . . . Lieutenant [John] McKinney, dashing fearlessly for-

> ward at the head of his troop, was met at the end of the canyon with a volley from the concealed foe ahead. Rider and horse both fell, mortally wounded by half a dozen bullets, while the leading fours of the troop were shot down at the same time.[71]

"Bullets were flying every way and mity thick to," added Private Smith. "I had my Pistell in my hand and felt a little rattled, I must say, for this was the first time i had ever hird them so close. As I was going around a hill I saw an old Indin and a boy makeing for the hill. I took a shot at him with my pistell and he caught hold of his leg and limped off."[72]

With the enemy driven beyond the village, a deadly long-range duel ensued. One soldier near John Bourke foolishly raised up from cover; a Cheyenne sniper "put a bullet through his jaws [and] knocked him senseless against the bank in front of him. The blood from his wound poured down his throat and choked him to death."[73] Another Indian marksman was just as determined to draw blood for every foot of ground gained. Luther North:

> This fellow must have been a crack shot, for in the afternoon a couple of soldiers started across a little valley from one hill to another, and they were at least six hundred yards from where he was hiding behind a rock. The soldiers were about one hundred yards apart, and were running. When the first man got about half way across, the Indian shot and the soldier dropped. The other soldier ran on, and when he was within twenty feet of the first man the big gun boomed out again, and he went down.[74]

While random firing continued, many attackers turned to other matters. Henry Bellas:

> Our Indian allies, who had . . . fought, recklessly, beside the soldiers, against their own race, now taking advantage of the lull in the fight, returned to the village and, having already secured the main herds, commenced to plunder the encampment from one end to another. One or two squaws were found secreted in the lodges, unable to escape, and now refusing to come out and surrender were, in spite of the remonstrances of the soldiers, quickly shot and scalped . . . . All regrets, if any existed, for the destruction of the encampment vanished, as many relics of the ill-fated Custer expedition now came to view . . . . Several beaded necklaces, decorated with dried human fingers—one having 10 others 5, 6, or eight of these horrible mementoes—were likewise found and identified by our furious allies.[75]

Scouts were not the only ones looting. Private Smith:

> I went down in among the teepes to see what I could find . . . . I went into one teepe and hear I found an old squaw with a nice pipe. Well thinks I I must have that and so I make moshens to let me see it. But she would not do it. I could of shot hir but did not like to do that so when she stuck it out a little to one side i made a grab and caught it by the bowl and she hung onto the stem. She would of made at me now but I stuck my pistell in her fase and she did not like the looks of it and she lade down and roled up in a nice Buflow robe. I had a noshen to take that, but I went out and left hire to her fate.[76]

During the long standoff, Lieutenant Bourke recorded an incident that stood out boldly in his memory.

> There was one notably daring warrior or chief, a powerful looking man, riding a fine white horse and himself bearing on his left arm a circular shield of buffalo hide and upon his head a war bonnet, whose pendant eagle plumes swept the ground at his horse's feet. Bullets struck the ground before him, behind him, beside him . . . but each and all spared the grim Cheyenne who serenely rode along the front of our line, venting derision in the teeth of his foes, until the cool, deadly aim of Lieutenant Allison . . . knocked him lifeless from his charger.
>
> Before the cheers from the whites and their Indian allies had died away, there issued from the Cheyenne line a young warrior . . . . This brave Cheyenne charged recklessly into the face of death . . . chanting loudly the war-song proclaiming his determination to save from profane hands the corpse of his comrade and friend . . . . Many were the expressions of admiration from our side as he lifted the body across the withers of the pony, and then springing lightly into the saddle, plied vigorously the quirt . . . and turned back to regain the friendly shelter of the rocks and gulches. Escape seemed secure but . . . [a]lmost within handshake of his people, the heroic Cheyenne and his sturdy pony . . . fell pierced with many wounds.[77]

"Towards evening," Luther North recalled, "General McKenzie [*sic*] called a council of his officers and talked over the advisability of charging up the mountain, and driving the Indians out of the rocks . . . . [I]t was decided that . . . it was not worth the lives it would cost to get them out, so we went into camp."[78] William Earl Smith:

[T]here was no more firring done to amount to anything and I took a walk down among the teepes. Our Indins had birnt a good menney of them. I come to the teepe where I had goot the pipe in the morning. And hear I saw the old squaw shot all to pieces. I found after words that some of the boys in my company had done it for to get the Bufflow robe. I saw lots of ded Indins now laying a round all over. I went back and watched the boys carring in the ded and wounded some skelpt and some striped of all their clothing.[79]

The following morning, with five dead and seventeen wounded, Mackenzie retraced his steps down the canyon. In his wake lay dozens of dead Indians and a large village in ashes—the power of the Northern Cheyenne had been broken forever. At least one sympathetic soldier well understood what the victory meant for the vanquished: "The thermometer never got higher than 25 below . . . . Those poor Cheyennes were out in that weather with nothing to eat, no shelter . . . and hardly any clothing. It was said that many children died. It makes me sort of sick to think of it."[80]

For the remaining Indians, the winter of 1876–77 got no better. From one seemingly secure camp to the next, the relentless white hunters hounded their trail. And dogging the steps of all—-white man and red man alike—was the deadly Western winter. Wrote one officer to his mother:

I am now wearing two flannel and a buckskin shirt, one pair of drawers, trousers of buckskin and a pair of army trousers, two pairs woolen socks, a pair of buffalo overshoes and big boots, a heavy pair of blanket leggings, a thick blouse and heavy overcoat, a heavy woolen cap that completely covers my head, face and neck except nose and eyes and still I am not happy . . . . [W]hen I am all fixed out I am a sight to behold and have all I can do to mount my horse.[81]

The officer did not exaggerate. Bundled for winter, the U.S. soldier was an almost immobile target. The situation would have been ludicrous had a war not been in progress. "As I saw him in his long Buffalo overcoat," another officer commented as he gazed upon a dead comrade, "I realized how perfectly helpless he must have been against a savage stripped for the fight."[82]

On January 8, 1877, in the Wolf Mountains of Montana, a small force under the tenacious Nelson Miles engaged a much larger force of warriors led by Crazy Horse. The resulting defeat and demoralization triggered massive Indian surrenders over the next several months. By May, even the legendary Crazy Horse saw the folly of further resistance.

With Crazy Horse at last on a reservation and the mighty Sitting Bull a refugee in Canada, only one band stood between the U.S. military and complete victory on the High Plains. Gathering several hundred recalcitrants from various tribes, the Sioux leader Lame Deer let it be known that he would never surrender. At dawn on May 7, Miles and a column of cavalry swooped down on the chief's camp near the Rosebud. Sergeant John McBlain:

> As soon as the camp had been attacked General Miles had it made known to the hostiles that they could surrender and be properly taken care of. Lame Deer and Iron Star . . . seemed desirous of taking advantage of this offer, and approached to within a few yards of General Miles. Lame Deer placed his gun on the ground as an earnest of his good intentions, and Iron Star seemed about to follow his example, when one of the citizen scouts near the General fired at the Indian; immediately Iron Star fired at the group with the General, and Lame Deer, grasping his gun, stepped back about five yards, and taking deliberate aim fired directly at the General. How the bullet missed the one it was fired at is one of those mysterious things that happen in all battles . . . . [T]he bullet hit a soldier . . . who was in line with the General . . . killing him instantly.
>
> The audacity of the move and the suddenness with which it took place . . . so occupied the attention of those with the General, that the two chiefs made good their retreat to the hills . . . . [T]he Indians fought stubbornly . . . but . . . Lame Deer was killed within a few minutes thereafter. Iron Star . . . was killed . . . within thirty yards of . . . his chief.
>
> From that time until the hostiles finally got down into the valley of the Rosebud, the fight was a running one, the Indians making stands at every place presenting good opportunities of checking the advance of the troops, to cover the retreat of their families . . . .
>
> The defeat of the Indians was most complete. Everything they owned, aside from what little they had on, was abandoned in the wild rush for the hills . . . . Their entire camp was destroyed, together with large stores of dried meat, and all at the expense of four soldiers killed and one officer and five soldiers wounded . . . . This was the last of the fights in that long series incident to the Sioux War.[83]

16

Bloody Road Back

At the conclusion of the great war for the northern Plains, the once-mighty Sioux were finally forced onto their Dakota reservations. The Cheyenne, however, "the most reckless, uncalculating, uncompromising and obstinate fighters of any of the northern Indians," were compelled by the federal government to join their southern brothers in far-off Indian Territory.[1] Some whites, including Nelson Miles, regarded the exile as barbarous. "I consider the banishment of a body of people . . . from a cold region to a warm, malarial district like the Indian territory to be unwise, unjust and cruel," protested the general. "It is like going to Quebec and taking a village of men, women, and children from there and removing them to North Carolina. The change is as great."[2]

Nevertheless, by August 1877, more than 1,000 Northern Cheyenne had made the long journey south and were resettled near Fort Reno. From the outset, the Indians despised their new surroundings. The heat, dust, and dryness were strange and depressing to northern spirits. When they were permitted to leave the reservation that fall and hunt buffalo, the Cheyenne found not a single animal. In their misery and frustration, the newcomers, particularly Chief Dull Knife, taunted their southern neighbors and called them fools for working like whites and conforming to their ways.

"Dull Knife could with less provocation stir up more strife with less raw material to start with than any Indian I ever knew or heard of," wrote an observer. "He complained bitterly all winter, but on ration day he was there with the rest."[3] Unfortunately, when ration day did arrive, little of what had been promised was delivered. One officer at Camp Supply was appalled by what he saw.

> While here a portion of them killed and ate their ponies, while the remainder feasted on their dogs—an Indian never eats his dog except when served up as a kind of state dinner or when he is driven to the wall by hunger. They applied to [the] commanding officer for food; but the military establishment having no authority to issue rations to Indians, they were refused. Dull Knife appealed so persistently for aid that the commanding officer, seeing their condition and fearing trouble from them . . . ordered a few rations to be issued to them which were eagerly accepted and greedily devoured.[4]

During the summer of 1878, conditions among the Cheyenne worsened until many, like the leader, Little Wolf, dreamed only of old homes in the north.

> A great many have been sick, some have died. I have been sick a great deal of the time since I have been down here—homesick and heartsick and sick in every way. I have been thinking of my native country and the good home I had up there where I was never hungry, but when I wanted anything to eat I could go out and hunt buffalo. It makes me feel sick when I think about that, and I cannot help thinking about that.[5]

Finally, in early September, more than 300 Cheyenne men, women, and children bolted the hated reservation. With Dull Knife and Little Wolf to lead, the long trek north began. Many in America, including the department commander, Brigadier General John Pope, commiserated with the fugitives.

> Who is responsible I can't say; but I know the Indians have suffered more privations and hardships, and endured them more patiently and with less grumbling, than would the same number of white men . . . . Like the same number of white men would do, when they found the Government wasn't keeping its promises . . . they resolved to go back to their old hunting grounds in the north.[6]

All the same, and in spite of similar sentiments elsewhere, the army had the task of arresting the Indians and forcing them back to the reservation. On September 13, two companies of cavalry under Captain Joseph Rendlebrock caught up with the Cheyenne near the Cimarron River, forty miles northwest of Camp Supply. Dull Knife and Rendlebrock rode forward to parley.

"I don't want to attack you," said Rendlebrock. "I don't want to engage in battle with you. Some of your warriors and some of my men will necessarily be killed; but you must go back to your reservation, and it would be better all around for you to come without resistance."[7]

"Nor do we want to fight you," Dull Knife replied. "We went on the reservation because the Government promised to furnish us with supplies and provisions. We have waited patiently and long . . . . We can not starve. We are going back to our old hunting grounds. Before we return to our reservation we will die in our tracks."[8]

A correspondent for the Leavenworth *Times* described the scene.

> The Indians were drawn up in line, occupying a position in the passes of the bluffs. Captain Renderbrock [*sic*] not thinking of any strategy on the[ir] part . . . moved his command properly within the gulch, when he learned to his complete surprise, that he was surrounded on all sides. About this time an Arapahoe scout with the cavalry named Chack espied two or three of his ponies in the hands of the Indians, which they had stolen from him. He seized a revolver from one of the soldiers and mounted a horse belonging to another and made a charge for the ponies, which were guarded by seven Cheyennes. Chack commenced firing, and killed four Indians and wounded two more, when he was brought to the ground, shot through the thighs and bowels. This opened the battle. The Indians charged from every direction before the cavalry had taken positions; but . . . a counter charge was made, which, for the time being, nonplused the Cheyennes; but they soon rallied again, and kept up the fight for thirty-six hours. The cavalry were completely hemmed in and isolated from water, and every moment subject to a general massacre. Had the troops shown but one weak part in their lines, it is evident that not one would have been spared to tell the tale. At daylight on the morning of the 14th, the troops became desperate. No water or rations and their ammunition almost exhausted, they determined to break through the lines . . . . [W]ith one last effort [they] charged against the lines of the enemy, and broke through, and made a hasty march for water. The Indians followed for a distance of four miles; keeping up a skirmish fire.[9]

With three dead and many wounded, the terrorized troopers continued their flight while the Cheyenne turned back to press north once more.

Soon after entering Kansas, the Indians ran amok—looting ranches, slaughtering hundreds of cattle and sheep, and murdering several unwary settlers. When news of the raids reached the rest of the state, "a terrible storm of excitement ensued."[10]

"As we write," warned a nervous editor in Kinsley, a full fifty miles from the scene, "the blood thirsty fiends are roaming at will, almost in sight of Kinsley, butchering the honest, unsuspecting pioneer, whose wreaking scalp is thonged to the belt of those satanic fiends who are armed today better than any army in Europe."[11]

To meet the threat, a company of cavalry and twenty-five "cow boys" hurried aboard freight cars at Dodge City and rushed down the Santa Fe Railroad to Cimarron Station. Soon after unloading, the party was joined by the two companies under Captain Rendlebrock. Rattled by his earlier encounter, the officer was in no mood to force the issue when he came upon the Cheyenne at Sand Creek. According to one civilian:

> The cattle men . . . drove the Indians from the ridge they occupied and were clamorous for a general charge. Captain Raundebrook [*sic*] sent one company to assist them, but retained two companies to guard his camp. A skirmish of half an hour was kept up with the Indians, who hid and dodged behind the rocks, after which the troops withdrew. The soldiers were anxious for a general fight, while the officers seemed haunted by the ghost of Custer.[12]

"The troops are now following," the civilian quipped in disgust, "using precaution to prevent the track from becoming too fresh."[13]

At length, near Pierceville, the Indians crossed the Santa Fe unmolested. As the Cheyenne moved ever closer to the Kansas Pacific, hundreds of troops rushed west by train to prevent a crossover. While telegraph wires crackled with the latest reports, trains heavily laden for war were kept under a full head of steam to be dispatched at a moment's notice. Even so, John Pope was not optimistic.

> The absence of cavalry in the department is severely felt, and may make it impracticable to intercept these Indians. I do not believe that they will kill anyone or do any damage, except to kill what cattle they need for food on the way. I hope we shall be able to arrest them before they cross the Kansas Pacific railroad, and every measure possible has been taken to do so.[14]

While the army was focusing on the Kansas Pacific, another large force under Lieutenant Colonel William Lewis was crowding the Cheyenne from the rear. On September 26, George Brown was in front of the column scanning the ground. "The Indian trail was very broad and easy to follow," the scout recalled. "We marched all day over a level prairie, about forty miles, and made a dry camp that night."

> Next morning we marched about ten miles until we came to [Famished Woman] Creek. We crossed the creek and saw there where the Indians had been in camp. I scratched in the ashes and found live coals of fire. This convinced me that the Indians were not far away . . . . The command followed down the creek after them, the scouts about two or three hundred yards in advance. We had gone down about a mile and Amos [Chapman] said, "Brown, you go back and show the wagons how to get around that big canyon." I started back and found Colonel Lewis riding at the head of his command. I rode up to him and said, "Have you got any flankers out?" He said he had not. I said, "Colonel, I believe those Indians are right in here close." He said the Indians were all gone. I went on and met the wagon train, and just as I was getting the lead wagon around the big canyon I heard some shooting up in front. The Indians had fired on the scouts. I knew then the fight was on.[15]

Again, as the hidden Cheyenne fired down from the canyon walls, the army found itself trapped. A correspondent for the Hays *Sentinel* told what happened:

> Col. Lewis . . . led his men in person . . . . Wherever the fight was the hottest, he was at the head. Being the only mounted man on the field, he was, consequently, a target for the braves. His saddle-blanket was scarlet, which rendered him doubly conspicuous. He was importuned to dismount; but he desired to be where only a horse could carry him from point to point . . . . Finally his horse was wounded. A Pawnee scout, wild with agony, lest its heroic rider should fall also, pulled him bodily off his horse; but a few moments later [Lewis] received . . . [a] wound—a shot penetrating his thigh, tearing open the femoral artery. He was carried off, amid a shower of bullets, to have his wound dressed; but twenty minutes elapsed before the surgeon was able to reach him; and then . . . it was too late . . . . Col. Lewis said: "Doctor, I have my death wound. Do not expose yourself so; remember your wife and children; you can do nothing for me."[16]

With dark descending over the canyon and with those below pinned down, the Cheyenne silently slipped away into the night. A short time later—despite scouts, soldiers, locomotives, and telegraph lines—Dull Knife's elusive band crossed the Kansas Pacific near Carlyle without opposition.[17]

For many Indians, the Plains had changed greatly since last they trod it. Cattle and sheep grazed tamely where before only buffalo and elk had roamed. Trails had given way to well-rutted roads lined with fences and sign posts. Homes, ranches, and schools now sat in valleys where only tepees once stood. And even the prairie itself, with its wildflowers and life-giving grass, was being plowed into tracts of raw and ugly sod.

Whatever national sympathy the Cheyenne had garnered thus far in their hopeless yet heroic bid for freedom was completely shattered by their bloody behavior while fleeing through northwestern Kansas. Many victims, some of whom were Texas cattlemen on drives or recent immigrants, either had not heard the news or felt it was greatly exaggerated. Twelve-year-old Anton Stenner was helping his father plow near Beaver Creek when a group of warriors rode up.

"[T]he indian on [the] north shot father through [the] chest," the youth said. "I knew the bullet went clear through, I seen father slap his hand on his chest, but he didn't fall, he stood for a moment, then the indian shot again and hit him again just below the right eye, then father fell."[18] When the marauders finally left and the frightened mother and children emerged from the creek bank, they not only found their home destroyed, but discovered a neighbor dead in the doorway. "I could see 4 nails drove in [the] left side of his head," young Stenner noted.[19]

Nearby, a woman, her husband, and six-month-old child, along with the man's younger brother and a friend, were fleeing afoot from another war party. In the words of the wife:

> My husband was carrying the baby . . . . just then they shot the men. I ran out about 30 steps . . . . my husband dropped the baby in the road . . . . the other indian kept on shooting at my husband, he kept calling to me and kept on crawling out toward me, he said I can't see, the indians shot 6 shots . . . . every time they hit him, he would holler out, after the last shot was fired, he only crawled just a little ways.[20]

The next morning, September 30, William Laing, his fifteen-year-old son, Freeman, and two young female friends set out by wagon for a nearby town to pay for preempted land. According to the Omaha *Republican*:

They had proceeded on their journey about eight miles, when they were met by a band of twelve Indians, who rode up to them at a gallop . . . . They immediately surrounded the wagon, and began to salute Mr. Laing with the usual greeting, "How!" Two of them, with seeming cordiality, grasped the hands of the father and son, while two others fired from behind; killing both instantly—the father falling back into the lap of one of the young ladies, and the boy sinking upon his knees in the wagon. Provisions had been prepared for the long journey; and while the Indians were eating these, the young ladies were compelled to hold the horses. After satisfying their hunger, they cut the horses loose, and took the trembling girls to the creek . . . where the band was encamped. Here they were ravished by as many as a dozen of the fiendish devils . . . . [T]hey were [then] ordered to go to a house about half a mile distant [but] they feared to go, lest when they turned their backs their treacherous ravishers would kill them. After some little expostulation on the part of the savages they went to the house . . . .

About sundown on the same day, as William and John Laing, two older sons of the murdered man, were leaving their work to return to the house, they saw what they supposed to be some Texans trying to catch wild horses. However, they were not alarmed, even when they came close enough to be distinguished; as they supposed they were friendly Indians. Shortly two . . . rode up to the wagon with the characteristic greeting. Three little girls, their sisters, aged twelve, nine, and seven years, were in the wagon; having gone out to ride home with their brothers. The Indians shook hands, and were invited to go to the house with them. They started, as if to accept the invitation; but, after riding along a short distance, one of the Indians said, "Look there," and, as the boys turned their heads, the Indians shot them—killing them instantly. The little girls were ordered to get out of the wagon and go to the house. The eldest girl, upon arriving at the house told the poor mother what had befallen her brothers. She had scarcely uttered the sad words before the savages surrounded the house. They compelled the frightened mother to give every thing that took their fancy . . . . Five of the party then ravished the mother; four, the oldest girl; and three, the second one . . . . Having satisfied their beastly lust, they placed the three girls between the feather ticks of the bed, kindled a fire in different parts of the room, and threw into the flames what they did not carry away. The mother, almost despairing, stood by wringing her hands,

> and entreating for the lives of her little ones. As if Providence had interfered, they took fright, probably at the rapidly advancing flames, and left their victims. The mother and her three children escaped from the burning house, and in the night walked eight miles to [a] house . . . about a quarter of a mile from the spot where the husband and brother met their death in the morning.[21]

"[T]he Indians captured an entire family of settlers . . . consisting of the mother . . . and three daughters, aged nineteen, seventeen and fourteen respectively," added a local newspaper. "The fiends ravished the shrieking women before the very eyes of the father and two brothers, and then slew the entire family, throwing the dead bodies into the burning house."[22]

As the Cheyenne continued their bloody sweep through Kansas, the army abandoned its line of defense along the railroad and set off in pursuit. "Our sympathies were . . . with them at first," confessed Second Lieutenant Calvin Cowles to his father, "but when we reached their trail of murder, rapine and desolation our blood rose against them."[23] Moving in their wake along Beaver and Sappa creeks, Cowles and others were stunned by what they saw. Revealed a young trooper:

> In one place . . . I saw the bodies of three men about a hundred yards from the house which they had evidently occupied; the men were lying on the ground with their brains knocked out; two had apparently been running from the house when they received these blows from the Indians. The house, inside, was all torn to pieces; the feather beds were strewn all over the yard; the dogs, cats, geese, ducks, every living thing belonging there had been killed, and was lying there dead.[24]

Added scout George Brown:

> They . . . killed every man they could find on . . . those creeks. They went to a schoolhouse and killed all the larger boys. [Capt. Clarence Mauck's] command found, about seven miles north of Beaver creek, a young lady lying on the prairie destitute of any clothing. She had lain there all night . . . . [T]he young lady was pretty badly chilled and almost dead. They wrapped her up in some blankets and sent her back to the settlements. They went on about three miles further and found three little children running around on the prairie, all too small to get anywhere.[25]

Other dazed women and children were found wandering about, "one of whom, a school teacher," Lieutenant George Palmer wrote in his journal, "had been stretched on the ground and secured by stakes driven in the ground and outraged by fifteen of the fiends. Her hair was cut off and after the Indians left her she crawled into the creek."[26]

By early October 1878, the raiders had finally left Kansas and entered Nebraska. As was the case to the south, George Crook established his line of defense in the north along the Union Pacific Railroad. And as before, the Indians crossed the tracks unscathed. For troopers who had been in the saddle since leaving Indian Territory, the halt at Sidney Station was the first rest in thirty days. "We arrived . . . completely worn out, not a man having had a chance to change clothes . . . [since] leaving Reno," said one dirty and disgusted soldier, "having often but one meal a day, having lost 40 horses and five engagements with the enemy."[27]

With hundreds of troops on their trail, the Cheyenne soon split into two bands—Little Wolf leading one into the broad expanse of the Nebraska Sand Hills and Dull Knife steering the other toward the Badlands of Dakota. The farther the Indians traveled, the more America was amazed. "It seems miraculous," Lieutenant Palmer admitted, "that two or three brigadiers, four or five colonels, majors and about a thousand men in good positions with wagons, rail roads and telegraphs were unable to stop the march of this [small] party of . . . warriors who carried their women and children with them . . . from the Indian Territory away into Nebraska."[28]

A correspondent for the Dodge City *Globe* was even more astonished:

> While we look the matter squarely in the face it must be conceded that Dull Knife has achieved one of the most extraordinary coups d'etat of modern times and has made a march before which even Sherman's march to the sea pales. With a force of 130 warriors this untutored but wily savage encounters and defeats, eludes, baffles and outgenerals ten times his number of American soldiers . . . and marched almost unmolested a distance of 1,000 miles. Of course, most of the country passed through by Dull Knife was sparsely settled; but with the number of military posts—six—lying almost directly in his path, and the great number of cattle men, cowboys, freighters, etc., scattered over the plains that came in contact with his band, it does seem strange that he slipped through the schemes and plans that were so well laid to entrap him . . . . Dull Knife has thoroughly demonstrated the fact that 130 desperate warriors can raid successfully through 1,000 miles of territory . . . steal stock and perpetrate outrages too vile and horrible to print.[29]

Finally, in late October, the inevitable occurred when Dull Knife found his path barred by a company of cavalry. After lengthy negotiations, bloodshed was averted when the 149 men, women, and children agreed to accompany the soldiers to Camp Robinson. "Now the fighting is over. We are friendly with one another," announced the post commander to Dull Knife.

> You must stay here for three months before the government will decide whether to send you south or to send you to the Sioux. While you are here, nothing bad will happen to you, but you must stay for three months. You will have the freedom of the post and may even go off into the mountains, but each night at supper time you must be here.[30]

While many felt that the captives should be allowed to remain in the north, some, including General Sheridan, were concerned that other tribes might follow suit and abandon their agencies for home. "Unless they are sent back," Sheridan argued, "the whole reservation system will receive a shock which will endanger its stability."[31]

On January 9, 1879, after it was learned they were to be sent south, Dull Knife and his band barricaded their barracks at the fort and declared they would sooner die than return. George Crook:

> It was supposed of course that the Indians had no arms other than a few knives. During the evening the building was as quiet as a grave, and the six sentinels who surrounded it suspected no danger. At ten minutes before 10 o'clock four shots were fired from the west end of the building killing two of the sentinels; shots were also fired from a front window into the guard-room wounding a Corporal. Simultaneously a rush was made through all the windows, the Indians sallying out resolved to kill and be killed.[32]

"I had just gotten into bed," recalled Captain Henry Wessells.

> I got up, put on my pants . . . my overcoat and hat and ran down to the East end of the Indian building. The Indians were all out running away . . . . The Indians fired at us repeatedly with carbines, and we killed five bucks in a few moments . . . . I passed two wounded squaws . . . . I went on a gallop to where Captain [Peter] Vroom was fighting the Indians in the bluffs about four miles out on the Laramie road . . . . I found . . . they had killed about eight Indians at that spot.[33]

Poorly armed, poorly clad, and weighed down by women and children in winter, the warriors were easy prey. As Crook reported to Sheridan one week later:

> Of the escaped Cheyennes there are fully forty-five not yet accounted for by death or capture. Of these nineteen are bucks. When last heard from on the evening of thirteenth they were about twenty-two miles distant going north-west. Many of them must be wounded, they travelled very slowly and . . . it is probable that the troops will over take nearly all of them.[34]

From the powerful alliance that had caused an entire army to tremble, resistance to the white invasion had dwindled to a handful of ragged refugees struggling through a winter wilderness. When it was over, half were dead and another score had been rounded up and shipped back to Indian Territory. Fifty-eight others, however, including the fugitive band under Little Wolf, were granted their prayers and allowed to remain in their beloved northland forever. Thus, mercifully, even as the last of the wild Indians of the High Plains melted away like snow in the sun, the survivors knew one lasting and well-earned victory.

Epilogue

Time . . . healing time. As with any tragic event, time cooled passions and allowed sharp, cruel memories to fade and soften. While such wounds in another corner of the world might remain raw for centuries, hardly a generation passed before Americans had "buried the hatchet." In its heedless, headlong rush to empire, the burgeoning Western giant simply had no time to harbor grudges or allow hatred to sap strength needed for challenges that lay ahead. Indeed, the healing began almost before the blood stopped flowing.

Hardly had the embers in Kansas cooled from the Dull Knife raid when the rapprochement commenced. In spite of the atrocities, a palpable sense of passing swept America when the Cheyenne were finally killed or caged, for with it came the realization that a colorful, dramatic epoch had drawn to a close. Far from being treated as monsters, when several raiders were brought back to Kansas for trial on murder charges, their return at times resembled a triumphal march. Reported one visitor from the Dodge City jail:

> I called upon those notable characters while they were supposed to be in durance vile, and found them the most conspicuous and best entertained men in prison. The representatives of different illustrated dailies were there, sketching their pictures, and treating them to cigars . . . . I cannot refrain from remarking that, if a white man, or body of white men, had been guilty of one-tenth of the crimes perpetrated by these Indians they would have been hanged as high as they could be raised . . . or shot to pieces in the streets.[1]

After their transfer to Lawrence, the prisoners, according to a local editor, were treated to a day at the circus.

> When the clowns appeared they smiled approval of their antics; and when the lean clown flung the fat clown over the ring bank, and then threw a colored boy upon him, [one brave] laughed until he cried, while his companions shook their sides . . . . They were provided with lemonade; and each one got away with two glasses, and when the third was offered they simply pressed their abdomens, and used the only English word they knew,—"heap."[2]

In sum, the editor said, "They enjoyed the performance thoroughly."[3]

The treatment of Dull Knife's warriors and their predictable acquittal was no aberration. After his return from exile, the most implacable Indian of all, Sitting Bull, became a hero among whites and a figure to rival Buffalo Bill, in whose "Wild West Show" the old chief proudly performed. Terrible as the Indian wars had been, in their wake Americans demanded to see and honor these men who had so long and heroically defied one of the mightiest powers on Earth.

Ironically, those closest to the Indian, the soldiers and scouts who had fought him, were some of the first to make peace. Indeed, many of these very whites who had laughed so long and loud at the myth of the "noble red man" were quick to reinstate that myth to an eager and gullible public. When the books, articles, and memoirs began to emerge years after the fighting, memories of Indians torturing the living, mutilating the dead, raping women, and murdering children had dimmed. Instead, the warrior grew in memory as a courageous, solitary figure who fought without stint or compromise—a ferocious individual who struggled against fate and overwhelming odds with little more than his bare hands and the simple tools of nature, holding back for more than a decade the inexorable tide of a steam, steel, and electric juggernaut.

"The courage with which they fought against the irresistible march of civilization," one backward-glancing officer wrote, "will always command the admiration of the soldiers who conquered them."[4]

Thus, the Indian of the High Plains gained in defeat a lasting and ever-expanding victory that he could never have won in war. Unfortunately, for the equally proud and courageous U.S. officers and men, there was never a chance that they would savor a true and total triumph. Praised by some and reviled by others, they would never receive a grand review through the streets of Washington when their long and bloody war was over. Nor was one expected.

Even amid the struggle, many soldiers realized that, with the nation divided over the issue, they were engaged in a no-win contest.

"If we punish the indians we are butchers and murderers," explained one angry young soldier, "and if we fail to do so we are cowards . . . . To be killed by an indian[,] burried in a ditch and have one's name spelt wrong in the papers is what any of us had reasonable grounds to expect."[5]

John Bourke also understood. As the lieutenant lay wet and shivering during one cruel campaign, replaying in his mind his years of service on the Plains, a scrawled diary entry reveals the haunting suspicion that all his sacrifices had been in vain.

> It made me feel old, as well as sad . . . . [M]y chequered life during the past fourteen years passed rapidly in review before my mind. I reflected how thankful I ought to be that I held the position I held . . . and I tried to make myself believe it was a grand thing to have my garments saturated with water, my feet cold and wet, my miserable straw hat torn by the breezes, no tent, no blanket, no supper to speak of. This, I said to myself, is heroism and I am a first-class hero; but it wouldn't work. Like Banquo's ghost, the thought would not go down that a good hot stove, with plenty of champagne and oysters would be good enough for the likes of me and it was then I made up my mind, if I ever married an heiress, to live for the remainder of my days in a brown stone front and retire from the hero business forever.[6]

It was only later, when time had smoothed the edges, that many, like Bourke, would look back to their years on the Plains with nostalgia. Gone were the harsh memories of Crook's "starvation march." Gone was the frozen white hell of Wyoming in winter. Gone too was the furnace of Texas in August and the sun that broiled the head from above and the sands that "cooked a man from the feet up." While young soldiers had cursed the cactus and dust and flies and mosquitoes and the stagnant green puddles unfit even for coffee, in later years, gray veterans enraptured listeners with the splendor of a High Plains sunset or the silver glint of morning sun on the snow-crowned Rockies or the wild game that teemed along the milky Powder River or the miles of prairie flowers that graced the broad Platte.

Then too, for many a lonely old man who had little else to show for his service to his country but lingering wounds, broken health, and a paltry pension, there was a rich, warm glow from within that money could not buy nor fame replace. It was the sweet satisfaction that he had, indeed "seen stirring times," a golden dawning that he had not only been a part of, but had played a prominent role in, one of the most romantic dramas the world had ever known—the winning of the West.

> Soon the landscape began to open out a little, and between the sand dunes and hummocks on the right I could get a glimpse of open prairie and hills in the distance. Finally, after passing around a bunch of such dunes, there opened up before us an immense valley and plain. The eye roamed for scores of miles over an unbroken wilderness. That splendid scene is still vivid in my memory though more than fifty-five years have passed away . . . . Today, villages and towns, surrounded with fields of grain and hay, probably cover the scene. Automobiles are darting here and there over good roads, and doubtless there is a railroad or two cutting across the country, while I, as an old man, am living in a small flat in a large Eastern city, with but little hope of ever seeing this wonderful transformation. Still, it is a source of satisfaction and great delight to me to think that I am one of the thousands of boys and men who in those days "did their bit" to make it possible for the good people of today to enjoy all these comforts in their pursuit of "life, liberty, and happiness."[7]

Notes

PROLOGUE

1. Stan Hoig, *The Sand Creek Massacre* (Norman: University of Oklahoma, 1961), 59.
2. Ibid., 150.
3. Ibid., 179.
4. Ibid., 188.
5. Senate Executive Documents for the Second Session of the Thirty-Ninth Congress, 1866–67 (Washington: Government Printing Office, 1867), 129–30.
6. Robert W. Mardock and Robert W. Richmond, *A Nation Moving West—Readings in the History of the American Frontier* (Lincoln: University of Nebraska, 1966), 250.
7. Denver *Weekly Rocky Mountain News*, December 14, 1864.

CHAPTER ONE

1. William E. Unrau, ed., *Tending the Talking Wires—A Buck Soldier's View of Indian Country, 1863–1866* (Salt Lake City: University of Utah, 1979), 261.
2. Casper (Wyoming) *Star Tribune*, July 27, 1970.
3. Unrau, 267.
4. Ibid., 252.
5. Earl A. Brininstool and Grace Raymond Hebard, *The Bozeman Trail* (Cleveland, Ohio: Arthur H. Clark, 1922), I: 180–81.
6. Ibid., 183–84.
7. Isaac B. Pennock Diary, entry for July 26, 1865 (Topeka: Kansas State Historical Society).
8. Kansas Scrapbook, II: 355–66. (Topeka: Kansas State Historical Society).
9. Brininstool, *Bozeman*, 187–90.
10. George M. Walker, "Eleventh Kansas Cavalry, 1865, and Battle of Platte Bridge," *Kansas Historical Collections* vol. 14 (1915–18): 338.
11. Brininstool, 194.
12. Ibid., 199.
13. Leavenworth (Kansas) *Daily Conservative*, August 2, 1865.
14. Donald F. Danker, "The North Brothers and the Pawnee Scouts," *Nebraska History* vol. 42, no. 3 (September 1961): 164.

15. D. Alexander Brown, *The Galvanized Yankees* (Urbana: University of Illinois, 1963), 125.
16. Benjamin Franklin Cooling, III, ed., *Soldiering in Sioux Country: 1865* (San Diego, California: Frontier Heritage, 1971), 36.
17. Brown, *Galvanized Yankees*, 129–30.
18. Myra E. Hull, ed., "Soldiering on the High Plains—The Diary of Lewis Byram Hull, 1864–1866," *Kansas Historical Quarterly* vol. 7, no. 1 (February 1938): n. 47.
19. Mardock, *Nation Moving West*, 251.
20. Brown, 187–88.
21. Mardock, 252; Brown, 188.
22. Hull, *Diary*, n. 47.
23. Cooling, *Soldiering*, 44–45.
24. Ibid., 47.
25. Ibid., 47–52.
26. Ibid., 50.

CHAPTER TWO

1. Merrill J. Mattes, *Indians, Infants and Infantrymen—Andrew and Elizabeth Burt on the Frontier* (Denver, Colorado: Old West, 1960), 254.
2. John S. Gray, *Custer's Last Campaign—Mitch Boyer and the Little Bighorn Reconstructed* (Lincoln: University of Nebraska, 1991), 38–39.
3. Ibid., 41.
4. Margaret I. Carrington, *Absaraka—Home of the Crows* (1868; reprint, Chicago: Lakeside, 1950), n. 88–89.
5. Ibid., 142–48.
6. Ibid., n. 145.
7. Stephen E. Ambrose, *Crazy Horse and Custer—The Parallel Lives of Two American Warriors* (New York: New American Library, 1975), 233.
8. *Massacre of Troops near Fort Phil. Kearney* (Fairfield, Washington: Ye Galleon, 1974), 8–9.
9. J.W. Vaughn, *Indian Fights—New Facts on Seven Encounters* (Norman: University of Oklahoma, 1966), 41.
10. Carrington, *Absaraka*, 324–25.
11. Ibid., 228.
12. Vaughn, *Indian Fights*, 48.
13. Carrington, 198.
14. Vaughn, 45.
15. Ibid., 46–47.
16. Carrington, 229–30.
17. Ibid., 330.
18. Ibid., 331.
19. Ibid., 231–34.
20. Ambrose, *Crazy Horse and Custer*, 242.
21. Carrington, 331–35.
22. Vaughn, 70.
23. *Massacre of Troops*, 10.
24. Mardock, *Nation*, 253.
25. Mattes, *Indians, Infants and Infantry*, 124.
26. Ibid., 128.
27. Ibid., 128–29.
28. Ambrose, *Crazy Horse*, 295.
29. Connie J. White, *Hostiles and Horse Soldiers—Battles and Campaigns in the West* (Boulder, Colorado: Pruett, 1972), 167.

30. Don Rickey, Jr., *Forty Miles a Day on Beans and Hay—The Enlisted Soldier Fighting the Indian Wars* (Norman: University of Oklahoma, 1963), 313.

CHAPTER THREE

1. Rickey, *Forty Miles a Day*, 28.
2. Elizabeth Bacon Custer, *Tenting on the Plains, or General Custer in Kansas and Texas* (reprint, 1887; Norman: University of Oklahoma, 1971), III: 686.
3. Mattes, *Indians*, 46.
4. Robert M. Utley, *Life in Custer's Cavalry—Diaries and Letters of Albert and Jennie Barnitz, 1867–1868* (New Haven, Connecticut: Yale University, 1977), 39.
5. DeB. Randolph Keim, *Sheridan's Troopers on the Border—A Winter Campaign on the Plains* (reprint, 1885; Lincoln: University of Nebraska, 1985), 49.
6. Raymond L. Welty, "Supplying the Frontier Military Posts," *Kansas Historical Quarterly* vol. 7, no. 2 (May 1938): 154.
7. Elizabeth Custer, *Tenting*, 688–89.
8. Unrau, *Talking Wire*, 261.
9. Utley, *Diaries and Letters*, 178.
10. Ibid., 132.
11. Custer, 657.
12. Rickey, *Forty Miles*, 129.
13. Leavenworth (Kansas) *Daily Times*, July 26, 1867.
14. Rickey, 180.
15. Ibid., 180–81.
16. Blaine Burkey, *"Custer, Come at Once!"—The Fort Hays Years of George and Elizabeth Custer—1867–1870* (Hays, Kansas: Thomas More Prep, 1976), 98.
17. Rickey, 183.
18. Sherry L. Smith, *The View from Officers' Row—Army Perceptions of Western Indians* (Tucson: University of Arizona, 1990), 5.
19. Utley, *Diaries*, 184.
20. Ibid., 203.
21. Smith, *Officers' Row*, 56–57.
22. Rickey, *Forty Miles*, 131.
23. Alson B. Ostrander, *An Army Boy of the Sixties—A Story of the Plains* (New York: World Book, 1924), 114.
24. Utley, 189.
25. Ibid.
26. Ostrander, *Army Boy*, 159.
27. Carrington, *Absaraka*, 214.
28. Ibid., n. 215.
29. Vaughn, *Indian Fights*, 229.
30. Richard G. Hardorff, *The Custer Battle Casualties—Burials, Exhumations and Reinterments* (El Segundo, California: Upton and Sons, 1991), 113.
31. Paul Wellman, *Death on the Prairie—The Thirty Years' Struggle for the Western Plains* (reprint, 1934; Lincoln: University of Nebraska, 1987), n. 36.
32. Rickey, 232.
33. Brown, *Galvanized Yankees*, 183–84.
34. Rickey, 315.
35. Paul Andrew Hutton, *The Custer Reader* (Lincoln: University of Nebraska, 1992), 266.
36. Ibid.
37. Rickey, 305.
38. Cooling, *Soldiering in Sioux Country*, 50.

CHAPTER FOUR

1. Brown, 52–53.
2. Ibid., 194–95.
3. "The Diary of Samuel Kingman at Indian Treaty in 1865," *Kansas Historical Quarterly* vol. 1, no. 5 (November 1932): 446.
4. John M. Carroll, ed., *General Custer and the Battle of the Washita—The Federal View* (Bryan, Texas: Guidon, 1978), 123.
5. Ibid., 210.
6. Lawrence A. Frost, *The Court-martial of General George Armstrong Custer* (Norman: University of Oklahoma, 1968), 16.
7. Carroll, *General Custer*, 130–31.
8. Utley, *Diaries*, 30–31, 34.
9. Milo Milton Quaife, ed., *My Life on the Plains* (Lincoln: University of Nebraska, 1966), 44–47.
10. Utley, 32.
11. Carroll, *Custer*, 127.
12. Ibid., 127–28.
13. John H. Monnett, *The Battle of Beecher Island and the Indian War of 1867–1869* (Niwot: University Press of Colorado, 1992), 51.
14. Ambrose, *Crazy Horse*, 265.
15. Quaife, *My Life on the Plains*, 62.
16. Ibid., 64; Custer, *Tenting*, 578.
17. Custer, 578; Utley, *Diaries*, 35.
18. Custer, 578.
19. Frost, *Court-martial*, 30.
20. Custer, 564.
21. Ibid., 576.
22. Carroll, 144.
23. Utley, 36.
24. Quaife, *My Life*, 94; Custer, 570.
25. Custer, 578.
26. Carroll, 117.
27. Mardock, *Nation*, 255.
28. Ibid., 255–56.
29. Ibid., 258.
30. Marysville (Kansas) *Enterprise*, August 17, 1867.
31. Monnett, *Beecher Island*, 31.
32. Denver *Weekly Rocky Mountain News*, April 12, 1866.
33. Oliver Knight, *Following the Indian Wars—The Story of the Newspaper Correspondents Among the Indian Campaigners* (Norman: University of Oklahoma, 1960), 21–22.

CHAPTER FIVE

1. Carroll, *Custer*, 101.
2. Burkey, *Fort Hays*, 14.
3. Carroll, 139.
4. Leavenworth (Kansas) *Daily Times*, July 2, 1867.
5. Monnett, 93.
6. Leavenworth *Daily Times*, August 27, 1867.
7. Monnett, 97; Donald F. Danker, *Man of the Plains—Recollections of Luther North, 1856–1882* (Lincoln: University of Nebraska, 1961), 74.
8. Topeka (Kansas) *State Record*, May 13, 1868.

9. Utley, *Diaries*, 68–69.
10. Mrs. Frank C. Montgomery, "Fort Wallace and its Relation to the Frontier," *Kansas Historical Collections* vol. 17 (1926–28): 209.
11. Utley, 71–73.
12. Ibid., 71–78.
13. Leavenworth *Daily Times*, July 17, 1867.
14. Utley, 76.
15. Quaife, *My Life*, 135–38.
16. Ibid., 138–39.
17. Ibid., 140–42.
18. Ibid., 192–200. Hutton, *The Custer Reader*, 103.
19. Marguerite Merington, ed., *The Custer Story—The Life and Intimate Letters of General George A. Custer and his Wife Elizabeth* (reprint, 1950; Lincoln: University of Nebraska, 1987), 196.
20. Marysville (Kansas) *Enterprise*, August 3, 1867.
21. "The Letters of John Ferguson, Early Resident of Western Washington County," *Kansas Historical Quarterly* vol. 12, no. 4 (November 1943): 345-46.
22. Monnett, 78.
23. Utley, *Diaries*, 80.
24. Leavenworth *Daily Times*, July 7, 1867.
25. Burkey, *Fort Hays*, n. 25.

CHAPTER SIX

1. Quaife, *My Life on the Plains*, 112.
2. Keith Wheeler, "The Scouts," 24 (Alexandria, Virginia: Time/Life, 1978), 15.
3. J.W. Vaughn, *The Reynolds Campaign on Powder River* (Norman: University of Oklahoma, 1961), 62.
4. Brown, *Galvanized Yankees*, 203.
5. Burkey, 21.
6. Olive K. Dixon, *Life of 'Billy' Dixon—Plainsman, Scout and Pioneer* (Dallas, Texas: P. L. Turner, 1927), 87.
7. Keim, *Sheridan's Troopers*, 166.
8. Carrington, *Absaraka*, 131.
9. Ostrander, *Army Boy*, 102–03.
10. Joseph G. Rosa, *They Called Him Wild Bill—The Life and Adventures of James Butler Hickok* (Norman: University of Oklahoma, 1964), 92.
11. Ibid., 109.
12. Burkey, 58.
13. Ibid., 20.
14. Ibid.
15. Brown, *Galvanized Yankees*, 203.
16. Burkey, 20.
17. Quaife, *My Life*, 234–38.
18. Ibid., 239.
19. Jerome A. Greene, *Slim Buttes, 1876—An Episode of the Great Sioux War* (Norman: University of Oklahoma, 1982), 27.
20. Elizabeth B. Custer, *Boots and Saddles, or Life in Dakota with General Custer* (reprint, 1885; Williamstown, Massachusetts: Corner House, 1974), 240–41.
21. Greene, *Slim Buttes*, 54.
22. Vaughn, *The Reynolds Campaign*, 41.
23. Martin F. Schmitt, *General George Crook—His Autobiography* (Norman: University of Oklahoma, 1946), 213.

24. W.A. Graham, *The Custer Myth—A Source Book of Custeriana* (Harrisburg, Pennsylvania: Stackpole Books, 1953), 179.

25. John F. Finerty, *War-path and Bivouac—The Big Horn and Yellowstone Expedition* (Chicago: R.R. Donnelley and Sons, 1955), 104.

26. Danker, "The North Brothers," 170–71.

27. Edgar I. Stewart, ed., *The March of the Montana Column—A Prelude to the Custer Disaster* (Norman: University of Oklahoma, 1961), 92–93.

28. Wheeler, "The Scouts," 116.

29. Finerty, *War-path*, 79.

30. Brininstool, *The Bozeman Trail*, 193.

31. Finerty, 234.

32. Wheeler, 203.

33. Greene, *Slim Buttes*, 75.

34. William F. Cody, *An Autobiography of Buffalo Bill* (New York: Rinehart, 1920), 287–88.

35. King, *Campaigning With Crook* (Norman: University of Oklahoma, 1964), 106.

36. Rickey, *Forty Miles*, 211; Finerty, *War-path*, 230.

37. King, 105.

38. Custer, *Boots and Saddles*, 79.

39. Brown, *Galvanized Yankees*, 159.

40. Rosa, *Wild Bill*, 117.

41. Robert C. Carriker, ed., "Thompson McFadden's Diary of an Indian Campaign, 1874," *Southwestern Historical Quarterly* vol. 75, no. 2 (October 1971): 199–200.

42. Dixon, *Billy Dixon*, 116–17.

43. Custer, *My Life*, 233.

CHAPTER SEVEN

1. Topeka (Kansas) *State Record*, December 23, 1868.

2. Ibid.

3. Leavenworth (Kansas) *Times and Conservative*, September 22, 1868.

4. Ambrose, *Crazy Horse*, 247.

5. Leavenworth *Daily Times*, June 21, 1867.

6. George A. Forsyth, "A Frontier Fight," *Harper's New Monthly Magazine* vol. 91 (June–November 1895): 42.

7. Sigmund Shlesinger, "The Beecher Island Fight," *Kansas Historical Collections* vol. 15 (1919–22): 540–41.

8. Forsyth, "A Frontier Fight," 44–45.

9. Ibid., 45.

10. John Hurst, "The Beecher Island Fight," *Kansas Historical Collections* vol. 15 (1919–22): 531.

11. Monnett, *The Battle of Beecher Island*, 125.

12. Ibid., 126.

13. Forsyth, 45.

14. Monnett, 126.

15. Forsyth, 46–47.

16. Hurst, 532.

17. Forsyth, 47.

18. Monnett, 132.

19. Forsyth, 47.

20. Hurst, 532.

21. Monnett, 133.

22. Hurst, 533.

23. Forsyth, 47–48.

24. Ibid., 48.
25. Hurst, 533.
26. Keim, *Sheridan's Troopers*, 52.
27. Hurst, 534.
28. Monnett, 139.
29. Forsyth, 50.
30. Keim, 53.
31. Hurst, 534.
32. Forsyth, 49–51.
33. Monnett, 106.
34. Forsyth, 51–54.
35. Ibid., 54.
36. Ibid., 54–56.
37. Ibid., 56.
38. Hurst, 536.
39. Monnett, 152.
40. Ibid., 152–53.
41. Forsyth, 57.
42. Monnett, 154–55.
43. Ibid., 155.
44. Hurst, 536; Monnett, 162.
45. Monnett, 155.
46. Ibid., 161.
47. Ibid., 160.
48. Forsyth, 60.
49. Hurst, 536.
50. Monnett, 160–61.
51. Forsyth, 60–61.
52. "Diary of Chauncey B. Whitney," *Kansas Historical Collections* vol. 12 (1911–12): 298.
53. Monnett, 163.
54. Hurst, 537.
55. Forsyth, 61.
56. Monnett, 165.
57. Hurst, 537.
58. "Diary of Chauncey B. Whitney," 302.
59. Forsyth, 61.
60. Monnett, 165–66.
61. Shlesinger, 545.
62. Monnett, 177–78.
63. Ibid., 178.
64. Ibid., 178–79.
65. Ibid., 179; Shlesinger, 546.
66. Shlesinger, 543–44.

CHAPTER EIGHT

1. Grace Meredith, ed., *Girl Captives of the Cheyennes—A True Story of the Capture and Rescue of Four Pioneer Girls, 1874* (Los Angeles: Gem, 1927), 16.
2. Fanny Kelly, *Narrative of My Captivity Among Sioux Indians* (reprint; Chicago: R.R. Donnelley and Sons, 1990), 4.
3. Ibid., 12.
4. Meredith, 17–19.
5. Kelly, 12–20.

6. Brown, *Galvanized Yankees*, 98.
7. Marysville (Kansas) *Enterprise*, August 11, 1866.
8. Leavenworth (Kansas) *Daily Times*, September 26, 1868.
9. Meredith, 20, 22.
10. Kelly, 46–49.
11. Ibid., 58, 61–62.
12. Ibid., 78.
13. Meredith, 25–26.
14. Ibid., 31–32.
15. Kelly, 86.
16. Brown, *Galvanized Yankees*, 34.
17. James L. Haley, *The Buffalo War—The History of the Red River Indian Uprising of 1874* (Garden City, New York: Doubleday, 1976), 202–03.
18. Brown, 98.
19. Leavenworth *Daily Times*, December 3, 1874.
20. Kelly, 141.
21. Meredith, 36.
22. Brown, 34.
23. Kelly, 191.
24. "Life and Adventure of George W. Brown—Soldier, Pioneer, Scout, Plainsman and Buffalo Hunter," *Kansas Historical Collections* vol. 17 (1926–28): 109.
25. Kelley, 345.
26. Ibid., 253–54.
27. Robert C. and Eleanor R. Carriker, eds., *An Army Wife on the Frontier—The Memoirs of Alice Blackwood Baldwin, 1867–1877* (Salt Lake City: University of Utah, 1975), 40–41.
28. Olive A. Clark, "Early Days Along the Solomon Valley," *Kansas Historical Collections* vol. 17 (1926–28): 728.
29. Marysville *Enterprise*, March 21, 1868.
30. Kelly, 175.
31. Stewart, *The March of the Montana Column*, 112–13.
32. Meredith, 49–50.

CHAPTER NINE

1. Samuel J. Crawford, *Kansas in the Sixties* (Chicago: A.C. McClurg, 1911), 291.
2. Monnett, *Beecher Island*, 68; Crawford, 292.
3. Burkey, *Fort Hays*, 41.
4. Topeka (Kansas) *State Record*, December 23, 1868.
5. Ibid.
6. Wellman, *Death on the Prairie*, 82.
7. Carroll, *Custer*, 26.
8. Merington, *The Life and Intimate Letters of General George A. Custer*, 217–18.
9. Utley, *Diaries and Letters*, 197, 199.
10. Merington, *Letters*, 217.
11. Hutton, *Custer Reader*, 163–64.
12. Merington, 218–19.
13. Hutton, 165–66.
14. Ibid., 167.
15. Custer, *My Life on the Plains*, 311, 313–15, 318–19.
16. Utley, *Diaries*, 218–19.
17. Ibid., 220, 223–24.
18. Custer, 333–34.
19. Utley, 225.

20. Custer, 334–35.
21. Utley, 225–28.
22. Keim, *Sheridan's Troopers*, 117.
23. Carroll, *General Custer and the Battle of the Washita*, 38.
24. Custer, 339–40.
25. Hutton, 171–72.
26. Custer, 336.
27. Hutton, 172.
28. Ibid., 173–74.
29. Merington, *Letters*, 222; Custer, 351–52.
30. Keim, 111.
31. Ibid., 121–22.
32. David L. Spotts, *Campaigning With Custer and the Nineteenth Kansas Volunteer Cavalry on the Washita Campaign, 1868–1869* (reprint, 1928; Lincoln: University of Nebraska, 1988), 66.
33. Keim, 122.
34. Hutton, *Custer Reader*, 177.
35. Keim, *Sheridan's Troopers*, 123.
36. Utley, *Diaries*, 229.
37. Ibid., 236.
38. Ibid., 243.
39. Keim, 143.
40. Ibid., 144–45.
41. Carroll, *General Custer*, 69.
42. Custer, *My Life on the Plains*, 426–27.
43. Keim, 154.
44. Custer, 427–28.
45. Custer, 429; Carroll, 70.
46. Carroll, 50.
47. Ibid., 72.
48. Ibid., 50–51.
49. Custer, 551–52.
50. Ibid., 554–56.
51. James Albert Hadley, "The Nineteenth Kansas Cavalry and the Conquest of the Plains Indians," *Kansas Historical Collections* vol. 10 (1907–08): 450.
52. Spotts, *Campaigning With Custer*, 152.
53. Hadley, "The Nineteenth Kansas," 450.
54. Spotts, 156.
55. Custer, 563.
56. Ibid., 564–71.
57. Ibid., 572–73.
58. Ibid., 581–82.
59. Spotts, 157–58.
60. Custer, *My Life*, 583–84.
61. Spotts, 157–58.
62. Custer, 585, 587–88.
63. Ibid., 589–90.
64. Spotts, 159–60.
65. Custer, 594.
66. Hadley, 453.
67. "A.L. Runyon's Letters from the Nineteenth Kansas Regiment," *Kansas Historical Quarterly* vol. 9, no. 1 (February 1940): n. 74.
68. Spotts, 160.
69. Custer, 595.

70. Spotts, 161.
71. Hadley, 445.
72. Smith, *The View From Officers' Row*, 128–29.
73. Carroll, *General Custer*, 60.
74. Ibid., 61.

CHAPTER TEN

1. Keim, *Sheridan's Troopers*, 167–69.
2. Thomas C. Battey, *The Life and Adventures of a Quaker Among the Indians* (reprint, 1875; Norman: University of Oklahoma, 1968), 93–95.
3. Ibid., 320–21.
4. Frost, *The Court-martial of General George Armstrong Custer*, 17.
5. Monnett, *The Battle of Beecher Island*, 106.
6. Spotts, *Campaigning With Custer*, 84–86.
7. Keim, 170, 194–95.
8. Smith, *Officers' Row*, 56.
9. Keim, 195–96.
10. Custer, *Boots and Saddles*, 134, 237.
11. King, *Campaigning With Crook*, 38.
12. Carroll, 96; Leavenworth (Kansas) *Daily Conservative*, July 8, 1862; Leo E. Oliva, *Soldiers on the Santa Fe Trail* (Norman: University of Oklahoma, 1967), 143, 147.
13. Utley, *Life in Custer's Cavalry*, 111.
14. Custer, *My Life on the Plains*, 252.
15. Keim, 217.
16. Battey, *The Life and Adventures of a Quaker*, 280–81.
17. Finerty, *War-Path and Bivouac*, 107.
18. Custer, *My Life*, 252, 254–55.
19. Ibid., 253.
20. Ambrose, *Crazy Horse and Custer*, 148.
21. Kelly, *Narrative of my Captivity*, 129–30.
22. Finerty, 105.
23. Knight, *Following the Indian Wars*, 19.
24. Utley, *Diaries and Letters*, 63.
25. Leavenworth (Kansas) *Daily Times*, July 24, 1867.
26. Utley, 112–13.
27. Keim, 216.
28. Custer, *My Life*, 488–89.
29. Keim, 216.
30. Knight, 20.
31. Smith, *Officers' Row*, 154.
32. Custer, 251.
33. Utley, *Diaries*, 202.
34. Custer, 336–38.
35. Danker, *Man of the Plains*, 51–52.
36. Ibid., 70.
37. Mattes, *Indians, Infants and Infantry*, 131–32.
38. Kelly, *Narrative*, 110, 113.
39. Mattes, 149–50.
40. Battey, *Quaker*, 257–58.
41. Kelly, 127.
42. Finerty, *War-Path*, 146–47.
43. Battey, 110–11.
44. Hays (Kansas) *Sentinel*, July 26, 1876; Smith, 38.

CHAPTER ELEVEN

1. Wheeler, "The Scouts," 208.

2. Donald F. Danker, ed. "The Journal of an Indian Fighter—The 1869 Diary of Major Frank J. North, Leader of the Pawnee Scouts," *Nebraska History* vol. 39, no. 2 (June 1958): n. 139.

3. Danker, *Man of the Plains,* 115.

4. Ibid., 115–18.

5. Wheeler, 208.

6. *Annual Report of the Commissioner of Indian Affairs to the Secretary of the Interior for the Year 1874* (Washington: Government Printing Office, 1874), 236.

7. Mardock, *A Nation Moving West,* 276.

8. Joe F. Taylor, "The Indian Campaign on the Staked Plains, 1874–1875—Military Correspondence from War Department Adjutant General's Office, File 2815-1874," *Panhandle-Plains Historical Review* vol. 34 (1961): 214.

9. Brenham (Texas) *Banner,* February 26, 1875.

10. Carriker, "*McFadden's Diary,*" 204–10.

11. Ibid., 230.

12. Robert C. Carriker, "Mercenary Heroes—The Scouting Detachment of the Indian Territory Expedition, 1874–1875," *The Chronicles of Oklahoma* vol. 51, no. 3 (Fall 1973): 320.

13. William H. Leckie, *The Military Conquest of the Southern Plains* (Norman: University of Oklahoma, 1963), 221.

14. Meredith, *Girl Captives of the Cheyennes,* 96–97.

15. Ibid., 86; *Life and Adventures of "Billy" Dixon of Adobe Walls, Texas Panhandle* (Guthrie, Oklahoma: Co-Operative, 1914), 296.

16. Taylor, *Indian Campaign,* 190.

17. Ibid., 208.

18. George Nellans, *Authentic Accounts of Massacre of Indians, Rawlins County, Kansas, 1875 and Cheyenne Indian Raid in Western Kansas, September 30, 1878.* pamphlet 3, no. 2, Kansas State Historical Society, Topeka, 2–3.

19. Homer W. Wheeler, *Buffalo Days—The Personal Narrative of a Cattleman, Indian Fighter and Army Officer* (reprint, 1925; Lincoln: University of Nebraska, 1990), 105–06.

20. Nellans, 4.

21. Ibid., 5.

22. Bernice Larson Webb, "First Homesteader and the Battle of Sappa Creek," *Kansas Historical Quarterly* vol. 10, no. 3 (Summer 1978): 56.

23. Taylor, 1.

24. Ellsworth (Kansas) *Reporter,* July 1, 1875.

CHAPTER TWELVE

1. Custer, *Boots and Saddles,* 73-74.

2. Ibid., 73–75.

3. Smith, *Officers' Row,* 144–45.

4. Mattes, *Indians, Infants and Infantry,* 20.

5. Ibid., 39, 42.

6. Custer, 82.

7. Mattes, 53–54.

8. Smith, 28.

9. Mattes, 54–55.

10. Custer, *Boots and Saddles,* 83.

11. Mattes, 50.

12. Custer, 85.

13. Sandra L. Myres, *Cavalry Wife—The Diary of Eveline M. Alexander, 1866–1867* (College Station: Texas A&M University, 1977), 63.

14. Mattes, *Indians, Infants and Infantry*, 117.
15. Denver (Colorado) *Rocky Mountain News*, June 7, 1865.
16. Carriker, *Army Wife*, 30–31.
17. Mattes, 142.
18. Utley, *Diaries and Letters of Albert and Jennie Barnitz*, 56–57.
19. Ibid., 57.
20. Dodge City (Kansas) *Ford County Globe*, August 20, 1878.
21. Burkey, *Fort Hays*, 58.
22. Mattes, 87–88.
23. Smith, *Officers' Row*, 29.
24. Custer, 226.
25. Carriker, 49.
26. Ibid.
27. Mattes, 85.
28. Ibid., 88–89.
29. Smith, 57.
30. Ibid., 66–67.
31. Ibid., 67.
32. Carriker, *Army Wife*, 99–100.
33. Smith, 28.
34. Mattes, *Infants*, 143.
35. Custer, *Boots and Saddles*, 155–56.
36. Mattes, 159–60.
37. Custer, *Tenting on the Plains*, 619–20.
38. Ibid., 484–85.
39. Mattes, 21.
40. Custer, 485.

CHAPTER THIRTEEN

1. Hutton, *The Custer Reader*, 266–67.
2. J.W. Vaughn, *The Reynolds Campaign on Powder River* (Norman: University of Oklahoma, 1961), 15.
3. O.W. Coursey, ed., *The First White Woman in the Black Hills, As Told by Herself* (Mitchell, South Dakota: Educator Supply, c. 1923), 38.
4. Vaughn, *Reynolds Campaign*, 4.
5. Ambrose, *Crazy Horse and Custer*, 392–93.
6. Vaughn, 7.
7. Ambrose, 393.
8. Vaughn, 7.
9. Cody, *Autobiography*, 297.
10. Vaughn, 10.
11. Ibid., 15.
12. Ibid., 45.
13. Ibid.
14. Ibid., 49.
15. Ibid., 80.
16. Ibid., 81–82.
17. Ibid., 83.
18. Ibid., 82.
19. Ibid., 98–99.
20. Ibid., 153.
21. Ibid., 162.
22. Ibid., 159.

23. Edward J. McClernand, *On Time for Disaster—The Rescue of Custer's Command* (reprint; Lincoln: University of Nebraska, 1989), 147–48.
24. Custer, *Boots and Saddles*, 261–63.
25. Ibid., 263–65.
26. Ibid., 265.
27. Charles M. Robinson III, *A Good Year to Die: The Story of the Great Sioux War* (Norman: University of Oklahoma, 1995), 133.
28. Jerome Greene, ed., *Battles and Skirmishes of the Great Sioux War, 1876–1877—The Military View* (Norman: University of Oklahoma, 1993), 26–27.
29. Knight, *Following the Indian Wars*, 183.
30. Ibid., 182–83.
31. Finerty, *War-Path and Bivouac*, 124.
32. Greene, *Great Sioux War*, 27–28.
33. Finerty, 26–27.
34. Rickey, *Forty Miles a Day*, 285.
35. Martin F. Schmitt, ed., *General George Crook—His Autobiography* (Norman: University of Oklahoma, 1946), 194.
36. Finerty, 128–29.
37. B.W. Allred, et al, eds., *Great Western Indian Fights* (Lincoln: University of Nebraska, 1960), 231.
38. Knight, 188.
39. Ibid.
40. Finerty, *War-Path*, 130–31.
41. Greene, 29, 31.
42. Ibid., 32–33.
43. Finerty, 132–33.
44. Ibid., 134, 136.
45. Ibid., 135–36.
46. Neil C. Mangum, *Battle of the Rosebud—Prelude to the Little Bighorn* (El Segundo, California: Upton and Sons, 1991), 84–86.
47. Ibid., 140.
48. Ibid., n. 142.
49. Ibid.
50. *Eli S. Ricker Collection*, M58, Nebraska State Historical Society, Lincoln, Tablet No. 15.

CHAPTER FOURTEEN

1. Merington, *The Life and Intimate Letters of General George A. Custer*, 309.
2. Jeffry D. Wert, *Custer: The Controversial Life of George Armstrong Custer* (New York: Simon and Schuster, 1996), 327.
3. Richard Upton, *The Custer Adventure—As Told by its Participants* (El Segundo, California: Upton and Sons, 1990), 16.
4. John M. Carroll, *Camp Talk—The Very Private Letters of Frederick W. Benteen of the 7th U.S. to his Wife, 1871 to 1888* (Bryan, Texas: John M. Carroll, 1983), 14.
5. Wheeler, "The Scouts," 96.
6. Rickey, *Forty Miles a Day*, 230.
7. Graham, *The Custer Myth*, 235.
8. Knight, *Following the Indian Wars*, 206.
9. Merington, 308.
10. Wheeler, 132.
11. Upton, *The Custer Adventure*, 21.
12. Robert M. Utley, *Cavalier in Buckskin—George Armstrong Custer and the Western Military Frontier* (Norman: University of Oklahoma, 1988), 168.
13. Graham, *Myth*, 187.

14. Merington, 307.
15. Upton, 22–23.
16. Ibid., 24.
17. Ibid., 24–26.
18. Kenneth Hammer, ed., *Custer in '76—Walter Camp's Notes on the Custer Fight* (Provo, Utah: Brigham Young University, 1976), 187.
19. Greene, 43–44.
20. Upton, *The Custer Adventure*, 26.
21. Greene, 45.
22. Upton, 28.
23. McClernand, *On Time for Disaster*, 168.
24. Greene, *Great Sioux War*, 45, 47.
25. Hammer, *Walter Camp's Notes*, 231.
26. Graham, 241–42.
27. Richard G. Hardorff, *The Custer Battle Casualties—Burials, Exhumations and Reinterments* (El Segundo, California: Upton and Sons, 1991), 144.
28. Graham, 242.
29. Greene, 48.
30. Hutton, *The Custer Reader*, 287.
31. Hammer, 232–33.
32. Graham, 242.
33. Greene, 49.
34. Hammer, *Camp's Notes*, 112.
35. Greene, 49–50.
36. Hutton, 289–90.
37. Carroll, *Camp Talk*, 22.
38. Hardorff, *Custer Battle Casualties*, 127–28.
39. Ibid., 128.
40. Hammer, 133–34.
41. Hardorff, 131.
42. Ibid., 136.
43. Graham, 243.
44. Hardorff, 149.
45. Upton, *The Custer Adventure*, 49.
46. Merington, *Life and Intimate Letters*, 316.
47. Hutton, *The Custer Reader*, 290–93.
48. Utley, *Cavalier in Buckskin*, 191.
49. Hutton, 293–95.
50. Graham, *Myth*, 244.
51. Ibid.
52. Hutton, 295.
53. Ibid.
54. Robinson, *Good Year to Die*, 201.
55. Ibid., 296–97.
56. Graham, 244.
57. Hutton, 296.
58. Greene, *Great Sioux War*, 52–53.
59. Upton, *The Custer Adventure*, 45.
60. Graham, 244.
61. Hutton, *The Custer Reader*, 297.
62. Hardorff, *The Custer Battle Casualties*, 164.
63. Rickey, *Forty Miles*, 292.
64. Hammer, *Walter Camp's Notes*, 114.
65. Hammer, 136.

66. Gordon Browne, "At the Little Bighorn the Unrecognized Hero of Reno Hill was not Major Reno, but Captain Benteen," *Military History* (August 1995): 90.
67. Ibid.
68. Hammer, 136.
69. Hutton, 297–98.
70. Graham, *Myth*, 182.
71. Hutton, 298.
72. Hammer, 114.
73. Hardorff, 162.
74. Hammer, *Notes*, 114.
75. Ibid., 114–15.
76. Ibid., 115.
77. Ibid., 225.
78. Hutton, *The Custer Reader*, 299.
79. Hammer, 235–36.
80. Greene, *Great Sioux War*, 59.
81. Hutton, 299–300.
82. Hammer, 116.
83. Graham, 246.
84. Robinson, *Good Year to Die*, 206–7.
85. Upton, *The Custer Adventure*, 85–86.
86. Ibid., 86.
87. McClernand, *On Time For Disaster*, 60.
88. Upton, 86.
89. McClernand, 60–61.
90. Hardorff, *Custer Battle Casualties*, 16–17.
91. Hutton, 309.
92. Hardorff, 157.
93. Ibid., 132–33.
94. Ibid., 161.
95. Ibid., 149.
96. Ibid., 149–50.
97. Ibid., 158.
98. Ibid., 159.
99. Hutton, *The Custer Reader*, 309.
100. Hardorff, 97.
101. Ibid., 18.
102. Hutton, 309.
103. Hardorff, 19, 106.
104. Ibid., 98.
105. Hammer, *Walter Camp's Notes*, 236–37.
106. Hardorff, 106.
107. Hammer, 136–37.
108. Hutton, 310.
109. Hardorff, *Custer Battle Casualties*, 19.
110. Hutton, 310.
111. Hardorff, 21.
112. Ibid., 105.
113. Ibid., 106.
114. McClernand, *On Time for Disaster*, 94.
115. Ibid.
116. Ibid., 148.
117. Upton, *The Custer Adventure*, 104–05.

CHAPTER FIFTEEN

1. Knight, *Following the Indian Wars*, 220.
2. Finerty, *War-Path and Bivouac*, 174.
3. Ibid., 176–78.
4. Ibid., 180–83.
5. Ibid., 184.
6. Ibid., 185–86, 188–89.
7. Ibid., 189–90.
8. Ibid., 191.
9. Ibid., 191–92.
10. Ibid., 193.
11. Ibid., 194–95.
12. Ibid., 197–98.
13. Wheeler, "The Scouts," 222; Paul L. Hedren, *First Scalp for Custer: The Skirmish at Warbonnet Creek, Nebraska, July 17, 1876* (Glendale, California: Arthur H. Clark, 1980), 37.
14. King, *Campaigning With Crook*, 22–23.
15. Ibid., 23.
16. Ibid., 32–33.
17. Ibid., 33–34.
18. Wheeler, 225.
19. Cody, *Autobiography*, 265.
20. Wheeler, 225.
21. *Ricker Collection*, Tablet No. 13.
22. Finerty, 230.
23. King, 35.
24. Ibid., 38.
25. Knight, *Following the Indian Wars*, 233.
26. McClernand, *On Time for Disaster*, 96–97.
27. Finerty, 235.
28. Greene, *Slim Buttes*, 30.
29. Schmitt, *Crook Autobiography*, 206.
30. Finerty, 267.
31. Ibid., 278.
32. Schmitt, 206.
33. Utley, *Cavalier in Buckskin*, 157.
34. Greene, 17.
35. Finerty, *War-Path and Bivouac*, 276–77.
36. Rickey, *Forty Miles*, 263.
37. Finerty, 277.
38. Ibid., 278–79.
39. Schmitt, 206.
40. Greene, 132–33.
41. Greene, *Great Sioux War*, 113.
42. Greene, *Slim Buttes*, 133–34.
43. King, *Campaigning With Crook*, 108.
44. Greene, *Slim Buttes*, 75.
45. King, 108–09.
46. Finerty, 285.
47. Ibid., 286–88.
48. Greene, *Slim Buttes*, 79.
49. Finerty, 289, 291.
50. Greene, *Great Sioux War*, 115.
51. Finerty, *War-Path and Bivouac*, 291–92.

52. Greene, *Slim Buttes*, 134.
53. Finerty, 297–98.
54. King, 122–23.
55. Hadley, "The Nineteenth Kansas Cavalry," 455.
56. Greene, *Slim Buttes*, 112.
57. Sherry L. Smith, *Sagebrush Soldier—Private William Earl Smith's View of the Sioux War of 1876* (Norman: University of Oklahoma, 1989), 111–12.
58. Stewart, *March of the Montana Column*, 121.
59. Mattes, *Indians, Infants and Infantry*, 157.
60. Ostrander, *An Army Boy of the Sixties*, 202–03.
61. Danker, *Man of the Plains*, 221.
62. King, 79.
63. Greene, *Great Sioux War*, 134–37.
64. Wheeler, "The Scouts," 106.
65. Greene, *Great Sioux War*, 137–39.
66. Ibid., 147.
67. Danker, 211.
68. Smith, *Sagebrush Soldier*, 66.
69. Ibid.
70. Greene, 177.
71. Smith, 72.
72. Greene, 178.
73. Smith, 72.
74. Ibid., 77–78.
75. Danker, 217.
76. Greene, *Great Sioux War*, 179–80.
77. Smith, 77.
78. Ibid., 78–79.
79. Danker, *Man of the Plains*, 216.
80. Smith, 81.
81. Danker, n. 217–18.
82. Rickey, *Forty Miles*, 256–57.
83. Greene, *Great Sioux War*, 189.
84. Ibid., 209, 211, 212.

CHAPTER SIXTEEN

1. *Eli Ricker Collection*, Tablet No. 15.
2. William D. Mather, "The Revolt of Little Wolf's Northern Cheyennes," master's thesis, University of Wichita (June 1958), Kansas State Historical Society, Topeka: 52.
3. Allred, *Great Western Indian Fights*, 296.
4. Dodge City (Kansas) *Ford County Globe*, October 29, 1878.
5. Allred, 297.
6. Hays (Kansas) *Sentinel*, October 19, 1878.
7. Ibid.
8. Ibid.
9. Ibid., September 28, 1878.
10. Hays *Sentinel*, September 28, 1878.
11. Ramon S. Powers, "The Dull Knife Raid of 1878: A Study of the Frontier," master's thesis, Fort Hays State College (1963), Kansas State Historical Society, Topeka: 77.
12. Dodge City *Ford County Globe*, September 24, 1878.
13. Ibid.
14. Montgomery, "Fort Wallace," 272.

15. George W. Brown, "Kansas Indian Wars," *Kansas Historical Collections* vol. 17 (1926–28): 136.
16. Hays *Sentinel*, October 5, 1878.
17. Ibid.
18. Fred and Wilma Wallsmith, *Reminiscences and Recollections of Anton Stenner, Jr.*, manuscript No. 1, Kansas State Historical Society, Topeka: 17.
19. Ibid., 18.
20. Jerome A. Greene and Peter M. Wright, eds., "Chasing Dull Knife: A Journal of the Cheyenne Campaign of 1878, by Lieutenant George H. Palmer," *Heritage of Kansas—A Journal of the Great Plains* vol. 12, no. 1 (Winter 1979): 29.
21. Hays *Sentinel*, November 23, 1878.
22. Beloit (Kansas) *Weekly Democrat*, October 11, 1878.
23. Weymouth T. Jordan, Jr., "A Soldier's Life on the Indian Frontier, 1876–1878: Letters of 2Lt. C.D. Cowles," *Kansas Historical Quarterly* vol. 38, no. 2 (Summer 1972): 154.
24. Powers, "The Dull Knife Raid," 91.
25. Brown, "Kansas Indian Wars," 137–38.
26. Greene, "Chasing Dull Knife," 29.
27. Powers, 95.
28. Greene, 30.
29. Dodge City *Ford County Globe*, October 29, 1878.
30. Powers, 99.
31. Ibid., 113.
32. Crook to Sheridan, January 15, 1879, Letters Received by the Office of the Adjutant General (main series), 1871–80, Roll 449, National Archives, Washington.
33. Letter of Captain Wessells, Fort Robinson, Nebraska, January 12, 1879 to the assistant adjutant general, headquarters, Department of the Platte, Fort Omaha, Nebraska National Archives, Washington.
34. Crook to Sheridan, January 16, 1879.

EPILOGUE

1. Powers, "The Dull Knife Raid," 113.
2. Hays (Kansas) *Sentinel*, August 1, 1879.
3. Ibid.
4. Smith, *Officers' Row*, 155.
5. Jordan, "A Soldier's Life," 154.
6. Vaughn, *The Reynolds Campaign*, n. 14.
7. Ostrander, *An Army Boy of the Sixties*, 121.

Bibliography

Allred, B.W., et al, eds. *Great Western Indian Fights*. Lincoln: University of Nebraska, 1960.

Ambrose, Stephen E. *Crazy Horse and Custer—The Parallel Lives of Two American Warriors*. New York: New American Library, 1975.

Annual Report of the Commissioner of Indian Affairs to the Secretary of the Interior for the Year 1874. Washington: Government Printing Office, 1874.

Battey, Thomas C. *The Life and Adventures of a Quaker Among the Indians*. 1875. Reprint. Norman: University of Oklahoma, 1968.

Browne, Gordon. "At the Little Bighorn the Unrecognized Hero of Reno Hill was not Major Reno but Captain Benteen." *Military History* (August 1995): 82–90.

Brininstool, Earl A., and Grace Raymond Hebard. *The Bozeman Trail—Historical Accounts of the Blazing of the Overland Routes into the Northwest and the Fights with Red Cloud's Warriors*. Cleveland, Ohio: Arthur H. Clark, 1922.

Brown, D. Alexander. *The Galvanized Yankees*. Urbana: University of Illinois, 1963.

Burkey, Blaine. *Custer, Come at Once!—The Fort Hays Years of George and Elizabeth Custer, 1867–1870*. Hays, Kansas: Thomas More Prep, 1976.

Carriker, Robert C. "Mercenary Heroes: The Scouting Detachment of the Indian Territory Expedition, 1874–1875." *The Chronicles of Oklahoma* vol. 51, no. 3 (Fall 1973): 309–24.

———, ed. "Thompson McFadden's Diary of an Indian Campaign, 1874." *Southwestern Historical Quarterly* vol. 75, no. 2 (October 1971): 198–232.

Carriker, Robert C. and Eleanor R. *An Army Wife on the Frontier—The Memoirs of Alice Blackwood Baldwin, 1867–1877.* Salt Lake City: University of Utah, 1975.

Carrington, Margaret I. *Absaraka—Home of the Crows.* 1868. Reprint. Chicago: Lakeside, 1950.

Carroll, John M. *Camp Talk—The Very Private Letters of Frederick W. Benteen of the 7th U.S. to his Wife, 1871 to 1888.* Bryan, Texas, and Mattituck, New York: John M. Carroll, 1983.

———, ed. *General Custer and the Battle of the Washita: The Federal View.* Bryan, Texas: Guidon, 1978.

Clark, Olive A. "Early Days Along the Solomon Valley." *Kansas Historical Collections* vol. 17 (1926–28): 719–30.

Cody, William F. *An Autobiography of Buffalo Bill.* New York: Rinehart, 1920.

Cooling, Benjamin Franklin, III, ed. *Soldiering in Sioux Country: 1865.* San Diego, California: Frontier Heritage, 1971.

Coursey, O.W., ed. *The First White Woman in the Black Hills, as Told by Herself.* Mitchell, South Dakota: Educator Supply, c. 1923.

Crawford, Samuel J. *Kansas in the Sixties.* Chicago: A.C. McClurg, 1911.

Custer, Elizabeth Bacon. *Tenting on the Plains, or General Custer in Kansas and Texas.* 1887. Reprint. Norman: University of Oklahoma, 1971.

Custer, Elizabeth B. *Boots and Saddles, or Life in Dakota with General Custer.* 1885. Reprint. Williamstown, Massachusetts: Corner House, 1974.

Danker, Donald F., ed. "The Journal of an Indian Fighter—The 1869 Diary of Major Frank J. North, Leader of the Pawnee Scouts," *Nebraska History* vol. 39, no. 2 (June 1958): n. 139.

———. *Man of the Plains—Recollections of Luther North, 1856–1882.* Lincoln: University of Nebraska, 1961.

———. "The North Brothers and the Pawnee Scouts," *Nebraska History* vol. 42, no. 3 (September 1961): 161–79.

"The Diary of Samuel A. Kingman at Indian Treaty in 1865." *Kansas Historical Quarterly* vol. 1, no. 5 (November 1932): 442–50.

Dixon, Olive K. *Life of "Billy" Dixon—Plainsman, Scout and Pioneer.* Dallas, Texas: P.L. Turner, 1927.

Finerty, John F. *War-Path and Bivouac—The Big Horn and Yellowstone Expedition.* Chicago: R.R. Donnelley and Sons, 1955.

Forsythe, G.A. "A Frontier Fight." *Harper's New Monthly Magazine* vol. 91 (June–November 1895), 42–62.

Frost, Lawrence A. *The Court-Martial of General George Armstrong Custer*. Norman: University of Oklahoma, 1968.

Graham, W.A. *The Custer Myth—A Source Book of Custeriana*. Harrisburg, Pennsylvania: Stackpole Books, 1953.

Gray, John S. *Custer's Last Campaign—Mitch Boyer and the Little Big Horn Reconstructed*. Lincoln: University of Nebraska, 1991.

Greene, Jerome A. *Slim Buttes, 1876—An Episode of the Great Sioux War*. Norman: University of Oklahoma, 1982.

Greene, Jerome A., ed. *Battles and Skirmishes of the Great Sioux War, 1876–1877—The Military View*. Norman: University of Oklahoma, 1993.

Greene, Jerome A. and Peter M. Wright, eds. "Chasing Dull Knife: A Journal of the Cheyenne Campaign of 1878, by Lieutenant George H. Palmer." *Heritage of Kansas—A Journal of the Great Plains* vol. 12, no. 1 (Winter 1979): 25–36.

Hadley, James. "The Nineteenth Kansas Cavalry and the Conquest of the Plains Indians." *Kansas Historical Collections* vol. 10 (1907–08): 428–56.

Haley, James L. *The Buffalo War—The History of the Red River Indian Uprising of 1874*. Garden City, New York: Doubleday, 1976.

Hammer, Kenneth, ed. *Custer in '76—Walter Camp's Notes on the Custer Fight*. Provo, Utah: Brigham Young University, 1976.

Hardorff, Richard G. *The Custer Battle Casualties—Burials, Exhumations and Reinterments*. El Segundo, California: Upton and Sons, 1991.

Hedren, Paul L. *First Scalp for Custer: The Skirmish at Warbonnet Creek, Nebraska, July 17, 1876*. Glendale, California: Arthur H. Clark, 1980.

Hoig, Stan. *The Sand Creek Massacre*. Norman: University of Oklahoma, 1961.

Hull, Myra E., ed. "Soldiering on the High Plains—The Diary of Lewis Byram Hull, 1864–1866." *Kansas Historical Quarterly* vol. 7, no. 1 (February 1938): 3–53.

Hurst, John. "The Beecher Island Fight." *Kansas Historical Collection* vol. 15 (1919–22): 530–38.

Hutton, Paul Andrew. *The Custer Reader*. Lincoln: University of Nebraska, 1992.

———, ed. *Ten Days on the Plains*. 1871. Reprint. Dallas, Texas: Southern Methodist University, 1985.

Jordan, Weymouth T., Jr. "A Soldier's Life on the Indian Frontier, 1876–1878: Letters of 2Lt. C.D. Cowles." *Kansas Historical Quarterly* vol. 38, no. 2 (Summer 1972): 144–55.

Kansas Scrapbook. Kansas State Historical Society, Topeka. 2:355–56.

Keim, DeB. Randolph. *Sheridan's Troopers on the Borders—A Winter Cam-*

paign on the Plains. 1885. Reprint. Lincoln: University of Nebraska, 1985.

Kelly, Fanny. *Narrative of My Captivity Among the Sioux Indians.* Chicago: Lakeside, 1990.

King, Charles. *Campaigning With Crook*. Norman: University of Oklahoma, 1964.

Knight, Oliver. *Following the Indian Wars—The Story of the Newspaper Correspondents Among the Indian Campaigners*. Norman: University of Oklahoma, 1960.

Leckie, William H. *The Military Conquest of the Southern Plains*. Norman: University of Oklahoma, 1963.

"The Letters of John Ferguson, Early Resident of Western Washington County." *Kansas Historical Quarterly* vol. 12, no. 4 (November 1943): 339–48.

"Life and Adventures of George W. Brown—Soldier, Pioneer, Scout, Plainsman and Buffalo Hunter." *Kansas Historical Collections* vol. 17 (1926–28): 98–134.

Mangum, Neil C. *Battle of the Rosebud: Prelude to the Little Bighorn*. El Segundo, California: Upton and Sons, 1987.

Mardock, Robert W. and Robert W. Richmond, eds. *A Nation Moving West—Readings in the History of the American Frontier*. Lincoln: University of Nebraska, 1966.

Massacre of Troops near Fort Phil. Kearney. Fairfield, Washington: Ye Galleon, 1974.

Mattes, Merrill J. *Indians, Infants and Infantry—Andrew and Elizabeth Burt on the Frontier*. Denver, Colorado: Old West, 1960.

Mather, William D. "The Revolt of Little Wolf's Northern Cheyenne." Master's thesis, University of Wichita, 1958. Kansas State Historical Society, Topeka.

McClernand, Edward J. *On Time for Disaster—The Rescue of Custer's Command*. Lincoln: University of Nebraska, 1989.

Meredith, Grace E. *Girl Captives of the Cheyennes—A True Story of the Capture and Rescue of Four Pioneer Girls*. Los Angeles: Gem, 1927.

Merington, Marguerite, ed. *The Custer Story—The Life and Intimate Letters of General George A. Custer and his Wife Elizabeth*. 1950. Reprint. Lincoln: University of Nebraska, 1987.

Millbrook, Minnie Dubbs. "The West Breaks in General Custer." *Kansas Historical Quarterly* Vol. 36, no. 2 (Summer 1970): 113–48.

Monnett, John H. *The Battle of Beecher Island and the Indian War of 1867–1869*. Niwot: University Press of Colorado, 1992.

Myres, Sandra L., ed. *Cavalry Wife—The Diary of Eveline M. Alexander, 1866–1867.* College Station: Texas A&M University, 1977.

Nellans, George. "Authentic Accounts of Massacre of Indians, Rawlins County, Kansas, 1875 and Cheyenne Indian Raid in Western Kansas, September 3, 1878." Manuscript. Kansas State Historical Society, Topeka.

Olivia, Leo E. *Soldiers on the Santa Fe Trail.* Norman: University of Oklahoma, 1967.

Ostrander, Alson B. *An Army Boy of the Sixties—A Story of the Plains.* New York: World Book, 1924.

Pennock, Isaac B. Diary. Kansas State Historical Society, Topeka.

Powers, Ramon S. "The Dull Knife Raid of 1878: A Study of the Frontier." Master's thesis, Fort Hays State College, 1963. Kansas State Historical Society, Topeka.

Quaife, Milo Milton, ed. *My Life on the Plains.* Lincoln: University of Nebraska, 1966.

Eli S. Ricker Collection. M58. Tablet 15. Nebraska State Historical Society, Lincoln.

Rickey, Don, Jr. *Forty Miles a Day on Beans and Hay—The Enlisted Soldier Fighting the Indian Wars.* Norman: University of Oklahoma, 1963.

Robinson, Charles M. III. *A Good Year to Die: The Story of the Great Sioux War.* Norman: University of Oklahoma, 1995.

Rosa, Joseph G. *They Called Him Wild Bill—The Life and Adventures of James Butler Hickok.* Norman: University of Oklahoma, 1964.

"A.L. Runyon's Letters from the Nineteenth Kansas Regiment." *Kansas Historical Quarterly* vol. 9, no. 1 (February 1940): 58–75.

Schmitt, Martin F. *General George Crook—His Autobiography.* Norman: University of Oklahoma, 1946.

Schneider, George A., ed. *The Freeman Journal—The Infantry in the Sioux Campaign of 1876.* San Rafael, California: Presidio, 1977.

Senate Executive Documents for the Second Session of the Thirty-ninth Congress, 1866–67. Washington: Government Printing Office, 1867.

Shlesinger, Sigmund. "The Beecher Island Fight." *Kansas Historical Collections* vol. 15 (1919–22): 538–47.

Smith, Charles. *Campaigning With Crook.* Norman: University of Oklahoma, 1964.

Smith, Sherry L. *Sagebrush Soldier—Private William Earl Smith's View of the Sioux War of 1876.* Norman: University of Oklahoma, 1989.

———. *The View from Officers' Row—Army Perceptions of Western Indians.* Tucson: University of Arizona, 1990.

Spotts, David L. *Campaigning With Custer and the Nineteenth Kansas Volunteer Cavalry on the Washita Campaign, 1868–1869*. 1928. Reprint. Lincoln: University of Nebraska, 1988.

Stewart, Edgar I., ed. *The March of the Montana Column—A Prelude to the Custer Disaster*. Norman: University of Oklahoma, 1961.

Taylor, Joe F. "The Indian Campaign on the Staked Plains, 1874–1875—Military Correspondence from War Department." *Panhandle-Plains Historical Review* vol. 34 (1961): 7–216.

Unrau, William E., ed. *Tending the Talking Wire—A Buck Soldier's View of Indian Country, 1863–1866*. Salt Lake City: University of Utah, 1979.

Upton, Richard. *The Custer Adventure as Told by its Participants*. El Segundo, California: Upton and Sons, 1990.

Utley, Robert M. *Life in Custer's Cavalry—Diaries and Letters of Albert and Jennie Barnitz, 1867–1868*. New Haven, Connecticut: Yale University, 1977.

Utley, Robert M. *Cavalier in Buckskin—George Armstrong Custer and the Western Military Frontier*. Norman: University of Oklahoma, 1988.

Vaughn, J.W. *Indian Fights—New Facts on Seven Encounters*. Norman: University of Oklahoma, 1966.

Vaughn, J.W. *The Reynolds Campaign on Powder River*. Norman: University of Oklahoma, 1961.

Walker, George. "Eleventh Kansas Cavalry, 1865, and Battle of Platte Bridge." *Kansas Historical Collections* vol. 14, 332–40.

Wallsmith, Fred and Wilma. "Reminiscences and Recollections of Anton Stenner, Jr." Manuscript. Kansas State Historical Society, Topeka.

Webb, Bernice Larson. "First Homesteader and the Battle of Sappa Creek." *Kansas Quarterly* vol. 10, no. 3 (Summer 1978): 52–57.

Wellman, Paul. *Death on the Prairie—The Thirty Years' Struggle for the Western Plains*. 1934. Reprint. Lincoln: University of Nebraska, 1987.

Welty, Raymond L. "Supplying the Frontier Military Posts." *Kansas Historical Quarterly* vol. 7, no. 2 (May 1938): 154–69.

Wert, Jeffry D. *Custer: The Controversial Life of George Armstrong Custer*. New York: Simon and Schuster, 1996.

Wheeler, Keith. "The Scouts," Vol. 24, *The Old West*. Alexandria, Virginia: Time/Life, 1978.

Wheeler, Homer W. *Buffalo Days—The Personal Narrative of a Cattleman, Indian Fighter and Army Officer*. c. 1925. Reprint. Lincoln: University of Nebraska, 1990.

White, Connie J. *Hostiles and Horse Soldiers—Indian Battles and Campaigns in the West*. Boulder, Colorado: Pruett, 1972.

"The Diary of Chauncey B. Whitney." *Kansas Historical Collections* vol. 12 (1911–12): 296–302.

NEWSPAPERS

Beloit (Kansas) *Weekly Democrat*, 1878.

Brenham (Texas) *Banner*, 1875.

Casper (Wyoming) *Star Tribune*, 1970.

Denver (Colorado) *Weekly Rocky Mountain News*, 1864–1865, 1876.

Dodge City (Kansas) *Ford County Globe*, 1878.

Ellsworth (Kansas) *Reporter*, 1875.

Hays (Kansas) *Sentinel*, 1876, 1878.

Leavenworth (Kansas) *Daily Conservative*, 1865, 1868.

Leavenworth (Kansas) *Daily Times*, 1867.

Marysville (Kansas) *Enterprise*, 1866–1868.

Topeka (Kansas) *State Record*, 1868.

Index

(Pages with photographs are indicated by italics.)

Adams, Pvt. Charles, 15, 16
Adams, Pvt. Jacob, 252, 261, 262
Adobe Walls, Texas, 186
Alderdice, Susanna, 181, 182–183
Alexander, Col. Andrew, 201
Alexander, Eveline, 201-202
American Horse, 282
Anderson, Maj. Martin, 10, 13
Apache Indians, 48, 144, 148, 161, 181
Arickaree (Colo.), Battle of the, 97–107
Army and Navy Journal, 73
atrocities, 10, 13, 43, 44, 112, 129; against Indians, 4, 9–10, 18, 44–45, 129, 190; murder of captives, 44, 112, 124, 125, 148–149, 181, 291; mutilations, 3, 12, 13–14, 18, 29–30, 42–44, 47, 56, 66, 72–73, 147–148, 260–262, 300; rape, 3, 53, 93, 119–120, 124, 301–303

Baldwin, Alice, 127–128, 198, 203–204, *204*, 209, 210
Baldwin, Lt. Frank, 191, 198, *204*
Barnitz, Capt. Albert, 36, 40, 41–42, 50, 52, 56, 65–68, 74, 133, *134*, 137–138, 139, 140–141, 143, 146–147165–166, 170, 172, 206
Barnitz, Jennie, 40, 41, 133, *134*, 146, 205–206
Battey, Thomas, 161, 162, 166, 177
Bearstooth, 176–177
Becker, John, 268
Beecher, Henry Ward, 57, 95
Beecher, Lt. Frederick, 95, 96, 99, 103
Behale, Baptiste, 173
Bellas, Lt. Henry, 290–291
Bennett, Joseph, 73
Bent, William, 48
Benteen, Capt. Frederick, 84, 173, 234, 235, 241, 245, 246, 247, 253, 254, 263
Big Head, 153, 155, 157
Big Squaw, 122
Big Timber, Colorado, 62
Bingham, Lt. Horatio, 25
Bishops Ranch, Colorado, 74
Bismarck, Dakota Territory, 235
Black Bear, 16
Black Foot, 124
Black Kettle, 3, 142, 148, 149, 158
Bloody Knife, 234, 237, 238–239, 240, 241, 244
Boston (Mass.) *Banner of Light*, 93
Bourke, Lt. John, 215, 218, 219, 220–221, 229, 265, 280, 290, 291, 292, 309
Bouyer, Mitch, 237, 240, 241
Bowers, Sgt. G.R., 25
Box, Josephine and Margaret, 126
Bozeman Trail, 21, 23, 24, 31, 32, 33, 218
Bradley, Lt. James, 85, 129
Brewster, Dan, 152, 156, 157
Bridger, Jim, 77, 79, 80, 133, 135
Brown Springs, Wyoming, 24
Brown, Capt. Frederick, 25, 30
Brown, George, 299, 302
Buffalo Springs, Wyoming, 24
Buntline, Ned, 87
Burke, Martin, 107
Burt, Elizabeth, 199, 200, 201, 202, 204–205, 207, 208, 209, 210–212, 213, 286
Burt, Maj. Andrew, 32, 176–177, 207, 211, 227

Caddo, 165
Cahoon, Thomas, 65
Camp Robinson, Nebraska, 216, 304
Camp Supply, Indian Territory, 135, 144,187, 189, 206, 296, 297
captives. *See* Atrocities; *also see* Women
Carpenter, Capt. Louis, 111
Carr, Maj. Eugene, 181–182
Carrington, Col. Henry, 23–24, 25–26, 27, 28, 29–30, 43
Carrington, Margaret, 24, *26*, 27, 28–29, 79
Carson, Kit, 48, 79
Carter, Capt. R.G., 45
Chack, 297
Chapman, Amos, 299
Cheyenne (Wyo.) *Argus*, 65
Cheyenne, Wyoming, 90, 215
Chicago (Ill.) *Journal*, 14
Chicago (Ill.) *Times*, 84, 167
Chivington, Col. John, 1, *2*, 3, 5, 57, 132
Cimarron Station, Kansas, 298
Cincinnati (Ohio) *Commercial*, 146
Clark, Ben, 111
Clark, Lt. William, 280

Clarke, Charles, 66
Cody, William F. ("Buffalo Bill"), 86–88, *88*, 89–90, 91, 181–183, 217, 273, 274–276, 277, 308
Collins, Col. William O., 168
Collins, Lt. Caspar, 10, 13–14
Colorado *Tribune*, 62
Colorado, ix, 2–3, 74, 201
Comanche, 7, 48, 87, 131, 144, 148, 159, 165, 181, 186
Comstock, Will, 70, 71, 77, 78, 81–82
Connor, Brig. Gen. Patrick, 14, 15, 16, 18, 20
Cooke, Lt. William, 151
Cooper, James Fenimore, 40, 41, 59, 81
Council Grove, Kansas, 49
Cowles, Lt. Calvin, 302
Crawford, Gov. Samuel, 131–132, 133
Crawford, Jack, 83, 279
Crazy Horse, 216, 227, 230, 233, 238, 273, 293, 294
Crazy Woman's Fork, Wyoming, 202
Crook, Brig. Gen. George, 84, 85–86, 218, 220, 221–224, 225–231, *228*, 249, 250, 265, 266, 272, 273, 274, 276, 277–285, 287, 304, 305
Crooked Creek (Kansas) Massacre, 186
Crooked Hand, 174
Crow, 84–85, 168, 174, 175, 176, 210, 221, 224–225, 235, 238, 276–277
Culver, George, 101, 102
Cushing, Capt. Sylanus, 182
Custard, Sgt. Amos, 12
Custer, Elizabeth (Libbie), 54, *54*, 55, 57, 81, 83, 90, 135, 164–165, 197, 198, 199, 200, 201, 202, 206–207, 208–209, 211, 212–213, 222–223, 236, 264
Custer, Lt. Col. George Armstrong, 49, 50–51, 52–53, *54*, 61, 68–69, 135–144, 145, 146, 147, 148, 149– 150, 151–156, 157, 158, 166, 167–168, 171–172, 173, 178, 179, 197, 198, 209, 222, 265, 266, 273, 276, 298; at the Kidder Massacre, 70–73; 75, 77, 81, 82, 91, 133; at the Little Bighorn Campaign, 233–263
Custer, Lt. Thomas, 68, 143, 201, 262

Dakota Territory, 199, 215
Dallas (Tex.) *Herald*, 186
Darlington Agency, Indian Territory, 191
Davenport, Reuben, 224, 225, 227–229, 276
Davis, Theodore, 78, 81
Deadwood, Dakota Territory, 286
Delaware, 55, 70, 71, 72, 187
Denver (Colo.) *Rocky Mountain News*, 21, 218
Denver, Colorado, 5, 58, 74, 90
DeRudio, Lt. Charles, 244, 250, 251
DeWolf, Dr. James, 234, 259
Dixon, Billy, 78–79, 91
Dobytown, Nebraska, 38
Dodge City (Kan.) *Globe*, 303
Dodge City, Kansas, 39, 298, 307
Dodge, Col. Richard, 43, 58, 170, 172, 285
Dog Soldiers, 181, 183
Donovan, Jack, 108, 110
Doolittle, Sen. James R., 58
Dorman, Isaiah, 260
Dose, Henry, 234, 262
Douglas, Maj. Henry, 48–49, 62
Downer's Station, Kansas, 47
Drew, Lt. William, 9–10, 12–13, 86
Dry Fork, Wyoming, 24
Dull Knife, 153, 155, 295, 296, 297, 300, 303, 304, 305, 307

Edgerly, Lt. Winfield Scott, 233, 247, 253
Edmundson, William, 65
Egan, Capt. James, 217, 219
Elliott, Charley, 19
Elliott, Maj. Joel, 136, 138, 139, 142, 143, 147
Erhardt, Pvt. Ferdinand, 11–12
Essahavit, 160
Eubanks, Lucinda, 124, 125

Famished Woman Ck. (Kan.), Battle of, 299–300
Far West, 233, 234, 263
Farley, Louis, 99
Ferguson, John, 74
Fetterman Massacre (Wyoming), 27–30
Fetterman, Capt. William, 27, 28, 29, 30
Fifth U.S. Cavalry, 87, 89, 181, 273, 276
Fifth U.S. Infantry, 287
Finerty, John, 84, 167, 168, 178, 224–231, 267–273, *269*, 277–278, 279, 280–282, 283, 284
Fisher, Isaac, 30
Forsyth, Maj. George, 94, *95*, 96, 97, 98–99, 100, 101, 102–103, 105, 106, 107, 108, 109, 110, 111, 114
Fort Abraham Lincoln, Dakota Terr., 197, 208, 222, 263
Fort Arbuckle, Indian Territory, 210
Fort Bridger, Wyoming, 207
Fort C.F. Smith, 24, 31, 44, 210, 211, 286
Fort Cobb, Indian Territory, 149, 162
Fort Dodge, Kansas, 48, 62, 87, 90, 126, 135, 146, 172
Fort Ellis, Montana, 222
Fort Fetterman, Wyoming, 218, 222
Fort Harker, Kansas, 73, 127
Fort Hays, Kan., 36, 39, 56, 87, 135, 205, 206, 212
Fort Kearny, Nebraska, 80
Fort Laramie, Wyoming., 21, 23, 30, 39, 79, 116, 200, 210
Fort Larned, Kansas, 38, 49, 87, 209
Fort Leavenworth, Kansas, 49
Fort Lyon, Colorado, 62
Fort Marion, Florida, 192
Fort Phil Kearny, Wyo., 23, 25–27, 29, 31, 286
Fort Reno, Indian Territory, 295, 303
Fort Reno, Wyoming, 24, 31
Fort Riley, Kansas, 79
Fort Sedgwick, Colorado, 36, 39, 70
Fort Sully, Dakota Territory, 126
Fort Wallace, Kansas, 36, 65–68, 74, 77, 96, 105, 111, 113, 114
Frank Leslie's Illustrated Weekly, 24

French, Capt. Thomas, 249

Gatling guns, 187, 234
German, Addie, 120, 124–125, 191, *192*
German, Catherine, 115, 116–117, 119, 120, 122–123, *123*, 124, 125, 126, 129–130, 186, 191–192, 194
German, Julia, 120, 124–125, 191, *192*
German, Sophia, 115, 120, 191
German, Stephen, 115, 116, 117
Gibbon, Col. John, 221, 235, 257, 258, 259, 286
Gibson, Lt. Frank, 246, 253
Girard, Fred, 241, 242, 244, 250, 251, 256, 261, 262
Glenn, Pvt. George, 253, 261
Glover, Ridgeway, 24
Godfrey, Lt. Edward, 44–45, 135–136, 142, 143, 146, 235, 236–237, *237*, 239, 240, 244–245, 246–247, 249–250, 252, 253, 254, 256, 259, 260, 262
Golden, Pat, 254
Goldin, Pvt. Theodore, 260
Gordon, Pvt. Dave, 246
Grant, Gen. Ulysses, 32, 33
Grimm, Cpl. Henry, 12
Grouard, Frank, 78, 84, 267–272, 279, 280, 281, 284
Grover, Abner, 95, 96, 102, 103, 105–106
Grummond, Frances, 24–25
Grummond, Lt. George, 27–28

Haddam, Kansas, 73
Hadley, Sgt. James, 152, 157, 158
Half Yellow-Face, 237–238
Halstead, Murat, 146–147
Hamilton, Alexander, 136
Hamilton, Capt. Louis M., 40, 136, 143
Hancock, Maj. Gen. Winfield Scott, 49–50, 52, 55, 57, 62, 75
Hare, Lt. Luther, 247, 258
Harper's, 66, 67, 78, 81, 170
Harris, Cpl. Prentice G., 66
Harvey, Jack, 90
Hays (Kansas) *Sentinel*, 299
Hays City, Kansas, 38
Henely, Lt. Austin, 193, 194
Henry, Capt. Guy, 229
Herendeen, George, 256, 259, 260
Hesselberger, Lt. G.A., 127
Hickok, James Butler ("Wild Bill"), 80, *81*, 86, 87
Hines, Dr. C.M., 25
Hodgson, Lt. Benjamin, 245
Holman, Albert, 14–15
Horseshoe Creek Station, Wyoming, 116
humanitarianism, 48, 57, 58, 132, 158; *See also* Quakers
Hummell, Pvt. John G., 66
Humpy, 229
Hurst, John, 96, 97–98, 99–100, 101–102, 105–106, 107–108, 110–111

Indian Territory, 133, 151, 165, 185, 186, 295, 303, 305
Indians, 16, 143, 159–164, 165–166, 166–168, 172–173, 200, 209–210, 219; as captives, 16, 146, 148, 307–308; as scouts. *See* Crow, Pawnee, Shoshoni, Delaware, Ree, and Osage Indians; attacks, 62, 63–65, 202–203; death among, 177–178, 210; "Hangs-around-the-forts," 40–41, 207; marksmanship, 27, 170, 291; scalp dance, 175–176; signals, 171–172; tactics of, 14–15, 41–42, 172, 173; war dance, 168–170; weapons, 42–43, 170
Iron Bull, 174
Iron Star, 294

Jackson, Billy, 238–239, 240–241, 242, 243–244, 250–251, 256, 257
Janis, Nick, 79, 80
Johnson, Cpl. Hervey, 8–9, 37
Johnson, Peter, 24
Johnson, Pres. Andrew, 131
Julesburg, Colorado, 38, 43
Junction Cut Off, Colorado, 74

Kansas Pacific Railroad, 62, 116, 298, 299, 300
Kansas, 48, 93, 131, 181, 186, 197, 298, 300–303
Kaw, 165
Keim, DeBenneville, 100, 101, 141, 144–145, 146, 147–148, 159–160, 161, 163–164, 166, 171, 172
Kellogg, Mark, 234–235, 263
Kelly, Fanny, 116, 117–119, 120–122, 123–124, 129
Kelly, Mary, 116, 117, 119, 120, 125
Kelly, Sgt. James, 19
Keogh, Capt. Myles, 40, 82, 284
Kidder Massacre (Kansas), 70–73
Kidder, Lt. Lyman, 70–72
King, Capt. Charles, 89, 165, 273–276, 280–281, 284, 287
Kinney, Col. N.C., 174, 175
Kinsley, Kansas, 298
Kiowa, 7, 48, 62, 87, 131, 132, 144, 148, 149, 162, 165, 166, 177, 178, 181, 186, 209, 210

Laing, Freeman, 300
Laing, John, 301
Laing, William Jr., 301
Laing, Willaim, 300–301
Lame Deer, 294
Lane, M.R., 107, 109
Lawrence, Kansas, 308
Lawson, Lt. Joseph, 278, 279
Leavenworth (Kans.) *Times*, 94, 297
Leavenworth, Kansas, 87, 90
Lewis, Lt. Col. William, 299
Little Beaver, 135, 145
Little Big Man, 217
Little Raven, 148
Little Robe, 154
Little Wolf, 296, 303, 305

Lockwood, James, 31, 43
Lookout Station, Kansas, 56
Lord, Hank, 12
Lorentz, Pvt. George, 243

MacKenzie, Col. Ranald, 190, 289, 290, 292, 293
Mathey, Lt. E.G., 136
Mauck, Capt. Clarence, 302
McBlain, Sgt. John, 294
McCall, Sgt. William, 99, 101, 102, 103
McCaskey, Capt. William S., 264
McClellan Creek (Texas), Battle of, 191
McClernand, Lt. Edward, 258–259, 263, 276–277
McFadden, Thompson, 90–91, 186–190
McIntosh, Lt. Donald, 236, 246
McKinney, Lt. John, 290
McLoughlin, Louis, 97
Medicine Arrow, 151, 152
Medicine Water, 153
Merritt, Col. Wesley, 273, 274, 275, 276
Metzler, Adolph, 30
Meyer, Pvt. Bill, 246
Miles, Col. Nelson, 185, 187, 192, 287, 288, 293, 294, 295
Mills, Capt. Anson, 279–280, 283–284; at the Battle of the Rosebud, 225, 226, 230–231
Milner, Moses, 82–83, 90, 91, 136, 137, 144–146
Montana, 21, 39, 41, 44, 193, 204, 219, 265, 287
Mooers, Dr. J. H., 101
Morgan, Anna Belle, 126
Morris, James, 45
Morris, Pvt. William, 245, 246
Morris, Sarah, 119, 124
Moylan, Lt. Myles, 137
Murphy, Pvt. William, 31, 39
Musgrove, Capt. Richard, 78
mutilation. *See* atrocities

Navajo, 160
Nebraska, 303
Neill, Lt. Col. Thomas, 192
New York *Herald*, 2, 79, 159, 191, 224, 234, 265, 276
New York Times, 282
Nineteenth Kansas Volunteer Cavalry 132, 135, 139, 145, 147, 151, 152, 156, 158, 162
North Platte River, 8
North, Maj. Frank, 85, 181, 183
North, Lt. Luther, 173, 174, 181, 182–183, 286–287, 290–292
Northern Arapahoe, 7, 14, 16, 183, 185, 191, 218
Northern Cheyenne, 7–9, 13, 14, 20, 178, 183, 185, 191, 216, 218, 274, 276, 277, 289

O'Brien, Pvt. Timothy, 27
O'Kelly, James, 265
O'Neil, Pvt. Thomas, 244, 250
Oaks, George, 107
Old Crow, 224, 225
Omaha (Nebr.) *Republican*, 300
Omaha, Nebraska, 64, 90
Oregon Trail, attacks on, 7–9, 21, 116
Oregon Trail, The, ix
Osage, 135, 137, 141, 145, 146, 149
Ostrander, Pvt. Alson, 41, 42, 286
overland route. *See* Oregon, Santa Fe, and Smoky Hill Trails

Palmer, Capt. Henry, 15–16, 43, *44*
Palmer, Lt. George, 303
Palo Duro Canyon (Texas), Battle of, 190
Parkman, Francis, ix, x
Pawnee Fork, Kansas, 50, 52, 56
Pawnee, 85, 174, 181, 182, 290, 299
Pawnee Killer, 69–70
Pawnee Rock, Kansas, 47
Peace councils, 21–23, 48, 49, 209, 216–217
Peate, Jack, 111–112
Petring, Pvt. Henry, 245–246, 251
Phillips, Wendell, 57
Pierceville, Kansas, 298
Platte Bridge (Wyoming), Battle of, 9–14
Platte Bridge Station, Wyoming, attacks on, 9
Pliley, Allison, 102, 108
Plum Creek (Nebraska) Massacre, 63–64
Pond City, Kansas, 36
Pond Creek Station, Kansas, 65–66
Pope, Alexander, 40
Pope, Brig. Gen. John, 296, 298
Pope, Lt. James, 287–288
Porter, George, 128
Porter, Lt. James, 257
Postlewaite, Joseph, 24
Pouier, Baptiste, 267, 279, 281, 282
Powder River (Wyoming) Campaign, 14–20
Powder River (Wyoming), Battle of, 219–221
Powell, Capt. James, 26, 32

rape. *See* Atrocities
Randall, Maj. George, 229
Red Bead, 70, 72
Red Cloud, 21–25, *23*, 31, 33, 208, 216 , 286
Red Dog, 216–217
Red River War, 185–194
Ree Indians, 235, 238
Rendlebrock, Capt. Joseph, 296, 297, 298
Reno, Maj. Marcus, 233, 234, 241, 242, *243*, 245, 246, 247, 248 251, 253, 254, 258, 259, 260, 261, 263
Reynolds, Charley, 83–84, 91, 234, 239, 240, 244
Reynolds, Col. Joseph, 219, 220, 221
Robbins, Sam, 40
Robertson, Jack, 90
Roman Nose, 52, 102–103
Rosebud (Montana), Battle of the, 225–231
Roy, Cpl. Stanislas, 254–255, *255*, 256
Running Antelope, 208–209
Ryan, Sgt. John, 241, 242, 243, 246, 248–249, 250, 251, 257

Sand Creek (Colo.) Massacre, 3–4, 48, 50, 52, 142
Sand Creek (Kansas), Battle of, 298

Santa Fe Railroad, 298
Santa Fe Trail, 21, 47, 49, 62
Sappa Creek (Kansas), Battle of, 193–194
Satanta, 48, 49, 62, 148, 149, *150*
Saunders, Pvt. George, 8
scalping. *See* Atrocities: mutilations
Schuyler, Lt. Walter, 278, 279
Schwatka, Lt. Frederick, 280
scouts, 77–79, 90, 186–190; "Forsyth Scouts." *See* Forsyth, Maj. G.; Indians as. *See* Crow, Pawnee, Osage, Shoshoni, and Delaware
Seventh U.S. Cavalry, 49, 52, 53, 55, 65, 133, 147, 151, 158, 197, 222, 233, 235, 257, 284
Sheridan, Kansas, 36, 38
Sheridan, Maj. Gen. Philip, 22, 83, 87, 89, 94, 132, 133, 135, 144, 146, 147, 149, 151, 158, 185, 186, 190, 194, 273, 304, 305
Sherman, Maj. Gen. William T., x, 36, 37, 75, 90, 93–94,114, 221
Shlesinger, Sigmund, 95, 98, 106, 107, 108–109, 110–111, 112–113, *113*, 114
Shoshoni (Snake), 178, 207, 224–225
Sibley, Lt. Frederick, 265–266, 268, 270, 272, 273
Sidney Station, Nebraska, 65, 303
Sioux, 7, 8, 13, 14, 18, 20, 48, 50, 53, 62, 69, 70, 73, 168, 173, 174, 175, 177– 178, 208, 215, 216, 217–218, 277, 280, 282, 295
Sitting Bull, 216, 217, 223–224, 234, 238, 267, 273, 276, 287, 288, 294, 308
Slaper, Pvt. William, 241–242
Slim Buttes (Dakota Terr.), Battle of, 279–284
Smiley, Lt. Philip, 18, 19
Smith, "Salty," 40
Smith, Col. A. J., 49
Smith, Maj. Benjamin, 32
Smith, Pvt. Patrick, 24
Smith, Pvt. William Earl, 290, 291, 292–293
Smoky Hill Trail, 21, 47, 49, 61, 62, 116, 170, 186
Solomon River (Kan.) Massacre, 132
Southern Arapahoe, 3, 7, 48, 49, 62, 131, 132, 144, 148, 151, 181, 297
Southern Cheyenne, 3, 48, 49–50, 62, 68, 73, 131, 132, 144, 148, 151, 173, 181, 186, 191, 192, 209
Spotted Tail, 216
Spotts, Pvt. David, 145–146, 152, 155, 156, 157, 162–163
Springer, Lt. Charles, 14, 18–19, 20, 45
Stanley, Henry Morton, 53, 64, 74
Steele, Lt. James, 40–41, 164
Stenner, Anton, 300
Stillwell, Jack, 97, 106, 108
Strahorn, Robert, 218, 219–220, 224, 226–227
Summit Springs (Colo.), Battle of, 181–183
Sun Boy, 177
Sweetwater Creek, Texas, 151

Tait, Ed, 274
Tall Bull, 49, 50, 181, 183
Tallent, Annie, 216
Taylor, Nathaniel, 21, 22
Ten Eyck, Capt. Tenodor, 28, 29
Terry, Brig. Gen. Alfred, 222, 234, 235, 256, 257, 258, 263, 276
Texas, 2, 48, 186, 191
Thompson, Pvt. Peter, 254
Thompson, William, 63–64
Tongue River (Wyo.), Battle of, 15–16
Trudeau, Pierre, 106, 108
Tweed, Tom, 261

U.S. Army, 24, 35–37, 38–40, 94; artillery, 14, 19, 28, 32, 49, 50, 288; cowardice, 25, 45, 62, 67, 253; desertions, 35, 37
Ulbrick (Mr.), 73
Union Pacific Railroad, 62–63, 173, 303
Ute, 160

Van Moll, Sgt. John, 229
Varnum, Lt. Charles, 241
Vilott, Fletcher, 109
Vogdes, Ada, 200, 208, 210
Vroom, Capt. Peter, 304

Wagon Box Fight (Wyoming), 31–32
Walker, Lt. George, 13
Wallace, Lt. George, 236, 240, 258
Wands, Lt. Alfred, 25, 27, 28
Warbonnet Creek (Nebr.), Battle of, 274–276
Ware, Capt. Eugene, 42–43
Washakie, 207, *208*, 224, 229
Washington (D.C.) *Chronicle*, 36
Washita (Indian Terr.), Battle of the, 138–143, 173
Washita Campaign, 218, 288
Weichell, George, 181
Weichell, Maria, 181, 182
Weir, Capt. Thomas, 260
Wessells, Capt. Henry, 304
Westerners, 48, 58–59, 132
Wheatly, James S., 30
Wheeler, Homer, 193–194
White Horse, 49
White, Charles, 87–88, 273, 274, 275, 279, 281
White, Sarah, 126
Whitney, Chauncey, 109
"Wild West Show," 308
Williams, Stockley, 24
Wilson, Lem, 190
Windolph, Pvt. Charles, 235, 249, 252, *252*
Wolf Mountains (Mont.), Battle of the, 293
women, 28, 29, 30, 203–209, 210–213; as captives, 120–128, 151–157, 181, 183, 191–192; murder of, 182–183; revenge against Indians, 128–129
Wyllyams, Sgt. Frederick, 66, *67*
Wynkoop, Edward, 50, 57
Wyoming, 8, 39, 199

Yellow Hand, 275

Ziegler, Eli, 98, 100, 106, 109–110